HOW TO WATCH THE OLYMPICS

Scores and laws, hcrocs and zeros –
an instant initiation into every sport

DAVID GOLDBLATT

and JOHNNY ACTON

Diagrams by Belinda Evans

P

PROFILE BOOKS

This paperback edition published in 2012

First published in Great Britain in 2011 by
PROFILE BOOKS LTD
3A Exmouth House
Pine Street
London EC1R 0JH
www.profilebooks.com

10 9 8 7 6 5 4 3 2 1

Printed and bound in Great Britain by
Clays, Bungay, Suffolk

A CIP catalogue record for this book is available from the
British Library.

ISBN 978 1 84668 476 0
eISBN 978 1 84765 758 9

The paper this book is printed on is certified by the © 1996 Forest
Stewardship Council A.C. (FSC). It is ancient-forest friendly. The printer
holds FSC chain of custody SGS-COC-2061

CONTENTS

INTRODUCTION 5

THE OPENING CEREMONY 9

ARCHERY 21

ATHLETICS 31

BADMINTON 71

BASKETBALL 81

BOXING 93

CANOEING 109

CYCLING 120

DIVING 131

EQUESTRIANISM 139

FENCING 149

FOOTBALL 160

GYMNASTICS 171

HANDBALL 193

HOCKEY 202

JUDO 211

MODERN PENTATHLON 220

ROWING 229

SAILING 239

SHOOTING 250

SWIMMING 260

SYNCHRONISED SWIMMING 275

TABLE TENNIS 284

TAEKWONDO 298

TENNIS 308

TRIATHLON 317

VOLLEYBALL 324

WATER POLO 334

WEIGHTLIFTING 343

WRESTLING 355

THE MEDALS CEREMONY 367

THE CLOSING CEREMONY 369

APPENDIX 1: DISCONTINUED OLYMPIC SPORTS ... 378

APPENDIX 2: THE 26 PREVIOUS OLYMPIC GAMES .. 382

INDEX 389

THANKS

David and Johnny would like to thank: Sally for sealing the deal; Jonathan 'Surely Not?!' Buckley for his unique style of editing, his inhuman fastidiousness and for saving us from ourselves; Henry Iles for his delightful layout; and our illustrator Belinda Evans for undergoing such a demanding crash course in the world of Olympic sport and drawing such nice stick people.

Special thanks for inspiration, amusement and diversion to, in no meaningful order: Lady Perce, Lady Sarah, Bunners, Mooers, Jefris 'More Bir' Pakpahan, Lionel Richie, Paul Moss, and John from the *Cock and Bottle* pub. Last and most definitely not least, thanks, love and praise to the white-gloved impressario of the whole show, the incomparable Jeeves to our flustering Bertie Wooster, the one and only Mark 'Frasier Crane' Ellingham. Bless them all.

INTRODUCTION

For two and a half weeks every fourth summer, the planet reliably goes sports crazy. The most watched event in history wasn't the 1969 moon landing, the episode of *Dallas* which revealed who shot JR., or Charles and Di's wedding. It was the opening ceremony of the Beijing Summer Olympic Games. Over a billion people tuned in to at least part of the extravaganza. And 4.7 billion of us - around 70 per cent of the world's population — watched the sporting festival at some point over the next two and a half weeks.

In July 2012, we will all be at it again. Yet if we're honest, there's a gaping hole at the heart of the Olympic experience: most of us know remarkably little about most of the sports we've suddenly gone nuts about. Of course, you could just plonk yourself down on a sofa and keep your eyes open. No harm in any of that, but to get the most out of the Olympics it really helps to know HOW TO WATCH the proceedings. Which is where this book comes in: a training programme for the Olympics, or, to be precise, a five-point-plan of crucial need-to-know information for each sport.

The first, overarching question is WHY WATCH any given sport? Why exactly do South Koreans turn out in their tens of thousands to watch the nation's leading archers? Why do Turks venerate a 4ft-11in weightlifter? Are they all mad? Sometimes, the thrill is straightforward. Other times, you need to know the STORY OF A SPORT — why it has mattered and to whom. Only then will you grasp why Denmark comes to a standstill during the women's handball or why it seems so terribly important to the Hungarians to beat the Russians in that water polo match.

Next, you need a grasp of the BASICS. To make sense of what is going on, you have to know the object of the exercise and understand the constraints the participants are operating under. How does one win, how does one lose, how does one score and how long will it all go on for? In other words, you've got to know the rules. Once you've cleared this hurdle, you are ready to take on board some of the FINER POINTS. This will enhance your enjoyment immeasurably. Understanding the different spins, for example, will improve your experience of table tennis no end. Appreciating the tactical stratagems of basketball will turn the blur of bodies into a sharply focused and thrilling encounter.

At this point, you will be in good enough shape to move on to the OLYMPIC HISTORY of the sport. This section provides historical context and introduces you to the legends, scandals and rivalries, showing how the sport's trajectory at the Games has reflected and occasionally shaped our times.

Finally, there are some Olympic topics that are so interesting, controversial or otherwise important that they merit sections of their own. You will find the main text sprinkled with features devoted to everything from the history of drugs in weightlifting to the peculiar antics of the man who popularised recreational canoeing. Oh – and there's a useful appendix at the end of the book listing the 26 PREVIOUS OLYMPIC GAMES, with details of their host cities, their key events ... and, naturally, their mascots.

We hope you will treat this book as an amusing, knowledgeable and bizarrely passionate friend – on hand to help you get the most out of the Games. We realise you're not an expert on the finer points of dressage; we won't laugh at you if you confuse a kayak with a canoe; and we know there's something faintly ridiculous about competitive walking, or a cycling race in which the competitors can sit still on their bikes for half an hour. But we have the greatest respect for what THE GAMES are about – a cosmopolitan celebration of humanity, a demonstration of the universal power of sport and play, a showcase for the wonders of the human body and spirit – and we want to help you to enjoy them.

David Goldblatt and Johnny Acton

PS: THE IOC

Olympic sports are littered with JARGON and ACRONYMS. You don't need to know the half of it to enjoy the sports, though where you do, you'll find the low-down under each relevant section of this book. The one key acronym, which crops up in any discussion of the Olympics, is the IOC. This is the INTERNATIONAL OLYMPIC COMMITTEE, created by BARON PIERRE DE COUBERTIN in 1894 to oversee what we know as the 'modern Olympics'. The IOC is made up of senior figures from international sports federations (Sepp Blatter from FIFA, for example), prominent former Olympians, and the great and the good (it helps to have a royal connection). The IOC runs both the Summer and Winter Games, selects the host cities and approves the inclusion of new and existing sports (each of which are governed by their own international federations).

There are also 206 NATIONAL OLYMPIC COMMITTEES, which organise their countries' teams and officials. Their number is rather more than the 193 states represented at the UN, as it includes such 'nations' as Aruba, Guam and Cook Islands. Palestine is also recognised as an Olympic nation.

THE OPENING CEREMONY

27 JULY 2012

OLYMPIC STADIUM

Athletes: 12,000 (if they all show up)

OLYMPIC PRESENCE

THE 1896 GAMES OPENED WITH SPEECHES AND HYMNS. PARIS failed to put on an opening ceremony in 1900 and ST LOUIS wasn't much better in 1904. But since LONDON 1908 the ceremony has been a permanent fixture.

OLYMPIC FORMAT

LIKE SYNCHRONISED SWIMMING AND DIVING, THE OPENING ceremony has a fixed and a free programme. The fixed programme is set by Olympic protocol and includes a parade of athletes, flames, torches, flags and oaths. The free section is open to artistic interpretation by the host city.

PAST CHAMPIONS

LONDON, PARIS, ATHENS, LOS ANGELES: 2 EACH.

WHY WATCH THE OPENING CEREMONY?

WHAT EVENT GETS THE BIGGEST TV AUDIENCE AT EVERY Olympics? Which tickets are the most oversubscribed? The OPENING CEREMONY of course. It is the moment at which after four years and more of relentless hype, cynicism, argument, scandal and uncertainty the curtain finally goes up. And it's a show that has changed out of all recognition since its first appearance at the 1896 Games, becoming along the way a strange amalgam of global ritual, military march-past, TV spectacular, Broadway musical and circus.

The ARTISTIC PROGRAMME, with which an Olympic opening ceremony now always begins, can be seen as a costumed folly or as a message of the host nation's self-image – or both. And after that, there are the old favourites of the COMPULSORY PROGRAMME to look forward to – the PARADE OF NATIONS, the ARRIVAL OF THE OLYMPIC FLAG, the LIGHTING OF THE CAULDRON. The pleasures here are many: the extraordinary national costumes of the athletes, the partisan response of crowds to a nation's foes, friends and favourites ... and, not least, the possibility that something might go a bit wrong.

OPENING CEREMONY BASICS

THE ORGANISERS AND CHOREOGRAPHERS OF THE OPENING ceremony for LONDON 2012 have made it clear that they won't try to compete with Beijing – which featured over 15,000 perform-ers and cost around $100 million. The 2012 director's gig for both the opening and closing Olympic ceremonies went, somewhat surprisingly, to the Oscar-winning film director DANNY BOYLE (*Trainspotting, Slumdog Millionaire*). Very little has leaked as to what will be on show. But here's a taste of the main ingredients ...

THE ARTISTIC PROGRAMME

IN THE ERA OF THE GIGANTIC STADIUM SCREEN AND GLOBAL television coverage the opening ceremony of the Olympic Games is choreographed down to the last detail. This even applies to the COUNTDOWN to the start of the show. At BEIJING 2008 LED-embedded drums not only beat out the seconds in the countdown to the Games but spelled out the numbers themselves in Chinese and Arabic numerals.

Once we reach zero it really is anyone's guess what's coming next. Since MOSCOW 1980 raised the stakes with a gigantic, apparently

BEIJING 2008 PRESENTS FIVE MILLENNIA OF CHINESE HISTORY, WITH A CAST OF THOUSANDS

endless, array of formation dancing, marching and gymnastics and a cast of many thousands, the artistic programme has run riot. LOS ANGELES 1984 opened with the entire stadium holding up coloured squares to form the flags of each participating nation; SEOUL 1988 started in the middle of a river; and SYDNEY 2000 went with a formation horse troupe. Thematically, the ambition has often been overweening – the story of humanity, five millennia of Chinese history, a treatise on balance and entropy in the universe.

THE COMPULSORY PROGRAMME

ATHLETES ON PARADE

THE ARTISTIC PROGRAMME IS FINALLY DONE. THE LAST MIME artistes and creatures from the black lagoon have gone. It time for the athletes. The form now is for each team to be led out by a STANDARD BEARER provided by the hosts plus a team member who carries the national flag. The GREEKS always open proceedings and the HOSTS bring up the rear. In between, countries go in alphabetical order according to the host language. It's once around the track and then the teams line up in the centre of the stadium. The costumes worn by the (usually female) standard bearers have often proved divertingly kitsch, as at SEOUL 1988, where they were decked out in white leather boots and peaked caps.

The response of the crowd to the teams is always interesting. ATHENS 2004 proved particularly partisan, with Turks, Israelis and Macedonians getting the silent treatment while the Palestinians and the Serbs received very positive vibes. The biggest cheers were reserved for Greece, countries with big Greek populations like Cyprus and Australia, and war-torn Afghanistan and Iraq.

THE SPEECHES

NOW FOR THE SPEECHES: THREE OF THEM! PRESUMABLY THEY are scheduled here to give the audience a chance to get a drink or go to the toilet after the marathon of the athlete's parade. There'll be something anodyne from the head of the local organising committee and something in a similar vein from the PRESIDENT OF THE IOC – it is their Olympics after all. Finally, the host's head of state or their representative declares the Games open. Mercifully there is strict protocol on what the head of state can say, and it isn't much.

THE OLYMPIC ANTHEM

SOMETIMES THEY PLAY THE OLYMPIC ANTHEM NEXT, SOMETIMES they bring the flag in and play it during or after the flag has been raised. Either way they are going to play it. The anthem was composed for the first modern Games in 1896 with music by SPIROS SAMARAS and words by the poet KOSTIS PALAMAS, but it didn't become a fixed feature of the ceremony until 1960. Some hosts, like the Chinese in 2008, go with the original Greek version; others get it translated into their own language, like the Italians at ROME 1960 or the Japanese version sung at TOKYO 1964. Language politics being a complicated thing in Spain, at BARCELONA 1992 the anthem was sung part in Catalan, part in Spanish and part in French.

MUNICH 1972 featured an instrumental version. In Anglophone countries an English version has been sung, with various attempts to put old school Greek poesy into some kind of plausible modern English. It does go on rather, with a lot of choral work, but the first two stanzas should give you the drift of things.

Immortal spirit of antiquity
Father of the true, beautiful and good
Descend, appear, shed over us thy light
Upon this ground and under this sky
Which has first witnessed thy unperishable fame

Give life and animation to these noble games!
Throw wreaths of fadeless flowers to the victors
In the race and in the strife
Create in our breasts, hearts of steel!

FLY THE FLAG

THE FLAG IS UP NEXT AND IT IS INVARIABLY CARRIED BY A selection of the host nation's great Olympians – eight seems to be the preferred number for ease of manoeuvre. Outfits vary, but all-white has been the look most organising committees have gone for.

FLAME ON

IN LINE WITH TRADITION, THE CAULDRON CONTINUES TO BE lit by the final torchbearer, but there has been a turn to novelty acts. In 1988 SEOUL went with three torchbearers, four years later BARCELONA's flame was lit by the flight of a flaming arrow. At SYDNEY 2000 the cauldron was ignited by a flame that passed through water, while at ATHENS 2004 it was lowered down to the torchbearer on a long pivot. In BEIJING a gymnast was flown by wire around the stadium before lighting a long fuse that initiated the conflagration.

Whatever the method, the lighting of the cauldron is a peak moment of the ceremony. Over the years, the criteria used to decide who should be the final torchbearer have varied wildly. GIANCARLO PERIS lit the flame in ROME in 1960 having won a junior cross-country race to secure the honour. Schoolteacher KIM WON-TAK was one of three torchbearers who lit the flame in SEOUL in 1988 – she had won a marathon. In TOKYO in 1964 YOSHINORI SAKAI was chosen as he was born on the day the Hiroshima bomb was exploded. MONTREAL 1976 went with two teenage torchbearers representing French and English speaking Canada; a symbolic point that did not go unnoticed among First Nation Canadians. Leading Olympians have made obvious choices, like PAAVO NURMI at HELSINKI in 1952. The choice of the aboriginal Australian runner CATHY FREEMAN at SYDNEY 2000 and MUHAMMAD ALI in 1996 at ATLANTA were acknowledgements of the contested ethnic and national identities of the hosts.

CATCH THE DOVES

AT ONE POINT IT WAS USUAL FOR THE DOVES TO BE RELEASED prior to the lighting of the Olympic flame. However, in SEOUL in 1988, many of the birds came to rest on the rim of the Olympic cauldron and were incinerated when it was lit. The doves now follow the lighting of the flame. At BEIJING, the Chinese decided to dispense with the birds altogether and symbolically substituted them with yellow fireworks.

FORTUNATELY, LIVE PIGEON SHOOTING WAS NO LONGER A SPORT AT LA 1932

NO CHEATIN', PROMISE!

NEXT UP ARE THE ATHLETE'S AND OFFICIAL'S OLYMPIC OATHS. They are taken by one person on behalf of everyone, sometimes while holding a corner of the Olympic flag. The athlete's oath was first said at the 1920 Games, while 1972 saw the introduction of the official's oath. Time has not been kind to the language of the Olympic oath. The first version, taken by the fencer VICTOR BOLIN, had an old fashioned grace to it:

> We swear, we will take part in the Olympic Games in a spirit of chivalry, for the honour of our country and for the glory of sport.

The most recent version has been amended by committee:

> In the name of all the competitors I promise that we shall take part in these Olympic Games, respecting and abiding by the rules which govern them, committing ourselves to a sport without doping and without drugs, in the true spirit of sportsmanship, for the glory of sport and the honour of our teams.

At LA 1984 hurdler EDWIN MOSES stalled midway through the oath and was forced to repeat the same sentence three times before he finally remembered the rest of the oath. Today's autocues make a repeat unlikely.

FIREWORKS AND MIMING

IT'S BECOME STANDARD FOR EACH OLYMPIC OPENING CEREMONY to culminate in a FIREWORK DISPLAY. These have grown progressively longer, louder, larger and more expensive – though it is hard to imagine how any display could surpass the gigantic cascades of colour coming from the roof of the Bird's Nest stadium at BEIJING 2008. That said, what most of the world saw on TV was in fact a computer-generated version of the display, the organisers having panicked that weather conditions might adversely affect the real one.

Such obsessive control freakery had been foreshadowed at SYDNEY 2000, where the SYDNEY SYMPHONY ORCHESTRA mimed its way through the ceremony. At Beijing the singer LIN MIAOKE mimed as the Chinese flag entered the stadium. The real singer – a seven-year-old girl with buck teeth – was not considered suitable for display.

THE OPENING CEREMONY STORY

CEREMONIALLY, THE MODERN OLYMPICS GOT UNDERWAY WITH the unveiling of a statue of Georgios Averoff, the Greek tycoon who was footing the bill for the 1896 ATHENS GAMES. Dues paid, a few days later the focus moved on to the Olympic stadium, where 80,000 spectators endured a series of speeches before the massed bands of the Greek army, navy, Athenian municipalities and far-flung provinces struck up the newly composed OLYMPIC HYMN. A quick blast from the trumpet followed, the athletes arrived and the Games began.

The 1900 PARIS GAMES saw the Olympics reduced to a small athletic sideshow – a lost and chaotic component of the much grander WORLD FAIR that was running concurrently. Consequently there was no opening ceremony of any kind. The ST LOUIS GAMES of 1904 were hardly any better. This time the Games were subsumed within the LOUISIANA PURCHASE CENTENARY EXHIBITION. David Rowland Francis, president of the show's organising committee, came along to the first day of athletics with a few local worthies and conducted a brief inspection of the competitors lined up on the field,. The athletes then dispersed, warmed up and got on with the sport.

Flushed with success by their inaugural 1896 Games, the Greeks had agitated to host the Olympics every four years, while the IOC wanted the event to travel the world. As a compromise, Greece was permitted to hold the 1906 ATHENS OLYMPIC INTERNATIONAL EXHIBITION but the IOC has never recognised the Games held on that occasion. These largely forgotten 'INTERCALCATED GAMES' were in most ways a complete disaster, but they did feature an ATHLETES' PARADE in which teams were preceded by national flags.

The LONDON OLYMPICS of 1908 picked up on this and in the dark drizzle Edward VII and Queen Alexandra took the salute from the flags of every competing nation but the US. As the shot-putter Ralph Rose, carrying the Stars and Stripes, famously remarked, 'this flag dips to no earthly king'. At STOCKHOLM 1912 the Swedes added standard bearers with countries' names to the parade, but that was the only flourish. The rest of the ceremony was a sermon, a hymn and a few words from King Gustav V.

Baron de Coubertin had been beavering away at the Olympic logo for years and in June 1914 his FIVE INTERLOCKING RINGS device was approved by the IOC congress. Six years and a world war later, the logo got its first outing at the 1920 ANTWERP GAMES on a plain white flag. Since then this emblem of amateurism and internationalism has become one of the most fiercely guarded trademarks on the planet. (We're not allowed to reproduce it – nor any image of the Olympic torch – in this book.)

PIGEONS made their first appearance at the Olympics in 1900 when the Belgian Leon de Lunden led the carnage in the LIVE PIGEON SHOOT contest. De Lunden killed 21 birds and was entitled to a 20,000 francs prize but in a magnanimous and Olympian spirit the top four finishers agreed to split the winnings. The event was discontinued, which was just as well as the PARIS GAMES of 1924 saw the first mass release of doves as part of the opening ceremony – a gesture of peace rather than slaughter.

The 1928 AMSTERDAM GAMES retained all these elements of the ceremony but oddly decided to stage the athletes' parade separately from the rest of the show – a running order that has not been repeated since. More significant was the ARRIVAL OF FIRE. Given the ancient Greek love of symbolic and sacred flame it was only a matter of time and technology before the modern Olympics got in on the act. A FLAME was first lit inside the Olympic stadium in Amsterdam in 1928, though without great ceremony. LA in 1932 brought a little staging to the torch and flame, but it took BERLIN 1936 to make its ignition the big finale that the ceremony needed.

CARL DIEM, one of the leading organisers of the Berlin Games, tapped into the Nazi nation's obsession with classical Greece and arranged for a fire to be kindled and a torch to be lit using a parabolic mirror in Olympia. The flame was then carried by a relay of runners to Berlin through the Balkans, on a route uncannily similar (if in reverse) to the movement of German armies southwards just a few years later. No one was doing this stuff at the ancient Olympics, but Diem was tapping into a wider vein of Hellenic fire imagery: there were torch races in Greece, the myth of Prometheus' theft of fire from the gods was important and the sacred Olympic truce was communicated by runners across Greece. By the time the final torchbearer reached the stadium a real sense of drama had been created.

As one would expect of the austerity Games, the LONDON 1948 opening ceremony was a low key affair. Boy scouts served as stewards. The crowd, still living on rations, brought their own picnics and the British women athletes had to supply their own blouses for the parade: a 21-gun salute prior to the arrival of the torch bearer was the chief theatrical flourish. HELSINKI 1952 was equally unflamboyant, enlivened mainly by German peace activist BARBARA ROTRAUT PLEYER who, clad all in white, ran across the track and on to a podium in an effort to speak.

MELBOURNE's 1956 ceremony broke little new ground, though the equestrians, who had to compete in Stockholm due to the prohibitive expense of shipping horses to Australia, conducted their opening ceremony entirely on horseback. Over the next decade the stadiums would be become larger but ROME 1960 and TOKYO 1964 retained the same format. Tokyo's release of 10,000 balloons was the only notable change.

MEXICO 1968 was conducted in the shadow of the widespread political protest and vicious repression that had been conducted out on the streets of Mexico City just weeks before the Games. The ceremony was both chaotic and bombastic. With just half an hour to go, the audience was treated to screaming military music over the PA and last minute lawn mowing. Drum rolls and chants of 'Viva Mexico' accompanied almost everything, while unifomed marines carried in the Olympic flag. Pleasingly, the athletes broke ranks at the end, spreading across the track and forcing the final torchbearer to push her way through a scrum. Many of the 10,000 doves slated for release after this were too hot and too ill to fly.

MUNICH 1972 reacted strongly to this display of nationalism and militarism. Paranoiacally aware of the tarnished grandeur and hubris of Berlin 1936, the Munich organisers went to the other end of the spectrum. While the Berlin Games had used a great Teutonic bell to call the athletes to the stadium, Munich went with a Dutch glockenspiel playing easy listening classics like 'Jingle Bells'. The athletes' parade was accompanied by cheesy tunes specially selected for each team: the Turks got 'Turkish Delight', the Hungarians 'Gypsy Love' and the Cubans 'Habana Alegre'. Brightly-clad schoolchildren danced in circles and handed out flowers to the athletes.

The game changers in the history of the Olympic opening ceremony were MOSCOW 1980 and LOS ANGELES 1984, in which the two Cold War superpowers refused to go to each other's parties and in the other's absence tried to put on the biggest and best show yet. Moscow drew on the traditions of both the Red Square military parade and the gigantic COLLECTIVE GYMNASTIC DISPLAYS beloved of communist Europe. The ace in the pack was the very low tech use of colour-square cards, held by the audience above their heads. Choreographed with precision, one segment of the stadium provided a constant and changing visual commentary on events. The opening parade was a kitsch fest of Greek imagery and Russian style. Chariots, gods, and goddesses carrying the flag of Moscow rolled by. Later on there would be conversation with cosmonauts, mass displays of rhythmic gymnastics, dancing from all fifteen Soviet republics, and a stadium full of Mishas – the Games' ursine mascot. LA countered with high-tech razzamatazz and Americana in the sun, with a ceremony that included mass marching bands in candyfloss colours and toy solider uniforms, and a SPACEMAN with operational jet pack flying into the stadium.

While Moscow and LA had been statements of established power, SEOUL 1988 was a great big coming out party for South Korea. A country in ruins at the end of the Korean War, it had in just three decades transformed itself into a major industrial power. The opening ceremony was suitably enormous and the dance sequence – which purported to tell the story of balance and discord in the universe – marked a step change in the narrative ambition of this element of the ceremony.

In the twenty-first century, the soaring ambitions of Olympic hosts, allied to new staging and lighting technologies, have made for a series of increasingly spectacular and expensive opening ceremonies.

SYDNEY 2000 opened with 130 horses riding in formations (including the Olympic rings), used nearly 13,000 performers, had a band of 2000 musicians orchestrated by six conductors, and offered a tableau that went from the life of the ocean floor to the notion of eternity by way of Australia's aboriginal and colonial histories.

ATHENS 2004 threw the kitchen sink at the opening ceremony, Eros flew, a giant helix of DNA spun round, massed ranks of Bouzouki players were assembled and everyone from Alexander the Great to the Goddess Hera got a walk on part. The stadium floor was filled with over two million litres of water,

THE ANCIENT SPORT OF MINOAN BULL-JUMPING RE-ENACTED IN THE ATHENS OPENING CEREMONY

all of which had to be drained away in minutes to provide a hard surface for the parade of nations that followed.

All of this, however, was to pale in comparison with the blow-out in BEIJING 2008. Four hours long, and with over 15,000 performers, it trumped everything that had gone before. Its centrepiece was a visual retelling of Chinese history, emphasising the nation's great technological innovations – movable type, paper, gunpowder – while managing to avoid most of the twentieth century. It concluded with the rising of a phoenix and a celebration of the burgeoning Chinese space programme. The world got the message. China is big, back and it means business.

ARCHERY

27 JULY–3 AUGUST 2012

LORD'S CRICKET GROUND, LONDON NW8 8QN

Athletes: 128 | Golds up for grabs: 4

OLYMPIC PRESENCE

1900–20, 1972–PRESENT.

OLYMPIC FORMAT

THERE ARE FOUR ARCHERY GOLDS AT STAKE, IN INDIVIDUAL and team competitions for men and women.

CURRENT CONTENDERS:

THE SOUTH KOREANS' STRENGTH IN DEPTH MAKES THEM favourites for the team events and their women seem unstoppable. In the men's events, expect competition from the leading Americans, French and Ukrainians.

PAST CHAMPIONS:

SOUTH KOREA: 16 | USA: 14 | BELGIUM: 11

WHY WATCH ARCHERY?

WITH THE OLYMPIC STADIUM ON MONTJUIC PLUNGED INTO darkness, the climax of the opening ceremony of the BARCELONA 1992 Games was approaching. The Olympic torch made its final journey into the stadium, where Spanish paralympic archer Antonio Rebollo lit his arrow from it. He turned to face the high metal tower on which the Olympic flame was due to burn, and launched his burning arrow towards the top of the structure, where the arrow flew through a plume of gas, igniting a column of fire

DOUBLE OLYMPIC CHAMPION IM DONG HUYN. REMARKABLY, HE IS LEGALLY BLIND IN HIS NATIVE SOUTH KOREA

that rose high into the night sky. Not even a stadium-full rendition of Queen's *Barcelona*, specially written for the Olympics, could compete.

Target archery competitions may not pack quite the same spectacular punch, but each shot offers a sequence of excitement: the tension as the archer draws back the bowstring; the snap of the arrow's release; the swish of its 150mph flight; the split-second of impact. And archery often produces exceptional sustained drama, like the nail-biting final of the men's team bronze medal match in ATHENS 2004, in which Ukraine pipped the USA 237–235. Composure under pressure, perfect balance and focus – Olympic archery is like competitive meditation with lethal weapons.

In recent years, the sport has also bent over backwards to become more spectator (and TV) friendly. Simultaneous competition with dozens of archers firing together is out, allowing cameras and audiences to focus on the drama of head-to-head contests. Very long rounds of arrows have been replaced by short sets that make errors more costly and upsets more likely. Split screens, big screens and electronic scoring have all been introduced. In South Korea, the world's leading archery nation, this has produced huge TV audiences and very large and noisy crowds.

Lord's Cricket Ground is unlikely to generate quite such a raucous atmosphere, but – given that archery's competitive dynamics are not far from darts and its aural and visual pleasures not unlike golf – it would be good to think that the sport might get a bigger airing than it usually receives.

THE STORY OF ARCHERY

SKILL WITH A BOW AND ARROW HAS BEEN CRUCIAL TO THE development of humanity. Cave paintings in France and Spain, created around 25,000 years ago, depict archers in hunting scenes, while stone arrowheads litter numerous Neolithic archaeological sites. The first great civilisations may have relied on agriculture for subsistence, but archery was essential to hunting and organised warfare – bowmen were a central component of the armies of ancient China, Persia, Egypt, Greece and Rome.

Alongside hunting and warfare, archery had a ritual and competitive aspect: in Homer's *Iliad*, for example, the GREEKS hold a shooting contest at Patroclus' funeral games. Fourteenth-century records show that the archers of the OTTOMAN EMPIRE competed to see who could fire an arrow the furthest, while in JAPAN the medieval Oyakazu archery contest is widely recorded. In the only known form of MARATHON ARCHERY, competitors were required to fire as many arrows as they could in 24 hours through a hole in a wall. The record, set in 1886, was 8132 scores from 13,053 attempts.

In all of these cultures, gunpowder radically altered the status of archery. By the end of the sixteenth century, the longbow and crossbow had been abandoned by most European armies, and the rest of the world would soon follow. In Britain archery endured in high society as a quasi-militaristic recreation, but by the middle of the eighteenth century it was a dying art. Its revival was brought about largely through the efforts of the antiquarian and collector

Sir Ashton Lever, who, in addition to creating the largest aviary in Britain, founded in 1781 the Toxophilite Society, which combined target archery with an enormous amount of eating and drinking. Joseph Strutt, in his survey of Georgian sport, observed: 'I have seen the gentlemen who practise archery in the vicinity of London, repeatedly shoot from end to end, and not touch the target with an arrow'.

Although it was already attracting a rather select crowd to its events, the patronage in 1787 of George, the Prince of Wales, saw the status and membership of the Toxophilite Society boom. Aristocratic archery clubs sprang up all over England and for the next thirty years provided a space for conviviality and flirtation. The latter was assured when, in the early nineteenth century, the Royal British Bowmen permitted women to join. The decorum of archery was such that, as one contemporary wrote, 'it is the only field diversion they can enjoy without incurring the censure of being thought masculine'. Indeed, the *1829 Young Lady's Book: A Manual of Elegant Recreations, Exercises and Pursuits* suggested that 'the moment of the bending of the bow is particularly graceful'.

In the 1820s British archery peaked as a lordly pastime, with great gatherings of archery clubs on heaths and parks in huge tented enclosures. Competition was definitely secondary to the feasting and merry-making, and to the display of the extraordinary costumes invented by archery societies, many inspired by the period's cult of medievalism. In some cases, large crowds of the poor and curious would gather to watch the event.

Queen Victoria herself was a patron of the Royal St Leonards Archers, but archery never quite returned to the heady days of Georgian England. Over the next eighty years the sport lost much of its high-end glamour and settled down to a quieter life in garden parties and national meets. It did, however, evolve as sport, with issues of format, scoring, technique and etiquette becoming standardised. It was this more sober culture that spread to countries with a strong tradition of hunting – notably America, France and the Low Countries – and in turn led to archery's arrival at the 1900 Olympics.

GAME ON: ARCHERY BASICS

THE 1.2M DIAMETER TARGET IS DIVIDED INTO TEN CONCEN-
tric rings, with 1 point being awarded for hitting the outermost
ring and 10 points for hitting the bullseye, which is just 12.2cm
across. Arrows that land on a line score the higher of the two scores.
Within the bullseye there's a smaller ring called the x10. There are
no additional points for hitting this, but in the event of a tie, the
archer with the most x10s wins the contest. In all Olympic events,
the archer stands 70m from the target, which from that range appears to competitors to be the size of the head of a carpet tack held
at arm's length.

THE ARCHER WITH THE HIGHEST NUMBER OF POINTS WINS
– that much is straightforward. But the way the Olympic archery
events are structured is quite complicated.

Sixty four archers take part in the INDIVIDUAL competitions,
which begin with the RANKING ROUND, in which contestants
shoot 72 arrows (in 6 ENDS of 12 arrows), after which they are
ranked by score from 1 to 64. In the ELIMINATION ROUNDS, the 1st-
ranked archer competes against the 64th, the 2nd against the 63rd,
and so on. Archers shoot simultaneously, firing 18 arrows in 6 ends
of 3. In the QUARTER-FINALS, SEMI-FINALS and MEDAL MATCHES
each archer shoots 12 arrows, in 4 ends of 3, but contestants shoot
alternately, which makes for better drama. The losers of the semi-
finals play each other to determine the bronze medal.

Each TEAM in the team events consists of three archers who
have competed in the individual competition. Their scores in the
individual ranking round are added together to determine the
team's ranking score. Suitably seeded, teams play off in a series of
knock-out matches, which consist of 24 arrows per team, shot in
4 ends of 6 arrows, with each member of the team firing twice
per end.

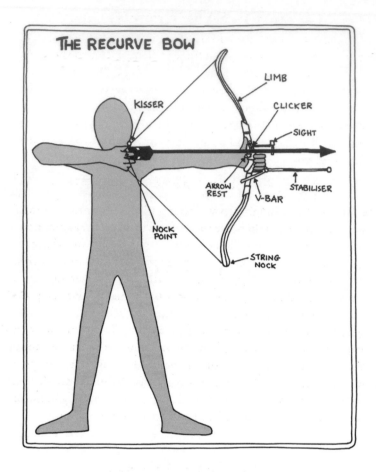

THE RECURVE BOW

LIMB

KISSER

CLICKER

SIGHT

ARROW REST

V-BAR

STABILISER

NOCK POINT

STRING NOCK

ETIQUETTE

AS ONE WOULD HOPE IN A SPORT THAT USES LETHAL WEAP-
onry, etiquette and safety are high on archery's agenda. Competitors
must wait for the command to start and are not allowed to collect
arrows while other people are shooting.

If you hear someone shouting 'Fast!' it is not an attempt to
increase the pace of shooting but to stop it. The call requires everyone to stop shooting immediately and return any unshot arrows to
their quivers. Rather quaintly, archers are expected to offer to pay
for any damage caused to a competitor's equipment.

THE RECURVE BOW

THE DEFINING FEATURE OF THE MODERN OLYMPIC BOW HAS been in existence for more than three millennia. Called the recurve bow, it has tips that curve away from the archer when the bow is unstrung. This allows the bow, when tense, to store more energy than a straight-limbed bow of the same size. Today's bows are made of complex layers of fibreglass, carbon and wood, with detachable limbs and all manner of additions and contraptions to aid stability and thus increase accuracy.

BOW PARTS

THUMB RING A twanging bow string and flying arrow can rough up your fingers. Archers use these small leather flaps as protection.

CLICKER Archers try and achieve the same strength of draw every time they fire. The clicker is a small wire attached to the central part of the bow to help them with this. The clicker sits on the arrow as it is drawn back and drops off it when it has been pulled back the correct distance.

KISSER Consistency is everything in archery. To ensure they get into the correct positions when drawing, competitors touch these little buttons placed on the strings to their faces or lips.

STABILISER Archers like their bows evenly balanced to fit their styles and postures. Stabilisers are rods of varying length and weight which are attached to bows to absorb vibration.

THE FINER POINTS

FOR THE SPECTATOR, MUCH OF THE PLEASURE OF ARCHERY comes from watching how an individual athlete or a team performs over a series of contests, each of which brings a higher level of tension. Most archers at the Olympics are hitting the bullseye most of the time, so the difference between winning and losing comes down to fractions of a centimetre, and tiny wobbles and movements when firing. Look for signs of cracking under pressure, such as fussing with the equipment. Competing at Olympic level requires all-round composure and a meditative poise and balance.

Archers compare using the bow to a golf swing. It can be broken down into tiny component parts, from the stance, to the raising of the bow, to the pattern of breathing. Each of these must be perfected and all of them must put together in a smooth automatic set of movements that can be executed faultlessly under the highest competitive pressure.

ARCHERY GOES TO THE OLYMPICS

ARCHERY APPEARED AT EVERY OLYMPICS BUT ONE BETWEEN 1900 and 1920 and took a different format every time. Unlike most other early Olympic sports, the archery event was open to women from the start: British archer Queenie Newall won a gold in 1908 at the age of 53, still the record for the oldest female champion in any Olympic sport. Archery's embrace of diversity has extended more recently to disabled athletes: in 1984, in Los Angeles, the archer Neroli Fairhall of New Zealand became the first paraplegic competitor in Olympic archery.

The star of the early Games was HUBERT VAN INNIS of Belgium, winner of six golds and four silvers between 1900 and 1920.

53-YEAR-OLD SYBIL 'QUEENIE' NEWALL AT LONDON 1908

However, archery was then ditched from the Olympics, on account of the low number of competitors it had attracted: only France, Belgium, the USA, the Netherlands and Great Britain had ever taken part.

Archery established an international federation for itself in 1931 but the sport was really sustained for the next half-century by the USA. In the mid-1950s *Sports Illustrated* reported that there were more than four million amateur archers in the country. FRED BEAR (his real name) and his TV descendants drew on backwoods nostalgia and the mystique of big-game hunting to keep archery in the public eye, while in Hollywood HOWARD HILL – the self-styled 'world's greatest archer' – advised ERROL FLYNN for his role as Robin Hood and offered dazzling bow-work and trickery in his own films. More recently, enthusiasts like WILLIAM SHATNER (Star Trek's Captain Kirk) and actress GEENA DAVIS (who just missed out on inclusion in the US Olympic team) have sprinkled some stardust on the sport.

When archery returned to the Olympics in 1972, the Americans swept the board, and they repeated the feat at Montreal in 1976. Only the US boycott of the 1980 Games prevented them from making it three in a row. American dominance continued in the men's events through the 1980s and 1990s. At Los Angeles, DARRELL PACE was so far ahead of the field that he held a press conference mid-event on the final day. In 1996 the gold went to twenty-year-old JUSTIN HUISH, who as a kid had learned the sport by firing arrows through his parents' garage from a neighbour's lawn. He turned up at the Olympics looking like a classic California slacker, with his beard, pony-tail and reversed baseball cap. First impressions weren't entirely incorrect, as in the run up to the 2000 Games Huish was busted for possession of marijuana; he quit the team and has since retired from the sport

American archery has been in decline ever since and at ATHENS 2004 the US team failed to win any kind of medal. The new masters of the sport are the SOUTH KOREANS. An Olympic gold secures a South Korean a generous life-long pension and huge public acclaim. The nation's women have dominated every team event since 1988 and often take all three medals in the individuals.

IN THE ZONE DUDE! JUSTIN HUISH SHOOTS FOR GOLD AT ATLANTA 1996

KIM SU-NYEONG, the most successful archer of the modern era, has taken four golds, one silver and one bronze at three different Olympics. The men's team, meanwhile, has won gold at four out of the last six Games. Solidarity in the Korean squad reached new heights in 2008 when PARK SUNG-HYUN and PARK KYUNG-MO, South Korea's top male and female archers, announced their impeding marriage – which made it three couples inside the national squad. Nothing suggests that they will all be anything less than brilliant in London.

ATHLETICS

3–12 AUGUST 2012

OLYMPIC STADIUM (Track, field and combined events)

LONDON, FINISH AT THE MALL (Road events)

Athletes: 2000 | Golds up for grabs: 47

OLYMPIC PRESENCE

MEN 1896–PRESENT; WOMEN 1928–PRESENT.

OLYMPIC FORMAT

24 TRACK EVENTS, 16 FIELD EVENTS (4 JUMPING AND 4 throwing for each gender), 5 road events (men's and women's marathons and 20km walks, men's 50km walk), and 2 combined events (men's decathlon and women's heptathlon).

CURRENT CONTENDERS:

AMERICA HAS TOPPED THE ATHLETICS MEDALS TABLE IN ALL but three of the 26 Modern Olympic Games and may well do it again in London. On the evidence of Beijing, however, their position is far from safe. RUSSIA, KENYA and JAMAICA each collected six golds in 2008, just one less than TEAM USA.

PAST CHAMPIONS:

USA: 311 | USSR/RUSSIA: 64 | GREAT BRITAIN: 49 | FINLAND: 48

WHY WATCH ATHLETICS?

ATHLETICS, BOXING AND WRESTLING ARE THE SPORTS THAT connect the ancient Games to the modern Olympics, and whether the yardstick is worldwide television audience or iconic historical moments, athletics is the biggest of the three. Does anyone not have an indelible image in their head of Fosbury flopping, Flo-Jo with her bionic physique and unworldly talons, or Usain Bolt annihilating his opponents in Beijing? And that's before you consider the politics – from Jesse Owens' defiance at Berlin to the Black Power salutes at Mexico 1968.

The hold Olympic athletics has on the global imagination is connected to the SIMPLICITY of the constituent disciplines. We can all relate to running, jumping and throwing, and there is an extraordinary thrill in watching individuals who can do these things better than anyone else on the planet. And while all sports are to some extent dramatic, the starkness of athletics magnifies the drama: little can compare with the despondency of the relay runner who lets down his team by dropping his baton, or the elation of the javelin thrower who produces a medal-winning personal best after a sequence of no-throws.

Another fascinating aspect of Olympic athletics is the POLITICAL dimension. The glory attendant on athletic success has always been co-opted by the powers that be, from the rulers of ancient Greek city states to the Third Reich and beyond. The stadium is an arena in which a nation can demonstrate its supremacy both to its citizens and to the rest of the world. The stakes may not now be quite as high as during the Cold War, when Olympic athletics amounted to a blatantly symbolic battle between opposing regimes, but there are still plenty of engrossing nationalistic and ideological subplots. How quickly are the Chinese catching up with the Americans, for example?

Although athletics is self-evidently elitist, it is also remarkably democratic. There are events tailored to short and nippy people (STEEPLECHASE), human stick insects (HIGH JUMP) and the super-sized (HAMMER and SHOTPUT). This diversity and the universality of athletics mean that everyone should be able to find something with which to identify, while at the more recherché end of the spectrum, some of the minority sports can make one marvel at the oddity of the competitors' excellence. How exactly does one go about becoming a champion at the POLE-VAULT, for example, and what can possibly induce a person to commit his or her youth to Olympic WALKING?

THE STORY OF ATHLETICS

THE ACTIVITIES AT THE HEART OF ATHLETICS ARE SO FUNDA-mental that providing dates for their origins is close to meaningless. Walking is an Olympic discipline, for example, and hominids are thought to have been at it for four million years. As for the javelin, even wild chimpanzees have been observed using spears.

We are on slightly firmer ground when we try to trace the roots of what might be termed organised athletic events. The oldest known example was the bizarre SED FESTIVAL, conducted in Egypt from the First Dynasty (3100–2890BC) onwards. After thirty years on the throne, pharaohs were expected to demonstrate their continued vigour by running between points representing the borders of their kingdom. They did this in public, with jackals' tails tied to their waists.

A related practice in many ancient societies was the use of athletic challenges for INITIATION. Young men of the Hamer tribe of south-western Ethiopia jump cattle to prove their virility (a man must leap over a bullock four times before he is permitted to get

PHARAOH DEN (c.2945 BC) SHOWS HE STILL HAS THE LEGS FOR THE JOB AT THE SED FESTIVAL

married), and have doubtless been doing it since their ancestors took to pastoralism back in the mists of time. Bull-leaping (in which both girls and boys took part) was similarly important to the Minoans of Crete (2700–1450BC).

The next stage in the evolution of athletics was the introduction of the crucial ingredient of COMPETITION. The emerging empires and city states of the Bronze Age naturally wanted their soldiers to be fit and proficient at throwing spears and so forth, and track and field events developed skills that were useful on the battlefield. At the same time, athletics worked in the other direction, by channelling aggressive impulses that might otherwise have led to fighting. To borrow George Orwell's phrase about football, it was 'war minus the shooting'. Rulers sponsored athletic competitions because this allowed them to demonstrate their power while diffusing the combative energies of their subjects, or of rival cities.

Many of the earliest recorded athletic meetings were held as part of FUNERAL CELEBRATIONS. According to legend, the Irish Tailte-ann Games, which included pole jumping, high jumping and spear throwing, were initiated by King Lugh in 1829BC to commemo-rate the death of his mother. Funeral games also play a prominent role in the *Iliad*, Homer's account of the Trojan Wars. Achilles, the hero of the Greek armies frequently referred to as 'the fast runner', responds to the death of his beloved friend Patroclus by holding commemorative games which feature a foot race, boxing, wres-tling and a spear-throwing contest. The competitions had a triple purpose: they established a basis for the distribution of the fallen warrior's possessions; they allowed his comrades to get his death out of their systems by asserting their strength and fitness; and they provided opportunities for 'immortal fame'.

GREECE was, of course, the seedbed of modern athletics. The great quadrennial meeting at OLYMPIA (see feature box), and the other pan-Hellenic sporting festivals at Corinth, Nemea and Del-phi, served many of the same functions as the modern Games. They fostered a sense of cultural unity, provided an opportunity for rival states to assess their relative strengths, and satisfied the perpetual quest for glory.

ATHLETICS AT THE
ANCIENT OLYMPICS

The ancient Olympic Games were part of a religious festival dedicated to Zeus, the king of the Greek gods. Conventionally dated to 776BC, they took place every four years at OLYMPIA in south western Greece, and endured until around the end of the fourth century AD, when they were suppressed by the Christian Byzantine emperors.

The festival was initially a local affair but by the fifth century BC it had expanded to receive competitors from the Black Sea to the western Mediterranean. A few months ahead of each Games, heralds would travel throughout the Greek-speaking world to invite athletes and spectators to travel to Olympia, declaring a sacred truce which guaranteed their safe passage. That this was generally observed during a period of almost perpetual warfare between city states illustrates the religious significance of the Games.

The ZEUS link was emphasised throughout the festival. On arrival at Olympia, the athletes had to swear in front of a fearsome image of the god that they were free Greek men who had been in training for at least ten months. A hundred oxen were sacrificed to Zeus during the gathering, and in around 432BC a colossal gold and ivory statue of the god, by Pheidias, was unveiled in his temple on the site. Standing thirteen metres high, it was one of the Seven Wonders of the ancient world.

In its early days, the sporting aspect of the festival consisted of nothing but athletics. Indeed, for the first fifty years or so there was only one event: the STADE, a 192-metre sprint along the length of the *stadion* or stadium. It was run bare-footed on a course of rolled sand. The winner of the first recorded race, in 776BC, was a cook from the nearby city of Elis called Koroibos.

Other events were gradually added to the schedule. In 724BC the authorities introduced the DIAULOS, a race to the end of the stadium and back, which was roughly equivalent to the 400m. The DOLICHOS or 'long race', which consisted of between 20 and 24 lengths of the *stadion*, made its debut four years later. Only in 708BC did the first non-athletics event, WRESTLING, get added to the menu. Later additions included CHARIOT RACING, BOXING, a nasty form of no-holds-barred combat called the PANKRATION

AND THEY'RE OFF ... GREEK RUNNERS ON A VASE, 6TH CENTURY BC

(which, alarmingly, has recently been revived), and the HOPLITODROMOS, a race of two lengths of the stadium run in armour.

More interesting from an athletics perspective was the PENTATHLON, which was introduced at the same time as wrestling. It consisted of a stade foot race, a jumping event, discus and javelin throwing, plus wrestling. On the evidence of a fifth century BC poem composed in honour of a pentathlete named Phallyos, which claims he leapt over sixteen metres in the course of winning the competition, the JUMPING event must have involved multiple bounds, like today's triple jump. The DISCUS, in contrast to modern practice, was launched from a platform with the feet in fixed position. Its weight and dimensions were not standardised: instead, competitors had to use the biggest projectile that any of them produced for the occasion. The JAVELIN was also thrown in a way that's unfamiliar to us now. It was wrapped in cord, one end of which was tied to the fingers of the thrower. At the moment of release, the cord would unwind at terrific speed, imparting a stabilising rotation to the javelin that allowed it to sail well over 100 metres.

Athletes initially competed clothed but in 720BC a sprinter called Orsippos became separated from his loincloth during the stade race and went on to win it. A Spartan named Akanthos figured this was no coincidence, and promptly won the double-stade in a similar state of undress. Thereafter, NUDITY became standard. It is tempting to think this is why unmarried women were not allowed to attend the Games but the real reason is likely to have been religious. Zeus was a macho god who wouldn't have taken kindly to the dilution of the testosterone-charged atmosphere.

Then as now, there were no financial rewards for the winners. They had to make do with OLIVE WREATHS, plus the right to have their statues installed at Olympia. But the spin-off benefits of success were considerable. Promising athletes were generously sponsored by their native city states and victors could expect to be showered with gifts, pecuniary and otherwise. Indeed, the kudos attached to having a winner at the Games was so great that athletes were frequently poached. Sotades, for instance, won the long race at the 99th festival as a Cretan, only to appear at the subsequent Games as an Ephesian. An early example of the big money transfer.

The main perk of victory, however, was IMMORTALITY. This wasn't entirely illusory: athletes like LEONIDAS of Rhodes, who won all three running events at four consecutive Games between 164 and 152BC, are still remembered today.

The ROMANS inherited the Greek taste for organised games, which they often linked to religious festivals. But they famously liked their sports bloody, preferring gladiatorial contests and chariot races to purely athletic disciplines. In PRE-COLONIAL AMERICA, by contrast, tribes like the Jicarilla Apache and Osage built running tracks to keep their warriors fit, while in the remoter parts of Europe throwing contests were used as tests of manhood. The VIKINGS, for example, used hammer-throwing as a method of divvying up newly conquered land – the further a warrior threw the implement, the more territory he could claim.

The most glamorous sporting competitions in MIDDLE AGES and RENAISSANCE EUROPE were the jousting tournaments, held to hone the fighting skills of the knights. But it was the activities of regular soldiers that fed more directly into the evolution of modern athletics. SHOT PUTTING, for instance, grew out of the practice of hurling cannon-balls.

By the seventeenth and eighteenth centuries, the main sponsors of athletic competition were the ruling classes of the British Isles. Aristocrats were much given to organising foot races between their employees, and gambling on the results. The Earl Bishop of Cloyne in County Cork famously held a curate's race to determine the winner of an ecclesiastical post in his gift, forcing the competitors to run through boggy ground for his amusement. It was the near worship of the classical world by the same British elite that provided the spur for the first pan-athletic meeting of the (reasonably) modern era. In 1612, a lawyer named Robert Dover established the annual COTSWOLD OLYMPICK GAMES near Chipping Campden in Gloucestershire, with King James I's blessing. The programme included running, jumping and sledgehammer throwing.

The classical revival also underpinned the OLYMPIADE DE LA RÉPUBLIQUE that was held in revolutionary France, as well as the attempts by the Greeks to revive the ancient Games in 1859, 1870 and 1875, and the GRAND OLYMPIC FESTIVAL held annually at Liverpool from 1862–7, which had a programme startlingly like that of the 1896 Games in Athens. Another symptom of admiration for the ways of ancient Greece was the incorporation of physical exercise into the curriculum of schools and colleges in Europe and the USA. This played a vital role in the development of modern athletics. The meetings held at Shrewsbury School in 1840 and Exeter College, Oxford in 1850, for example, were among the first pan-athletic competitions of the modern era.

Outside the academies, a two-man gravel running track was built around the perimeter of Lord's Cricket Ground in LONDON in 1837 and in 1863 the first known indoor athletics meeting was held at Ashburnham Hall in the same city, featuring four races and a triple jump competition. The next stage was the establishment of national associations and championships. The ENGLISH AMATEUR ATHLETICS ASSOCIATION kicked off the process in 1880 and was soon followed by the AMERICAN ATHLETIC UNION (1888) and the UNION DES SOCIÉTÉS FRANÇAISES DE SPORTS ATHLÉTIQUES (1889). The world governing body, the IAAF (International Amateur Athletics Federation) was founded in 1912, and continues to govern the disciplines, having relaxed its 'Amateur' rules in 1982. It finally changed the tag from 'Amateur Athletics' to 'Athletics Associations' in 2001.

GAME ON: ATHLETICS BASICS

THE DIVERSE DISCIPLINES THAT CONSTITUTE ATHLETICS FALL into five categories: running, jumping, throwing, walking and combined events. Unless stated otherwise, the events below are contested – separately – by both sexes.

The excitement of athletics events tends to be proportionate to the simplicity of the challenge. 'Jump as far as you can' is a clearer proposition than 'do as big a hop and skip as you can, leaving something in reserve for a huge jump'. Consequently, the long jump enjoys a higher status than the triple jump, except where the viewer's priorities are twisted by patriotism (as with the British and triple jumper JONATHAN EDWARDS). Similarly, being the FASTEST MAN ON EARTH is more liable to impress than being the best at negotiating various obstacles over 3km. But dismissing the minority disiplines would be a mistake. It may not be easy to think your way into the mind of a hammer thrower, but the skill and dedication of such competitors are invariably breathtaking.

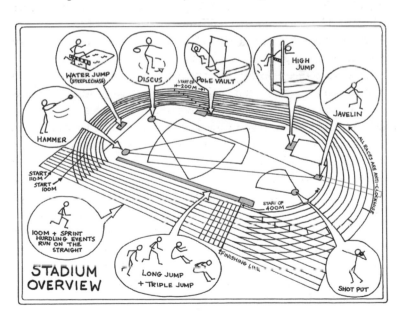

RUNNING

ALTITUDE MAKES A SIGNIFICANT DIFFERENCE TO PERFORMANCE. Runners at the 1968 Games at Mexico City (2240m above sea level) benefited from a reduction in air resistance that had a similar effect to a tailwind of 1.5m/sec. This was of benefit to the sprinters, but runners over longer distances suffered, as there was approximately 3 per cent less oxygen available to them than at sea level. Athletes who live and train at altitude, such as those from Africa's RIFT VALLEY, have a definite advantage in distance events as their bodies become accustomed to using oxygen more efficiently. When they come down to sea level, their lungs are supercharged with the gas.

Races up to 400 metres are run in LANES, as is the first 100m of the 800m, after which the athletes 'BREAK' – they are allowed to leave their starting lanes and move to the inside of the track, which offers the shortest and quickest route. In the longer races, athletes break from the start. The race time of an athlete is determined by the moment at which his or her torso breaks the finishing line.

SPRINTING

IN EVENTS OF 400M OR LESS, ATHLETES BEGIN IN STARTING BLOCKS. Explosiveness is the name of the game as they aim to spring out of their blocks and reach top speed as soon as possible. A FALSE START is registered if a runner leaves his or her blocks less than a tenth of a second after the starting gun is fired (the time it takes for the information to be relayed from the ears to the brain and muscles). It used to be that athletes were each allowed one false start but the rules were amended to allow just one false start by anyone in a race – and instant elimination thereafter. Then in 2010 they were further tightened so that just one false start led to dis-qualification: an absurd decision that soon had major repercussions, when Usain Bolt false started at the 2011 world championships in Korea and was unable to defend his 100m title.

A GOOD START is vital in the sprints, though perhaps not as vital as people tend to think. A bad start is only about five hundredths of a second slower than a good one and a top runner may be able to make up the difference during the race. But the psychological

USAIN BOLT CASUALLY SHATTERS THE 100M RECORD AT BEIJING

advantage of getting away quickly is invaluable. Mental condition is one of the key determinants of sprinting performance. Watch how the athletes PSYCH THEMSELVES UP before their races, posturing, blocking out crowd noises and indulging in 'hundred metre stares'.

Note that RECORDS do not count in the 100m and 200m (and the sprint hurdle events, long and triple jump) if a TAILWIND of 2.1m/second or more is recorded at any point during the race.

100M

THE ULTIMATE EXPRESSION OF HUMAN SPEED IS RUN OVER A straight course. To save surveyors and building contractors from going nuts, international 100m courses are allowed to deviate by up to 2cm in length and to rise or fall up to 10cm between start and finish.

At Olympic level, men usually complete the course in 43 to 46 strides and women in 47 to 52. A top male sprinter typically reaches a maximum speed of around 12 METRES PER SECOND (26.8mph) between 60 and 70m into a race. The equivalent figures for women are about 11m/s (24.6mph) at 50–60 metres. During the acceleration phase, both sexes run about 4.6 strides per second.

100M OLYMPIC RECORDS
MEN: 9.69 SEC, USAIN BOLT (JAMAICA), BEIJING 2008.
WOMEN: 10.62 SEC, FLORENCE GRIFFITH JOYNER (USA), SEOUL 1988.

··· **200M** ···

THE 200M IS SIMILAR IN DISTANCE TO THE ANCIENT STADE but is actually derived from the furlong (220 yards, one eighth of a mile). Throughout modern Olympic history, the event has been run on a 400m track with athletes going round a full bend, but prior to 1960 Americans competing in domestic competitions ran the 200m on straight tracks. Evidence accumulated before that date suggests that the technical demands of running around a bend add about one-third of a second to race times.

The athletes are still going flat out – USAIN BOLT's world record time is almost exactly twice his equivalent in the 100M – but there is a noticeable decline in speed in the second half of the race.

200M OLYMPIC RECORDS
MEN: 19.30, USAIN BOLT (JAMAICA), BEIJING 2008.
WOMEN: 21.34, FLORENCE GRIFFITH JOYNER (USA) SEOUL 1988.

RACING AND RACE

There are two elephants in the locker room of international athletics. One is the role of drugs in the sport, the other the relationship between race and athletic performance. Almost everyone agrees about the former (the use of artificial chemicals as contrary to the competitive spirit), at least in theory. The second subject is highly controversial.

What are the facts? As of 2011, the world record for every Olympic men's running discipline was held by an athlete of AFRICAN DESCENT. Indeed, aside from the 100m, 200m and 400m and the hurdling events, they were all held by Africans. The comparable statistics for women are much less clear cut but both sprint records currently belong to black athletes. There are lies, damned lies and statistics, but are black people simply better runners than everyone else?

The answer is 'yes and no': yes, in that it clearly helps to have African ancestry; no, because the notion that people in that category form a single ethnic group couldn't be more erroneous. Africa is, by a distance, the most genetically diverse continent, and Zulus and Berbers, for example, have about as much in common physically as Scandinavians and the Chinese.

THE EAST AFRICAN EXPRESS: KENENISA BEKELE OF ETHIOPIA SHOWING THE WAY
HOME TO KENYAN ELIUD KIPCHOGE AT BEIJING 2008

What is incontrovertibly true is that two ethnic groups overwhelmingly
boss Olympic running. The best SPRINTERS have WEST AFRICAN ancestry
and the top LONG DISTANCE RUNNERS are almost invariably EAST AFRICAN.
Remarkably, a huge proportion of them come from just one area – the
Kalenjin region of the Upper Rift Valley in Kenya. Scientists point to the
typical physiologies of the ethnic groups concerned. West Africans and
their American, Caribbean and European descendants tend to have narrow hips, well-developed musculature and an unusually high proportion of
fast-twitch muscle fibres – all qualities that are advantageous to sprinting.
Kalenjins, on the other hand, are usually small and light, with muscles packed
with slow-twitch fibres. They also come from a high altitude region, which
makes for more efficient use of oxygen. In other words, they are ideally
equipped for endurance running.

Interestingly, the Chinese openly embrace the concept of racial differences in athletic ability. In 2004, the *People's Daily* reported that the CHINESE

have 'congenital shortcomings' and 'genetic differences' that mitigate against track and field success. This might be seen as a case of getting the excuses in early. However, the doctrine allows the success of the likes of Liu Xiang, winner of the 110m HURDLES in Athens, to be attributed to stereotypical Chinese virtues like discipline, hard work and clever technique. It's also interesting to note that the JAPANESE have always produced strong MARATHON runners – their trainers often put their success down to a combination of low body fat and a very good attitude to pain.

One thing is certain: only a fool would bet on a non-East African winning the men's 10,000m, or a white man winning the 100m. But a Jamaican winning the former or an Ethiopian the latter is just as unlikely.

400M

THE 400M MAKES DEMANDS ON COMPETITORS THAT HAVE led the IAAF to describe the event as an 'endurance sprint'. Even the fittest athletes are incapable of running at top speed for more than 30–35 seconds before they start to suffer the effects of oxygen depletion. At this stage the body begins to respire anaerobically to make up the deficit, and the consequence is a build-up of lactic acid in the muscles. As anyone who has experienced a 'stitch' can testify, this is decidedly uncomfortable. Successful 400m runners therefore need to be cussed individuals with an ability to ignore pain. Needless to say, they must also be extremely quick.

Once upon a time, top 400m runners could be divided into 200/400m and 400/800m specialists, the latter including the great Cuban ALBERTO JUANTORENA, who won both events at Montreal 1976, and the former MICHAEL JOHNSON, who won both 200m and 400m at Atlanta 1996. It seemed inconceivable that either feat would be repeated, until it was revealed that USAIN BOLT is considering a move up to 400m.

400M OLYMPIC RECORDS
MEN: 43.49, MICHAEL JOHNSON (USA), ATLANTA 1996.
WOMEN: 48.25, MARIE-JOSÉ PÉREC (FRANCE) ATLANTA 1996.

MIDDLE DISTANCE

MIDDLE DISTANCE RUNNING IS MUCH MORE TACTICAL THAN sprinting, because athletes cannot go flat out all the way through their races. They must conserve as much energy as possible until the final bend, while constantly monitoring what their opponents are doing.

This is what's fun to try to assess. Do the athletes look as though they have something left in the tank for a sprint finish? Or are they feeling the strain? If an athlete BREAKS AWAY from the main pack before the end, have they gone too soon or timed it to perfection? You can expect to see the best runners cruise up from mid-pack to second or third as they pass the bell – unless they are oddballs like Kenya's 1970s star HENRY RONO, who used to accelerate every second lap or so, to break all resistance well in advance of the last lap.

800M

THE SHORTEST OF THE MIDDLE DISTANCE RACES CONSISTS OF two laps of the stadium. Competitors start off in lanes but 'break' after 100 metres. A bell is rung at the beginning of the final lap, as it is in all multi-lap races. At this point the pace picks up via a para-Pavlovian reaction which adds considerably to the drama.

800M OLYMPIC RECORDS
MEN: 1:42.58, VEBJØRN RODAL (NORWAY) ATLANTA 1996.
WOMEN: 1:53.43, NADEZHDA OLIZARENKO (USSR) MOSCOW 1980.

1500M

THE 'METRIC MILE' IS THE BLUE RIBAND EVENT OF MIDDLE distance running. It demands greater stamina than the 800m but almost as much leg-speed – to compete at this level a male competitor needs to run consecutive laps in an average time of 55 seconds – plus an ability to gauge the precise moment to break out of the pack and hit the front. The 1500m and to a lesser extent the 800m are often rough races, with plenty of jostling and barging. Britain's Steve Ovett used to create space for himself by shoving the runner in front with a straight arm. Competitors in big 1500m races have been known to come to blows.

1500m Olympic Records
Men: 3:32.07, Noah Ngeny (Kenya), Sydney 2000
Women: 3:53.96, Paula Ivan (Romania) Seoul 1988.

-------------------------------- **STEEPLECHASE** --------------------------------

The steeplechase – which began as a form of Irish cross country in which participants raced between churches – is a muscle-sapping 3000m race with 28 hurdles and 7 water jumps. The obstacles are 36in high in men's steeplechasing and 30in in women's; they don't collapse if you crash in to them, so some competitors deliberately land on the top of the fences to help themselves get over them. The water jump consists of a hurdle followed by an upward sloping pit of water 12 feet long. The further the athletes jump, the less wet they get, but they nearly always land with one foot in the water, on the upper part of the slope, to reduce the jarring.

Steeplechase Olympic Records
Men: 8:05.51 Julius Kariuku (Kenya) Seoul 1988.
Women: 8:58.81, Gulnara Galkina (Russia) Beijing 2008.

Long Distance

The Olympics host 5000m, 10,000m and Marathon events. In earlier times there was also cross country but this was dropped after the catastrophic Paris 1924 event, in which the competitors were poisoned by fumes from a power plant.

-------------------------------- **5000M & 10,000M** --------------------------------

Long-distance running is like middle distance running, only more so. It is extremely tactical, with the athletes either trying to break their opponents by building up unassailable leads or making damned sure they have something left in the tank for the last lap. Despite the energy-sapping earlier stages of these races, the last few hundred metres are often thrillingly fast.

5,000M OLYMPIC RECORDS
MEN: 12:57.82, KENENISA BEKELE (ETHIOPIA) BEIJING 2008.
WOMEN: 14:40.79, GABRIELA SZABO (ROMANIA) SYDNEY 2000.

10,000M OLYMPIC RECORDS
MEN: 27:01.17, KENENISA BEKLE (ETHIOPIA) BEIJING 2008.
WOMEN: 29:54.66 TIRUNESH DIBABA (ETHIOPIA) BEIJING 2008.

MARATHON

THE MARATHON WAS DEVISED AS A HEADLINE-GRABBING centrepiece for the Athens Olympics in 1896. It was inspired by the legend of PHEIDIPPIDES, a Greek soldier who in 490BC supposedly ran 26 miles to Athens to deliver news of the Greek victory over the Persians at the Battle of Marathon, only to drop dead of exhaustion. The standard distance was extended at the London Games in 1908 at the behest of the British royal family, who wanted the race to begin beneath the windows of the nursery at Windsor Castle and to finish opposite the royal box in White City Stadium, 26 miles and 385 yards away.

Marathon runners obviously need great STAMINA. They also have to SHIFT. The men's world record time of 2:03:59 and the women's 2:15:25 equate to 26 sub-five-minute miles in a row. Until the 1970s you could be a top-class male marathon runner on stamina alone, but it has since become the domain of men who can do a sub-four-minute mile, not just sub-five – and you now have to be able to sprint at the finish. Women's marathon racing likewise. In the light of which, it's no surprise that 10,000M RUNNERS often double up in the marathon, or move on to marathon when they've finished with the 10k – notably the sublime HAILE GEBRSELASSIE.

MARATHON OLYMPIC RECORDS
MEN: 2:06:32, SAMUEL WANJIRU (KENYA) BEIJING 2008.
WOMEN: 2:23:14 NAOKO TAKAHASHI (JAPAN) SYDNEY 2000.

HURDLING

RHYTHM AND TECHNIQUE ARE EVERYTHING IN HURDLING. The best performers seem to float over the barriers, expending the minimum of energy and not disrupting their step patterns in the slightest. The world record times for the women's and men's 400m hurdles are less than four seconds slower than those for regular races over that distance. Maintaining a consistent STRIDE PATTERN is extremely difficult. The standard way of clearing a hurdle, with the leading leg extended and the other one bent either sideways or underneath the body, is also very demanding.

The HURDLES themselves are designed to collapse if they are hit sufficiently hard and there are no penalties for doing this, provided the contestants make reasonable attempts to jump them. They often are hit, although this is something hurdlers seek to avoid. A collision disrupts RHYTHM and slows progress in proportion to its severity. In extreme cases it can cause a highly unpleasant fall. But hurdlers learn to cope with knocking a few over in the course of a race if that's what it takes.

When watching the hurdling events, attempt to get an early fix on who is running with the best rhythm. The smoothness or otherwise of their LEADING LEG movements is the key – if a runner has to stutter to correct their STRIDE PATTERN, they're finished.

······· 110M (MEN), 100M (WOMEN), 400M (MEN AND WOMEN) ·······

ALL OLYMPIC HURDLES RACES CONSIST OF TEN JUMPS. THE women's sprint is 100m, the men's 110m. There are differences too in the height of the hurdles (1.067m in the men's race, 0.8m in the women's) and the distances from starting line to the first hurdle, one hurdle to another and the last hurdle to the finish. The hurdles used in the 400m races are lower – 0.914m and 0.762m for men and women respectively – but this time the course is laid out in the same way for both sexes: a 45m dash to the first obstacle, 35m between subsequent hurdles and a 40m sprint at the end.

110M HURDLES OLYMPIC RECORDS
MEN: 12.91, XIANG LIU (CHINA) ATHENS 2004.
WOMEN: 12.37, JOANNA HAYES (USA) ATHENS 2004.
400M HURDLES OLYMPIC RECORDS
MEN: 46.78, KEVIN YOUNG (USA) BARCELONA 1992.
WOMEN: 52.64, MELANIE WALKER (JAMAICA) BEIJING 2008.

RELAYS: 4 x 100M, 4 x 400M

OLYMPIC TEAMS ARE COMPOSED OF EACH NATION'S FASTEST runners, but speed alone is not enough: smooth HANDOVERS are essential to success. Exchanging a baton with a colleague without substantially reducing the speed of its progress is an art, and teams often come to grief under pressure. Batons must be passed within a transition zone which extends ten metres each side of the nominal distance of each leg. The recipient must start on the inside of the first line and time his or start so as to be going as fast as possible when the baton is handed over. They mustn't go too fast however, or they will have to slow down dramatically to ensure that the handover occurs before they cross the front of the zone.

The 4 x 100m is run in lanes staggered as for a regular 400m race. The first leg of the 4 x 400m is also run in lanes, which continue through the transition zone to a point 100 metres into the second leg. At this stage the runners BREAK, seeking a good position on the inside of the track. The transition zones thereafter can look extremely chaotic, with the teams jostling for position along the nearside line of the zone and several athletes often taking off from much the same point at much the same time.

Traditionally, the FIRST LEG of a relay is run by the second fastest member of a team, the SECOND by the third fastest, the PENULTI-MATE by the slowest and the final leg – the ANCHOR LEG – by the quickest.

4 x 100M RELAY OLYMPIC RECORDS
MEN: 37.10, JAMAICA, BEIJING 2008.
WOMEN: 41.60, EAST GERMANY, MOSCOW 1980.
4 x 400M RELAY OLYMPIC RECORDS
MEN: 2:55.74, USA, BARCELONA 1992.
WOMEN: 3:15.17, SOVIET UNION, SEOUL 1988.

JUMPING

SPEED OF APPROACH IS THE KEY TO LONG- AND TRIPLE-JUMP-
ing success. Pay careful attention to the consistency of the
competitors' TAKE-OFF POINTS. If they are erratic, or if they are
repeatedly taking off too early, it is likely to prey on their minds
during the run-up. For HIGH JUMPERS it is a question of getting
in the zone, bouncing jauntily and smoothly on the approach and
gauging the optimum launching point. For all of them, it's vital to
make a good start. A jumper rarely recovers from a series of bad
jumps in the early rounds.

As with sprinters, jumpers' PRE-PERFORMANCE RITUALS are
worthy of attention. Long jumpers in particular are known for their
strange psyching techniques, acting out a complete jump in their
minds, with accompanying jerks and twitches, before setting off.
Jumpers also often encourage the crowd to clap a rhythm to which
they can match their stride – runners tend to shut out the noise,
whereas jumpers like it.

Rather sadly, contests for STANDING JUMPS were abandoned
in 1912, depriving us of such exponents as RAY EWRY, aka 'THE
HUMAN FROG', who made a clean sweep of the standing jump events
at three consecutive Games between 1900 and 1908. Paradoxically,
the key to his success was a bout of childhood polio. The young
Ewery exercised his way out of his wheelchair, developing legs so
powerful that he was able to leap more than nine feet backwards.

···························· **HIGH JUMP** ····························

EACH CONTESTANT HAS A MAXIMUM OF THREE ATTEMPTS AT
every height, after which the BAR IS RAISED until only one jumper
is left in the competition. In the case of a TIE, the jumper with the
fewest failures at the last cleared height prevails. If these are identical, the number of failures in the whole competition is taken into
account and if all else fails there is a JUMP-OFF.

TAKE-OFF POINT is crucial in the high jump. Too close to the bar
and the jumper will clip it as they rise. Too far and they will hit it
as they fall. The angle of approach is equally critical. Most top high
jumpers arrive at an angle of 30–40 degrees. The aim is for the

DICK FOSBURY DEBUTS HIS FLOP AT MEXICO CITY, 1968

body to reach its highest point just as it reaches bar level, which is easier said than done.

Prior to 1968, high jumpers typically crossed the bar facing downwards. After DICK FOSBURY won the Mexico City event with his face pointing skywards, his revolutionary 'FLOP' technique became standard almost overnight.

HIGH JUMP OLYMPIC RECORDS
MEN: 2.39M, CHARLES AUSTIN (USA) ATLANTA 1996.
WOMEN: 2.06, YELENA SLESARENKO (RUSSIA) ATHENS 2004.

.... **LONG JUMP** ....

SUCCESS HINGES ON SPEED ON THE RUNWAY AND TRANSLATING it into forward motion through the air. This explains why many top sprinters – notably CARL LEWIS and MARION JONES – have adapted quite easily to long jump.

TAKE-OFF POINT is again critical. Competitors must take off from a point on or before a 20cm-wide board laid flush with the running track – ideally, the front foot leaves the ground a few millimetres from the forward edge. FOUL JUMPS frequently occur and are verified by a slab of putty in front of the take-off board, which takes on an imprint of the foot of any jumper who goes over the line.

Each jumper gets THREE ATTEMPTS, then the eight with the longest jumps to date go through to the final, where they get another three goes. The longest jump of the day wins the competition.

LONG JUMP OLYMPIC RECORDS
MEN: 8.90M, BOB BEAMON (USA) MEXICO CITY 1968.
WOMEN: 7.40, JACKIE JOYNER-KERSEE (USA) SEOUL 1988.

··· **TRIPLE JUMP** ···

THE RULES AND STRUCTURE OF THE TRIPLE JUMP ARE MUCH the same as those for the long jump. Smooth transitions between the HOP, SKIP AND JUMP are vital. In the hop phase, competitors must land on the foot with which they took off. They then take a giant step, landing on the opposite foot, before jumping in such a way as to land on two feet. As in long jumping, the distance of a jump is taken from the mark in the sand nearest to the launching board.

TRIPLE JUMP OLYMPIC RECORDS
MEN: 18.09M, KENNY HARRISON (USA) ATLANTA 1996.
WOMEN: 15.39, FRANÇOISE MBANGO (CAMEROON) BEIJING 2008.

··· **POLE VAULT** ···

THE POLE VAULT INVOLVES RUNNING DOWN A TRACK WHILE holding one end of a long, flexible pole, planting the other end in a small box and using the energy of the unbending pole to climb as high as possible. Skilful exponents are able to push themselves upwards from the top of the pole just as it reaches a vertical position, which allows them to clear heights of 6m or more. The rules are much the same as in the high jump – THREE FAILURES at a given height and you're out.

POLE VAULT OLYMPIC RECORDS
MEN: 5.96M, STEVEN HOOKER (USA) BEIJING 2008.
WOMEN: 5.05, YELENA ISINBAYEVA (RUSSIA) BEIJING 2008.

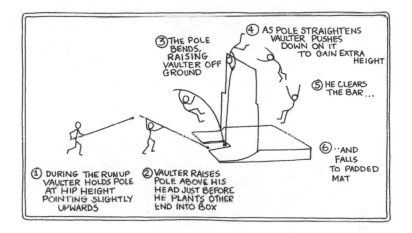

④ AS POLE STRAIGHTENS VAULTER PUSHES DOWN ON IT TO GAIN EXTRA HEIGHT

③ THE POLE BENDS, RAISING VAULTER OFF GROUND

⑤ HE CLEARS THE BAR...

⑥ ..AND FALLS TO PADDED MAT

① DURING THE RUN UP VAULTER HOLDS POLE AT HIP HEIGHT POINTING SLIGHTLY UPWARDS

② VAULTER RAISES POLE ABOVE HIS HEAD JUST BEFORE HE PLANTS OTHER END INTO BOX

THROWING

STRENGTH IS OBVIOUSLY VITAL IN THE THROWING EVENTS, but speed is equally important. The distance an object is thrown is directly related to the speed of the relevant parts of the body at the instant of release. In the javelin and shot put, the VELOCITY OF THE THROWING ARM is what matters; in the discus and hammer, what matters is the rate at which the whole BODY IS SPINNING at the moment of truth. Top performers glide across the launching circles like twenty-stone ballet dancers. Getting your ANGLES RIGHT is also essential. If the trajectory of a throw is too high, its energy will be wasted on vertical climb rather than horizontal distance; too low and the projectile will come to ground prematurely. SMOOTHNESS OF DELIVERY is another imperative. The best javelin throwers make their implements slice through the air with scarcely a flutter.

Olympic athletes have THREE INITIAL ATTEMPTS in all the throwing events. The eight athletes who register the longest distances during this phase of the competition go through to the final, where they are allowed another three attempts.

DISCUS

MEN USE A 2KG DISCUS 22CM IN DIAMETER, WOMEN A 1KG model, which explains why the women's Olympic record is

NO ATHLETE, MALE OR FEMALE, HAS THROWN THE DISCUS AS FAR IN THE MODERN OLYMPICS AS EAST GERMANY'S MARTINA HELLMANN

superior to the men's – uniquely in Olympic sport. Competitors skip-spin across a 2.5m throwing circle, turning one and a half times, before using their momentum and the torsion generated by rapidly twisting their bodies to hurl the discus as far as possible. The optimum ANGLE OF RELEASE is around 35 degrees. For a throw to count, the discus must land within 20 degrees of a line projecting straight forward from the throwing circle.

DISCUS OLYMPIC RECORDS

MEN: 69.89M, VIRGILIJUS ALENKA (LITHUANIA) ATHENS 2004.
WOMEN: 72.30M, MARTINA HELLLMANN (EAST GERMANY) SEOUL 1988.

··· **JAVELIN** ···

BY THE 1980S, JAVELIN THROWERS HAD BECOME SO GOOD (the top men were hurling their weapons over 100m) that their efforts were starting to threaten athletes on the running track. The IAAF responded by changing the design specifications of competition javelins, altering their centres of gravity to make them plunge to earth sooner than they otherwise would. For a throw to count, the tip of the javelin must strike the ground before any other part of it, but it's not necessary for it to actually stick in the ground.

Men's javelins must weigh at least 800g and be 2.6–2.7m long. The comparable figures for women are 600g and 2.2–2.3m.

A fast but controlled RUN-UP is essential, as is launching the javelin at the optimum angle: it should be pointing upwards by 30–40 degrees. The throwing arm should move smoothly but rapidly and the follow-through should generate as much power as possible. Javelin throwers typically perform a little skip before braking and launching. And they often wear huge support belts to reduce the stress these movements put on their lower backs.

Javelin Olympic Records
MEN: 90.57M, ANDREAS THORKILDSEN (NORWAY) BEIJING 2008.
WOMEN: 71.53, OSLEIDYS MENENDEZ (CUBA) ATHENS 2004.

··· **SHOT PUT** ···

THE MEN'S SHOT PUT WEIGHS 7.26KG AND HAS A DIAMETER OF 110–130mm, while the women's is 4kg and 95–110m across. The aim of the exercise is to launch the projectile solely by a rapid extension of the throwing arm, which initially cradles it under the thrower's chin. Putters add OOMPH to their throws by moving rapidly across a 2.135m throwing circle and slamming the leading foot into a 10cm high stop board, thus setting up a Newtonian counter-reaction that adds energy to their puts. Some putters glide across the circle in a straight line, others spin once before releasing the metal ball.

Shot Put Olympic Records
MEN: 22.47M, ULF TIMMERMAN (EAST GERMANY) SEOUL 1988.
WOMEN: 22.41, ILONA SLUPIANEK (EAST GERMANY) MOSCOW 1980.

··· **HAMMER** ···

THE HAMMER CONSISTS OF A METAL WEIGHT OF THE SAME mass and dimensions as the shot put attached to a wire 1.17–1.215m in length, with a grip at the far end. As with the shot, the throwing circle is 2.135m in diameter. Athletes ROTATE up to four times, using a heel–toe–heel footwork sequence, before launching the hammer. They wear gloves to prevent the handle from skinning their fingers.

Of all the throwing events, the hammer offers the highest chance of mayhem. If a competitor releases the projectile prematurely, the PROTECTIVE CAGE that surrounds much of the throwing circle is likely to be demolished.

Hammer Olympic Records
MEN: 84.80, SERGEY LITVINOV (USSR) SEOUL 1988.
WOMEN: 76.34, OKSANA MENKOVA (BELARUS) ATHENS 2004.

WALKING

RACE WALKING GREW OUT OF A CRAZE FOR COMPETITIVE 'pedestrianism' in the UK and USA in the eighteenth and nineteenth centuries. Huge wagers were staked on how long it would take selected individuals to walk between specified points. Celebrity walkers ranged from mutton-chop whiskered men to elderly women. In 1749, an 18-month girl walked the half a mile length of Pall Mall in 23 minutes, to the delight of her backers.

······ 20KM WALK (MEN & WOMEN), 50KM WALK (MEN) ······

COMPETITORS MUST HAVE ONE FOOT IN CONTACT WITH THE ground at all times and the ADVANCING LEG must be straight from the moment it touches the ground to the point where it is in a vertical position. Several judges are on hand along the course to monitor the walkers and issue RED CARDS if they infringe the rules. If a competitor receives three such cards (each judge can only issue one per athlete), he or she is disqualified.

20KM Walk Olympic Records
MEN: 1:18:59, ROBERT KORZENIOWSKI (POLAND) SYDNEY 2000.
WOMEN: 1:26:31, OLGA KANISKINA (RUSSIA) BEIJING 2008.
50KM Walk Olympic Records
MEN: 3:37:09, ALEX SCHWAZER (ITALY) BEIJING 2008.

COMBINED EVENTS

'IS THE WORLD'S SECOND GREATEST ATHLETE GAY?' ASKED Daley Thompson's T-shirt at a press conference following his victory in the DECATHLON at LA in 1984. Clearly aimed at Carl Lewis, the jibe wasn't the most charming moment of the Games, but beneath the yobbishness lay a valid question. Was Lewis, who had just won golds in the 100m, 200m, long jump and 4 x 100m relay, really the best male athlete in the world or did that title properly belong to the man who had outdone all-comers over ten different events? A similar question could be asked of women heptathletes with reference to their specialist sisters.

·········· DECATHLON (MEN), HEPTATHLON (WOMEN) ··········

THE MEN'S DECATHLON IS HELD OVER TWO DAYS. ON DAY one the 100M, LONG JUMP, SHOT PUT, HIGH JUMP and 400M are contested, while the 110M HURDLES, DISCUS, POLE VAULT, JAVELIN and 1500M take place on day two, in that order.

The WOMEN'S HEPTATHLON also takes two days to complete. The order of events is 100M HURDLES, SHOT PUT, HIGH JUMP and 200M on the first day; LONG JUMP, JAVELIN and 800M on the second.

Competitors in both disciplines need to pace themselves carefully. It's no good exhausting yourself in the 110m hurdles if you have to compete in the discus, pole vault, javelin and 1500m later in the day. As a consequence of the punishing schedules, performances tend to be more pedestrian than they would be if the events were more spread out. The top athletes aim for CONSISTENCY and keeping the leader in their sights. POINTS are awarded for distances thrown and times registered, and the decathlete/heptathlete who accumulates most points over the course of the competition is the winner.

DECATHLON OLYMPIC RECORD
MEN: 8893 POINTS, ROMAN ŠEBRLE (CZECH REPUBLIC) ATHENS 2004.
HEPTATHLON OLYMPIC RECORD
WOMEN: 7291 POINTS, JACKIE JOYNER-KERSEE (USA) SEOUL 1988.

Athletics Goes to the Olympics

Athletics have been at the heart of every Olympic Games. Here's a summary of some of the highlights.

·· **1896** ··

The first event of the modern Olympic era was a heat of the men's 100m, which was won in 12.2 seconds by Frank Lane of the USA. His compatriots went on to collect nine of the twelve winners' medals on offer (silver rather than gold). For home fans, the victory of Spyridon Louis in the marathon was the highlight. Some 70,000 euphoric Greek spectators cheered home the 24-year-old water-carrier, who was joined on the last lap by the nation's two crown princes.

·· **1900** ··

Nobody would call the 1900 Paris Olympics a triumph of organisation. Most of the athletic events were held in an uneven field dotted with trees, with a grass track 500 metres long. Nevertheless, heroes managed to emerge, most of them American. Ray Ewry (the frog man – see 'Jumping') won all three standing jumps and Alvin Kraenzlein became the first modern Olympic great, winning the 60m sprint, the 110m and 200m hurdles and the long jump in the space of three days. In the process, he introduced the world to the extended leg method of hurdling (athletes had previously bunny-hopped over the obstacles with both legs tucked under their bodies) and narrowly avoided being beaten up by the man he defeated in the long jump after reneging on a promise not to compete on a Sunday (Alvin turned up, his trusting rival didn't).

·· **1904** ··

US dominance of athletics continued in St Louis, not least because 197 of the 233 competitors were American. George Poage and Joseph Stadler became the first African-American medallists (in the 400m hurdles and the standing high jump respectively) and Ray Ewry again sprang his way to a clean sweep of the

standing jump titles. The apparent winner of the MARATHON, a New
Yorker named FRED LORZ, was discovered to have covered eleven
miles of the course in a car. The gold medal was snatched from his
neck and awarded to THOMAS HICKS of Massachusetts, who completed the race fortified with brandy and strychnine.

··· **1908** ···

THE MARATHON AGAIN STOLE THE HEADLINES IN LONDON IN
1908. The first runner to appear in front of the 90,000 crowd was an
exhausted Italian waiter named DORANDO PIETRI. In his delirium
he tried to run around the track the wrong way, collapsed five times
and was eventually helped over the line by officials. Not surprisingly,
the American runner-up JOHNNY HAYES lodged a complaint. It was
upheld and he was awarded the gold. (Pietri was, however, given a
silver cup by Queen Alexandra – oddly enough, at the suggestion of
Arthur Conan Doyle). As had become the norm, the USA won far
more athletic gold medals than anyone else (sixteen) but the British
and Irish team did manage to claim seven of their own.

··· **1912** ···

THE 1912 OLYMPICS IN STOCKHOLM PRODUCED FURTHER
evidence that the Europeans might be beginning to close the gap
between themselves and the Americans. This time the main challengers were the FINNS, who won six athletics titles compared with
the USA's sixteen – a thrashing on paper but a stunning victory
on a per capita basis. HANNES KOLEHMAINEN was the pick of the
bunch, winning the 5,000m, 10,000m and cross-country. But the
biggest story of the Games was JIM THORPE, who won both the
pentathlon and decathlon, breaking the world record in the latter
with a score that would have still have earned him silver in 1948.

··· **1920** ···

THE ANTWERP GAMES INTRODUCED THE WORLD TO PAAVO
NURMI. The original and greatest 'FLYING FINN' won gold medals
in the 10,000m and the individual and team cross country events,
helping his nation to match the USA's total of nine athletics victories. He also won a silver in the 5000m.

··· **1924** ···

NURMI COLLECTED FIVE MORE GOLDS IN THE SECOND PARIS Games, which coincided with a fierce heatwave. He would almost certainly have won a sixth had the Finnish authorities not prevented him entering the 10,000m out of concern for his health. Long jumper WILLIAM DEHART HUBBARD became the first BLACK ATHLETE to win an individual gold, although the shine was slightly tarnished by the fact that his fellow American ROBERT LEGENDRE had broken the world record for the discipline the previous day while competing in the pentathlon.

··· **1928** ···

AS WELL AS INSPIRING *CHARIOTS OF FIRE*, THE AMSTERDAM Olympics threw up two significant firsts. WOMEN were finally allowed to compete in track and field events, though their programme was soon drastically cut (see box) and Japanese triple jumper MIKIO ODA of Japan won Asia's first gold medal.

'ELEVEN WRETCHED WOMEN': THE 1928 WOMEN'S 800M

Although the IOC had graciously allowed females to compete in the relatively demure disciplines of tennis, golf and sailing since 1900, with archery added to the list in 1904 and swimming and diving in 1912, there were no Olympic WOMEN'S TRACK AND FIELD EVENTS until the 1928 GAMES IN AMSTERDAM. Even then, the decision to include them was controversial.

The prevailing view in certain circles was that women were not biologically suited to strenuous exercise, an attitude supported by spurious scientific claims that athletic activity threatened women's fertility by jiggling their internal organs around. Harold Abrahams, the winner of the 1924 100m, as immortalised in *Chariots of Fire*, spoke for many when he wrote: 'I do not consider that women are built for really violent exercise of the kind that is the essence of competition. One has only to see them practising to realise how awkward they are on the running track.' Heaven knows what he would have made of JARMILA KRATOCHVILOVA, the 1980s Czech middle distance runner, who had pecs like Arnold Schwarzenegger. Unfortunately, the women's 800m final at Amsterdam played into the hands of those who saw such events as abominations. One old-school sports reporter wrote that, 'Below us on the cinder path were eleven wretched women, five of whom dropped out before the finish, while five collapsed on reaching the tape.' In fact, footage of the event shows that there were only nine runners, all of whom finished the event. But several of them did then collapse in exhaustion.

As more progressive observers pointed out, this would have been considered routine in a men's

AN UNDIGNIFIED SPECTACLE? LINA RADKE (GERMANY) LEADING THE FIELD HOME IN 1928'S INFAMOUS WOMEN'S 800M

race, where competitors were expected to give their all. The event had also been won (by LINA RADKE of Germany) in a world record time of 2:16.8, and so might have been expected to be rather draining. But the dinosaurs seized on the 'unfeminine' sight of spent females sprawled on the ground and banned women from racing further than 200m, a ruling that was not rescinded at Olympic level for 32 years.

······························· **1932** ·······························

IN LOS ANGELES, AUTOMATIC TIMING MADE ITS FIRST APpearance, ditto the PHOTO FINISH, which was used to correct the result of the 110m hurdles. The bronze medal was initially awarded to Jack Keller of the USA, then to Donald Finlay of Great Britain. The great all-rounder BABE DIDRIKSON qualified for all five women's events on her home soil and won golds for the javelin and 80m hurdles, and a silver for the high jump.

1936

BERLIN 1936 IS BEST REMEMBERED FOR JESSE OWENS, who made a mockery of the Third Reich's theory of racial superiority with victories in the 100m, 200m, 4 x 100m relay and the long jump. The local crowds took Owens to their hearts and Germany's Luz Long publically befriended him during the long jump competition, to the dismay of the Nazi authorities. They weren't best pleased with the medals table either – Germany came second with five golds while the Americans racked up fourteen.

JESSE OWENS ON HIS WAY TO A FOURTH OLYMPIC GOLD AT BERLIN

1948

THE STAR OF THE SHOW AT LONDON'S SECOND GAMES WAS Dutch housewife FANNY BLANKERS-KOEN, who won golds in the 100m, 200m, 80m hurdles and 4 x 100m relay. USA's ALICE COACHMAN won the high jump to become the first BLACK FEMALE Olympic champion, while the men's decathlon title was claimed by seventeen-year-old American BOB MATHIAS, who remains the YOUNGEST MALE Olympic athletics champion. When asked how he intended to celebrate, he said 'I'll start shaving I guess.' MICHELINE OSTERMEYER, a French concert pianist, used her delicate fingers to win the first women's Olympic shot put competition – as well as winning a gold for the discus and a bronze in the high jump.

1952

WITH THEIR FINE RECORD IN LONG-DISTANCE RUNNING, THE Finns had every reason to expect a hatful of victories on their home soil. They had reckoned without Czech phenomenon EMILE ZÁTOPEK. Having collected golds in the 5000m and 10,000m, he thought it might be worth trying his hand at the marathon, a distance he had never attempted before. He won it by more than two and a half minutes.

1956

THE HOME NATION GOT OFF TO A STORMING START IN THE athletics at Melbourne, with BETTY CUTHBERT completing a double in the women's 100m and 200m and anchoring Australia's victory in the 4 x 100m relay.

1960

AFTER 64 YEARS, A RUNNER FROM A NON-ANGLOPHONE NAtion – Germany's ARMIN HARY – won the men's 100m in Rome. ABEBE BIKILA of Ethiopia broke the marathon record, running in his bare feet, becoming the first black African gold medallist. Women were finally allowed to run more than 200m again, with LYUDMILLA SHEVTSOVA (USSR) claiming the first women's 800m since 1928. The athletics cold war also heated up, as the SOVIET UNION came within a whisker of matching the American haul of victories – the final tally was eleven golds to twelve.

1964

THE TOKYO GAMES PRODUCED TWO STUNNING VICTORIES from the walking wounded. BIKILA won the marathon again, in another record time, just six weeks after having his appendix removed, and American AL OERTER collected his third men's discus title while wearing a neck brace.

1968

THE ATHLETIC EVENTS IN MEXICO CITY WERE MARKED BY THE effects of high altitude. BOB BEAMON of the USA sailed through the thin air to break the WORLD LONG JUMP RECORD by almost

TWO GLOVES, ONE STRUGGLE: TOMMIE SMITH AND JOHN CARLOS GIVE BLACK POWER SALUTES ON THE PODIUM

two feet (his record stood until 1991 and remains the Olympic record). Five of the male triple jumpers exceeded the existing record distance and there were world records in all the men's races up to and including 400m. Contrariwise, the distance races were won in slow times due to the exhaustion produced by the low-oxygen atmosphere; the great RON CLARKE was nearly killed by the 10km race. Other highlights included DICK FOSBURY introducing the world to the 'flop' method of clearing the high jump bar; KIP KEINO, first of the world-beating Kenyans, who won the 1500m by a (still unrivalled) margin of 20m; and sprinters TOMMIE SMITH and JOHN CARLOS being kicked out of Olympic village after their infamous BLACK POWER SALUTES at the men's 200m award ceremony.

·········· **1972** ··········

A NEW GREAT FINNISH LONG-DISTANCE RUNNER EMERGED IN Munich, when LASSE VIREN claimed the men's 5000m and 10,000m, a feat he would repeat in Montreal. ULRIKE MEYFARTH of West Germany became the youngest individual athletics champion by winning the women's high jump at the age of sixteen. East German WOLFGANG NORDWIG brought a sequence of sixteen US victories in the pole vault to an end and the USSR finally managed to come first in the athletics medals table, with VALERI BORZOV achieving a sprint double in the 100m and 200m.

1976

ALBERTO JUANTORENA (CUBA) BECAME THE FIRST MAN TO complete the 400m/800m double (he was a newcomer to the latter event). VIKTOR SANEYEV (USSR) won his third triple jump title and Hungarian javelin thrower MIKLOS NEMETH became the first son of an Olympic gold medallist to win one of his own – his father Imre had won the hammer in 1948. The top nation was the GDR (EAST GERMANY), with eleven athletics golds. The GDR would enjoy stunning athletics success until its demise in 1989, much of it attributable to a systematic doping policy.

1980

THE USA BOYCOTTED THE MOSCOW GAMES IN PROTEST AT the Soviet invasion of Afghanistan, and the absence of American athletes gave other nations a chance to shine – among them Great Britain. STEVE OVETT and SEBASTIAN COE's battle in the middle distance races ended with each winning the event for which the other was the favourite (Ovett the 800m, Coe the 1500m).

1984

THE ATHLETICS IN LA WAS COLOURED BY A TIT-FOR-TAT SOVIET-led boycott. The introduction of the WOMEN'S MARATHON was a belated slap in the face to the school of 1928 (see p.60). CARL LEWIS matched Jesse Owen's achievement in Berlin with victories in the 100m, 200m, 4 x 100m and the long jump, and ED MOSES extended his 400m hurdles winning streak to an incredible 102 races. ULRIKE MEYFARTH now became the *oldest* winner of the women's high jump at the age of 28, and Britain's SEBASTIAN COE retained the 1500m – some achievement in the blue riband event.

The (now discontinued) women's 3000m is remembered for the clash between MARY DECKER, darling of the LA crowd, and a shy, tiny 'British' South African named ZOLA BUDD. Seventeen hundred metres into the final, Decker bumped into Budd, who had to stretch her left leg outwards to avoid falling. The American promptly tripped over the Budd's other leg, pitching off the track and out of the contest. The crowd booed Budd for the remainder of the race, which was won by Romania's MARICICA PUICA.

1988

THE STORY OF THE SEOUL OLYMPICS CAN BE SUMMED UP IN two words: BEN JOHNSON. The Canadian athlete astonished the planet by storming to victory in the men's 100m final in a world record time of 9.79 seconds, then plunged it into dismay by failing a drug test. There was a strong shadow of suspicion, too, over FLORENCE GRIFFITH JOYNER's scarcely credible performance in the women's 100m final, winning the race in 10.54 seconds (still the Olympic record). FLO-JO had arrived at the Games having improved inexplicably in the course of the preceding year, and one look at her was enough for many sceptics. As the US coach Bill Dellinger had remarked at the US team trials (albeit not about Flo-Jo): 'That wasn't a sprint – that was chemical warfare.'

1992

THE FIRST OLYMPICS SINCE THE FALL OF THE BERLIN WALL SAW Britain's LINFORD CHRISTIE become the oldest winner of the men's 100m by a margin of four years. DERARTU TULU of Ethiopia became the first black female African Olympic champion with victory in the women's marathon. The most emotional episode of the Games began 150 metres into the semi-final of the men's 400m, when Britain's DEREK REDMOND felt his right hamstring pop and collapsed to the ground. His father Jim raced down from the stands, put his arm around his stricken son and told him 'We started your career together so we're going to finish this race together.' The 65,000 crowd gave the two Redmonds a standing ovation as they hobbled their way to the finishing line. The USA's EVELYN ASHFORD won a remarkable fourth gold (for the 4 x 100m relay) in three Olympic Games; she might well have won more had it not been for Flo-Jo.

1996

ATLANTA PRODUCED TWO ASTONISHING DOUBLES: MICHAEL JOHNSON took the 200m and 400m double (the first by any male athlete in a non-boycotted Games), while MARIE-JOSÉ PÉREC of France matched him in the women's division. Men's 10,000m champion HAILE GEBRSELASSIE ran the second half of the race in a time which would have won every Olympic 5000m final bar one.

2000

WHEN MARIE-JOSÉ PÉREC CRACKED UP AND FLED SYDNEY under the weight of media scrutiny, the way was clear for Australian CATHY FREEMAN to win the women's 400m. Her victory, achieved in a hooded bodysuit in front of a record Olympic crowd of 112,524, was of huge significance to the nation's Aboriginal people. Another highlight was American athlete MARION JONES' drive for five Olympic titles. She won three of them – the 100m, 200m and 4 x 400m – but in 2007 admitted taking performance-enhancing drugs and was stripped of her medals. Her husband, the gargantuan shot putter C.J. HUNTER, tested positive for nandrolone at Sydney.

2004

THE GREEK HOSTS HAD HIGH HOPES OF VICTORY FOR SPRINTER KONSTANTINOS KENTERIS and EKATERINI THANOU, but to intense local embarrassment, the pair failed to turn up for a drugs test the day before the opening ceremony, claiming they had been involved in a motorbike accident. LIU XIANG became the first male Chinese athlete to win an Olympic athletics gold with victory in the 110m hurdles. Britain's KELLY HOLMES notched up a double in the 800m and 1500m. Her compatriot PAULA RADCLIFFE had bad luck in the women's marathon, forced to withdraw 36km into the race due to stomach trouble. Brazilian VANDERLEI DE LIMA had an even worse time in the men's equivalent – he was attacked by an Irish priest – though he still managed to finish third. The Moroccan HICHAM EL GUERROUJ – perhaps the greatest ever middle distance runner – took golds in the 1500m and 5000m.

2008

ATHLETICS AT BEIJING'S GAMES BELONGED UNQUESTIONABLY TO USAIN BOLT. The 6ft 5in Jamaican produced the most exciting outcome the sport can offer – a world record in an Olympic 100m final. Even more impressive in some ways was his performance in the 200m. Many witnesses of Michael Johnston's annihilation of the field in the event in Atlanta believed he had set a world record that would stand for fifty years. In fact it lasted just eight, as Bolt justified his surname in a time of 19.30sec.

10 Athletic Greats

TEN OF THE GREATS – IN ORDER OF APPEARANCE.

1. JIM THORPE, USA (GOLD 2)

When King Gustav of Sweden placed a gold medal around the neck of the winner of the 1912 pentathlon and decathlon, calling him the greatest athlete in the world, Thorpe replied 'Thanks, King.' This alone would have secured him immortality. The part-Native American, part-Caucasian was given a ticker-tape parade on his return to New York but things turned sour when it emerged that he had earned $25 a week in 1909 and 1910 playing minor league baseball in North Carolina. This was deemed an intolerable breach of the 'amateurs only' rules. The IOC asked Thorpe to return his gold medals and struck his name from the record books. In 1983, thirty years after his death, the decision was reversed.

2. PAAVO NURMI, FINLAND (GOLD 9, SILVER 3)

The Flying Finn's haul of nine gold medals ties him with Carl Lewis as the most successful male Olympic athlete. In 1924, he won the 1500m in a world record time, rested for 26 minutes and then repeated the feat in the 5000m.

3. MILDRED 'BABE' DIDRIKSON, USA (GOLD 2, SILVER 1)

At the Los Angeles Games in 1932, the Texan all-rounder won the javelin and 80m hurdles and tied for the high jump (she was relegated to silver by the judges for a style contravention). Such was her versatility that she became, under her married name of Mildred Zaharias, the most successful female golf player of all time. She was pretty damned good at basketball, too.

4. JESSE OWENS, USA (GOLD 4)

One afternoon in May 1935, Owens set six world records in 45 minutes. But the sprinter and long jumper from Cleveland, Ohio is most celebrated for his four victories at the Berlin Olympics in 1936. Adolf Hitler actually treated him marginally better than the leader of his own country, sending him an inscribed photograph. 'It wasn't Hitler

TWO OF THE GREATS: MILDRED DIDRIKSON THROWING THE JAVELIN AT LA 1932 AND THE INELEGANT BUT DEVASTATING EMIL ZÁTOPEK AT HELSINKI 1952

who snubbed me,' Owens later said. 'It was FDR who snubbed me. The President didn't even send me a telegram.'

5. FANNY BLANKERS-KOEN, NETHERLANDS (GOLD 4)

The 'Flying Housewife' from the Netherlands is still the only female athlete to have won four golds at one Games, triumphing in the 100m, 200m, 80m hurdles and 4 x 100m relay in London in 1948. She wasn't even at her peak when she did it. Having competed in the 1936 Olympics as an eighteen-year-old, FBK's best years overlapped with the Second World War, a period during which she broke world records for the high and long jumps and various sprint and hurdling events. At the grand old age of 33 she registered another record, in the pentathlon.

6. EMIL ZÁTOPEK, CZECHOSLOVAKIA (GOLD 4, SILVER 1)

Known as the 'Czech Locomotive', Zátopek was the toast of the Helsinki Games of 1952, with victories in the 5000m, 10,000m and the marathon (he was carried aloft by the Jamaican relay team after this last victory). He is a rare exception to the rule that a beautiful style is the most efficient: his head rocked from side to side, his torso twisted, and he made a hell of a racket (his loud wheezing was one reason for the nickname). Zátopek was promoted to the rank of lieutenant colonel in the Czech army in recognition of his athletic exploits but was sent to do manual labour in a uranium mine after he lent his support to the 1968 uprising.

7. ABEBE BIKILA, ETHIOPIA (GOLD 2)

Abebe Bikila, the winner of the 1960 and 1964 Olympic marathons only failed to win one race at the distance during his career – the 1963 Boston Marathon. A member of the Imperial Bodyguard of Haile Selassie, the great Ethiopian has a stadium named after him in Addis Ababa. Tragically, he was rendered quadriplegic in a car accident in 1969 and died four years later.

8. CARL LEWIS, USA (GOLD 9, SILVER 1)

The only man to successfully defend Olympic titles in the 100m and long jump, Lewis is the joint most successful Olympic athlete of the modern era (with Paavo Nurmi). At the 1984 Olympics he equalled Jesse Owens' haul of four golds.

9. MICHAEL JOHNSON, USA (GOLD 4)

No athletics coach would encourage his charges to run like Johnson, who took extraordinarily short steps and leaned backwards. But nobody could argue with the results. Olympic 400m champion in 1996 and 2000, he also knocked an astounding third of a second off the 200m world record in the final at Atlanta. And that record – Pietro Mennea's 1979 time in Mexico – was widely regarded as the toughest in athletics

10. USAIN BOLT, JAMAICA (GOLD 3)

The laid-back Jamaican showman has taken sprinting into a new dimension, regularly beating top class fields by margins of several metres, and with an apparently casual air. Many believe him capable of running the 100m in less than 9.5 seconds. And he seems to be considering a move up to 400m, to bag further records. He recently announced that he would like to play football for Manchester United when he retires from international athletics.

BADMINTON

28 JULY – 5 AUGUST 2012

WEMBLEY ARENA

Athletes: 172 | **Golds up for grabs:** 5

OLYMPIC PRESENCE

BADMINTON WAS A DEMONSTRATION SPORT IN 1972 AND 1988, and became a full Olympic sport in 1992.

OLYMPIC FORMAT

THERE ARE FIVE EVENTS: MEN'S SINGLES AND DOUBLES, WOMEN's singles and doubles, and mixed doubles.

CURRENT CONTENDERS:

CHINA IS IN A DIFFERENT LEAGUE FROM EVERYONE ELSE. South Korea, Indonesia and Malaysia offer some opposition, while what little European challenge there is comes from Great Britain and Denmark.

PAST CHAMPIONS:

CHINA: 11 | SOUTH KOREA: 6 | INDONESIA: 6

WHY WATCH BADMINTON?

IN 1876, ENGLISHMAN HENRY JONES SET OUT AN EARLY version of the rules for what he called 'The Anglo-Indian Game of Badminton'. He concluded by suggesting that: 'Any garden that has a small lawn provides the suitable locus .., given a fair sky and a happy, light-hearted company, Badminton will furnish healthy enjoyable recreation and amusement for both old and young of both sexes for many an afternoon'. You might think him right. Badminton is a gentle, slow-moving, recreational affair, is it not?

Think again. The SHUTTLECOCK may be mere cork and feathers but struck correctly it can split a watermelon in two. Shuttlecocks have been recorded flying at SPEEDS in excess of 260km an hour – faster than the fastest tennis serves (currently Ivo Karlovic's 251kmh, followed by Andy Roddick's 249kmh). One time and motion study asserted that top-class badminton players cover twice as much ground as tennis players and are engaged in rallies for twice as long. And the speed and power of badminton is more than matched by its tactical complexity, virtuoso technique and compelling court battles.

In ASIA, where people have been playing shuttlecock games for over two thousand years, this sport really matters. When in 1992 badminton stars Susi Susanti and Alan Kusuma returned from the Barcelona Olympics with INDONESIA's first gold medals in any sport, the whole of Jakarta turned out to see the recently engaged couple parade through the city in an open-topped car, to which was fixed a gigantic shuttlecock. At the Athens and Beijing Olympics, the CHINESE love of the game gave badminton the biggest TV audiences of any single event and in 2008 the locals packed the badminton arena to see their heroes. Lin Dan, notionally a lieutenant colonel in the People's Army, celebrated his victory in the men' singles by throwing his shoes and racquet into an ecstatic crowd.

So forget the world of genteel English garden parties and take a look at Olympic badminton – 250 million Indonesians and 1.2 billion Chinese can't be entirely wrong.

THE SHUTTLECOCK

The shuttlecock is a remarkably stable device, almost always flying with the cork bottom forward, however it is struck. It is thus capable of great speed, but once the energy of a stroke has been spent the drag imparted by the feathers makes the shuttlecock decelerate very sharply. This makes lobs and lofts and drop-shots possible, strokes that are enhanced by the shuttlecock's tendency to fall at a steeper angle than it rises.

Most of us manage with the nylon varieties but these are far too slow and insensitive for competition play. Top-level shuttlecocks are made from sixteen feathers embedded in a rounded cork base covered with leather. Goose feathers are the best. Duck feathers are sometimes used but they have a tendency to dry out and break. The feathers – nearly all from China, where there is a strong taste for goose – must come from the left wing of the bird, and each wing provides only seven or eight feathers of the requisite size. They are easily bent and broken, so players may get through a dozen or more in the course of a match. Shuttlecocks also have to be used quickly: they cannot be vacuum-packed and begin to degrade after a couple of months on the shelf.

THE STORY OF BADMINTON

THERE IS EVIDENTLY A SPECIAL PLEASURE THAT HUMANS DErive from the arc of an object that appears to float through the air, for there are versions of the shuttlecock all over the world. The Native American Zuni, who lived in what is now New Mexico, played with dried corn husks set with feathers. The pre-Inca Mochi of northern Peru tossed a shuttlecock as part of their fertility rites while in Amazonia people still play *Paetec*, using a coin-weighted corn husk with feathers attached.

In ancient China *Ti Jian Zi* was the shuttlecock game, in which players used their feet to keep the sophisticated feathered shuttlecocks aloft. Crossing the social divides of imperial China, it was played by soldiers, children and ladies of the court alike for almost two millennia, and spread to Thailand, Vietnam, Laos and Malaysia. In medieval Japan the shuttle (known as the 'small barbaric demon') was struck with a bat or *hagoita*.

Europeans began to play shuttlecock games in the early sixteenth century. In the royal courts of France and Sweden and in the streets of London, the flight of the shuttle had the same cross-class and cross-gender appeal it had in Asia. In England the game was known as battledore and shuttlecock, and was played with racquets covered in vellum. It was a fashionable pastime at the court of James I, but was also played by children in the streets, who would sing nursery rhymes and counting games as they kept the shuttle aloft. It became popular in France, too, where as a rare example of a game played by both sexes, it was seen as full of erotic potential. Count Rivarol, enjoying the game in Versailles, wrote with some relish, 'How I'd like to be a shuttlecock to be able to stroke uncovered generous breasts and come to rest at the foot of young beauties.'

Despite their love of shuttlecock games none of these civilisations moved beyond forms of competitive KEEPY-UPPY, transfixed by the deceleration and fall of the shuttlecock, and almost oblivious to the possibilities of speed, power and confrontation. All this changed in the mid-nineteenth century, when British army officers and imperial officials discovered the many variants of the game that were played in Madras, Bombay, Calcutta and Peshawar. Though their rules varied greatly, the Anglo-Indian hybrids that emerged all included court markings, a high net, oppositional playing and a system of scoring.

It appears that these versions were first tentatively combined at a weekend party in the 1860s at BADMINTON HOUSE, home of the Duke of Beaufort. The association between this country house and the game became fixed in 1873, when an extensive correspondence began in the sporting journal *The Field* over the precise rules of the 'Badminton game of battledore'. In response a Major Forbes submitted a pamphlet published in Calcutta by the Great Eastern Hotel Company that decreed an hourglass-shaped court and allowed up to three a side. Two years later in 1875 the first badminton club was opened in Folkestone, Kent. Similar clubs sprung up in other English seaside resorts and in towns where the officers of the British Raj chose to retire, and just over a decade later the Badminton Association was established in SOUTHSEA and the game's rules were codified and published.

By the eve of the First World War badminton had found new blood in the rest of the British Isles, northern France and Denmark. In the inter-war years the sport made its way down the social scale to the British lower middle classes, and travelled back out to India and Malaysia, where the game was played by the last generation of imperial officials and the local elites. It was picked up in Australia and New Zealand and spread among the middle classes of continental Europe.

However, badminton enjoyed its most sustained popular craze in the UNITED STATES in the 1930s, where leading baseball and football players took to it the way they play golf today. Enthusiasts included Hollywood stars Douglas Fairbanks Jr, Joan Crawford, James Cagney, Boris Karloff and Ginger Rogers. Despite this kind of fan base, though, the sport never achieved the social cachet of tennis – badminton clubs were never exclusive enough to provide the kind of deal making opportunities offered by the country club. More emblematic was the New York hair salon that put a badminton court on its flat roof so customers could play while they waited.

260KM AN HOUR ... CHINA'S LIN DAN STRIKES AT BEIJING 2008

BADMINTON ON ICE: HUGH FORGIE

Badminton became big enough in the USA in the 1930s to sustain a small number of professionals who made a living playing exhibition games. Most famous of them was Hugh Forgie, who abandoned professional ice hockey for the new craze. 'I did for badminton what the Harlem Globetrotters did for basketball,' he recalled, and for a time he even worked as the Globetrotters' half-time show.

He began touring in 1935, challenging all comers, before teaming up with British trick-shot artist Ken Davidson in a show so spellbinding that they sold out a 38-week run

PRE-WAR BADDERS TRICKSTER
KEN DAVIDSON

at the London Palladium, where the audience included King George and Queen Elizabeth. Forgie went on to star in two badminton movies – *Flying Feathers* and *Volley Oops!* – but after the war the public tired of comedy badminton and he was forced to up the ante, putting his act on ice. In his travelling revue show of the early 1950s, *Ice Capades*, Forgie would play extraordinary rallies on skates, culminating in a frenzied one-man game in which he would serve and receive, skidding back and forth around the net.

GAME ON: BADMINTON BASICS

THE GAME BEGINS WITH A SERVE. SERVES MUST BE MADE from below the waist, with the racquet head below the hand and with both feet on the ground. Serves that are not touched by the receiver must land in the SERVICE AREA to win the point. If they touch the net, and land in, a LET is called and the point replayed.

RALLIES

RALLIES ARE WON WHEN THE SHUTTLE TOUCHES THE FLOOR of a demaracted area on the opponent's side of the court or if it goes out of play. Shuttles that land on the line are considered in play. Shuttles that clip the net but go over it are considered legal. Whoever wins the rally gets the next serve; points are won whether one is serving or receiving (a change from original practice).

GAMES AND MATCHES

GAMES ARE WON BY THE FIRST PLAYER TO REACH 21 POINTS. If the score is tied at 20-all the game continues until someone is two points clear. If the game reaches 29 all, then the next point decides the game.

MATCHES are the best of three games.

THE FINER POINTS

THE SERVE IS NOT KING

UNLIKE TENNIS, SERVICE DOES NOT GIVE AN OVERWHELMING advantage nor does it produce the fastest strokes. Players tend to opt for serves that that go low over the net, and use flicks and spin to deceive the receiver.

MAKING SPACE FOR THE SMASH

IN SINGLES, PLAYERS SPEND MUCH OF THEIR TIME TRYING TO manoeuvre their opponents around the court, hoping to open up space for a decisive winning shot – an unplayable SMASH, perhaps, or a lethal DROP SHOT.

FORCING THE LOB

IN DOUBLES, WHERE THERE IS LESS SPACE ON THE COURT, players try to force their opponents into making HIGH LOBS, thereby setting up SMASHING OPPORTUNITIES for themselves. They do this by playing drop shots close to the net.

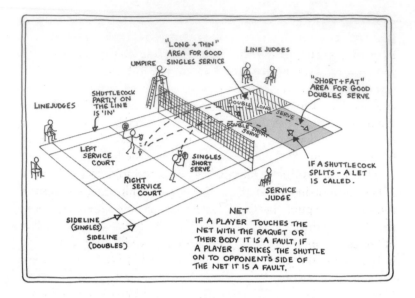

FORCING ERRORS

THE TOP PLAYERS ARE SO GOOD THAT SPACE RARELY OPENS up and RETURN LOBS are brilliantly placed. Therefore, most points are won on mistakes, where a return is put into the net or out of play.

THE IMPORTANCE OF DECEPTION

GIVEN HOW HARD IT IS TO HIT A WINNER, THERE IS A PRE-mium on deceiving your opponent, gaining an advantage by disguising your shot or changing it at the last moment. A split-second shift of the angle of the racquet head produces a SLICE, dropping the shuttlecock short, a result that can also be achieved by abruptly shortening the hitting action. The best players can also get a certain amount of SPIN on to their shots and will sometimes produce a DOUBLE MOTION SHOT, in which the stroke begins in one direction before the player suddenly snaps into a different one.

BADMINTON GOES TO THE OLYMPICS

IN 1934 A TINY INTERNATIONAL BADMINTON FEDERATION was set up in Southsea but with just nine members its global reach was limited. In fact, it took badminton until 1972 to gain a place as a demonstration sport and another twenty years to achieve full Olympic status. What changed its standing was the rise of the game in Asia, which has made possible a small but sustainable world professional circuit. The shuttlecock game has gone home.

The balance of badminton power began tilting eastward in the 1960s. In post-independence Malaysia and Indonesia, badminton acquired huge public status. The game had arrived in INDONESIA in the 1920s via the gyms and games halls of the Chinese communities of Singapore and Malaya. By the 1930s rival clubs were competing in Jakarta and the game had spread across all of Java. While Chinese participation was high, the game served as a rare arena in which Chinese, Javanese and other ethic groups could socialise, and from which the colonial Dutch elites were absent. Indeed, given the long folk memory of Asian shuttlecock games, badminton did not appear to be a foreign sport at all. In the years after independence this culture nurtured world class players like RUDI HARTONO, who was among Indonesia's few global sports stars.

In the 1970s the game became popular in SOUTH KOREA. As with the American craze of the 1930s, under conditions of rapid urbanisation and rising affluence the lower middle classes, who were excluded from golf and tennis clubs, opted for badminton. CHINA had its badminton boom in the 1980s and 1990s. The government sports system relentlessly focused on nurturing champions, making the sport even more popular.

The rising power of Asian badminton was heralded by the creation of the breakaway WORLD BADMINTON FEDERATION in 1978. In a direct challenge to the control exercised over world badminton by the four British national associations, the WBF called for the expulsion of Taiwan as a precondition of Chinese membership, the expulsion of apartheid South Africa and the introduction of one nation one vote decision-making. They then established the Independent World Championships and called for a boycott of the

All-England tournament. Three years later the IBF gave in to the inevitable, and signed a union with the WBF on the latter's terms.

Now a truly global game, with the weight of Asian numbers behind it, badminton was introduced at the Seoul Olympics and took its permanent place at the Games in 1992. South Korea and Indonesia shared the gold medals that year and in 1996 the Dane POUL-ERIK HØYER LARSEN won Europe's only badminton gold in the men's singles. Nearly everything else has been won by the CHINESE, who have received nearly half of all the medals awarded at the Olympics for badminton, including eleven golds. This is the new world order: expect more of the same.

BASKETBALL

28 JULY–12 AUGUST 2012

BASKETBALL ARENA, OLYMPIC PARK
PRELIMINARIES AND WOMEN'S QUARTER-FINALS

NORTH GREENWICH ARENA
ALL OTHER MATCHES

Athletes: 288 | Golds up for grabs: 2

OLYMPIC PRESENCE

MEN SINCE 1936 (DEMONSTRATION SPORT 1904, 1924); WOMEN since 1976.

OLYMPIC FORMAT

IN BOTH MEN'S AND WOMEN'S TOURNAMENTS, TWELVE TEAMS play in two groups of six. The top four from each group go into the knock-out stages.

CURRENT CONTENDERS:

IN THE MEN'S EVENT, THE USA WILL AS USUAL BE THE TEAM to beat – the young NBA stars who won the 2010 World Basketball Championships are looking very good. However, with so many foreign players in the NBA these days, as well as strong leagues in Europe, there will be stiff competition from ARGENTINA, SPAIN, SERBIA and TURKEY. In the WOMEN'S TOURNAMENT the AMERICANS are even further out in front and looking for their fifth straight gold medal, but again SPAIN will be competitive, as will the RUSSIANS.

PAST CHAMPIONS:

USA: 19 | USSR/RUSSIA: 5 | ARGENTINA & YUGOSLAVIA: 1

WHY WATCH BASKETBALL?

WHY WATCH BASKETBALL? WHY EVER NOT? IN FACT, IF YOU have got tickets and are in two minds about going, call us and we'll work something out. For those lucky enough to be attending, expect something amazing. On the basketball court, human beings almost fly: the best can hang in the air, seemingly making split seconds expand to create time in which to move the ball between their hands before shooting.

If the game's vertical dimension inspires awe, its horizontal axis releases adrenaline, even if you're only watching on TV. Basketball is a game of incessant flow and action that demands complex and high-speed teamwork as well as moments of individual genius. In the tight spaces of the basketball court, INSPIRATION, SPONTANEITY and TRICKERY are constant, as players, unable to barge or push, must seek out space, throw no-look passes, steal the ball, turn and switch direction in an instant.

The rules require teams to SHOOT AT THE BASKET at least every 24 seconds. This creates a pulsating ebb and flow of advantage and disadvantage, and huge scores too – often over 100 points on each side (the last Olympic final finished 118-107). There may not be much midfield, but every game is a blizzard of action, punctuated with jump shots and the high-energy surges of players hard-driving to the net. And all of this in an arena where the crowd is closer to the benches and the action than in any other. Still want to sell those tickets?

THE STORY OF BASKETBALL

BY THE CLOSING YEARS OF THE NINETEENTH CENTURY THE YMCA had established a network of sports halls and gymnasiums all over Europe and North America. However, in the United States it was rapidly losing members to the great outdoor sports of the era – American football and baseball – while its commitment to gymnastics was proving a little too rigorous for the youth of America. It was in this context that LUTHER GULICK, head of the training school for YMCA instructors in Springfield, Massachusetts, encouraged his students and staff to develop indoor games that could bring the punters back to the YMCA's 'halls of health'.

JAMES NAISMITH, a thirty-year-old Canadian, was one of those students, and after considering and rejecting variants of American football, soccer and lacrosse, he formulated a 13-rule game that would soon become BASKETBALL. The first recorded game was played NINE-A-SIDE in December 1891, with a peach basket nailed to the rafters as the goal. It was an instant hit, and over the next decade Springfield's instructors did such a good job of promoting the new sport that it was soon second only to baseball in terms of national participation. The rules were quickly and systematically adapted – nine-a-side quickly became FIVE-A-SIDE, the basket was replaced by a backboard and a net, regulations on fouls and free throws were introduced – but it was still essentially the same basic no-contact game of passing, dribbling and shooting that Naismith had invented.

Thereafter, the game grew through two different channels. In the USA, the school and college sport was accompanied by the emergence of a huge urban basketball culture, especially amongst the ethnic enclaves of America's great industrial cities, and by a growing circuit of professional leagues and exhibition matches. These somewhat chaotic leagues, which featured roughhouse play and courts surrounded by wire mesh, eventually coalesced to form the NATIONAL BASKETBALL ASSOCIATION (NBA) in 1949.

In the rest of the world, basketball arrived via the YMCA or the American army, or both. In urban gyms and sports clubs in the Mediterranean, Eastern Europe, Australia, Japan, the Philippines and China, basketball took hold as an immensely popular recreational game. However, it never acquired elite professional status, and the communist nations (China has an estimated 30 million players) could challenge only at American college level. Meanwhile, the NBA – the apex of global basketball – remained in a league of its own.

The readmission of professionals into the Olympics in 1992 brought these worlds back together, to an extent. While the Americans remain the dominant force in both men's and women's basketball, the professionalisation of the game in Europe and China and the flow of talent from overseas into the NBA have made the Olympic contest rather more equal.

Game On: Basketball Basics

SCORING: 3-2-1

THE AIM OF THE GAME IS TO SCORE MORE POINTS THAN THE opposing team. This is done by putting the ball through the net that they are defending. The number of points scored depends on where the ball was released. If it was thrown from outside the 6.25m line (a LONG BASKET), it's a 3-POINTER. More common is the 2-POINT FIELD GOAL, scored from open play inside the line. Finally, a FREE THROW, taken unimpeded from the free throw or foul line in front of the basket, scores 1 POINT.

TIME IN, TIME OUT

THE GAME IS FIVE-A-SIDE. EACH TEAM HAS ANOTHER SEVEN players on the bench and SUBSTITUTIONS are unlimited. Though the starting five on a team are generally the strongest unit and play the most minutes, it is virtually unheard for anyone to play a complete match. At the Olympics, the game is played in FOUR QUARTERS, each ten minutes long, with a half-time interval of fifteen minutes. In the event of a tied score at the end of the fourth quarter five minutes of OVERTIME are played. Coaches can call a one-minute TIME OUT, during which play is suspended, once in each of the first three quarters, twice in the fourth quarter and once in overtime.

MOVING AND DRIBBLING

PLAYERS CAN THROW, BOUNCE, ROLL AND PAT THE BALL, BUT they must not kick or punch it. They are allowed to take THREE STEPS with the ball but must then shoot or pass. If they bounce the ball, one handed, they can DRIBBLE an unlimited distance with the ball. If the ball goes over the sidelines, the last team to touch it loses possession. Their opponents then have five seconds to get

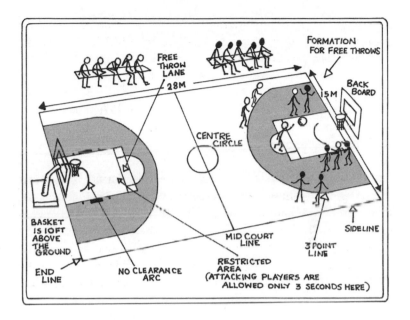

FORMATION FOR FREE THROWS

FREE THROW LANE
28M

BACK BOARD

5M

CENTRE CIRCLE

BASKET IS 10FT ABOVE THE GROUND

SIDELINE

MID COURT LINE

3 POINT LINE

END LINE

NO CLEARANCE ARC

RESTRICTED AREA
(ATTACKING PLAYERS ARE ALLOWED ONLY 3 SECONDS HERE)

the ball to the place where it passed out of play and five seconds
to release it.

FOULING UP

BASKETBALL IS, THEORETICALLY, A NON-CONTACT SPORT.
Players are not allowed to impede the movement of their opponents with their arms, elbows or hips, nor are they allowed to grab,
charge, barge or trip them. However, there is a great deal of hidden
contact and the officiating can be rather uneven.

FOULS committed by a team result in possession passing to the
opposition. If the foul was committed on a player in the act of
shooting, a FREE THROW (see diagram above) is given. If the team
has already accumulated four TEAM FOULS in a quarter then any
additional foul results in TWO FREE THROWS for their opponents.
Players also have fouls counted against them individually. When
they reach five PERSONAL FOULS they are excluded from the game
(though they can be subbed). TECHNICAL FOULS are also awarded
for acts of violence and unsportsmanlike behaviour.

·············· NO GOAL HANGING, NO GOALTENDING ··············

BASKETBALL HAS DEVELOPED A SERIES OF RULES TO ENSURE THAT the balance between attack and defence is maintained. To prevent GOAL HANGING, the coloured rectangle in front of the basket – referred to as the PAINT or the KEY – is designated a restricted area. Attacking players can spend no longer than three seconds inside it. Another flaw in the old basketball rules was that a very tall player could stand close to the basket and swat everything away. To prevent this kind of GOALTENDING, players are not allowed to block shots on the downward element of their arc nor are defensive players allowed to try to gain an offensive foul from their opponents inside the small arc drawn 1.25m in front of the basket. This prevents defenders from simply impeding players who are driving towards the basket.

································ THE SHOT CLOCK ································

ONE TACTIC THAT TEAMS USED TO EMPLOY WAS TO PLAY keep-ball, thereby wasting time and grinding down the opposition; effective perhaps, but terminally dull. To prevent this, the NBA introduced the SHOT CLOCK, which is usually positioned above the backboards and on the scoreboard. Once a team takes possession they have 8 SECONDS to get the ball into the opponents' half and 24 SECONDS to make an attempt on goal. Failure to do either results in possession passing to the other side.

THE FINER POINTS

···· THE SHOT LOCKER: JUMP, FADE, SPIN AND LAYUP ····

THE BREAD AND BUTTER OF BASKETBALL IS THE JUMP SHOT. A player leaps into the air and at the high point of the jump launches the ball in an arc towards the basket, over the hands of jumping defenders. Look out for variations that give players a little more space or time in which to make the shot. Playing with their back to the basket, players often leap and SPIN through 180 degrees before shooting. This can be combined with a FADE, in which a player jumps up and drifts backwards away from the defender. Closer to the basket, players use the LAYUP. As they leap, the ball is sent vertically up towards the backboard and SPIN imparted by the fingers makes it drop directly into the net or bounce off the backboard and through the hoop.

########## **THE DUNK** ##########

THE MOST SPECTACULAR SCORE IS THE DUNK, some times known as the SLAM DUNK, in which the player drops or pushes the ball through the hoop from ABOVE THE RIM. Even in its most basic versions it is an extraordinary display of athletic power and strength, often completed with the most emphatic of flourishes, leaving a player swinging from the edge of

HIS AIRNESS MICHAEL JORDAN IN ACTION AT BARCELONA 1992

the hoop. This play wasn't envisaged as an aspect of the game that Naismith devised and the American college game banned it for a decade. However, it's been a staple of the modern sport, especially since it became the preserve of giants (the famous 1992 USA Dream Team had only one player under 6ft 6in). For converse reasons, the slam dunk remains rare in the women's game.

Most dunks come from a drive by a player towards the hoop and a massive leap, but look out for a high ball passed above the hoop, caught by a player in flight, and slammed into the net: this is the ALLY-OOP. Most spectacular of all, a leap combined with a spin produces the OVERHEAD REVERSE DUNK. Dunks can, on occasion, muster enough power to break the whole structure holding up the basket or shatter the glass backboard.

GIMME BACK MY BALL: THE REBOUND

GIVEN THAT MOST TEAMS WILL SCORE ON MOST POSSESSIONS in basketball, getting hold of the ball is a crucial part of the game. Occasionally defences will STEAL the ball, by intercepting a pass or capitalising on an opponent's mishandling. But more commonly – and crucially – shots bounce off the rim or the backboard and are seized as REBOUNDS.

THE FURIOUS FIVE: PLAYER POSITIONS

DIVISION OF LABOUR IN BASKETBALL IS FLUID: ALL PLAYERS participate in nearly every attacking and defensive move. That said, teams play with two back court players (the GUARDS), a CENTRE and two FORWARDS, each of whom – as the diagram below explains – has particular duties.

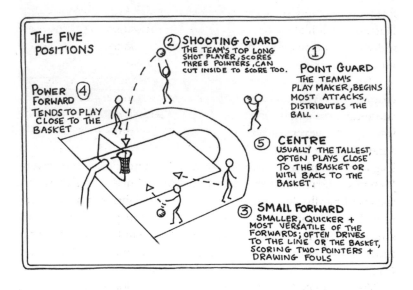

THE FIVE POSITIONS

② SHOOTING GUARD
THE TEAM'S TOP LONG SHOT PLAYER, SCORES THREE POINTERS, CAN CUT INSIDE TO SCORE TOO.

① POINT GUARD
THE TEAM'S PLAY MAKER, BEGINS MOST ATTACKS, DISTRIBUTES THE BALL.

POWER FORWARD ④
TENDS TO PLAY CLOSE TO THE BASKET

⑤ CENTRE
USUALLY THE TALLEST, OFTEN PLAYS CLOSE TO THE BASKET OR WITH BACK TO THE BASKET.

③ SMALL FORWARD
SMALLER, QUICKER + MOST VERSATILE OF THE FORWARDS; OFTEN DRIVES TO THE LINE OR THE BASKET, SCORING TWO-POINTERS + DRAWING FOULS

PICK AND ROLL

PICK AND ROLL IS THE MOST WIDELY USED ATTACKING PLOY in basketball and you will see every Olympic team use it. When a ball carrier is being marked by a defender, a second member of the attacking team will move so as to put himself between the two, sometimes called SETTING A SCREEN. At this point the defender has a choice: if they continue to mark the ball carrier, the screen setter can pivot and roll around them into space to receive the ball; if the defender goes with the screen setter then the ball carrier is suddenly in space to shoot or make a decisive pass – THE PICK AND POP.

BASKETBALL GOES TO THE OLYMPICS

JUST THIRTEEN YEARS AFTER BEING INVENTED, BASKETBALL appeared as a demonstration sport at the 1904 St Louis Games. There were collegiate, YMCA and schools tournaments, plus an amateur six-squad competition that was the closest thing to an Olympic contest. It was won by the BUFFALO GERMAN YMCA from upstate New York. In the years before the First World War the Buffalo team, like all of the early semi-professional barnstorming squads, was permanently on the road, and racked up a 111-game winning streak.

The global network of YMCAs was spreading the game to the cities of East Asia, Latin America and Europe, and at PARIS 1924 it was recalled as a demonstration sport. Basketball didn't make it as a full sport, however, until BERLIN 1936. By this time it had acquired a global ruling body (FIBA), a whole raft of professional American leagues and a place in the sporting cultures of dozens of countries. JAMES NAISMITH himself came to present the medals in Berlin, but the event hardly showed the sport in its best light, as matches were played outside on a tennis court that had been packed hard with sand and clay. The final, played in wet and windy conditions that made dribbling impossible, was particularly dismal. The USA beat Canada 19-8.

The LONDON Games of 1948 were held indoors and the USA, now able to play the game properly, showed the world how it was done. In the official report it was noted that the Americans possessed 'the agility of bantams', and that 'as soon as these giants entered the arena, opposing teams seemed to wilt and fade away'. In the final they thrashed France 65–21.

HELSINKI 1952 saw the arrival of the SOVIET UNION and Cold War politics. The Soviets went all the way to the final, where, in a dour and mean-spirited game, they tried to play keep-ball; the Americans beat them anyway, 36-25. A rather more spirited approach to the game was taken by the URUGUAYANS. In their game against France they had lost so many players to personal fouls that they played the final minutes of the game with just three on the court. When the referee called a further foul against them he was rushed by the bench; two Uruguayans were eventually banned from the Games as a result. Things were little better the next day, when a game between a four-man Uruguay and three-man Argentina culminated in a massive on-court brawl.

In MELBOURNE in 1956 the USSR team arrived with JAN KRU-MINSH, a 7ft 3in Latvian centre, but the AMERICANS, including the great BILL RUSSELL (five-time winner of the NBA Most Valuable Player Award), ran rings around them and everyone else, beating the USSR 89-55 in the final. Rome, Tokyo and Mexico City all went the same way, though the Yugoslavs and Soviets were getting closer.

In 1972, at the MUNICH Games, the gap finally closed. The USSR led the USA for almost the whole of the final game, but with three seconds to go American DOUG COLLINS was bundled out of the court and the US was awarded two free throws. Looking battered but composed, Collins sunk them both and for the first time the USA was in the lead, 50-49. The Soviets restarted, a long ball went nowhere, the buzzer went and the Americans exploded with joy and relief. Then chaos erupted on the court when one of the officials claimed a time out had been called with one second left on the clock. The game was restarted and the Soviets again failed to score, only for the officials to insist that a third restart was required but with three seconds rather than one second on the clock. At the third attempt the Soviets launched a huge court-length pass to SASHA BELOV whose simple layup made it 51-50. The Americans refused to show for the medal ceremony.

Over the next four Games, the Cold War pendulum swung back and forth. In MONTREAL in 1976 the Americans were de-nied a full measure of revenge when the YUGOSLAVS knocked the Soviets out in the semi-final. The USSR did, however, win

PREMATURE U.S CELEBRATIONS IN THE CONTROVERSIAL 1972 MEN'S FINAL

the inaugural women's gold medal and went on to dominate the Olympic tournament until 1988, when the Americans took over. In fact, the USA WOMEN are currently on an unbroken streak of five consecutive gold medals.

With the Americans boycotting the 1980 MOSCOW Games, the Soviets were expecting to wrap up their second men's gold, only to be knocked out again in the semi-finals by the eventual champions YUGOSLAVIA. The USSR were absent from LA 1984, where the USA cruised to victory, but at SEOUL, four years later, the Soviets outplayed the Americans to win 82-76 in the semi, before beating the Yugoslavs in the final.

Four years later, the world of Olympic basketball looked wholly different: the Soviet Union had ceased to exist; Yugoslavia, America's other chief basketball competitor, was being riven by war; and the

IOC had decided to allow professionals to compete in all sports. The NBA exploited the situation to the maximum, assembling the greatest pool of basketball talent ever to go to the Games. Including such stellar players as MICHAEL JORDAN, MAGIC JOHNSON, LARRY BIRD and CHARLES BARKLEY, the so-called 'DREAM TEAM' won every game, by an average of 43.8 points. Their smallest margin of victory was in the final, in which they beat Croatia 117-85.

ATLANTA 1996 and SYDNEY 2000 brought more of the same, but the opposition was getting stronger and more confident while the Americans became a little complacent, almost blowing it in the semi-finals against Lithuania in 2000. Sydney was a warning not taken, and in ATHENS the Americans were narrowly beaten in the semi-finals by a fleet-footed ARGENTINA team, led by NBA star MANU GINÓBILI. The US team at BEIJING 2008 was, termed, inevitably, the 'REDEEM TEAM'. Equipped with leading lights KOBE BRYANT, LEBRON JAMES and Dwyane Wade, they duly swept to victory.

BOXING

28 JULY–12 AUG 2012

EXCEL ARENA

Athletes: 286 | **Golds up for grabs:** 13

OLYMPIC PRESENCE

MEN 1904–1908, 1920 PRESENT; WOMEN ARE COMPETING for the first time at London 2012 (though women's boxing was a demonstration sport in 1904).

OLYMPIC FORMAT

MEN COMPETE IN TEN WEIGHT DIVISIONS; WOMEN IN THREE. One boxer per nation is allowed in each weight category. Each competition is seeded and proceeds on a knock-out basis, culminating in a final. There is no third place fight – the losing semi-finalists both receive bronze medals.

CURRENT CONTENDERS:

THE BOXING IN BEIJING WAS THE MOST OPEN IN OLYMPIC history. The eleven golds on offer went to fighters from nine different nations, including first ever Olympic boxing triumphs for CHINA (2), MONGOLIA and DOMINICAN REPUBLIC. The London event is expected to produce a similar diversity of winners, though the traditional powerhouses CUBA and the USA will be looking to put the record straight after failing to win a single title in Beijing.

PAST CHAMPIONS:

USA: 48 | CUBA: 32 | USSR/RUSSIA: 32

WHY WATCH BOXING?

IT ISN'T A BAD QUESTION. WHY WOULD YOU WANT TO SET-
tle down in a comfy chair to watch a pair of adults systematically
knock seven bells out of each other? But to its fans, boxing is the
very essence of sport, pitting man against man (or woman against
woman) with no tools at their disposal but their fists and their wits
– a purity of proposition that gives boxing a fundamental honesty.
And if sport is about asserting dominance over other people, and
people are in some sense their bodies, what could be more sporting
than an activity that involves attacking and defending the body?

One thing Olympic level boxing emphatically is not is crude.
A thug wouldn't last 11 seconds out there. Boxing isn't just about
hitting people – it's at least as important not to be hit. To achieve a
winning balance requires immense skill, speed and guile, as well as
boundless courage. The sport is not so much an exercise in savagery
as a recognition and containment of it. It takes the unpleasant primal urge to beat the daylights out of someone and turns it into a
discipline. Boxing is therefore best thought of as a Western martial
art – or, as it is sometimes called, the 'sweet science'.

For all its virtues, boxing has had a chequered history. Fortunately for the Olympic watcher, most of the negatives have applied
to the professional game. Tainted by associations with organised
crime and pitifully punch-drunk ex-fighters who didn't know or
weren't told when to stop, it has fragmented into numerous and often meaningless 'world championships' in pursuit of cash. Amateur
boxing – the kind practised at the Olympics – is different gravy.
Though not always squeaky clean, it is a great deal safer than the
professional version, largely because the fighters wear head protectors and there are fewer rounds. It is also refreshingly unbefuddled
– there is only one Olympic champion per weight division and
competitors can't duck out of facing opponents they don't fancy.

The fact that the stakes are so high, both in terms of the prizes
on offer and the risk of getting seriously hurt, makes Olympic boxing electrifyingly tense. It can draw you in like no other sport, its
visceral nature allowing you to 'feel' a smidgen of what the fighters are going through. And there is a good chance of a legend

emerging. Olympic boxing has consistently thrown up magnificent warriors, among them SUGAR RAY LEONARD, JOE FRAZIER and the incomparable MUHAMMAD ALI.

A final excellent reason to watch the boxing in London is the introduction of an Olympic tournament for WOMEN. Is this a triumphant achievement of equality or a demeaning folly? There's only one way to form your own opinion ...

THE STORY OF BOXING

BOXING GOES WAY BACK. THE SPORT WAS KNOWN TO THE ANCIENT EGYPTIANS and SUMERIANS, and made its first appearance at the ANCIENT GAMES in Olympia in 688BC, where contestants bound their hands with leather straps for protection and fought on until one of them surrendered or was rendered unable to continue. The Romans came up with a typically dark variant of the sport, which used a metal studded glove known as a *cestus*. Losing a fight was often fatal.

After the collapse of the Roman Empire, boxing disappeared from view in much of Europe. The carrying of arms became much more common in the absence of a powerfully policed state, and history suggests an inverse relationship between the popularity of boxing and the prevalence of weapons. In a nutshell, you don't want to start a public fight if everyone is armed to the teeth, and the authorities won't like it either. Nevertheless, various forms of folk boxing survived, some of them pretty hard-core. In INUIT HEAD PUNCHING, the combatants took it in turn to hit each other as hard as they could, with the receiver offering no defence whatsoever. RUSSIAN FIST FIGHTING, first mentioned in the thirteenth century, also had a variant of this extreme form of the sport, as well as regular two-way boxing and organised team brawls.

The modern sport developed out of PRIZE-FIGHTING, which rose to prominence in England in the seventeenth century. The participants fought for money, with BARE KNUCKLES and minimal rules – there were no weight divisions or limits on the number or duration of rounds. The cash was often put up by aristocrats – the first recorded bout (1681) involved the butler and the butcher of the 2nd Duke of Albemarle – but prize-fighting was also popular in less illustrious circles, where it was often the subject of huge wagers.

The Englishman JACK BROUGHTON is credited with the introduction of BOXING GLOVES, or 'mufflers' as he called them, although their use was initially restricted to training and exhibition matches. BROUGHTON'S RULES, published in London in 1743, aimed to bring some order to the chaos that characterised unregulated prize-fighting. Hitting a man when he was down was forbidden, as was grasping an opponent below the waist. A boxer who was floored was given 30 seconds to recover – if he failed to beat the count he lost the contest. Canny fighters could exploit this rule by dropping to one knee when they felt the need for a breather, although this was not approved. Manliness or 'nobility' was the central ideal of the emerging sport, both in Europe and the USA. 'The manly stand-up fight is surely far preferable,' opined the American *Spirit of the Times* in August 1837, 'to the insidious knife, the ruffianly gang system or the cowardly and brutal practice of biting, kicking or gouging now so prominent.'

The LONDON PRIZE RING RULES, published in 1838, brought further gentlemanliness to the proceedings, specifying a ROPED SQUARE RING and forbidding head-butting, biting and HITTING BELOW THE BELT. But the event that catapulted boxing into the modern era was the publication, in 1867, of the MARQUESS OF QUEENSBERRY CODE. The eponymous aristocrat, later responsible for the downfall of Oscar Wilde, didn't actually write the famous Rules – he published them. They were penned in 1867 by a Cambridge University athlete called JOHN GRAHAM CHAMBERS for the first amateur championship of the sport, held at Lillie Bridge in London. The twelve rules stipulated the wearing of gloves, introduced the 10 COUNT for fallen boxers and established the system of THREE-MINUTE ROUNDS with one-minute rest periods. They form the basis of the laws that govern boxing today.

Initially designed for amateur boxing, the Queensbury Rules were eventually adopted by the professional game too, a process hastened in England by an 1882 court ruling that declared bare knuckle fights to be criminal assaults, irrespective of the participants' consent. Spectators also became vulnerable to the charge of aiding and abetting. The subsequent almost universal ADOPTION OF GLOVES had far reaching effects. As the huge mitts could be used to block punches, the 'forearms upright' style of the bare knuckle boxer fell out of favour. Bouts became longer and more tactical, with a greater emphasis on defence. From the perspective of the punch receiver, gloves were a mixed blessing. They diffused the impact but allowed the aggressor to punch harder as there was less risk of damaging the hand.

The organisers of the amateur championships at Lillie Bridge in 1867 had deliberately sought to exclude 'riff-raff' from the sport but the British AMATEUR BOXING ASSOCIATION, founded in 1880, was happy to allow blue collar workers to compete. It also did not bar boxers on the grounds of race. The establishment of the ABA was a crucial moment in a battle for the soul of the sport between the upper and working classes. This was to be emphatically won by the latter but the process took much longer in the USA than in Britain. Wealthy club men controlled the amateur sport in America until the *Chicago Tribune* started the GOLDEN GLOVES TOURNA- MENT in 1926.

The late nineteenth and early twentieth centuries were characterised by a widening split between the amateur and professional codes. The former featured shorter rounds and an emphasis on sparring (the demonstration of skill) rather than fighting (continuing to the point of exhaustion or knock-out). Many now see amateur boxing as the perfect grounding for the huge payday that the professional sport can be.

The spread of Queensbury Rules boxing was gradual – FRANCE, in the years leading up to the First World War, was the first nation other than Britain, Ireland and the United States to take to the sport in a big way – but ultimately comprehensive. The first global body for the amateur boxing, the FÉDÉRATION INTERNATIONALE DE BOXE OLYMPIQUE founded in Paris in 1920, had only five member nations – England, France, Brazil, Belgium and the Netherlands – but by the time the AMATEUR INTERNATIONAL BOXING ASSOCIATION (AIBA)

THE AFGHAN WOMEN'S BOXING TEAM TRAINING FOR LONDON 2012

came into existence in London in 1946, the number had grown to 25. The first WORLD AMATEUR BOXING CHAMPIONSHIPS were held in 1974. The USA and to a lesser extent Great Britain and Ireland have continued to be major forces in the amateur sport but they have been joined by the likes of Cuba and the ex-Warsaw pact nations, with boxers from Latin America and the Far East doing particularly well in the lighter divisions.

·· **WOMEN'S BOXING** ··

ASTONISHINGLY, GIVEN THAT THE EVENT IS ONLY JUST NOW about to make its Olympic debut, women's boxing was a demonstration sport at the St Louis Games in 1904. The competitors look like extras from *Upstairs Downstairs* in their knickerbockers but they could doubtless pack a punch.

And by that stage, women's boxing was already almost two centuries old. The earliest record of an all-female bout dates from 1722, when Elizabeth Wilkinson defeated Martha Jones at an inn near Oxford Circus in London. By the second half of the nineteenth century, WOMEN'S PRIZE-FIGHTING was well enough established for it to be banned by law in several European nations and American states. In Britain, the sport became illegal in 1880. It never disappeared entirely, however.

In 1954, a fight involving Barbara Buttrick was broadcast on American national television, but the real breakthrough in the women's sport came in the 1970s and 1980s as a result of legal challenges to the bans in operation in many countries. It took still longer for women's boxing to be sanctioned by the sport's governing bodies. In 1996, the British Amateur Boxing Association voted to allow women to fight under its auspices and five years later the first AIBA World Championships were held in Scranton, USA.

GAME ON: BOXING BASICS

OLYMPIC BOXING IS A SIMPLE SPORT AT HEART: THE FIGHTER who lands the most scoring punches wins. Alternatively, a bout may be won by way of KNOCK-OUT, in which a floored opponent fails to get up from the canvas before the referee has counted to ten, or via disqualification or withdrawal. Punches below the belt or to the back are forbidden, as are holding, wrestling and tripping. To count, a blow must be landed with the white portion of the glove, which denotes the knuckles and the first bone of the fingers. Thumbs should rest on the upper joints of the next two fingers.

·············· **THE RING AND THE SECONDS** ··············

BOXERS FIGHT IN AN ELEVATED RING – 20 FT SQUARE, WITH a padded post in each corner. The edge of the ring is defined by a 'fence' made of four ropes. Men fight three 3-minute rounds; women do four bursts of 2-minutes. There is a rest period of sixty seconds between each round.

Each boxer is allowed two assistants, known as SECONDS. Both are allowed to mount the apron of the ring and one is allowed to enter the ring between rounds. Their jobs include advising and encouraging their boxer, towelling them dry of sweat between rounds, attending to minor injuries and, if necessary, withdrawing them from the fight by THROWING IN A TOWEL.

WEIGHT DIVISIONS

THERE USED TO BE JUST EIGHT WEIGHT DIVISIONS IN BOXING BUT at the Olympics the figure has risen as high as twelve. In London there will be ten for men (from Light-flyweight at 46–49kg through to Super Heavyweight at 91kg plus), and three for women.

Competitors are required to attend a general WEIGH-IN at the start of the tournament, at which boxers must register weights within the parameters of the divisions they are entered in. They are also subject to a weigh-in on the morning of every day they are fighting. Any boxer who fails to make the necessary weight is eliminated from the competition.

WAYS OF WINNING

THE CLASSIC MEANS TO WIN A BOUT IS A KNOCK-OUT, WHEN a fallen boxer fails to get back on his feet within a count of 10. Boxers can also win through the retirement of their opponent, indicated by their second literally 'THROWING IN THE TOWEL' into the ring, or by the referee stopping a contest and eliminating a contestant. Most commonly, though, bouts are won on POINTS. If both boxers are still standing at the end of a bout, the one who has accumulated the most points (registered the most valid punches) is declared the winner.

A referee can stop a contest for a number of reasons, including: BOXER OUTCLASSED (where the referee deems one boxer to be taking excessive punishment); HEAD BLOWS (where a fighter is unable to defend themself after receiving one or more blows to the head); or DISQUALIFICATION. Referees can also issue a WARNING, for serious or persistent fouls. If a boxer is issued with a warning, two points are awarded to the opponent. Three warnings and you're out.

SCORING

ALL CLEAN HITS TO THE BODY OR SIDE OR FRONT OF THE head score 1 point. For a hit to be valid under the old scoring system, which applied to every Olympics between 1992 and 2008, at least three of the FIVE RINGSIDE JUDGES had to register it within a second of the punch being landed by pushing an electronic button. This system was widely disliked because judges frequently failed to act in time, whether by accident or design. So in 2011, a new code of points was introduced. Judges now score each boxer during the rounds, with no time limit on recording hits (beyond having to relay their reckonings at the end of a round). The score for each round is calculated on the basis of the three most SIMILAR SCORINGS – the egregious verdicts of the other two judges are discounted. The 'similar scores' are then averaged. Moves are afoot to develop sensor packed boxing suits that register hits electronically, as in Taekwondo, but they will not be used in London.

SAFETY AND EQUIPMENT

BOXING IS POTENTIALLY DANGEROUS. THIS IS PARTICULARLY true of the professional game. You only have to look at a punch-drunk ex-pro to see the long-term effects of too many blows to the head. But at amateur level, extensive measures are taken to minimise the risks. These include FEWER ROUNDS, the wearing of HEAD GUARDS (and CHEST PROTECTORS for women), a maximum age of 34, and a 'ONE PUNCH, ONE POINT' scoring system with no bonuses for high impact blows or knockdowns.

There is also extensive medical supervision: for every bout, a boxer must be certified fit to fight by a doctor appointed by the AIBA Medical Commission, and there are complex rules about how long boxers who have suffered blows to the head of varying severity must wait before fighting again. One knock-out or RSCH (Referee Stops Contest due to Head-blows) leads to a bar on competing for thirty days; three within a twelve-month period leads to an enforced 360 day break.

THE FINER POINTS

STANCE

BOXERS TYPICALLY STAND SIDEWAYS ON TO THEIR OPPONENTS, with the left foot advanced. The fists are raised, the right one protecting the chin and the left one doing most of the work via JABBING. The active use of the right fist is largely restricted to HOOKS and UPPERCUTS. This stable position is maintained by the fighter moving around the ring with their left foot leading and right foot following without overtaking it. Fighters known as SOUTHPAWS reverse the limb positions, leading with their right feet and jabbing with their right hands.

Each boxer has a characteristic STANCE. Some fighters hold their hands at or slightly above the level of their heads. FLOYD PATTERSON was famous for using this 'Peek-a-Boo' stance. Other boxers hold their hands low. Most find a happy medium.

·· **PUNCHES** ··

MOST PUNCHES FALL INTO ONE OF FOUR CATEGORIES:

The JAB is the most commonly used punch and is made with a quick, straight extension of the lead hand.

The HOOK is a curving punch delivered in a sweeping arc. Usually made with the lead hand, it begins with the fist at waist level and ends (if all goes to plan) with it striking the side of the opponent's head.

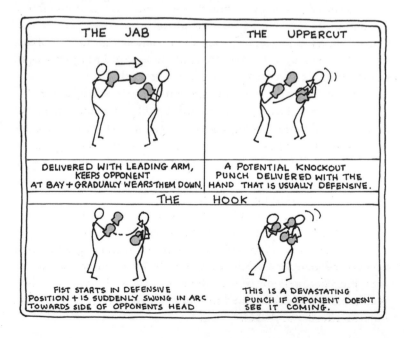

THE JAB	THE UPPERCUT
DELIVERED WITH LEADING ARM, KEEPS OPPONENT AT BAY + GRADUALLY WEARS THEM DOWN.	A POTENTIAL KNOCKOUT PUNCH DELIVERED WITH THE HAND THAT IS USUALLY DEFENSIVE.

THE   HOOK

FIST STARTS IN DEFENSIVE POSITION + IS SUDDENLY SWUNG IN ARC TOWARDS SIDE OF OPPONENTS HEAD	THIS IS A DEVASTATING PUNCH IF OPPONENT DOESNT SEE IT COMING.

The UPPERCUT is a punch typically made with the rear hand that moves rapidly upwards from the waist towards the opponent's chin.

The CROSS is often a surprise punch. It is thrown with the rear hand, with the lead hand simultaneously taking up a defensive position. It's like an orthodox fighter momentarily turning into a southpaw (or vice-versa).

.... **STYLE** ....

EVERY BOXER HAS A BASIC APPROACH TO THEIR ART, DETERmined by body type and personality, and each has its 'structural' strengths and weaknesses. Much of the character of a bout is de termined by the way the styles of the protagonists mesh. All other things being equal (which they never are), a SLUGGER will do well against an IN-FIGHTER but poorly against an OUT-FIGHTER.

However, it's not quite as simple as that. The best boxers are able to change style to suit the circumstances, and not all of the common styles are mutually exclusive. You can easily be an out-fighter/counter-puncher (though you can't be an out-fighter/in-fighter).

IN-FIGHTERS like to get in their opponents' faces. Classic examples include JOE FRAZIER and the great Hungarian light middleweight LASZLO PAPP.

OUT-FIGHTERS do the opposite, preferring to keep their distance and wear their opponents down with long range jabs. No one could call him typical, but MUHAMMAD ALI (who made his name at the Olympics as CASSIUS CLAY) fell into this category.

SLUGGERS (the most famous of whom was probably GEORGE FOREMAN) rely on power rather than finesse. They need good chins because they tend to get hit a lot.

PUNCHERS (take a bow, OSCAR DE LA HOYA) stay close to their opponents, looking to catch them with uppercuts and hooks.

COUNTER-PUNCHERS seek to exploit momentary lapses in their adversaries' defences while they are throwing punches, rapidly launching counter-punches of their own. This 'get yours in first' policy, brilliantly exemplified in the 1990s by ROY JONES JUNIOR, requires excellent reflexes.

Ali – The Greatest Ever Olympian?

Who is the greatest ever Olympian? There are several candidates: Jim Thorpe, Fanny Blankers-Koen, Larysa Latynina, Carl Lewis, Ian Thorpe (clearly a handy surname). But mention one name and their advocates are liable to say 'Oh yeah…I guess so', even if it is largely on the basis of what he did thereafter.

Cassius Clay – later Muhammad Ali – didn't fight like other boxers. He kept his hands low, ducking or swerving away from punches rather than blocking them, a tactic designed to make his trainers tear their hair out. But he trusted himself to evade the most savage hay-makers through reaction speed alone. Ali also threw out the rule book when it came to punching, aiming almost all his shots at his opponents' heads. But there was method in his madness. He was an 'out-fighter', who liked to keep his distance from the other boxer, evading every punch while landing stinging jabs. Some of them are too fast to see even in slow motion.

STINGING LIKE A BEE – CASSIUS CLAY AT ROME 1960

The eighteen-year-old boxer who won the light heavyweight gold at ROME 1960 was a long way from the finished article but all the ingredients were there to see. He faced a dangerous opponent in Poland's ZBIGNIEW PIETRZYKOWSKI (known as 'Ziggy' to nervous American commentators), a tricky southpaw with a monstrous right hook, but Clay was quick, smart and sassy enough to score a comprehensive victory.

At the after-fight press conference, a Soviet journalist posed a tricky question: how did the boxer feel about the fact that there were many places he, as a negro, was barred from in his own country? Clay robustly defended America, asserting that 'we've got qualified people working on that problem', but on his return to Louisville, Kentucky, he was forced to recognise that the Commie hack had a point. Having been refused service in a hamburger joint, despite a 'do you know who I am?' routine, he and his friend were pursued by bikers to Jefferson County Bridge on the Indiana border. The ensuing fight didn't go well for the bigots but for Clay the episode showed the hollow tokenism of his Olympic victory. He hurled his gold medal into the Ohio River in disgust.

Thirty-six years later, visibly shaking from the effects of Parkinson's disease, Muhammad Ali was given the honour of lighting the Olympic cauldron at Atlanta. He was also awarded a gold medal to replace the one he had jettisoned.

BOXING GOES TO THE OLYMPICS

GIVEN THE PRESENCE OF THE SPORT AT THE ANCIENT GAMES AND the classical-mindedness of the organisers, it is surprising that there was no boxing tournament in Athens in 1896. The explanation is that they felt the contemporary sport was too ungentlemanly. Boxing instead made its modern Olympic debut at ST LOUIS in 1904. The competitors were all American, an unsatisfactory arrangement blamed on a late decision to include the sport in the programme.

The boot was on the other foot at LONDON 1908. There were home victories in all five weight divisions but then nearly all the boxers were British. One rare exception was Australia's REGINALD 'SNOWY' BAKER, who won a silver in the middleweight but felt that he had been a victim of biased officiating. He may have had a point – the winner, JOHNNY DOUGLAS, was the referee's son. Baker lodged a complaint but to no avail.

The sport was absent from STOCKHOLM 1912, as it was banned in Sweden. But pugilism was back at ANTWERP 1920, with an expanded programme of eight weight classes. The USA won three of them, GREAT BRITAIN two. The same two nations finished top of the medals table at PARIS 1924, the first Games at which each country was limited to one entrant per weight category. At this stage, bouts consisted of three rounds, the first two 3 minutes long and the final one 4 minutes.

The extra minute in the last round was dropped for the AMSTERDAM Games in 1928, a tournament marked by unruly crowd behaviour. The most shameful episode occurred at the end of the flyweight semi-final. When South Africa's HARRY ISAACS was announced the winner, supporters of the USA's JOHN DALEY surrounded the judges and menaced them until they reversed their decision. The officials cravenly claimed they had got the fighters' scores mixed up.

LOS ANGELES 1932 was the first Olympics in which boxers were permitted to wear gum-shields and 'cup protectors', as groin guards are euphemistically known. At BERLIN 1936, the GERMAN hosts had to share top spot in the medals table with FRANCE, just as the USA had had to with ARGENTINA and SOUTH AFRICA at the previous Games.

Changes were afoot after the Second World War. BRONZE MEDAL FIGHT-OFFS took place for the last time at LONDON 1948, and four years later two new weight categories (light welterweight and light middleweight) were added to the Olympic programme. American boxers dominated the HELSINKI 1952 tournament, claiming half the gold medals.

SOVIET BOXERS had competed in Helsinki but MELBOURNE 1956 was the tournament in which they really made their mark, finishing with three gold medals to Great Britain and the USA's two each. But the star of the show was Hungary's LASZLO PAPP, who won the light middleweight division to become the first boxer to win three Olympic titles.

The tournament at ROME 1960 is best remembered for introducing the world to a cocky young Light Heavyweight called CASSIUS CLAY. As MUHAMMAD ALI, he was to secure immortality through contests with the winners of the heavyweight title at the next two Games: JOE FRAZIER (1964) and GEORGE FOREMAN (1968).

CUBA emerged as a major boxing power at the 1972 Olympics in Munich, winning three gold medals to the USSR's two. The Caribbean nation has topped the boxing table in five of the subsequent nine Games. It had to play second fiddle to the USA in 1976, though, when the American brothers MICHAEL AND LEON SPINKS both won golds, as did the great SUGAR RAY LEONARD in the light welterweight division. Meanwhile, bantamweight GU YONG JO won NORTH KOREA's first ever Olympic boxing title.

THE REVOLUTIONARY CUBANS

One of the most striking features of Olympic boxing over the last four decades has been the dominance of the Cubans. Seven of the last ten heavyweight champions have come from the island, and they have landed a stack of medals in most other weights.

The secrets of Cuba's success include a state system which identifies promising boxers at a young age and nurtures them carefully thereafter, plus a ban on professional fighting that came into effect in 1962. The cycle of victory is also self-reinforcing, with former champions turning to training and imparting their wisdom to the younger generation. But the country's biggest advantage in amateur boxing is cultural. Cubans regard Olympic boxing as their thing. Successful fighters are considered heroes of the Revolution and are feted accordingly.

The attitude that has powered so many Cuban boxers to the top of the podium was exemplified by TEÓFILO STEVENSON, heavyweight champion at three successive Games between 1972 and 1980. In the late 1970s, he was reportedly offered $5m to fight Muhammad Ali. Teófilo refused, saying 'What is one million dollars compared to the love of eight million Cubans?'

In the absence of American boxers, Cubans notched up five victories at Moscow 1980, including a third successive heavyweight crown for the awesome TEÓFILO STEVENSON. Cuba boycotted LA 84, a tournament which saw the wearing of head-guards made mandatory. The light heavyweight competition was mired in controversy when EVANDER HOLYFIELD was disqualified in the semi-final for allegedly throwing a knock-out punch after the referee had called 'break'. The eventual gold medallist, Yugoslavia's ANTON JOSIPOVIC certainly wasn't convinced – he hauled Holyfield on to his winner's podium at the medal ceremony.

SEOUL 1988 was marred by outrageous judging in the final of the light middleweight competition. The American ROY JONES JR landed almost three times as many punches as South Korea's PARK SI HUN but lost all the same. The host nation didn't come up smelling of roses in the bantamweight contest either. When local boxer BYUN JONG-IL lost to Bulgaria's ALEXANDER HRISTOV after having two points deducted for head-butting, his trainer got into the ring and walloped the referee, New Zealander Keith Walker, on the back. Cue general mayhem. Even one of the security guards called in to calm things down kicked Walker in the head. On a brighter note, KENYA's ROBERT WANGILA became the first black African to win an Olympic boxing gold.

The CUBANS were back at BARCELONA in 1992, winning seven golds including the first of three from Teófilo Stevenson's heavyweight successor FELIX SAVON. They have topped the medals table ever since, except in 2008, where CHINA entered the picture for the first time. It remains to be seen whether the nation's two gold medals in Beijing were a sign of things to come.

CANOEING

29 JULY–1 AUGUST 2012 (SLALOM);

6 –11 AUGUST 2012 (SPRINT)

LEE VALLEY WHITE WATER CENTRE (SLALOM),

ETON DORNEY (SPRINT)

Athletes: 330 | **Golds up for grabs:** 16

OLYMPIC PRESENCE

SPRINT CANOEING WAS A DEMONSTRATION SPORT AT THE 1924 Games, and became a full event in 1936; SLALOM arrived in 1972.

OLYMPIC FORMAT

OLYMPIC CANOEING IS DIVIDED INTO SPRINT AND SLALOM. IN both, heats are followed by semi-finals and then a final. There are four slalom (three for men, one for women) and twelve sprint events (seven for men, five for women), each designated by a letter plus a number: K stands for kayak and C for canoe, and the numeral denotes the number of occupants per boat. Distances range from 100m to 1000m (500m max for women).

CONTENDERS:

GERMANY WAS DOMINANT AT THE BEIJING GAMES AND IS likely to be so again. Central European nations are also powerful in both disciplines: watch out for Hungarians in the sprints and the Slovakian HOCHSCHORNER TWINS going for their fourth consecutive gold in the C2 slalom. Britain's TIM BRABANT is the reigning K1 1000m sprint champion but faces a stern challenge from Canada's ADAM VAN KOEVERDEN.

PAST CHAMPIONS:

USSR/RUSSIA: 29 | USA: 14 | BELGIUM: 11

WHY WATCH CANOEING?

WITH CONTESTANTS COMPETING DIRECTLY AGAINST EACH other, SPRINT CANOEING is exciting in much the same way as rowing, and for that matter all forms of racing in lanes. But there is also an atavistic thrill in watching paddlers going flat out, especially teams of them working in unison. There's something satisfyingly primitive about it, doubtless reflecting the importance of simple watercraft in the lives of our ancestors.

SLALOM CANOEING, by contrast, is like watching people flung into a gigantic washing machine. How are they going to make sense of their chaotic environment and assert dominion over the teeming waters? The answer: by becoming one with their boats. This is particularly true of KAYAKERS, who are organically coupled to their vessels via their spray decks. The two effectively become one organism – an aquatic centaur, if you like. As the boats go one at a time, slalom is more about battling the elements (albeit in contrived form) than direct competition with the other contestants. It demands strength, courage and quickness of thought, and makes excellent viewing.

THE STORY OF CANOEING

PREDATING THE INVENTION OF THE WHEEL BY SEVERAL MILLEN-nia, the canoe is one of the most ancient forms of transport: the oldest known example, displayed in a museum in Assen in the Netherlands, dates from around 8000BC. The first canoes were dugouts, made from hollowed-out tree trunks, but over time all manner of variations were developed, from the outrigger canoes of Polynesia to the birch bark constructions of eastern North America. The word 'canoe' is believed to be derived from *kenu*, the Carib term for a dugout.

The first kayaks – the word comes from the Inuktitut *qajaq*, meaning 'man boat' – were constructed by the Inuit around 4000 years ago. Made by stretching seal skin over driftwood frames, they were tailored to fit their owners, with a length typically three times that of their outstretched arms.

Canoes were used by European explorers in North America as early as 1615, when Samuel de Champlain, the founder of Québec, paddled his way through the Great Lakes. It was not until the second half of the nineteenth century, however, that canoeing was adopted as a middle-class sport. Tribal gatherings aside, the earliest SPRINT RACES were held at the inaugural regatta of the English Canoe Club in 1866, organised by the redoubtable John MacGregor. The New York Canoe Club was formed in 1871, followed by the American Canoe Association in 1880, and the Canadian equivalent ten years later.

Competitive SLALOM CANOEING arrived relatively late on the scene. The first competition, held in SWITZERLAND in 1932, was a sedate flat-water affair modelled on slalom skiing. Before long, enthusiasts realised that white-water racing offered far more thrills and spills. The first world slalom championship was staged, again in Switzerland, in 1949.

THE CHAPLAIN OF THE CANOE

The man who first popularised canoeing as a sport was an eccentric London barrister named JOHN MACGREGOR (1825–92). His aquatic adventures started in early infancy, when he and his parents were rescued from a burning boat en route to India. The next instalment came at the age of twelve, when he stowed on board a lifeboat dispatched to aid a ship in distress near Belfast.

A champion marksman as a young man, MacGregor seems to have acquired a taste for canoeing during a trip to the USA and Canada in 1858, though a journey to Siberia may also have played a part. His interest remained dormant until a train accident robbed him of the ability to hold a rifle steady.

Then, in 1865, he commissioned a firm of shipbuilders in Lambeth to build the first of his seven double-ended canoes, all named *Rob Roy*. The boat was 15 feet long, 28 inches wide and 9 inches deep, with an open cockpit and a cedar deck covered with rubberised canvas. Despite these canoe-like features, it was propelled kayak-style, with a double-bladed paddle.

THE CHAPLAIN IN A SPOT OF BOTHER

Thus equipped, MacGregor launched the maiden voyage of the Rob Roy from Gravesend in Kent. He lit a cigar and, to the astonishment of local bargemen, paddled down the Thames and into the English Channel, where he was joined by a school of porpoises. Inspired by this success, MacGregor had the canoe ferried to the continent, where he embarked on a tour of the waterways of Belgium, France, Switzerland and Germany. His account of the journey, *A Thousand Miles in the Rob Roy Canoe*, was a publishing phenomenon in 1866. Subsequent trips to the Baltic and the Middle East formed the basis of two more bestsellers.

MacGregor caused a sensation wherever he went, not least because he was 6ft 6in tall, and in the habit of paddling in a Norfolk jacket and straw boater. Ships would alter their courses to gawp at him. During his voyage down the River Jordan, a group of overexcited villagers plunged into the water, grabbed the Rob Roy and deposited it, with its occupant still in the cockpit, in the tent of the local sheikh. MacGregor was more than happy to play up to all the attention, performing magic tricks and sometimes lighting lengths of magnesium ribbon for the amusement of spectators. He did have a serious side though, notably a compulsion to distribute rabidly anti-Catholic religious tracts, hence his nickname 'The Chaplain of the Canoe'.

GAME ON: CANOEING BASICS

THE FIRST THING TO GET YOUR HEAD AROUND IS THE DIF-ference between CANOEING and KAYAKING. Not only will this help you make sense of paddle-related goings on at the Games; it will endear you to practitioners of both arts, who get heartily sick of people confusing the two or using the terms interchangeably (a situation not helped by Olympic nomenclature, which brackets them together as 'canoeing').

CANOES are propelled with single-ended paddles by people kneeling on one knee. KAYAKS are propelled with double-ended paddles by seated individuals. Whereas canoes are open in design, kayaks are 'closed' vessels, whose occupants seal themselves in by stretching skirt-like devices called spray decks over the rims of their cockpits. This was an essential precaution for the Inuit hunters who invented the craft, to prevent their boats filling up with icy Arctic water. They also invented an ingenious technique of righting themselves when they capsized, known as the ESKIMO ROLL.

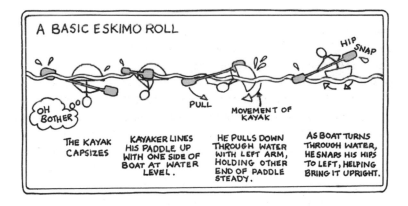

A BASIC ESKIMO ROLL

OH BOTHER

PULL

MOVEMENT OF KAYAK

HIP SNAP

THE KAYAK CAPSIZES

KAYAKER LINES HIS PADDLE UP WITH ONE SIDE OF BOAT AT WATER LEVEL.

HE PULLS DOWN THROUGH WATER WITH LEFT ARM, HOLDING OTHER END OF PADDLE STEADY.

AS BOAT TURNS THROUGH WATER, HE SNAPS HIS HIPS TO LEFT, HELPING BRING IT UPRIGHT.

The second key distinction is between SPRINT events, which take place on calm water on straight courses divided into lanes, and SLALOM, which involve negotiating series of gates on decidedly non-straight stretches of turbulent 'white' water. Whereas sprint canoeing and kayaking take the form of first-past-the-post races, slalom has a time trial format.

SPRINT CANOEING

MEN'S SPRINT RACES ARE HELD OVER 200M AND 1000M (CA-noes and kayaks), women's over 200 and 500m (kayaks only). There are no turns, just straight, lung-bursting charges to the finishing line. It takes around 30 seconds for each kind of boat to complete a 200m course.

There are eight boats in each Olympic heat, each allocated a nine-metre wide lane. To help prevent FALSE STARTS, the boats are aligned with their noses in small cones which automatically drop away at the start signal. Any boat guilty of two false starts is disqualified.

Throughout a race, competitors must endeavour to keep their boats within the FOUR-METRE-WIDE CENTRAL AREAS. If they de-viate, they must move back towards the centre. If one boat comes within five metres of another, it must take immediate remedial action or face the possibility of disqualification. If it leaves its al-located lane, this punishment is automatic; CAPSIZING also brings disqualification.

EQUIPMENT

SPRINT CANOES AND KAYAKS ARE COMPLEX DEVICES, TYPI-cally made from a combination of Kevlar, carbon fibre, fibreglass and sometimes foam, bonded in layers by epoxy or polyester resin. The emphasis in sprint canoeing is on speed rather than manoeu-vrability and this is reflected in the design of the boats, which are longer and more streamlined than their slalom cousins, with very narrow beams. This makes them easy to capsize.

The boats in the sprint classes are delineated as K1, K2 and K4 (kayaks with maximum lengths of 520cm, 650cm and 1100cm), and C1, C2 and C4 (canoes with maximum lengths of 520cm, 650cm and 900cm). Each also has a minimum weight.

Sprint kayaks are equipped with foot-controlled RUDDERS under their hulls, which are operated by the sole or front paddler. This removes the need for corrective strokes, allowing all the paddling energy to be channelled into forward motion. By contrast, sprint canoes are rudderless, which makes the use of corrective strokes essential.

SLALOM CANOEING

THE 2012 OLYMPIC SLALOM COURSE AT LEE VALLEY HAS (like four of the five courses in Olympic slalom history) been artificially constructed, dropping 5.5m along its 300-metre length, with a pump-powered water flow of 15 cubic metres per second.

THE COURSE

All slalom courses must have the following features:

LENGTH of 250 to 400 metres (generally navigable by a good single male canoeist in around 95 seconds).

EQUAL EASE/DIFFICULTY OF NAVIGATION for RIGHT- AND LEFT-HANDED canoe paddlers (kayakers, by definition, paddle ambidextrously).

18 TO 25 GATES, six or seven of which must be negotiated uphill. GREEN and WHITE gates must be crossed with the boat heading downstream, RED and WHITE ones in the opposite direction.

GATES must consist of either one or two SUSPENDED POLES between 1.2 and 4 metres apart. In the case of a one-pole gate, the other pole is placed on the bank of the course to define the gate line (the imaginary line a competitor must cross). The lower end of each pole must be about 20cm above the water line.

THE DISTANCE between the LAST GATE and the FINISH LINE must be between 15 and 25 metres.

The ideal Olympic course will also have at least one GATE COMBINATION which offers competitors several different options; constant CHANGES OF DIRECTION; and a gamut of daunting water features, including EDDIES, WAVES AND RAPIDS.

SCORING

COMPETITORS GET TWO RUNS IN THE HEATS, WITH THEIR better times determining progression. Semi-finals and finals are single-run affairs, which leaves no margin for error.

TIME PENALTIES, which are added to the time taken to complete the course, are incurred for failing to negotiate gates correctly. For a gate to be crossed successfully, it must be tackled from the right

SLOVAKIA'S HOCHSCHORNER TWINS PADDLING TOWARDS A THIRD SUCCESSIVE
GOLD IN THE C2 SLALOM, 2008

direction and in the right running order (Gate 2 comes after Gate
1 and so on); the head of each competitor must cross the gate line
at the same time as at least part of the boat; and neither of the gate
posts must be touched by boat, paddle or body. If either or both the
poles are touched, a 2-SECOND PENALTY is incurred.

If a gate is missed, a 50-SECOND PENALTY is incurred. A gate
is deemed to be missed if any part of a competitor's head breaks
the gate line in the wrong direction; part of the head breaks the
gate line without part of the boat doing the same simultaneously;
a competitor intentionally pushes a gate pole to aid negotiation; a
competitor's head is underwater when the gate line is crossed (this
isn't unheard of); or the gate is tackled out of sequence or omitted
altogether.

In practice, MISSING A GATE is fatal to hopes of a medal. The
same is true of CAPSIZING, which is deemed to have occurred if a
competitor has left his or her boat altogether. Turning a boat upside down does not in itself constitute capsizing. If the occupant(s)
manage(s) to execute an ESKIMO ROLL, there is no penalty and the
boat can continue.

LIKE THE SPRINT EQUIVALENTS, SLALOM CANOES AND KAYAKS
are typically made from permutations of Kevlar, carbon fibre, fibreglass, foam and resin. At Olympic level, they are usually tailor-made
for the course they will be tackling. They are, however, invariably
designed with maximum manoeuvrability in mind, which comes
at the expense of stability.

The difference between slalom kayaks and canoes is less obvious than in sprint racing, as both are decked and equipped with
cockpits. The canoeists, however, must still kneel rather than sit.
Rudders are not permitted on either kind of boat.

The weight and length stipulations for Olympic slalom boats
are delineated in three classes: K1, C1 and C2 (kayak/canoes with
minimum lenghts of 3.5m, 3.5m and 4.1m; minimum widths and
weights are also stipulated).

LOVE AND LOSERS AMONG THE RAPIDS

The women's kayak slalom at the 1992 BARCELONA GAMES was enlivened by the (non-)performance of Costa Rica's GILDA MONTENEGRO,
who accumulated an impressive 470 penalty points on her first run. She
spent most of her next attempt upside down, breaking her helmet as
her head banged along the bottom of the course. It transpired that she
had never even trained for the event until a month before the Games.
Belatedly realising that his country had one more canoeing berth at
Barcelona than he had thought, Costa Rican coach Rafael Gallo had
decided to offer the place to the nice lady who had worked for him
as a raft guide.

Montenegro was so traumatised by the experience that she wouldn't go
near a kayak for eighteen months. She was made of stern stuff, however,
and reappeared at Atlanta determined to complete the course without
missing a gate. She achieved her ambition on her second run, finishing
28th of 30 competitors. Her gutsy attitude so impressed OLIVER FIX, the
German winner of the men's single slalom at Atlanta, that the couple
ended up married.

THE FINER POINTS

CANOE SLALOM IS FAR LESS NEAT THAN THE MORE FAMILIAR ski version: unlike snow, water doesn't stay put, and in canoeing some of the gates must be negotiated backwards, i.e. with the canoeist heading uphill. When this involves turning around into a waterfall, nerves of steel are required.

In SLALOM CANOEING, watch how the competitors use different kinds of stroke to manoeuvre their craft. Long wide sweep strokes are used to turn around, quick short strokes to move forward and push strokes to move backwards.

CANOEING GOES TO THE OLYMPICS

SPRINT CANOEING APPEARED AS A DEMONSTRATION SPORT AT the 1924 Games in Paris, with races featuring both canoes and kayaks. The medals were divided between the USA and Canada, scarcely surprisingly as all the competitors belonged to either the Canadian Canoe Association or the Washington Canoe Club.

When canoeing became a full medal sport at Berlin in 1936, AUSTRIA and GERMANY won the majority of the medals, setting a pattern of Central and Eastern European success that has continued ever since. Women joined the party at the London Games in 1948.

Two individuals stand out in the history of Olympic sprint canoeing. Sweden's GERT FREDRIKSSON accumulated six men's kayak gold medals between 1948 and 1960, repeatedly devastating his opponents with sprint finishes at both 1000m and the now discontinued marathon distance of 10km. Even he, however, must bow to the great BIRGIT FISCHER, who won a staggering eight sprint kayaking golds between 1980 and 2004, three for the GDR and five for the reunited Germany. Just as effective in team events as singles, she became both the youngest and oldest Olympic canoeing champion at the ages of 18 and 42 respectively. Had East Germany not boycotted the 1984 Games, her tally would have been even more impressive.

Various sprint events have fallen by the wayside in the course of Olympic history, including the men's 10km, which was never much of a sprint in the first place, and men's 500m races, which are being replaced by 200m equivalents at the London Games.

SLALOM CANOEING made its debut at the Munich Games of 1972. The West Germans spent 17m deutschmarks on the construction of an artificial slalom course at Augsburg, only to find that the East Germans had built an exact replica in Zwickau. The GDR duly won all four slalom medals.

Largely as a result of the expense involved in building consistent and spectator-friendly artificial courses, slalom was absent from the next four Olympics, but it reappeared at Barcelona and has been a permanent fixture ever since.

CYCLING

ROAD: 28 JULY–1 AUG 2012, START/FINISH THE MALL
TRACK: 2–7 AUG 2012: VELODROME, OLYMPIC PARK
BMX: 8–9 AUG 2012: BMX CIRCUIT, OLYMPIC PARK
MOUNTAIN BIKE: 11–12 AUG 2012: HADLEIGH FARM

Athletes: 593 | Golds up for grabs: 18

OLYMPIC PRESENCE

TRACK CYCLING AND ROAD RACING FOR MEN MADE THEIR debut in 1896 and cycling has been present at every Games since. Women's road racing arrived in 1984 followed by track racing in 1988. Mountain bike was added to the Olympic programme in 1996 and BMX racing in 2008.

OLYMPIC FORMAT

THERE ARE FOUR CYCLING DISCIPLINES: TRACK RACING ON A banked indoor circuit (featuring five different events), BMX, MOUNTAIN BIKING and ROAD RACING. The last of these is held on public roads and comprises two different events: individual time trialing and straight racing. There are men's and women's events in all categories.

CONTENDERS:

ON THE TRACK, THE BRITISH TEAM WILL BE THE ONE TO watch and beat. On the road, the men's competition will feature the world's top professional cyclists, fresh from the Tour de France. In the new classes, BMX and mountain biking, the leading riders come from FRANCE, GERMANY, the USA and EASTERN EUROPE.

PAST CHAMPIONS:

FRANCE: 40 | ITALY: 32 | GREAT BRITAIN: 18

WHY WATCH CYCLING?

OLYMPIC CYCLING OFFERS MANY AND DIVERSE PLEASURES. For techno heads, the sport provides a showcase for the latest designs and newest materials; speed freaks can enjoy the sight of teams sprinting flat-out on the high banking of the velodrome; and the more sadomasochistically inclined will take to the gruelling spectacle of the road racing. The recent addition of mountain biking to the schedule is good for those who like something closer to rallying, while the BMX competition combines a tricksy urban edge with manic multi-rider racing.

For its sheer variety of races, cycling offers even more than athletics: SPRINTS, MIDDLE-DISTANCE RACES and ENDURANCE events; all-against-all racing, individual TIME-TRIALING against the clock, individual and team PURSUITS AND CHASES; 'devil take the hindmost' competitions in which the BACK MARKER is eliminated every time the pack crosses the line; the wild gyrations of POINTS RACES, in which the cyclists score points on a one-lap sprint every ten laps. All of these formats can be seen at the Olympics.

THE STORY OF CYCLING

SOME HAVE CLAIMED THAT THE FIRST BIKE WAS SKETCHED BY Leonardo da Vinci, others to have found a prototype in a stained glass church window in Stoke Poges, Buckinghamshire, but the earliest properly documented ancestor of the bike is the two-wheeled wooden scooter designed by German engineer Baron Karl Freidrich von Drais in 1818. Sitting astride his contraption, the Baron pushed the vehicle with his feet and steered using his revolutionary pivoting front wheel and handle bars. On a good day the Baron could keep up a steady 8mph. The machine was briefly fashionable, but soon disappeared.

The key technological advance came in 1866 when the Parisian carriage manufacturers Michaux experimented with putting pedals on the front wheel of what they called the *velocipede*. It was an instant hit. Within a year or two the Michaux factory was turning out hundreds of VELOCIPEDES, while copies were beginning to be made in the USA and in Coventry in England. That said, the bikes of the 1860s and 1870s were novelties and luxuries – and riding them was a tricky business. Known as boneshakers, they lacked suspension, had hard rubber tyres and were difficult to steer. This did not, however, deter a large number of wealthy young men from racing their new toys.

The first CYCLE RACE on a track was held in France in 1868 at Saint-Cloud, and in 1869 the first race on public roads was held between Paris and Rouen. Given that the pedals were attached to the front axle of these bikes, the inevitable trajectory of technological change was to place the saddle over the top of the front wheel, which became progressively bigger to accommodate the rider's legs; the back wheel became progressively smaller. While capable of considerable speeds, these 'penny farthings' were tricky to balance and not very manoeuvrable.

In 1885 John Kemp Starley from Coventry designed his version of the safety bike, known initially as 'Rover'. This machine had equal-sized wheels, a pedal-driven chain that turned the back wheel and an early form of bike gear. Within a few years it had swept the high-wheel bike aside, a process accelerated by a flood of innovations in component design: pneumatic tyres, gears, brakes, and freewheels.

These changes, combined with the mass production of cheaper machines, made the bicycle a mass means of transport. Racing, like bike ownership, was soon no longer the preserve of a tiny minority, and a new generation of competitive cyclists found huge audiences for their races on both public roads and specially built tracks. By 1900 there were more than 300 VELODROMES in France alone and people were flocking to tracks in New York, London, Brussels, Milan and St Petersburg.

But almost as soon as the bike had emerged it was overtaken by the motor car, the new symbol of industrial speed. In response, cycling made ENDURANCE its calling card. In America, in particular, enormously long track races were established, while the TOUR DE FRANCE – first raced in 1903 – became the keystone of continental European ROAD RACING. In Britain, however, road racing was all but killed off by the response of the authorities, who considered bicycling a public menace. Indeed, in the Town Police Clauses Act of 1888 cyclists were made liable to arrest for 'furious pedalling'.

Both track and road events were actively supported by bike manufacturers, becoming openly professional. Consequently, the leading participants were excluded from amateur competitions like the Olympics. But the gents had to play second fiddle in the great races of the European season. This situation lasted until 1996, when the Olympic events were opened to professional cyclists.

The new classes, MOUNTAIN BIKING and BMX RACING, came of age as organised sports through their inclusion in the Games in 1996 and 2008 respectively.

GAME ON: CYCLING BASICS

··· **TRACK RACING** ·······································

INDIVIDUAL SPRINT IS A TWO-PERSON RACE OVER THREE LAPS of the velodrome. However, the racing rarely starts until the last lap: the previous two circuits are nearly always games of cat and mouse, with the riders staying close to each other as they seek out momentary advantage – a flicker of hesitation from an opponent is the signal to suddenly break away and sprint for the line. The FIRST LAP must be conducted at a minimum of walking pace, but after this riders may GRIND TO A HALT, balancing on the banking like a pair of samurai poised to begin a duel. At the 1964 Tokyo Games Italy's Giovanni Pettenella and France's Pierre Trentin balanced motionless on their bikes for a record 21 mins 57 seconds.

TEAM SPRINT has two teams of three riders racing over three laps (two riders over two laps for women), starting on opposite sides of the velodrome. In contrast to individual sprints, the teams race in line, at full tilt from the start, with each team member having to take the lead on one of the laps before peeling off. Just one rider is left to complete the final lap.

TEAM PURSUIT is contested by two teams; four riders for men, and three for women. They begin from mid-way on the velodrome's two straights, exactly opposite each other. The team whose third rider completes the distance first wins; alternatively, if a team manages to catch the opposition's third rider, it wins the race instantaneously.

KEIRIN was invented in Japan in the late 1940s, where it rapidly became a national betting craze. Eight riders contest the eight-lap race. The first five-and-a-half laps are led by a pace-setter on a motorcycle. The early circuits are raced at relatively leisurely 25kmh, then the pace-setter ratchets things up to 45kmh before leaving the track with around two-and-

PENDEL POWER! VICTORIA PENDELTON (GBR) DOING A LAP OF HONOUR AFTER WINNING THE SPRINT IN BEIJING

a-half laps to go; then the pack races for the line.

THE OMNIUM is track cycling's pentathlon in which cyclists compete in a variety of races accumulating points from each of them towards their grand total. There are six races in all, held over two days.

THE FLYING LAP is a 250m time trial in which contestants race separately, but are allowed a warm-up lap to build up speed.

THE POINTS RACE is a gruelling 30km for men, 20km for women, with a 250m sprint every ten laps for which points are awarded, and big bonuses available for lapping opponents. The winner is the cyclist who accumulates most points.

In the **INDIVIDUAL PURSUIT** men race for 4km, women for 3 km; the cyclists start on opposite sides of the track and chase each other.

THE SCRATCH RACE is a long-distance race on the track – no sprints, no points, just first over the line; 15km for men, 10km for women.

THE TIME TRIAL has cyclists racing separately from a standing start, against the clock; 1km for men, 500m for women.

Lastly, in the **ELIMINATION RACE** all 24 competitors start together, with the last cyclist over the line eliminated every two laps.

ROAD RACING

WITH THE LOSS OF TEAM COMPETITIONS, THE OLYMPICS' road racing programme has been reduced to just two events. In the INDIVIDUAL ROAD RACE all competitors start together and race over approximately 250km of public roads for men, and 140km for women: first across the line wins. In the TIME TRIAL, the riders start 90 seconds apart, and the winner is the rider with the fastest time over a shorter course; around 44km for men and 30km for women.

MOUNTAIN BIKE

THE MOUNTAIN BIKE COMPETITION IS A SCRATCH RACE ON A semi-landscaped loop that's around 40km long. It begins with a mass start, and first across the line wins. The final layout of the course will be decided at the last minute to take account of the weather but it is guaranteed to feature rough terrain, obstacles, sharp drops, jumps and a lot of mud.

BMX

BMX BIKES ARE RACED ON A PURPOSE-BUILT COURSE. THE cyclists start on a high ramp and descend into a circuit of tight corners, bumps, banking and jumps that will take around 40 seconds to complete. All riders will race the course once by themselves to determine seeding and then compete in eight-bike heats to determine the quarter-finalists. The semis and finals involve multiple races in which riders score points according to their finishing places.

THE FINER POINTS

THE MOST IMPORTANT THING TO REMEMBER ABOUT CYCLING is that the majority of the effort expended by a cyclist goes into overcoming air resistance. You use much less energy if someone else is in of front you, moving the air before you get there and shielding you from winds. This is called DRAFTING or SLIPSTREAMING and it explains a lot about how races are conducted. It makes a huge difference to speeds and energy consumption in all races except individual time trials, which are a test of the solo rider, unaided, against the clock.

On the track, time trails aside, slipstreaming is a vital part of racing. In the INDIVIDUAL SPRINT the advantage to be gained by slipstreaming is so huge that most of the race is a battle of wits at walking speed to be the cyclist following rather than leading. The KEIRIN, which begins at a flying start, is one way of avoiding these shenanigans and forcing riders to go all out. Even so, many riders will seek to be right behind the leader until the very last straight.

In TEAM EVENTS, staying in precise formation to create the most effective slipstream is vitally important; look out for the smoothness and regularity which the team members change position in-line, to share the workload at the front without losing speed or rhythm.

Slipstreaming is not a significant aspect of MOUNTAIN BIKING and BMX racing, because the courses are so bumpy and complex that there is barely any space to tuck in behind another rider. In these events, sharp acceleration and braking, brilliant balance and technical cornering are the skills to look out for. In both of these disciplines, cyclists will also jump small obstacles.

In mountain biking there is also the possibility on very steep, muddy courses that the riders may just have to PICK UP THEIR BIKES and run. They are also prone to mechanical failure and tyre damage on the rough circuits. Mountain bikers – alone among Olympic cyclists – are allowed to carry tool kits, and they must do their own running repairs.

CYCLING GOES TO THE OLYMPICS

AS WITH MOST SPORTS, CYCLING'S EARLY OLYMPIC YEARS
witnessed some odd and gentlemanly events. In ATHENS in 1896,
during the interminable 300km track race, the eventual gold medal
winner, LEON FLAMENG of France, stopped racing and waited for
his Greek opponent, who had encountered a mechanical problem.
(It is still etiquette in the Tour de France for the leaders to dawdle if
the Yellow Jersey has a mechanical problem). In the road race from
Athens to Marathon and back, the eventual winner, Greek cyclist
ARISTIDIS KOSTANTINIDIS, fell heavily three times and needed two
bikes to complete the course.

Given the enduring legal and policing restrictions on road racing
in Britain, cycling at the 1908 LONDON GAMES was a track event only.
The 1000m sprint saw four contestants in the final but no medals
awarded: two riders fell and withdrew, and the two who completed
the course failed to do so within the minimum specified time and
were disqualified. In ANTWERP in 1920 the road race was held over
a course that crossed six railway lines. Officials were on hand to note
how much time each cyclist lost at each crossing. Initially it appeared
that South African HENRY KALTENBRUN had won the gold, before

FRENCH DUO SCHILLES AND AUFFAY IN THE 2000M TANDEM AT LONDON 1908

officials worked out that Swede HENRY STENQUIST had lost so much time to the trains that his adjusted time was the fastest.

Many cycling formats have fallen off the track over the last century. Departed friends include the POINTS RACE, the TEAM ROAD RACE and the TANDEM. Perhaps the saddest casualty for the purist is the TEAM TIME TRIAL, for nothing can compare with the speed and spectacle of a time trial team in perfect formation.

In the years after the Second World War, Olympic cycling remained a small, men-only, amateur affair, though the Games served as a stepping stone for some, like Italy's ERCOLE BALDINI, the sprint champion in 1956, who went on to a very successful professional road racing career. The ROME GAMES of 1960 were the first for over thirty years held in a country in which cycling was anything more than a curiosity. The hosts saw local sprinting favourite SANTE GAIARDONI win two golds on the track, but the cycling is now mainly remembered for the road race, held in searing 34-degree heat. The Danish rider KNUT JENSEN, suffering from sunstroke, collapsed, fractured his skull and died – the first athlete to die during a competition at the Games since the 1912 marathon. At the autopsy, traces of a circulation stimulant were found in his blood.

The first DOPING TEST was introduced into Olympic cycling in 1964 and in 1972 two medallists tested positive for banned substances: the Spanish road racing bronze medallist Jaime Huelamo, and Aad van den Hoek, a member of the Dutch time trial team, who had also won a bronze.

ENGINEERING rather than pharmacy seemed to be the key to the West German success at the 1976 Games, where the team sported silk jerseys (banned by the IOC) and raced on helium-filled tyres (permitted). However, in 1980 and 1984 MEDICINE trumped the other technologies. In Moscow, safe from any meaningful doping checks, the Soviets and the East Germans ran amok. In 1984, at Los Angeles, the US team won four golds and five other medals – successes that were later tarnished by the revelation that some of the medallists had been given BLOOD TRANSFUSIONS before their races, a procedure that increased the concentration of red blood cells in their system, thereby boosting oxygen uptake to the muscles. The

CURRENT WOMEN'S MOUNTAIN BIKE CHAMPION, PAOLA PEZZO

practice was not then against Olympic rules, although the medical guidelines discouraged it.

More positively, 1984 saw the first WOMEN'S CYCLING EVENTS at the Olympics. There was a dramatic end to the road race when US cyclist CONNIE CARPENTER-PHINNEY won the gold in a photo-finish, jumping forward over the line in the manner of a street biker mounting the kerb. Change has come at fast pace since then. British cyclist CHRIS BOARDMAN's AERODYNAMIC BIKE helped him win gold in the 4000m pursuit at Barcelona in 1992 and initiated a complete redesign of track bikes to incorporate complex modern materials. In Atlanta in 1996 the professionals arrived and the great Spanish road racer MIGUEL INDURAIN, five times winner of the Tour de France, won gold in the individual time trial; an up-and-coming American rider called LANCE ARMSTRONG finished sixth.

The 1996 Games also saw the debut of MOUNTAIN BIKING. People had experimented with off-road cycling in California during the 1970s, and in the 1980s the first commercially produced mountain bikes appeared. They had sturdier frames than road bikes, plus robust suspension systems, wider tyres and upright riding positions, making them far easier to ride on irregular surfaces. They were a huge sporting and recreational hit: a World Championship was held in 1987 and within a decade mountain bikes were outselling every other type combined, though most were used on urban roads. An Olympic berth became inevitable.

The queen of mountain biking has been Italian rider PAOLA PEZZO, who won the gold medal in 1996 and 2000, staging an amazing comeback in Sydney after taking a big fall and dropping some way behind the leading pack. She also gained considerable notoriety for her appearances in fairy-tale costumes for her cycling shoe sponsor, and the Italian press's obsession with her cleavage.

BMX – short for Bike Moto Cross – completed the current quartet of cycling disciplines with its appearance at the Beijing Olympics in 2008. While mountain biking was the new mainstream, BMX bikes had more of a cult following. These small-wheeled, single-geared bikes – first ridden in Santa Monica, California in the late 1960s – and are prized for their lightness and manoeuvrability, qualities that account for the huge BMX freestyle trick-riding scene.

DIVING

29 JULY–11 AUGUST 2012

AQUATIC CENTRE, OLYMPIC PARK

Athletes: 136 | Golds up for grabs: 8

OLYMPIC PRESENCE

MEN, 1904–PRESENT; WOMEN, 1912–PRESENT

OLYMPIC FORMAT

MEN AND WOMEN COMPETE IN SPRING BOARD AND PLAT-FORM events, in both individual and synchronised competitions.

CONTENDERS:

ONLY AN AUSTRALIAN VICTORY IN THE MEN'S SPRINGBOARD prevented CHINESE divers from capturing every gold medal at Beijing 2008. Expect more of the same. BRITISH hopes are on TOM DALY, who won the 10m competition at the 2010 World Championships and keeps improving.

PAST CHAMPIONS:

USA: 48 | CHINA: 27 | SWEDEN: 16

WHY WATCH DIVING?

OF ALL THE SPORTS SHE COULD HAVE CHOSEN FOR THE climactic final sequence of *Olimpia*, Leni Riefenstahl chose diving. In the most controversial and innovative of all Olympic films, Riefenstahl created a series of stunning images that capture the many compelling facets of the sport: the iron nerve required to maintain poise when leaping from a platform higher than a two-storey house;

the grace and acrobatic brilliance of the diver's flight; the sensational moment of entry and engulfment, as the body strikes the water at more than thirty miles an hour.

It hasn't changed very much since, though new technologies create micro-ripples and bubbles to soften the water, lowering its surface tension. Still, get it a fraction wrong and diving can hurt – or worse. Russian diver Sergei Chalibashvili died after attempting a three-and-a-half reverse somersault in the tuck position during the World University Games in 1983; on the way down, he smashed his head on the board.

The Story of Diving

The earliest record of diving is a painting in a burial chamber south of Naples that dates from 480BC, but we can safely assume that people were doing it long before this. As an organised sport, diving began in northern Europe in the nineteenth century. In Sweden and Germany the nationalist gymnastic movements were part of a wide cultural current that venerated nature and called for athletes to embrace wild waters and the sea. Inevitably, diving became part of the curriculum.

It was in the municipal swimming pools of Victorian Britain that diving first assumed competitive form. In 1883 England's Amateur Swimming Association held the first PLUNGE DIVING CHAMPIONSHIPS, where competitors leapt from starting blocks into the pool and stayed underwater as long as possible. By 1895 the British National Diving Championships boasted separate events for standing and running dives, with springboards. Meantime, HIGH-BOARD DIVING was pioneered in Scandinavia by Otto Hageborge and CF Mauritzi, who came to London in the 1890s and put up a tower in Highgate Ponds, where they wowed the public with fancy dives and twists.

Diving arrived at the Olympics in 1904 in a state of flux. Different traditions in the Anglo-Saxon world and continental Europe remained unreconciled; the judging and scoring of dives was problematic, and equipment and techniques were primitive. The sport has been sharply rationalised since then, and the Olympics has provided a testing ground for its development.

GAME ON: DIVING BASICS

OLYMPIC DIVING COMES IN TWO DISTINCT FORMATS, USING 3-METRE SPRINGBOARDS and 10-METRE PLATFORMS. There are competitions in both formats for men and women and for INDIVIDUAL and SYNCHRONISED diving, which was introduced to the Olympics in 2000. Synchronised divers perform the same dive simultaneously, or mirror-image dives (PINWHEELING), and are judged on both the quality of the individual dives and their relationship to each other.

In all formats, there are two rounds: a COMPULSORY set of dives (chosen by the judges) and an OPTIONAL set (chosen by the athletes).

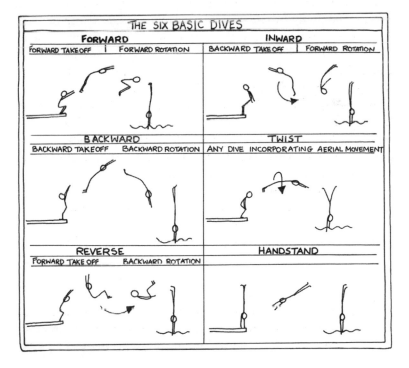

·············· **SCORING AND JUDGING** ··············

WHAT MAKES A GOOD DIVE? IT TOOK NEARLY THREE DECADES for Europeans and North Americans to agree. These days the consensus is that, out of a possible 10, a dive scores up to 3 points each for the quality of TAKE-OFF from the board, FLIGHT through the air and ENTRY into the water. The remaining point can be awarded as a bonus in any one of these three categories. The score is then multiplied by a degree of difficulty factor (DD) – so you get a lot more points for three twisting somersaults, for example, than for a quick half-pike. Olympic competitions have seven judges. To calculate the final score for a dive, the top and bottom scores are excluded and the remaining five averaged.

FOUR POSITIONS AND TWO ROTATIONS

STRAIGHT	PIKE
TUCK	FREE FLYING
SOMERSAULT	TWIST

·············· **BASIC DIVES** ··············

THERE ARE SO MANY DIFFERENT DIVES THAT THE SPORT HAS had to invent a complex alphanumeric code to describe them all. That said, the basics are simple. A dive is defined by three features: the form of the TAKE-OFF, the position of the diver during FLIGHT, and the ROTATIONS – somersaults and twists – performed during the dive. There are six ways in which divers spring from the board or platform: FORWARD; BACK; REVERSE; INWARD; TWIST; AND HANDSTAND.

There are four different POSITIONS that a diver can assume in flight: STRAIGHT; PIKE; TUCK; and FREE. And there are two kinds of rotation: SOMERSAULTS and TWISTS.

THE FINER POINTS

HERE ARE THE KEY POINTS TO LOOK OUT FOR IF YOU WANT to do your own scoring:

TAKE-OFF. Judges are looking for smoothness of approach and the steadiness of handstands.

FLIGHT. A high apex of flight is awarded extra points, while getting too close to the diving board or platform is penalised. Pointed toes score well, but if you let your feet drift apart you will be marked down.

ENTRY. The diver should enter the water at 90 degrees to the surface; the more acute the angle of entry the lower the score. Similarly the fewer splashes a diver creates on entry, the higher the score.

Finally, BEWARE OF GREEKS IN TUTUS. There should, perhaps have been one more gold medal for the Chinese in the synchronised diving competition at Athens 2004, where Bo Peng and Kenan Wang went into the final stretch of the event well ahead of their rivals. Before they could make it on to the boards, a man in the audience dashed on to a diving board and stripped off to reveal a PINK TUTU. After a couple of minutes of clowning and cheering, he dived into the pool before being apprehended. The arena calmed down but the rattled Chinese scored a zero for their next dive, handing the gold medal to the Greeks.

DIVING GOES TO THE OLYMPICS

DIVING IS AN UNLIKELY AND PERHAPS ERRATIC BAROMETER OF global politics, but since 1904 it has boiled down to a series of fights between the USA and its various challengers for political hegemony: first the Germans, then the Japanese in the inter-war period, followed by Cold War duels with the Eastern Bloc. Today, American diving is having to come to terms with the rise of China.

Diving made its Olympic debut in ST LOUIS in 1904, where the aquatic events proved to be a fractious affair, with the US and Germany quarrelling over the rules of almost every acquatic event. (US officials banned the Germans from the 4 x 50yd swimming relay on the grounds that they weren't all from the same club, clearing the path for American swimmers to claim all the medals.) In the dive events, the PLUNGE FOR DISTANCE competition – in effect, an underwater long jump, now sadly discontinued at the Olympics – was unproblematic. But the FANCY DIVING proved difficult.

The Germans had brought their own diving board – a plank covered with coconut matting – that was mounted on a floating pontoon in the lake. They also wanted dives to be marked only for acrobatic content and not for the quality of the entry or finish: the Germans twisted and rolled beautifully but were happy to crash into the water belly or back first. Some Germans refused to compete and, after a third place dive-off saw Alfred Braunschweiger walk off in a huff, the German delegation was so incensed that Dr Lewald, the Imperial High Commissioner to the World's Fair (of which the Games were a part), withdrew his offer of an honorary bronze statuette for the winners. The American winner, George Sheldon, refused to accept his medal at the time due to the chaos.

Over the next twenty years the format of the sport was steadily rationalised. TARIFF VALUES were introduced for different dives in 1908, a blend of COMPULSORY AND OPTIONAL ROUTINES became the norm. WOMEN began to compete in 1912, and springboard diving was added to the platform version.

Still, the complexity of the rules and the BIAS OF JUDGES created problems. At the women's platform competition in Paris in 1924, the Swedish judge awarded first place to the Swedish diver, the Danish judge awarded first place to the Danish diver, and the American judge awarded joint first place to all three American divers. The British and French judges went for CAROLINE SMITH (USA), whose consequent victory was the first of seven in a row for American female platform divers.

GREG LOUGANIS

Born to Swedish and Samoan parents, Greg Louganis was adopted by Greek-Americans in southern California. After early encounters with acrobatics and dancing, he became a teenage diving sensation, winning a silver medal at the Montreal Olympics at sixteen and winning the world championships two years later. After missing the 1980 Moscow Games, along with the rest of the American team, he excelled in Los Angeles, winning two golds with record scores. He repeated the feat

BRIEF ENCOUNTER: GREG LOUGANIS AT SEOUL 1988

in Seoul in 1988, but in the preliminary springboard competition smashed his head on the board after attempting a reverse pike somersault. Despite the concussion and the two-inch wound in his scalp, he performed the dive later in the competition and won the gold.

In 1994, Louganis made his comeback as an announcer and star turn at the Gay Games. He was out of the closet and the following year disclosed in his autobiography that he was HIV positive – a matter of some consternation to the diving fraternity, who panicked over the possible consequences of his blood leaking into the pool at the Seoul Olympics. He also revealed the shatteringly tough childhood he had endured – learning difficulties, bullying at school, sexual abuse at home, teen bingeing on drugs and alcohol.

Diving, it appeared, was not merely his vocation but his salvation. Since then, Louganis has appeared in a number of Hollywood movies, publicly campaigned on HIV issues and taken up competitive dog agility trials, in addition to coaching a new generation of divers.

Similar problems surfaced after the Second World War, but with a distinctly Cold War gloss to them. In Melbourne in 1956 Mexican JOAQUIN CAPILLA PÉREZ won the platform gold on his final dive, edging the American diver Gary Tobian by just 0.03 points. The US team claimed that the Soviet and Hungarian judges were biased but Perez kept his gold (which together with his two bronze and one silver medal, made him Mexico's most successful Olympian).

Thereafter, under American pressure, the authorities started to tighten up on judging. It was indicative of the new regime that a Soviet judge was removed from the Rome Games in 1960 after accusations of partiality. In fact, the USSR never broke American hegemony, and its gold medal in the men's springboard at Moscow 1980 required both the absence of the USA and some help from above. ALEKSANDR PORTNOV of the Soviet Union was allowed to repeat one of his dives after he claimed he was distracted by crowd noise. He went on to win gold, though three of his competitors protested that they were subjected to the same noise.

America's extraordinary domination of Olympic diving peaked in the Reagan years with the arrival of GREG LOUGANIS (see above). Since his retirement the balance of power in diving has shifted to the CHINESE, whose rise is attributable above all to the obsessive and meticulous XU YIMING. Working without books, equipment or facilities in the wake of the Cultural Revolution, Yiming constructed his own diving boards and trampolines in order to train his youngsters. His dedication has paid off spectacularly: since 1992 China has won eleven out of a possible sixteen men's gold medals, and thirteen out of sixteen for the women, including four for the brilliant FU MINGXIA – who in 1991 became world champion at the age of twelve, the youngest in any sport, ever.

EQUESTRIANISM

27 JULY–9 AUGUST 2012

GREENWICH PARK

Athletes: 200 | Golds up for grabs: 6

OLYMPIC PRESENCE

1900–PRESENT.

OLYMPIC FORMAT

THERE ARE INDIVIDUAL AND TEAM COMPETITIONS IN DRES-sage, show jumping and cross-country eventing. Equestrianism is the only sport at the Olympics in which men and women compete against each other on equal terms.

CONTENDERS:

IN RECENT YEARS THE STRONGEST EQUESTRIAN NATIONS have been Germany, the Netherlands, Spain, Britain and New Zea-land. Given recent doping problems and the consequent turmoil in several teams, however, all bets are off.

PAST CHAMPIONS:

GERMANY: 21 | SWEDEN: 17 | FRANCE: 12

WHY WATCH EQUESTRIANISM?

AT THE ROME GAMES OF 1960, ALL SEEMED LOST FOR THE Australians in the equestrian competition. One of their riders, BILL ROYCROFT, had fallen badly during the steeplechase section: his horse, OUR SOLO, had somersaulted over an obstacle, thrown him to the ground and then landed on him. Somehow, Roycroft had managed to remount and finish the course; then, after being administered oxygen and whisky, he'd been flown to hospital in a helicopter. The following day was the show jumping, the final discipline in the event, and Australia had only two fit horse-rider combinations left. They needed three, so Roycroft insisted on competing. Heavily sedated, he was hoisted on to his horse by the rest of the team, before producing a flawless round that brought him and his team a gold medal.

Olympic equestrianism is not for the faint-hearted: EVENTERS have to get their horses over more than thirty huge fences, ditches, banks and water jumps, while SHOW JUMPERS must, under pressure of time, negotiate some terrifyingly high barriers and gallop through a complex array of obstacles. The intricate movements of the DRESSAGE, which demand the appearance of effortless control, are executed under the highest levels of scrutiny. With its roots in military horsemanship and fox hunting, equestrianism was once the most exclusive sport at the Games, and it still retains an aristocratic and military cast. On the other hand, it's unique in allowing men and women to compete as equals, and increasingly the women are coming out on top.

THE STORY OF EQUESTRIANISM

FOR MORE THAN THREE MILLENNIA HUMAN BEINGS HAVE been training horses for transport, war, work and pleasure. DRESSAGE and EVENTING have their roots in the practical needs and competitive spirits of the cavalry regiments of early modern Europe. Dressage, an adaptation of the French word for 'training', was initially a means to an end, a system that prepared horse and rider for the parade ground and the battlefield by emphasising style, control and precision. Modern dressage was first systematised by the Neapolitan nobleman FEDERICO GRISSONE, who established his riding academy in Naples in 1532 and published *Gli ordini di cavalcare*, the defining guide to horsemanship for more than three centuries.

Grissone's influence spread to German-speaking Europe, Scandinavia, Russia and Britain, but it was his French disciples who proved the most enthusiastic. In the late eighteenth century the centre of world dressage was the court of Versailles, where dressage master FRANÇOIS ROBICHON embellished a strictly utilitarian military discipline with something of the artistry of the modern sport. In the nineteenth century the focus shifted to GERMANY, where dressage remained integral to military horsemanship. Indeed, proponents of classical dressage were not delighted when their discipline became an organised sport at the Olympics of 1912. The schism between competitive and non-competitive dressage continues to this day.

EVENTING was preceded by endurance races for cavalry officers, the earliest recorded instance being a race from Vienna to Wiener Neustadt in 1687. In the late nineteenth century, endurance racing took off in the American west, with the Pony Express, cow herders and the US cavalry all providing competitors for riding marathons. German and Austrian officers tested each other in a race held in 1895 between Vienna and Berlin, a distance of more than 330 miles, while in France cross-country cavalry dashes were popular amongst the officer class. A combination of endurance racing, steeplechasing and all the other equine disciplines – a test of the all-round horsemanship expected of cavalry officers – was held in France in 1902. This CHAMPIONNAT DU CHEVAL DES ARMES proved a massive success with the cavalry fraternity, and the format was instantly adopted across Europe. Like dressage, it made its debut at the Olympics in 1912.

SHOW JUMPING, as the name implies, has less practical origins. Equipped with the new hunter saddle for English-style riding, nineteenth-century fox-hunters took great pleasure in leaping over walls, brooks and all manner of natural obstacles in pursuit of their quarry. Jumping competitions were a natural progression. The Royal Dublin Society staged contests for wide and high leaps in 1865, and in 1883 American show jumping made its debut at Madison Square Gardens in New York. Something close to this style of competition was seen in 1907 with the inaugural International Horse Show at Olympia in London. Combined with dressage and eventing, it would form the basis of the Olympic sport that debuted in 1912.

Game On: Equestrianism Basics

Dressage

In the dressage, rider and horse have to perform a series of closely defined movements, displaying mastery in the TROT, WALK and CANTER as well as more complex moves like the HALF-PASS, in which the horse moves diagonally. Points are awarded by a panel of judges.

At the Olympics, team and individual events occur simultaneously over three rounds of competition: the GRAND PRIX serves as the whole team version and the first round of the individual competition. Teams count their three best scores, while the top twenty-five rider-horse combinations go through to the next round. The GRAND PRIX SPECIAL is the second individual qualifying round. Competitors perform a slightly shorter version of the Grand Prix movements and the top fifteen progress to the final round. This is the GRAND PRIX FREESTYLE, in which the leading riders perform an original sequence of MOVES SET TO MUSIC.

The judges SCORE each individual movement from zero to ten, and add in a difficulty factor. They also produce a score (called a collective mark) for four key qualities of the competitor's performance: the freedom and regularity of the horse's paces; the impulsion of the horse; the submission of the horse to the rider; and the posture of the rider. In the freestyle, marks are also awarded for interpretation and artistry.

Show Jumping

In the show jumping, horse and rider must complete a course of around FIFTEEN FENCES within a time limit, but not against the clock. PENALTY POINTS are accumulated for a variety of faults, and the rider or team with the lowest number of faults wins. At the Olympics there are five rounds of show jumping, grouped into three.

ROUND 1. This round, over a short course, is the first qualifying round of the individual event and also determines the starting order in the team event.

ROUNDS 2 AND 3. Both of these count towards individual qualification. The top 45 riders go through to the final round. Scores from round 2 also contribute to team scores; the cumulative scores after round 3 determine the team gold.

ROUNDS 4 AND 5. The 45 riders who made it through rounds 2 and 3 now face further rounds to determine the individual medals. The field is whittled down to 20 for the final round and the lowest cumulative score wins.

FAULTS IN SHOW JUMPING
Obstacle knocked down: 4
First disobedience of horse: 4
Feet in the water jump: 4
First fall of rider: 4
Second fall of rider: 8
Second disobedience of horse: ELIMINATION
Fall of horse: ELIMINATION
Exceeding the time limit: ELIMINATION

EVENTING

FORMERLY A THREE-DAY COMPETITION, NOW SPREAD OVER four days, eventing begins with two days of dressage, followed by a day of cross-country and a day of show jumping. The DRESSAGE and SHOW JUMPING phases are very similar to the pure dressage and show jumping competitions. In the CROSS-COUNTRY, riders must complete an obstacle course about 5.7km long, with up to 45 jumps; they must complete the course within a set time and accumulate as few faults as possible. Team and individual competitions run concurrently, with an additional jumping test at the end to determine the individual classifications.

SCORING is complex. DRESSAGE is marked in the same way as the stand-alone event, then mathematically converted to penalty

NOT FOR THE FAINTHEARTED: EVENTING AT MELBOURNE 1956

points – riders try to accumulate as low a score as possible across the three events. In both the JUMPING and CROSS-COUNTRY an optimum and a maximum time for completing the course are set. Riders who finish outside the maximum time are eliminated and for every second they go over the optimum time further penalty points are collected. Penalty points are collected in show jumping in the normal way. In the cross-country all falls lead to elimination, refusal and disobedience score twenty penalty points and five instances of disobedience (or three at the same fence) lead to elimination. It is, after all, a sport rooted in military discipline.

THE FINER POINTS

·················· SWING IS THE THING: DRESSAGE ··················

AS DUKE ELLINGTON PUT IT, 'IT DON'T MEAN A THING IF IT ain't got that swing.' Despite its stuffy image and the ramrod backs of the riders, dressage is all about swing and rhythm, or as the Germans more onomatopoeically put it, the *Schwung*. Horse and rider should move with ease, grace, suppleness and precision: hesitations, imbalance and shuffling are poor form.

Much of a dressage routine involves horse and rider effortlessly moving between different stride patterns – walk, trot and canter – while displaying technical variants of each of these gaits and performing diagonal movements, like the HALF-PASS, where the horse moves forward and sideways simultaneously. Look, too, for the PIROUETTE, in which horse and rider will rotate through 360 degrees.

CROSS-COUNTRY

THOUGH THE COMPETITION IS BUILT AROUND AN OPTIMAL time for the course, riding flat out is virtually impossible: all riders will need to decelerate and show caution in tackling the tougher obstacles. Look out for horses tiring towards the end of the course: clipping obstacles, skidding on landing and heaviness of movement all suggest an animal at its limits.

FAULTS AND FENCES: SHOW JUMPING

THE FENCES IN SHOW JUMPING ARE HIGHER AND WIDER THAN those in eventing. Don't be fooled by the TV pictures – they are gigantic, even if you are a horse. The riders must balance speed against accuracy of jumping – at the highest levels even a single fault can be disastrous. The best will be those that prepare the horse for each jump, approaching at the right angle and speed, while adjusting the mount's stride to find the right take-off point.

EQUESTRIANISM GOES TO THE OLYMPICS

EQUESTRIAN EVENTS DEBUTED AT PARIS 1900 BUT THEN went absent until the modern form of the sport was defined by the 1912 STOCKHOLM OLYMPICS. The Swedish court was anxious to bring the sport back to the Games, and the campaigning work of COUNT CLARENCE VON ROSEN, Master of the Horse to the King of Sweden, paid off. Dressage, eventing and show jumping were contested at Stockholm – albeit only by serving military commissioned officers. Sweden swept the medal board.

The 1912 DRESSAGE was a simpler affair than today's version, but the very existence of a judging system was a radical development in the rarefied world of elite cavalry regiments. SHOW JUMPING had an even more complex and idiosyncratic scoring system than today's, while the EVENTING course was extremely arduous. It became even harder: in 1932 the eventing was so difficult that only the USA and Netherlands teams finished it – the bronze was left unclaimed. As recently as 1968, in Mexico City, only three of fourteen teams completed the eventing course. The IOC introduced a trimmed version of the event at Athens in 2004.

ETIQUETTE was very strict too. At the 1920 Antwerp Games the Swede GUSTAF BOLTENSTERN, winner of the dressage gold in 1912, was disqualified for practising in the ring prior to the competition. Fellow Swede BERTIL SANDSTRÖM was disqualified from the 1932 dressage event for making a clicking noise to control his horse; he claimed that the judges had heard the creaking of his saddle.

The Swedes were in trouble again in 1948 when Sergeant GEHNÄLL PERSSON was promoted to Lieutenant just three weeks before the Games. As a commissioned officer he was now able to

THE AMAZING LIS HARTEL, HELSINKI 1952

compete, and the Swedes duly won the dressage gold. Two weeks later he was demoted. The IOC and the sport's ruling body reacted by stripping the Swedes of their medal and, thankfully, abandoning the officers-only rule. The leading Mexican show jumper HUMBERTO MARILES won gold in London. In later life he shot a man in a road rage incident and served five years in jail, only to be re-imprisoned for drug trafficking in France. He was found dead in his cell.

The post-war years were the final flourish for the military men. COLONEL HARRY LLEWELYN and his ride FOXHUNTER were the heroes in 1952, clinching an amazing last-minute comeback and gold medal for a British show jumping team that had looked totally beaten. At the same Games, the Danish rider LIS HARTEL, on JUBILEE, took silver in the dressage, becoming the first woman to win an equestrian medal at the Games – just as remarkably, she had suffered polio as a child and was paralysed below the knees.

SEND IN THE CAVALRY

Up to 1948, cavalry officers were the stars of Olympic equestrianism, and some were starrier than most. The show jumping in Los Angeles 1932 was won by Japanese cavalryman TAKEICHI NISHI on URANUS, a victory that made him such a celebrity that for a while he became a member of the Hollywood set around Mary Pickford and Douglas Fairbanks Jnr. He would later serve as a tank commander, and died in the defence of Iwo Jima in 1945. At the Berlin 1936 Games LIEUTENANT KONRAD FREIHERR VON WANGENHEIM, a member of the German eventing team, fell and broke a collar bone in the steeplechase. He clambered back on to his horse, jumped the remaining 32 obstacles, and presented himself for the following day's show jumping with his arm in a sling. Wangenheim then had another severe fall: his horse threw him and toppled on to him, but he still managed, in great pain, to complete the course and secure a gold medal for Germany in front of 100,000 spectators.

As with Nishi, the war was the ruin of him. After being captured on the Eastern front, Wangenheim was imprisoned for more than a decade and died in a Russian POW camp in 1953, just days before his planned release. He was found hanged.

In 1956 equestrianism achieved the unique feat of becoming the only Olympic event to have been held, in total, in a different country from the rest of the Games. Australia's strict quarantine laws made the equestrian competitions a logistical nightmare, so Stockholm was used as the venue.

In recent years, Olympic equestrianism has been riven by DOPING SCANDALS and conflicts with animal welfare groups. In 2004 CIAN O'CONNOR and his horse WATERFORD CRYSTAL were stripped of their show jumping gold medal (Ireland's only gold of the Athens Games) after the horse tested positive for a banned drug. The problem of doping appeared endemic when, on the eve of the show jumping competition in BEIJING in 2008, horses from the Irish, Norwegian, Brazilian and German teams failed their drug tests and were excluded from the event. A year later, the German equine sports federation went a stage further and dismissed all of their

CIAN O'CONNOR WINS GOLD ON THE DOPED-UP WATERFORD CRYSTAL

Olympic teams after show jumper MARCO KUTSCHER confessed to the press that his horse had been doped at Beijing.

The welfare of the horses has always been a contentious issue and it looks like it will be again this time round. In the run-up to London 2012 ANIMAL RIGHTS ACTIVISTS have called for a boycott of the equestrian events. Their campaign began when a video depicting the dressage training and warm-up technique *rollkur* went viral. Swedish rider PATRIK KITTEL was seen drawing his horse's neck round and down so that its nose was touching its chest. While many within the sport consider this a perfectly legitimate and cruelty-free form of training, viewers were alarmed at the state of the horse's tongue (which went blue) and Kittel received many death threats.

FENCING

28 JULY–5 AUGUST 2012

EXCEL ARENA

Athletes: 212 | Golds up for grabs: 10

OLYMPIC PRESENCE

MEN, 1896–PRESENT; WOMEN 1924–PRESENT.

OLYMPIC FORMAT

THERE ARE INDIVIDUAL CONTESTS FOR ÉPÉE, FOIL AND SABRE for both men and women. Men contest a team foil and a team sabre competition, women team foil and team épée.

CONTENDERS:

IN THE WOMEN'S EVENTS ALL EYES WILL BE UPON THE ITALIAN VALENTINA VEZZALI, who has won the last five golds in the foil. The sabre should prove a fierce battle between the winner in 2008, American MARIEL ZAGUNIS, and the young Ukrainian star OLGA KHARLAN. In the MEN'S EVENTS look out for China's LEI SHENG and Japan's YUKI OGTA in the foil, Germany's JOERG FIEDLER in the épée, and NICOLAS LIMBACH in the sabre.

PAST CHAMPIONS:

ITALY: 45 | FRANCE: 41 | HUNGARY: 34

WHY WATCH FENCING?

IT IS HARD NOT TO SEE COMPETITIVE FENCING THROUGH THE lenses of literature or film. The DUEL has been a staple dramatic device from Shakespeare through popular historical novels such as *The Count of Monte Cristo* to the swashbuckling movies of Douglas

THE FLASHING BLADE: MEN'S FOIL FINAL, TOKYO 1964

Fairbanks Jr. and Errol Flynn. And therein lies the problem: fencing's compressed and technical artistry can look colourless against the implausible flourishes of big-screen swordplay. To see the sport properly requires a recalibration of the mind. Fencing is a EUROPEAN MARTIAL ART: the stylish and refined remnant of an aristocratic code of masculine conduct – but not so refined that the dangers have been entirely eliminated, nor a code so strict as to prevent GAMESMANSHIP and cheating. Once the eye has adjusted to this extraordinary form of ritualised combat and recognised its sparse beauty, the *Three Musketeers* will look like a music-hall novelty turn.

THE STORY OF FENCING

EUROPE'S MEDIEVAL NOBILITIES WERE A WARRIOR CLASS AND their wills were enforced their will at the point of a sword. After the arrival of gunpowder, what kept the sword in business was its role as a marker of status: who could and couldn't publicly bear arms was a matter of considerable legislation. For those who were permitted to use a sword it became, through DUELLING, an instrument of dispute resolution in the aristocratic theatre of honour. Fencing, the structured art of swordsmanship, developed largely to serve this often illegal cult.

The oldest European guide to swordplay is a late thirteenth-century German manuscript in which a monk-like figure instructs a student who is armed with sword and a small shield known as a buckler. The arrival, in the fifteenth century, of the printing press in Europe saw a proliferation of FENCING MANUALS: printed in runs of more than a thousand, they were amongst the bestsellers of the day, with artwork from such luminaries as Dürer and Michelangelo.

Amongst the most widely read works of the Renaissance was Baldassare Castiglione's *The Book of the Courtier*, published in Venice in 1538. In this instruction manual for the social class one rung down from Machiavelli's *Prince*, Castiglione noted that skill with sword was central to the life of the courtier, 'for beside the use of them he shall have in war . . . There happen oft times enough variances between one gentleman and another, whereupon ensueth a combat.'

Demand for instruction was insatiable, and in the sixteenth and seventeenth centuries Italian masters supplied the market all over Europe. Achille Marozzo, author of *The New Text on the Art of Arms*, analysed the techniques of thrusting and parrying, while Camillo Agrippa's *Treatise on the Science of Arms* defined the stances (or guards) that remain in use today. ITALY was at that time an agglomeration of small states, each of which had its own school of swordsmanship, and it was only in the 1890s, after the creation of a united Italy, that a single style and set of rules was agreed upon. By that time Italy had long been eclipsed by FRANCE, a centralised nation whose nobility had proved even more enthusiastic about duelling.

When Louis XIII took the throne in the early seventeenth century the parkland of the Bois de Boulogne was awash with aristocratic blood. Duelling rules allowed multiple seconds to engage each other in combat, which resulted in mass fencing brawls. British ambassador Lord Herbert wrote home, 'There is scarce a

A EUROPEAN MARTIAL ART: FENCING AL FRESCO AT THE FIRST MODERN GAMES (ATHENS, 1896)

Frenchman worth looking on who has not killed his man in a duel.' Even Cardinal Richelieu could not eliminate duelling, despite edicts banning it. It was only when Louis XIV gathered the French nobility under the state's watchful eye at the Palace of Versailles that some kind of control was established. In the regimented world of the Sun King, FENCING was reinvented as a courtly practice. Fighters were encouraged to engage in a dialogue of blades rather than an unstructured melee. The FOIL, a lighter sword, was introduced and the legitimate areas of attack on the body were narrowed. Despite these measures, injuries abounded, and after three court masters lost eyes in the early 1700s MASKS were introduced.

The process of codification was completed in the nineteenth century. The illegal but widespread underworld of duelling was given its definitive form by the Comte de Chateauvillard of the Paris Jockey Club in his compendious *Essai sur le duel*, published in 1836. The official technical text of the public world of fencing was provided by the state: in 1877 the French Ministry of War issued its biblical *Manuel d'Éscrime*, which held sway over fencing practice for over half a century.

By the late nineteenth century fencing had assumed something close to its modern form, with weapons, protective clothing and rules broadly as they are today. Competitive fencing then found a new home in exclusive urban clubs. Fencing masters gave lessons and fought at gala exhibition events in front of thousands of well-heeled spectators. But the emergence of fencing as a sport would not only require new rules and technologies that made it a non-lethal activity (and less susceptible to cheating), it also required the destruction of the military and aristocratic milieus in which it had been forged. The First World War delivered both.

GAME ON: FENCING BASICS

FENCING BOUTS CONSIST OF THREE THREE-MINUTE SEGMENTS, fought out on a PISTE – a strip that must be between 1.5 and 2m wide. Fencers score when they hit the opponent's TARGET AREAS, which vary according to the kind of sword used. The winner is the one who scores MOST HITS, and in the event of a tie one minute OVERTIME is played. Lots are drawn before overtime to determine who wins in the event of another tie, in order to force fencers to be aggressive.

PENALTIES

PENALTIES CAN BE AWARDED FOR JOSTLING, DEFLECTING HITS with the hand and refusing to salute one's opponents. Referees award a YELLOW CARD and a warning for the first infringement, a RED CARD and a PENALTY POINT after this, and a BLACK CARD for a third offence, which means disqualification. It is illegal to parry a blade with the arm, but the practice is widespread. high-level fencing is so fast that referees rarely catch it.

CHOSE YOUR WEAPONS

THREE TYPES OF WEAPON ARE USED IN OLYMPIC AND INTER-national fencing, and different rules apply to each.

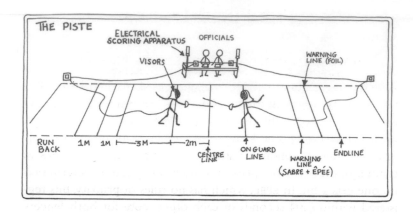

FOIL The lightest and most flexible of the swords was developed in eighteenth-century France as a training weapon. A hit is scored only with the point of the sword and only on the torso.

ÉPÉE Closer to the classic duelling sword of the nineteenth century, the épée may strike at any part of the body, but only with its tip – a style devised originally to draw blood but not to kill.

SABRE Derived from cavalry swords and duelling weapons like the rapier, the sabre is designed for cutting and slashing as much as thrusting. Points are scored with any part of the sword anywhere from the waist up – including the mask and back.

ELECTRONIC SCORING

KEEPING SCORE IS HARD IN FENCING, DUE TO THE SPEED OF THE action. In early Olympic contests, there were unsuccessful experiments with dye-tipped swords and points that snagged clothing to reveal hits. The ELECTRICAL ÉPÉE was first introduced into the European championships in 1935 and was considered a success. The foil equivalent arrived in 1955 and the sabre in 1988.

TEAM EVENTS

THREE-MEMBER TEAMS COMPETE WITH EACH FENCER FIGHTING all three opponents. The total hits from all the bouts are added up to determine the winners.

THE FINER POINTS

·········· WHO CAN HIT WHOM? RULES OF PRIORITY ··········

IF BOTH FENCERS SCORE A HIT SIMULTANEOUSLY, WHO GETS the point? To deal with this problem, FOIL AND SABRE fencing have RULES OF PRIORITY: the person who attacks first has priority and normally gets the point. Defenders can gain priority and become attackers after an opponent's strike fails, but they must be quick to claim it or they will lose priority. If no priority can be determined, no one gets a hit. In ÉPÉE, which has no rules of priority, hits registered within 0.04 seconds of each other score for both fencers, unless their scores are equal and one point from victory – in which case, no one scores.

···························· GETTING TECHNICAL ····························

AFTER A HIT HAS BEEN SCORED AND THE BOUT STOPPED, THE referees will describe the winning exchange in technical terms. Commentators may well use these terms too, so it's as well to know them.

ATTACK: the first offensive action

PARRY: a successful defence and deflection of an attacking blade

RIPOSTE: an attack that follows a successful parry

REMISE: an attack that follows a successful parry but with no withdrawal of the fencing arm

REDOUBLE: an attack after an opponent has lost his or her chance at priority due to inaction or slowness

···························· SWORDS AND STYLES ····························

FOIL Foil bouts are closely regulated by the rules of priority and are often technical affairs, with small and rapid movements the key to gaining advantage.

ÉPÉE The épée duel is closest in style to classical duelling: the whole body is the target, there are no rights of priority, and collisions are permitted. Counter attacking is often the preferred style. Look for fencers attempting to provoke rather than launch attacks and then responding when a gap opens.

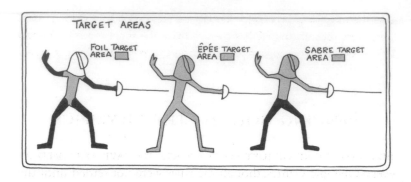

SABRE As the sabre can score a hit with any part of the blade and as parries are hard to execute, defence in this discipline is best conducted by footwork and positioning. Because cuts as well as thrusts are allowed, more flamboyant bladework is on display, and the flèche – a run and leap at the opponent with an outstretched sword – is also permitted.

PROTECT AND SURVIVE: KIT AND INJURIES

Fencing has a fatal past and remains a dangerous sport. A Russian contestant was run through the chest at the 1980 Olympics. At the 1982 World Championships VLADIMIR SMIRNOV was killed when a foil pierced his mask and his eye; three years later, at the same event, a Frenchman impaled his thigh on a broken blade and was saved by a Spanish doctor who leapt leaping from the audience to help him.

Consequently, fencing has gone to considerable lengths to design equipment that will prevent injury. Olympic athletes will have to put on a lot of kit. Their FENCING JACKETS are now partly made of Kevlar (used in bullet proof vests etc.). Women wear a plastic chest protector beneath this. An additional protective layer called a PLASTRON is worn under the ARMPIT (a weak point in past competitions) and regulations are so exacting that this cannot have a seam. GAUNTLETS are designed to prevent a blade running up a competitor's sleeve. The demands on FENCING MASKS have steadily risen and the VISORS must now be able to resist a force of 56kg. Fortunately these days the most likely injuries for fencers are twisted ankles and lower back pain. More recently, the FIE has tried to make the sport more TV-friendly by introducing coloured kit and clear masks that reveal the fencers' faces.

FENCING GOES TO THE OLYMPICS

FENCING IS ONE OF JUST FOUR SPORTS TO HAVE APPEARED AT every Olympic Games, though the rules were not settled until the foundation of the FIE (INTERNATIONAL FENCING FEDERATION) in 1913. Prior to this, fencing was a quirky Olympic presence. Unlike any other event, there were separate competitions for AMATEURS and FENCING MASTERS, who were deemed a special and permissible category of PROFESSIONALS. There were also competitions in which both groups took part – a kind of early pro-am fencing. Foil had been present since 1896 and épée and sabre were soon added, but there was experimentation in 1904 when a single sticks competition (fencing with wooden poles) was held, and in the non-recognised 1906 Games there were medals for the unorthodox three-pointed sabre. In 1904 the CUBAN fencers took gold in individual foil and épée but had to call in a New Yorker to make a trio, which went on to win the only Olympic medal for a MIXED TEAM.

The ARISTOCRATIC AMBIENCE of fencing is best captured by the record of the six-man British team at the 'Intercalated Games' of 1906, which included one knight and two peers of the realm. They sailed from England to Athens in a yacht called the *Branwen*, owned by Lord Howard de Walden. Theodore Cook, the team captain, wrote up a report of the expedition, which included the squad's favourite classical quotations in Greek and Latin, as well as architectural and historical discussions. Edward VII, who like most crowned heads of Europe attended the Games, was so excited by the fencing that he agreed on his return to become a patron of the art.

Aristocratic insouciance notwithstanding, fencing enjoyed some bitter feuding – notably at STOCKHOLM 1912. In the foil event the French insisted that the upper arm be included in the target area; the Italians refused to accept this and the French stormed out. The

WILL IT BE SIX? ITALY'S VALENTINA VEZZALI HAS WON THE LAST FIVE WOMEN'S
FOIL TITLES

Italians then argued for a rule change in the épée that would have
extended the permissible length of the sword; the French refused
and the Italians walked out.

Fencing in the 1920s was still a vocation rather than a sport,
typified by the NADI BROTHERS from Livorno. Relentlessly
schooled from an early age, NEDO NADI won his first gold medal
in 1912 and five at the 1920 Antwerp Games, before turning
professional. (His multiple haul of medals stood as a record for
fifty years, until Mark Spitz won seven swimming medals at the
1972 Games.) With his younger brother, ALDO, Nedo formed a
partnership that fought a celebrated series of exhibition bouts. He
lived the life of an itinerant playboy, moving to Hollywood, where
he trained movie stars and choreographed fights.

The 1924 Olympics saw the last contest that boiled over into a
real duel. In the final rounds of the sabre competition it was clear
that the Italian fighters were going soft on team favourite ORESTE
PULITI, easing his path to the medals. The tactic was denounced
by the French judge Lajoux and the Hungarian judge Kovacs.
Puliti responded by making threatening remarks to both and was
disqualified. Inevitably, Puliti and Kovacs met the following day at

the Parisian cabaret, the *Folies Bergères*, where the exchange turned violent and satisfaction was demanded. The two met on the Italian-Yugoslav border in November and duelled for over an hour, injuring each other seriously before the contest was stopped.

For much of the inter-war period fencing proved attractive to the elites of Europe's FASCIST STATES, satisfying their predilection for blood sports, warrior cults and medievalism. Oswald Mosley encouraged British fascists to embrace the foil, General Franco fenced with enthusiasm, and Reinhardt Heydrich, Himmler's deputy in the SS, was so obsessed with fencing that he had the archive of the FIE seized from Belgium and brought to his office in Berlin, from where he planned to run the global sport. MUSSOLINI had a penchant for duelling in his journalist days and when in power he liked to be seen practising by foreign journalists. The Italian fencing team received considerable support under his rule and the dictator enlisted Nedo Nadi – despite his anti-fascist convictions – as coach. In HUNGARY, the country's mastery of the sabre (it won every gold medal between 1924 and 1960) was incubated in the *salles* and clubs of the ultranationalist army.

Since the Second World War, the pre-eminence of France and Italy has been steadily whittled away. WEST GERMANY became a fencing power in the late 1970s and early 1980s, driven by their maniacal head coach Emil Beck, but perhaps the most significant change in the world of fencing came about as a result of the crushing of the 1956 uprising in Hungary, the nation that had dominated the sabre since the 1920s. The consequent exodus of top-class fencers led to the establishment of new schools in SWEDEN, POLAND, ROMANIA and, ironically, the SOVIET UNION – a legacy that has been bequeathed to RUSSIA, which is now among the strongest countries in the sport.

Between 1924 and 1960 individual foil was the sole WOMEN'S EVENT, though a team foil competition was introduced in Rome. However, it wasn't until 1996 that women's épée was added, followed by the sabre in 2004. While the USA, Switzerand and China have won medals in the women's events, the old fencing nations remain dominant.

FOOTBALL

25 JULY–11 AUGUST 2012
LONDON (WEMBLEY STADIUM)
BOTH MEN'S AND WOMEN'S FINALS
MANCHESTER (OLD TRAFFORD),
CARDIFF (MILLENNIUM STADIUM),
GLASGOW (HAMPDEN PARK),
NEWCASTLE (ST JAMES' PARK),
COVENTRY (CITY STADIUM)

Athletes: 504 | **Golds up for grabs:** 2

OLYMPIC PRESENCE

MEN'S FOOTBALL 1908–PRESENT; WOMEN'S 1996–PRESENT.

OLYMPIC FORMAT

THERE ARE SIXTEEN TEAMS IN THE MEN'S TOURNAMENT, twelve in the women's. Aside from up to three older players, all members of a MEN'S TEAM must be UNDER 23. There are no age restrictions for the women.

CONTENDERS:

ARGENTINA, URUGUAY, BRAZIL AND NIGERIA WILL BE THE favourites for the men's competition. The USA, GERMANY, CHINA, NORWAY and SWEDEN will be the teams to watch in the women's, as will 2011 women's world cup winners Japan.

PAST CHAMPIONS:

GREAT BRITAIN: 3 | USA: 3 | HUNGARY: 3

Why Watch Olympic Football?

Should the world's game be at the world's Games? Many think not. As with tennis, even the victors would acknowledge that the Olympic tournament is not the pinnacle of the sport. This is less true, however, of the WOMEN'S COMPETITION than the men's, as the former is open to footballers of any age. The MEN'S COMPETITION is something of a hotchpotch, being essentially an UNDER-23 TOURNAMENT. To make matters worse, as Olympics years coincide with the European Football Championships, the top European countries either do not take part or tend to field weakened teams. And the host nation — GREAT BRITAIN — doesn't have a team. Or at least it didn't until the English FA decided that it would invent one, in the face of strident opposition from the Scots, Welsh and Northern Irish.

The arrangements for the men's competition do have their merits, though. FIFA, the sport's governing body, organises global tournaments at under-20 and under-17 levels, but there is no under-23 equivalent, making the Olympics the closest thing to a World Cup for this age group. And for non-European nations, at least, the men's competition at the Olympics is a showcase for the best rising talent in the sport, seasoned with the experience provided by a smattering of older players. The BEIJING TOURNAMENT featured the likes of LIONEL MESSI and RONALDINHO. So while Brits may remain underwhelmed, or indeed unrepresented, for South American, Asian and African nations Olympic football is a very big deal indeed.

The Story of Football

The earliest recorded football-like game, played in China in the fifth century BC, involved kicking a ball through a hole in a piece of cloth suspended from two poles. As there were no teams, it was essentially a form of target practice. The ANCIENT GREEKS introduced passing and tackling in a game called *phaininda*, which was adopted by the ROMANS and renamed *harpastum*, but

WHO SAYS OLYMPIC FOOTBALL ISN'T IMPORTANT? MONTEVIDEO TURNS OUT EN MASSE TO GREET THE URUGUAYAN TEAM ON ITS TRIUMPHANT RETURN FROM THE 1924 GAMES

the sport probably had more in common with handball or rugby than with football. Feet don't appear to have played a particularly active part in the various forms of 'football' played in Europe during the MIDDLE AGES either, except as weapons. Typically played on Shrove Tuesday, these games were semi-formalised brawls in which two teams of indeterminate size vied to convey an inflated pig's bladder to one end or other of a village or town. The one medieval game that did concentrate on footwork was *kemari*, a ritualised form of keepy-uppy practised in Japan, which was itself derived from the Chinese game of *cuju*.

Football as we know it evolved in the public schools of ENGLAND during the nineteenth century, and in 1848 a common set of rules was drawn up. The key subsequent development was the restriction of the right to handle the ball to one player per team during the 1860s. By the beginning of the modern Olympic era, football had become a significant force – and a working-class passion – in Britain's industrial cities, with the first FOOTBALL LEAGUE founded in 1888. The sport soon took root in South America and continental Europe, courtesy of expat Brits and anglophile locals. And – for men's football, at least – the rest is history.

The story of WOMEN'S FOOTBALL is rather less well known. At the start, it developed very much in parallel with the men's game. The earliest recorded match was a 7-1 victory for a North of England eleven over the South in 1885. The first organised women's tournament was launched in the north-east of the country in 1917. Popularly known as the MUNITIONETTES' CUP, it was contested by workers in the region's armaments factories. The era's celebrated team was DICK KERR'S LADIES, formed in a Preston munitions factory. The team toured the USA and drew a crowd of 53,000 at a Boxing Day fixture at Goodison Park in Liverpool in 1920.

In 1921, the ENGLISH FA made a less than enlightened decision to BAN WOMEN'S TEAMS from playing at its affiliated stadiums, arguing that 'the game of football is quite unsuitable for females and ought not to be encouraged'. This led to the formation of the breakaway English Ladies Football Association and the establishment of a Challenge Cup. Although the tournament attracted much attention in its early days, women's football – lacking support from the powerful FA – gradually sank from prominence in the nation of its birth. Only when the governing body rescinded its ban in 1971 did its fortunes begin to revive.

By this stage, nations in which the women's game did not face the same kind of institutional resistance had surged ahead, notably GERMANY, CHINA, the USA and SCANDINAVIA. The first UEFA women's Championship was won by SWEDEN in 1982 and eight years later the USA captured the inaugural FIFA women's World Cup.

GAME ON: FOOTBALL BASICS

UNLESS YOU ARE A MARTIAN OR TRULY CAN'T STAND THE sport (in which case you are unlikely to want to read a long exposition of its laws), you'll be fully aware that the object of the exercise is to get the ball into the opponents' net more often than they get it into yours. You'll also have an inkling that the players, bar the goalkeeper, are not allowed to use their hands or arms. The one rule that can give trouble is offside ...

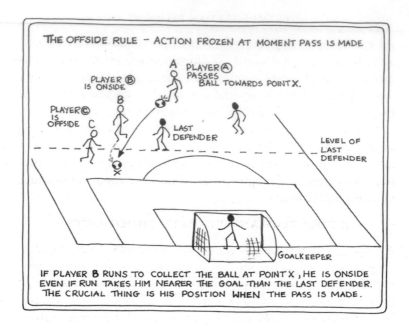

THE OFFSIDE RULE - ACTION FROZEN AT MOMENT PASS IS MADE.

PLAYER Ⓐ PASSES BALL TOWARDS POINT X.

PLAYER Ⓑ IS ONSIDE

PLAYER Ⓒ IS OFFSIDE

LAST DEFENDER

LEVEL OF LAST DEFENDER

GOALKEEPER

IF PLAYER B RUNS TO COLLECT THE BALL AT POINT X , HE IS ONSIDE EVEN IF RUN TAKES HIM NEARER THE GOAL THAN THE LAST DEFENDER. THE CRUCIAL THING IS HIS POSITION WHEN THE PASS IS MADE.

THE OFFSIDE LAWS

A PLAYER IS IN AN OFFSIDE POSITION IF THEY ARE IN THE opponents' half of the pitch, in front of the ball, and closer to the other team's goal line than the second-to-last opponent. This applies to any part of the player's body except the arms.

Crucially, however, a player will only be penalised if: they were in an offside position at the moment the ball was last touched by another player; they didn't receive the ball directly from a throw in, goal kick or corner; or they are deemed to be ACTIVELY INVOLVED IN PLAY.

Decisions relating to offside are frequently controversial for two reasons. First, it can be extremely difficult to judge whether a player is ahead of the second to last opponent at the moment the ball is played, particularly if the referee's assistant responsible for making the call isn't precisely parallel to the player at the time. Secondly, determining whether a player is active is far from straightforward and often more a matter of judgement than of incontrovertible fact.

COMPETITION FORMAT

As host nation, Great Britain has guaranteed places in both the men's and women's competitions. Everyone else has to qualify via preliminary continental tournaments. In the women's tournament, the European qualifiers are the two best performing European teams at the 2011 Women's World Cup

Both tournaments will begin with a GROUP STAGE (four groups of four for the men, three groups for the women), in which each nation will play the other three teams in its group. The top two from each group will progress to a KNOCK-OUT STAGE, culminating in a final at Wembley.

EXTRA TIME AND PENALTY SHOOT-OUTS

As with the World Cup, group matches will consist of two 45-minute halves with no extra time if the scores finish level. During the knock-out stages, 30 minutes of EXTRA TIME will be played if required, followed by a PENALTY SHOOT-OUT if no winner has emerged. (The 'golden goal' system, whereby the first team to score in extra time won the game there and then, was used in the Games in 1996 and 2000 but has now been dropped.)

In a PENALTY SHOOT-OUT each team takes five penalty kicks and the one that scores the most wins. If the scores are still level, the shoot-out enters 'sudden-death' – the first team to find itself ahead when both sides have taken the same number of penalties wins the match.

THE FINER POINTS

Should your first experience of football come at the 2012 Games, the following ought to increase your enjoyment of the spectacle.

WATCHING THE MIDFIELD BATTLES

Pay attention to how the players make and exploit space: good players are constantly moving into positions where they can receive passes while escaping the attention of opponents. The team which dominates the middle third of the pitch usually goes on to win the game. Possession isn't everything in football – what you do when you have the ball is what matters – but the ability to retain it is the hallmark of a good team. Chasing the ball is dispiriting and tiring; controlling it makes a team master of its own destiny.

······························· **WATCHING THE WATCHERS** ·······························

ASK YOURSELF WHETHER IT'S REALLY REASONABLE FOR THE individuals responsible for making the decisions about key incidents to be the only people on the planet without recourse to replays. The issue of whether and how much the officials should have access to technology burns continually.

······························· **WATCHING THE WOMEN** ·······························

SEASONED FANS MIGHT WANT TO TAKE A BREAK FROM THE men's game until the final stages and concentrate on the female tournament instead. The action is slower and less athletic but the levels of skill can be high.

TEAM GB?

The British invented football, are obsessed with it and happen to be hosting the 2012 Olympics. Yet getting a team together to compete at the London Games has been an uphill struggle. No Great Britain team has appeared at the Olympics since 1960 and none has even tried to qualify since the English Football Association abolished the distinction between amateur and professional players in 1974.

The root of the problem is a mismatch in the status accorded to constituent parts of the United Kingdom by the International Olympic Committee and FIFA, the governing body of world football. The IOC deems ENGLAND, SCOTLAND, WALES and NORTHERN IRELAND to comprise one nation, known as Great Britain, whereas FIFA, respecting the fact that the Home Nations have fielded separate teams since the sport's infancy, considers them to be four different countries. Technically, both are right, which clarifies the issue not at all.

This confusion is enhanced by a lack of enthusiasm by the natives for a British team – at least until 2012. To most Scotland or Wales fans the idea is anathema; the Northern Irish are divided; and the English, well the jury remains out ... though a lot of fans do fantasise about how tasty English-based sides augmented with the likes of Best, Dalglish and Giggs would have been.

If the fans aren't keen, the men who run the football associations of Scotland, Wales and Northern Ireland are considerably less so. In a nutshell, they fear that allowing their players to participate in a Great Britain Olympic side would be the thin end of a wedge that will ultimately lead to the loss of their individual identities on the international stage. FIFA President Sepp Blatter has frequently stated that their concerns are groundless, but he is not the world's most consistent man. In March 2008, in fact, he strongly implied the opposite. 'If you start to put together a combined team for the Olympics,' he said, 'the question will automatically come up that there are four different associations so how can they play in one team? If this is the case then why the hell do they have four associations and four votes and their own vice-presidency?'

It seems certain that some sort of Great Britain team will be cobbled together for the London Games, possibly under the stewardship of the thunder-thighed former England left-back Stuart Pearce. David Beckham, as ever, is gagging to take part. And there might even be a Welshman, Gareth Bale having expressed interest.

FOOTBALL GOES TO THE OLYMPICS

AFTER FEATURING AS AN EXHIBITION SPORT AT THE TWO PREVIOUS Games, football made its full Olympic debut at LONDON 1908. Only six teams took part, including two from France, and the quality was decidedly uneven. The Danes, who lost the final 2–0 to GREAT BRITAIN, scored 26 goals in their other two Games, including a 17–1 drubbing of France B, in which SOPHUS NIELSEN hit the net ten times. The number of participating nations rose to eleven in 1912, but in many respects the tournament mirrored its predecessor. Once again there was a handful of big scores, another player (GOTTFRIED FUCHS of Germany) bagged ten goals in a single match, and Great Britain again beat Denmark by a two–goal margin in the final.

The BELGIUM and CZECHOSLOVAKIA final at ANTWERP 1920 was the highlight of the Games for the locals, so when some youths dug a tunnel under the perimeter fence several thousand of them squeezed in for free. Their presence put such a strain on the already full 40,000-capacity stadium that a detachment of troops was stationed around the touchline to prevent the crowd spilling on to the pitch. The Czechs saw the soldiers' presence as deliberate intimidation, and were already disgruntled by the appointment of an English referee, John Lewis, whose decision-making had so outraged home fans during a qualifying match in Prague that they had physically attacked him. Czech morale did not improve when the Belgians quickly went two goals ahead. When Mr Lewis sent off their star player Karel Steiner in the 39th minute, the Czechoslovakian team stormed off the pitch and was disqualified.

The next two Olympic golds went to URUGUAY, inculcating the South Americans with a winning habit that they maintained at the first World Cup in 1930. The arrival of the World Cup, combined with America's lack of enthusiasm for soccer, led to the sport's being dropped for the Los Angeles Games in 1932, but it was back with a bang at BERLIN. Anyone who thinks BAD BEHAVIOUR in football is a modern disease should reflect on that 1936 tournament. During the opening encounter between ITALY and the USA, the Italian players prevented the German referee from sending off Achille Piccini by pinning his arms to his sides and clamping his mouth shut. Piccini stayed on the pitch and the Italians won 1-0, and went on to take gold.

The SWEDES won in 1948 with a side that boasted three firemen, but it was to be 36 years before another non-communist nation captured gold. The rise of professionalism in Western Europe and South America deprived countries from those parts of their best players, allowing state-sponsored teams of 'AMATEURS' from Eastern Europe to clean up. The Italians did their best to buck the trend in 1964, picking a team that included three members of the Inter Milan team that had recently collected the European Cup. When it was pointed out that not all of their players were strictly amateur, they withdrew from the competition in a huff.

In 1984, the IOC relaxed the participation criteria to allow PROFESSIONAL FOOTBALLERS from Europe and South America to compete, provided they hadn't previously played more than five times for their country. The final was duly contested by FRANCE and BRAZIL, with the French winning 2-0 in front of a 100,000 crowd, bringing to end the sequence of Warsaw Pact victories. The SOVIET UNION temporarily restored the old order at SEOUL 1988 but by then the Eastern Bloc was on its last legs.

The eligibility rules were changed again for the BARCELONA 1992 Games: from then on, a squad could be fully professional, as long as no more than three of its members were over 23. In Barcelona, SPAIN beat Poland 3-2 in a pulsating final.

Perhaps as a result of the absence of many of the top European players, due to their continental championships being held in the same summers as the Games, the African nations have broken through in the Olympics to a much greater extent than in the World Cup, providing three of the eight finalists and two of the four winners since the mid-1990s (NIGERIA in Atlanta and CAMEROON in Sydney). The last two golds, however, have fallen to ARGENTINA, which will remain the nation to beat in 2012.

USA KEEPER BRIANA SCURRY KEEPING HER KIT ON AT ATHENS 2004

WOMEN FOOTBALLERS finally joined the Olympic party in 1996 at ATLANTA, where the host nation collected gold, defeating China 2-1 in the final. This was a mixed blessing for American goalkeeper BRIANA SCURRY, who had unwisely pledged to a journalist from *Sports Illustrated* that she would run naked through the streets of Athens, Georgia, if the USA won the competition. Sure enough, in the wee hours of the night following the final, Scurry ran ten metres along a deserted side-street wearing nothing but her gold medal.

The 2000 women's final was won by NORWAY, who beat the USA courtesy of a 'golden goal' in extra time. The American women maintained their 100 per cent record of final appearances in Athens and Beijing, overcoming Brazil on both occasions. The second victory proved that there was life after the great MIA HAMM, who retired after the 2004 Games having scored more international goals (158) than any player of either sex, despite having been born with a club foot.

GYMNASTICS

28 JULY–12 AUGUST 2012

NORTH GREENWICH ARENA
ARTISTIC AND TRAMPOLINE

WEMBLEY ARENA
RHYTHMIC

Athletes: 324 | **Golds up for grabs:** 18

OLYMPIC PRESENCE

MEN: ARTISTIC SINCE 1896; TRAMPOLINE SINCE 2000.
WOMEN: ARTISTIC 1928–48 AND SINCE 1952; RHYTHMIC
since 1984; TRAMPOLINE since 2000.

OLYMPIC FORMAT

MEN'S AND WOMEN'S EVENTS IN ARTISTIC GYMNASTICS AND
TRAMPOLINE. RHYTHMIC GYMNASTICS is for women only.

CONTENDERS:

THE USUAL SUSPECTS – RUSSIA, UKRAINE, BELARUS, CHINA,
ROMANIA, JAPAN and the USA – are expected to do well in the
ARTISTIC division, but are they are likely to face sterner challenges
than previously from rising countries like BRAZIL and GREECE.
Russia will be heavily fancied to carry off both RHYTHMIC golds
and the smart money will be on the Chinese repeating the TRAM-
POLINE double they achieved in Beijing.

PAST CHAMPIONS:

USSR/RUSSIA: 81 | JAPAN: 29 | USA: 23

WHY WATCH GYMNASTICS?

AT THE HIGHEST LEVEL, OLYMPIC GYMNASTICS OFFERS THE fleeting illusion that the laws of gravity can be escaped. It requires immense self-discipline and grace, and, in the case of artistic gymnastics, great strength, courage and preternatural spatial awareness.

ARTISTIC GYMNASTICS, the classic form of the sport, involves fixed pieces of equipment plus the men's rings. In TRAMPOLINING, the competitors repeatedly launch themselves to heights of up to ten metres, which means they are in the air for much longer than divers, and thus can perform astounding acrobatic manoeuvres: quadruple somersaults are routine. RHYTHMIC GYMNASTICS often seems closer to dance than to a measurable sport, and there are many who question whether it should be in the Olympic programme. It is great spectacle nonetheless.

THE STORY OF GYMNASTICS

THE WORD 'GYMNASTICS' IS DERIVED FROM THE GREEK FOR 'exercise', which in turn derives from the word for 'naked', which is exactly how the men of ancient Greece liked to work out. Every self-respecting Greek city had a gymnasium, and records show that boxing, wrestling and swimming were all practised within their walls; what is less clear is the precise form of the activities that would now be classified as gymnastic.

The streams that fed into the modern gymnastics are numerous. The BULL-LEAPING MINOANS of Ancient Crete (2700–1450BC), for example, are known to have vaulted over the animals' backs by using HANDSPRINGS, a technique reminiscent of modern VAULTING. And the POMMEL HORSE can count among its ancestors the wooden horses used by ROMAN cavalrymen to refine their mounting and dismounting skills. Disciplines such as the floor exercise and rhythmic gymnastics are rooted in ACROBATIC DISPLAYS, which have a similarly long pedigree: they were held in CHINA as part of harvest festival celebrations, and at the Imperial Court by the seventh century BC. In addition to tumbling routines, these

NOT JUST A CUTE FACE: OLGA KORBUT ON THE UNEVEN BARS, MUNICH 1972

displays frequently involved props such as chairs, bowls and wicker rings, which can be seen as counterparts to the BALLS, RIBBONS AND ROPES used in the rhythmic form of the sport today. In medieval times, acrobatics was a regular entertainment in the castles and palaces of Europe.

Another source for modern gymnastics was the CIRCUS, which became popular in its modern form during the late eighteenth century. The influence of the trapeze is easy to detect in the

HIGH BAR, UNEVEN BARS AND RINGS. And it was the safety nets used by circus performers that prompted GEORGE NISSEN of the University of Iowa to build the first modern TRAMPOLINE in 1934. His invention had, in fact, been anticipated by the INUIT, who have a long tradition of bouncing on stretched walrus or bearded seal skins, as in the *nalukataq* (spring whaling festival) of northern Alaska.

The nineteenth century saw the emergence of various MASS GYMNASTIC MOVEMENTS in Central Europe, the most important of which was developed by FRIEDRICH LUDWIG JAHN, a Prussian nationalist who called his system TURNEN because he couldn't bear to use the Greek word 'gymnastics'. Jahn's initial motivation was to produce a generation of young Germans fit and disciplined enough to drive Napoleon's armies from his country. In 1811, he opened the first *Turnplatz* in a field outside Berlin, replete with platforms, ropes and rings. Jahn also invented the PARALLEL BARS (by removing the rungs from a ladder), created an early version of the HORIZONTAL BAR, and refined and developed the POMMEL HORSE and BALANCE BEAM.

In 1819, the Prussian authorities grew tired of Jahn's grandiosity and banned *Turnen* by means of an edict. But his ideas had taken root. In the run-up to the Franco-Prussian War of 1870, a curriculum based on Jahn's system was adopted by the German educational system and the DEUTSCHE TURNERSCHAFT was founded. By 1914 it boasted more than a million members.

The emphasis in the *Deutsche Turnerschaft* was firmly on paramilitary collective manoeuvres – competitive sports were despised as decadent English inventions. But there was less antipathy towards competition in the rival SOKOL movement that swept through the Slavic world in response to the *Turnen* explosion.

The other major nineteenth-century European gymnastic movement was based on the health-oriented teachings of PER HENRIK LING, who opened, in Stockholm, the Royal Gymnastic Central Institute in 1813. The so-called SWEDISH SYSTEM, like *Turnen*, was focused on synchronised team displays, but it shunned the use of apparatus. An Olympic discipline in its own right in 1912 and 1920, it made a particularly important contribution to the development of the FLOOR EXERCISE.

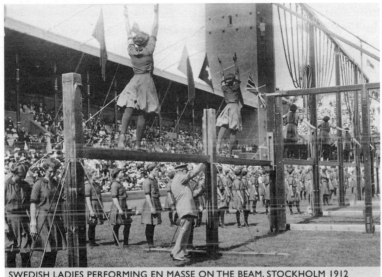

SWEDISH LADIES PERFORMING EN MASSE ON THE BEAM, STOCKHOLM 1912

RHYTHMIC GYMNASTICS grew from the eighteenth-century ideas of the likes of I.G. NOVERRE and FRANÇOIS DELSARTE, who believed that the best kind of exercise was based on freely expressive dance-like movements. The rejection of the rigidity of ballet by the great American dancer ISADORA DUNCAN also contributed to the emergence of the sport, as did the Swiss teacher ÉMILE JACQUES-DALCROZE, whose EURHYTHMIC SYSTEM (note that spelling, Annie Lennox) combined movement with music.

The final stage in the pre-Olympic evolution of gymnastics was the formalisation of its constituent disciplines into competitive sports. In the case of ARTISTIC GYMNASTICS, the organisation primarily responsible was the European Federation of Gymnastics; founded in 1881 in Liège, it was the world's first international sports organisation. It had just three member nations (France, Belgium and the Netherlands) until 1921, when non-European countries were admitted and the organisation changed its name to the FÉDÉRATION INTERNATIONALE DE GYMNASTIQUE.

The first competitive RHYTHMIC GYMNASTICS events were held in the Soviet Union, where a national championship was established in 1942. The FIG brought the discipline under its wing in 1961 and two years later the first world championship was held in Hungary. In 1948 the first national TRAMPOLINE CHAMPIONSHIPS were held in the USA. The inaugural World Championship took place in 1964 and in 1999 this sport, too, came under the umbrella of the FIG.

GAME ON: GYMNASTICS BASICS

ARTISTIC GYMNASTICS

THERE ARE FOUR DISCIPLINES IN WOMEN'S ARTISTIC GYM-nastics and six in men's. Two of the disciplines – the VAULT and the FLOOR EXERCISE – are contested by both genders. Women also compete in UNEVEN BARS and BEAM. Men add POMMEL HORSE, RINGS, HIGH BAR and PARALLEL BAR.

The Olympic programme consists of three competitions for each gender: TEAM, INDIVIDUAL ALL-ROUND and INDIVIDUAL APPARATUS. Qualification for the finals is determined by qualifying rounds in which five of the six competitors from each team perform on each piece of apparatus, and their scores are used to determine qualification for the individual all-round and apparatus finals as well as the team final. Scores from the preliminary round are not carried forward – competitors start each final with a clean slate.

In the TEAM FINAL, three gymnasts from each team compete on each piece of apparatus, and their scores contribute to their team's points total. A maximum of two competitors per nation take part in the INDIVIDUAL ALL-ROUND FINAL, in which each contestant performs on all pieces of apparatus, with their cumulative scores determining their finishing positions. A maximum of two gymnasts per nation also qualify for the INDIVIDUAL APPARATUS FINAL, which is contested by the eight gymnasts who scored highest on each piece of apparatus in the qualifying round.

In all the exercises, pay particular attention to the form of the gymnasts: limbs should be straight, toes should be pointed and there should be a general air of tightness about the body. HEIGHT is particularly important in airborne manoeuvres, as are perfect LANDINGS.

THE VAULT

THERE ARE SEVERAL STAGES TO A VAULT. A TYPICAL ROUTINE is the YURSCHENKO. In this, the gymnast sprints down a 25m runway and performs a HANDSPRING at the end, propelling themself towards the springboard in such a way that they land on it feet first, facing back in the direction they came from. During the spring, they do another half rotation to ensure that they land on the vaulting table in a hands–down position. During their brief contact with the table, they push downwards, which sends them still higher. This action, plus the forward momentum generated by their run-up, launches them into the flight phase, during which they perform a combination of twists and/or somersaults, before (hopefully) landing neatly on both feet.

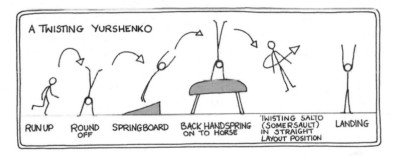

Prior to 2001, vaulting involved a canvas-covered 'horse' set at right angles to the runway for women and parallel for men. This has now been replaced by a more stable VAULTING TABLE 1.2m long and 95cm wide. It is set at a height of 1.25m for women and 1.35m for men. Gymnasts perform two vaults; only the one receiving the higher marks counts towards their score.

FLOOR EXERCISE

IN SOME WAYS THE FLOOR EXERCISE IS 'FREER,' THAN THE other disciplines in artistic gymnastics – it's the competitors doing what they can with their bodies on a 12 x 12m mat set on top of a sprung floor. Women's routines are longer – 70–90 seconds as against 60–70 seconds for the men – and are accompanied by MUSIC, whereas the men's are not. The differences are revealing: women are expected to incorporate DANCE-LIKE MOVEMENTS into their routines, whereas the emphasis in the men's version of the discipline is on STRENGTH. Competitors must use the whole area of THE MAT. The most spectacular elements of floor routines are the TUMBLING PASSES, which consist of a variety of somersaults, twists, handsprings and cartwheels performed in succession. The top women typically get four or five passes into their routines; the men rarely manage more than four because of the shorter time allotted to them.

UNEVEN BARS (WOMEN ONLY)

THIS DRAMATIC APPARATUS CONSISTS OF TWO PARALLEL BARS made of wood-sheathed fibreglass set at different heights (1.61m and 2.41m above the ground) and separated by a gap of between 130cm and 180cm (adjustible in 2cm increments to suit individual competitors). Back in the 1950s, gymnasts basically clambered between the bars, albeit gracefully. Now they fly around at scarcely believable speeds. To comply with Olympic specifications, a routine must include one AERIAL MANOEUVRE from the lower bar to the higher bar, one in the reverse direction and one which starts and finishes on the same bar. Competitors must also perform at least one HANDSTAND TURN.

BEAM (WOMEN ONLY)

MANY OF US WOULD STRUGGLE TO EVEN WALK ALONG A 5M strip of wood 10cm wide and 1.25m above the floor. The best Olympic gymnasts leap around on it as if they were performing on a piece of apparatus ten times wider. This discipline is all about courage, confidence and elegance. Competitors have a maximum of 90 seconds to impress the judges, during which time they must perform a variety of jumps, turns and balancing postures. They must also use the entire length of the beam.

POMMEL HORSE (MEN ONLY)

THE MILITARY ROOTS OF THE POMMEL HORSE ARE CLEAR: essentially you are watching cavalrymen showing off on their stationary mounts. The 'horse' is a leather-covered structure 1.6m long and 35cm wide, with a top surface 1.15m above the ground.

The pommels are a pair of 12cm high upward-standing 'D' handles set each side of the centre of the top of the horse.

The first commandment for gymnasts performing on the horse is not to touch the apparatus with their legs. Instead, they move around its surface (they must use all three sections) on their HANDS, while constantly swinging their legs, which sometimes are separated scissor-style – FLAIRS – and at other points are held together and moved in a circular or pendulum fashion. When circling his legs above the horse, the gymnast must lift his hands with immaculate timing to allow the limbs to pass.

Pommel routines end with a DISMOUNT, which must involves the gymnast dropping to the ground after a handstand.

TOO MUCH TOO YOUNG?
THE AGE OF TEEN GYMNASTS

Prior to the era of NADIA COMANECI, who was just fourteen when she wowed the world at Montreal 1976, champion Olympic female gymnasts were almost always in their twenties, and sometimes even older: AGNES KELETI of Hungary was 35 when she won four gold medals in Melbourne. But as the technical demands of the sport increased, the age of successful gymnasts started to plummet, because prepubescent girls, being smaller and lighter than fully grown women, found it is easier to overcome the force of gravity. The top two competitors in 1992, for example, were both 15 years old, 4ft 6in tall, and weighed around 31.5kg/70lbs.

Male gymnasts also tend to be on the small side – the great SAWAO KATO of Japan, who won eight gold medals between 1968 and 1976, was 5ft 3in and weighed 125lbs/56.7kg – but the emphasis on strength in the men's sport means that they aren't at their best until their musculature has fully developed.

Up to and including the Moscow Games, the minimum age for competing in senior FIG tournaments like the Olympics was 14. In 1981, amid growing concerns about the effect of intense competition on the muscular and skeletal development of young girls, the age limit was increased to exclude gymnasts who wouldn't have turned 15 by the end of the calendar year. In 1997, the age requirement was bumped up another year.

Opinion is divided about the rule changes. Supporters point to statistics showing that young female gymnasts are much more prone to stress fractures than their non-gymnastic peers. They also argue that girls in their early teens are ill-equipped emotionally to deal with the pressures of international competition. On the other side are former gymnasts like Nellie Kim, who argue that younger girls are better equipped for the sport as they are typically more fearless. Others point out that FIG under-16 competitiors are judged according to the same points system that applies to the seniors in the Olympics, so the rules are scarcely protecting younger gymnasts from the physical hardships that affect older competitors.

Not surprisingly, given the advantages possessed by gymnasts in their early teens, one effect of the rule changes has been a growing temptation to cheat. Daniela Silivas, who won three golds at Seoul in 1988, later revealed that the Romanian Gymnastics Federation had added two years to her age in 1985 (when she was actually 13) to make her eligible for that year's World Championships. Nicolae Vieru, head of the Romanian Federation at the time, later claimed that 'changing the ages was a worldwide practice'. The issue came up again in Beijing, when four Chinese gymnasts were strongly suspected of being under age, though an FIG inquiry exonerated them.

RINGS (MEN ONLY)

THE MOST DEMANDING PIECE OF APPARATUS, THIS INVOLVES A pair of rings with an internal diameter of 18cm suspended at a height of 2.75m by way of cables hanging from a bar 5.8m above the ground. The gymnast grips one ring in each hand and performs a variety of swings (e.g. from handstand to handstand), holds (such as L-SITS, in which the legs are extended forward with the body bent at the hips) and strength moves.

The latter include various forms of CRUCIFIX (or IRON CROSS), in which the body is held motionless by the fully outstretched arms. Competitors must endeavour to keep the rings stationary, except when moving them apart in a controlled manner when going into an iron cross or similar position. They are also expected to perform spectacular dismounts.

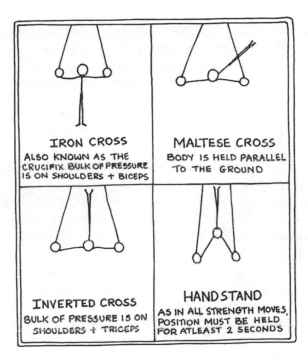

IRON CROSS
ALSO KNOWN AS THE CRUCIFIX. BULK OF PRESSURE IS ON SHOULDERS + BICEPS

MALTESE CROSS
BODY IS HELD PARALLEL TO THE GROUND

INVERTED CROSS
BULK OF PRESSURE IS ON SHOULDERS + TRICEPS

HANDSTAND
AS IN ALL STRENGTH MOVES, POSITION MUST BE HELD FOR ATLEAST 2 SECONDS

HIGH BAR (MEN ONLY)

ALSO KNOWN AS THE HORIZONTAL BAR, THIS PIECE OF APPARATUS consists of a steel bar 2.4cm thick and 2.4m long fixed 2.75m above the ground. Competitors swing from it continuously, except when performing RELEASES (aerial manoeuvres which involve temporarily letting go of the bar). Extra variation is provided by one-handed ROTATIONS, changes of grip, changing the direction of rotation and switching the lead part of the body from front to back. DISMOUNTS tend to be even more dramatic that those from the rings as the gymnasts are able to generate more momentum by means of GIANTS (powerful extended body rotations). TRIPLE TWISTING SOMERSAULTS are considered almost routine at Olympic level.

PARALLEL BARS (MEN ONLY)

THE PARALLEL BARS ARE WOODEN, 3.5M LONG, 1.95M HIGH and between 42 and 52cm apart (the distance can be adjusted

THE GREATEST MALE GYMNAST EVER? VITALY SCHERBO AT ATLANTA 1996

within this range to suit the gymnast). Competitors grip them with their hands, sometimes with their arms fully extended, at other times with them bent and the upper arms resting on the apparatus. No other part of the body is allowed to touch the bars. A gymnast is expected to make full use of the possibilities provided by the equipment, which include SWINGS, HANDSTANDS and AERIAL MANOEUVRES. For much of the time he will have a hand on each bar, leaving his body free to swing in the gap, but on occasion he will place them both on the same bar, which provides scope for UNDER-SWINGS. A typical DISMOUNT would be a double somersault either from the end of the bars or off to one side.

SCORING

THE ERA OF THE PERFECT 10, LED BY NADIA COMANECI, WAS certainly thrilling but it left the sport with nowhere to go. FIG has consequently revised the scoring system several times to dispense with the delightful but troubling notion of perfection. Performances on each piece of apparatus are currently marked by two panels of judges. The first, which has two members, calculates the DIFFICULTY OF THE ROUTINE on the basis of a standard list of values for its elements. The difficulty score is open-ended, which has led some critics to claim that the results of a competition can effectively be decided before it has started (though, of course, the harder the routine, the greater the risk of losing points in its execution).

The second judging panel, which has six members, marks the EXECUTION on a scale of 1 to 10. The highest and lowest scores are discarded and the remaining four scores are averaged. This figure is then added to the difficulty score to give a final mark for the performance. Any total of 16 or more is exceptional – even the phenomenal XIAO QIN scored only 15.875 in winning gold at Beijing

RHYTHMIC GYMNASTICS

RHYTHMIC GYMNASTICS TAKES PLACE ON A MAT WITH THE same dimensions and qualities as the floor exercise. Although practised by men in some countries, notably Japan, it is a WOMEN-ONLY DISCIPLINE at the Olympics. All routines are accompanied by MUSIC, which must be free of vocals and alarming sound effects. INDIVIDUAL ROUTINES must be between 75 and 90 seconds in duration. The parameters for TEAM ROUTINES are 60 seconds longer. The key to success is keeping the equipment CONTINUALLY IN MOTION, handling it with as much variety as possible, and producing routines that feel like unified performances. Demonstrations of BODILY FLEXIBILITY are also rewarded by the judges.

For rhythmic gymnastics there are separate qualifying rounds for the team and individual competitions. No more than two gymnasts from the same nation can qualify for the individual final, in which each gymnast performs with all four accessories: the ribbon, hoop, ball and clubs. The team final consists of two rounds: in the first, five of the six members of the team perform with the same piece of equipment (the ball at London 2012); in the second, two pieces of equipment are used simultaneously, three team members using one, two the other (hoops and ribbons respectively at London 2012).

HOOP

THE HOOPS USED IN RHYTHMIC GYMNASTICS MUST BE SEMI-rigid and 80–90cm in diameter. Competitors throw them, catch them, rotate them around their hands and bodies, swing them, jump through them and roll them along the ground. Any flutter while the hoop is travelling through the air is penalised.

BALL

SURPRISINGLY 'STREET', THE BALL EXERCISE COMBINES ELE-ments of basketball, freestyle soccer and seal-like joie de vivre. Gymnasts perform with a single ball 18–20cm in diameter. They are not allowed to grip the sphere but must let it rest on their hands, unless they are bouncing, throwing or rolling it, or balancing it on some other part of their anatomy. The ball is generally considered the most elegant of the rhythmic gymnastic disciplines.

CLUBS

THIS IS DRUM MAJORETTING TAKEN TO ANOTHER DIMENSION. Each gymnast performs with two wooden or synthetic clubs which are shaped like skinny bowling pins, with graspable 'knobs' on their heads. Successful performance requires many of the same skills as juggling, including high levels of hand and eye co-ordination and ambidexterity. In addition to throwing and catching the clubs, competitors balance them on their hands and swing them in a variety of visually appealing ways, while performing leaps and other acrobatic moves. Some rhythmic gymnasts grip them between their toes.

RIBBON

THE RIBBON IS A 7CM STRIP OF SATIN OR SIMILAR MATERIAL attached at one end to a 50–60cm stick. Visually this is perhaps the most appealing of the rhythmic disciplines, with competitors creating ever-shifting calligraphic shapes in the air. Large, free-flowing movements are rewarded and the gymnasts employ a wide range of throws and catches.

SCORING

RHYTHMIC DISPLAYS ARE GIVEN MARKS OUT OF 10 IN THREE categories: EXECUTION, in which deductions are made for mistakes such as losing control of the equipment; ARTISTIC EXPRESSION; and DIFFICULTY. There are four judges for each category, whose marks are averaged.

TRAMPOLINE

OLYMPIC TRAMPOLINES ARE 5.05M LONG, 2.91M WIDE AND 1 155m high. The bouncy bed is around 6mm thick and is made from nylon or string-based material. The centre of the bed – the springiest part – is marked with a cross to help competitors to position themselves. The closer they land to it the better, from both a safety and a technical perspective.

An Olympic routine consists of TEN ELEMENTS or bounces, although competitors are allowed to make preliminary bounces to achieve suitable heights, plus one manoeuvre-free bounce at the end to control their height and prepare to 'STICK' their landings. Each element must be different – if one is repeated, the second occurrence receives a difficulty score of zero.

While performing their elements, trampolinists must keep their legs together with the toes pointed. They should keep their bodies in one of three positions: STRAIGHT, in which the body and limbs are held as the adjective suggests, PIKE, in which the straightened legs are grasped near the ankles, and TUCK, in which the bent knees are clasped to the chest.

Competitors must start and end their routines on their feet. In theory they are allowed to land on their seats, fronts or backs at other stages, but this rarely happens in top-class competition. The final landing should be 'STUCK', i.e. ended abruptly and in a controlled manner with both feet on the bed. The gymnast must remain standing still for approximately three seconds.

Both male and female competitions start with two-routine qualification rounds. The best eight progress to the finals, where they perform another routine which determines their final placing. As with other gymnastic disciplines, no more than two finalists may come from any nation.

THERE ARE TWO ELEMENTS TO A CONTESTANT'S SCORE. THE DIFFICULTY SCORE is calculated by adding up the set tariffs of all the moves within a routine: manoeuvres like the QUADRIFFUS, a quadruple somersault with half a twist or more, are very valuable. Top male performers typically perform routines with difficulty values of around 16.5; the equivalent figure for women is 14.5. Five judges score each routine for EXECUTION, with a maximum of 10 points. The verdicts of the most and least generous judges are discarded; the remaining three are added together and this figure is added to the difficulty mark to give an overall score.

The more controlled a performance the higher it will be marked. Both feet should touch the bed simultaneously every time a gymnast lands, and they should land close to the cross.

GYMNASTICS GOES TO THE OLYMPICS

GYMNASTICS, IN ONE FORM OR ANOTHER, HAS FEATURED AT every modern Olympics, but it took some time for the authorities to establish its parameters. There were eight gymnastic events at the first modern Games in ATHENS, all of them for men: ROPE CLIMBING, TEAM HORIZONTAL BAR and PARALLEL BARS competitions, plus all the disciplines of today's male ARTISTIC GYMNASTICS except the floor exercise. GERMAN gymnasts carried off five of the eight gold medals but there were home victories in the rings and rope climbing.

There was just one event at PARIS 1900, a sixteen-exercise all-round competition. FRENCH gymnasts occupied the first eighteen places. The odds were stacked in their favour, as 108 of the 135 entrants were from the home nation, but it was an impressive performance nonetheless. The ratio of Americans to other competitors was even higher in ST LOUIS but one title did go to another nation: Switzerland's solitary gymnast ADOLF SPINNLER won the triathlon, which consisted of routines on the high and parallel bars plus the horse.

LONDON 1908 hosted two events: an all-round individual competition, won by ALBERTO BRAGLIA of Italy, and a group team event, won by SWEDEN. Braglia won the individual all-round title again in Stockholm, adding another gold to his collection in the apparatus-based team contest, while Sweden (predictably) won the Swedish System team event. They did it again at ANTWERP in 1920.

The list of events was expanded to nine for PARIS 1924, with individual apparatus titles back on the agenda. SWITZERLAND, ITALY and YUGOSLAVIA each notched up two wins. Swiss gymnasts won five gold medals at AMSTERDAM 1928, where women's synchronised calisthenics joined the party. This last event – the first Olympic gymnastics competition for women – was won by the DUTCH, four of whose team were Jewish; three were to perish in the Nazi gas chambers.

There were no women's events at LA 1932 but at BERLIN 1936 they competed individually for the first time in the Olympics, albeit in the context of a team competition. GERMAN gymnasts won six of the nine gold medals on offer. The FINNS did the same at LONDON 1948, in a tournament that was marked by weird scoring – one judge awarded 13.1 points out of 10 for a performance in the women's team competition. This event, which included the rings for the one and only time, was won by CZECHOSLOVAKIA, whose victory was made particularly poignant by the death from polio of intended team member ELISKA MISÁKOVÁ on the first day of the competition.

INDIVIDUAL WOMEN'S EVENTS (all-round and apparatus) made their debut at HELSINKI 1952, where the SOVIETS competed in the Olympics for the first time. They made an immediate impression, winning nine gold medals, including four for thirty-year-old VIKTOR CHUKARIN. The USSR's policy of hot-housing talented young children would ensure that this was no flash in the pan. The practice later spread to other Eastern Bloc nations (notably ROMANIA and EAST GERMANY), where generous state sponsorship went hand-in-hand – it is widely believed – with chemical assistance. Puberty-arresting drugs, among other substances, are thought to have been commonly administered to young female gymnasts during the 1970s and 1980s.

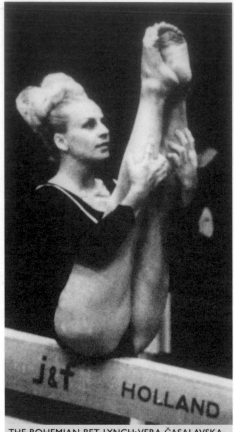

THE BOHEMIAN BET LYNCH: VERA ČASALAVSKA
ON THE BEAM AT MEXICO 1968

At MELBOURNE 1956, the star of the show was AGNES KELETI of Hungary, who won four gold medals at the age of 35 – she remains the oldest female Olympic gymnastics champion by quite a margin. She was pipped to the all-round title by LARYSA LATYNINA of the USSR. Viktor Chukarin showed age wasn't a barrier in the men's division, either. The great Soviet, now 34, added two golds to his collection, including a second successive men's all-round title.

In 1960, JAPAN won the first of five successive men's team titles, while Larysa Latynina took the women's all-round gold again. She claimed two more medals at Tokyo 1964, taking her total Olympic haul to eighteen, the most won by any competitor in any Olympic sport. But she lost her all-round crown to the rising star of the women's sport, VERA ČÁSLAVSKÁ of Czechoslovakia.

Čáslavská did it again four years later in MEXICO CITY, where she was a huge hit with spectators, partly because of the prominent part she had played in the Prague Spring that year, partly because she used the Mexican Hat Dance as the accompaniment for her floor routine. Čáslavská won four golds and two silvers at the 1968 Games, joining Latynina as the only female gymnast to have won the all-round title at two Olympics. She also managed to squeeze in a wedding to Czech 1500m champion Josef Odlozil. But things turned sour for her thereafter. Časlavaská's conduct at the Games – she had turned her back during the playing of the Soviet anthem at a medal ceremony – led the Czech authorities to banish her from gymnastics. Then in 1992, a son she and Odlozil had produced during their marriage murdered his father in a bar room brawl.

If Čáslavská had raised the profile of women's gymnastics, OLGA KORBUT sent it into orbit at MUNICH 1972. The coquettish seventeen-year-old Belarusian won golds in the team competition, floor and beam, and performed the first ever back flip on the uneven bars, but what secured her popularity was her bursting into tears after falling twice on the uneven bars during the all-round competition. Many purists, however, preferred the elegance of her compatriot LUDMILLA TOURISCHEVA, who won the all-round title.

In 1976, at Montreal, Romania's NADIA COMANECI became the first gymnast to score a PERFECT 10 in the Olympics – she went on to score six more in the course of securing three golds, a silver and a bronze. Her great Soviet rival, NELLIE KIM, also achieved two perfect scores, and took three golds and a silver.

But it was the exploits of Japan's SHUN FUJIMOTO in the men's team competition that were the most remarkable. During the last tumbling pass of his floor exercise routine, he fractured his knee-cap. As the Japanese were going for their fifth successive victory in the face of stern competition from the heavily fancied Soviet team, he decided not to tell the team medics. He proceeded to score 9.5 on the pommel horse and a life-time best of 9.7 on the rings, albeit at terrible cost – when he landed, after a twisting somersault dismount from a height of eight feet, he dislocated the broken knee-cap. His efforts proved enough to secure victory for his team; when asked if he would do it all again, Fujimoto tersely replied 'No.'

Fujimoto wasn't the only Japanese hero in Montreal. SAWAO KATO's victories in the team competition and parallel bars brought him his 7th and 8th Olympic golds, establishing a record that still stands.

NADIA AND THE PERFECT TENS

Nadia Comaneci had been awarded perfect scores in competitions preceding the Montreal Games, but it was nonetheless one of sport's transcendent moments when, on 18th July, 1976, the scoreboard finally registered 10 at the Olympics – or 1.00 as it actually read, the designers not having considered the possibility of perfection.

THE SCOREBOARD BLOWS A FUSE AS NADIA COMANECI SCORES TEN, MONTREAL 1976

Comaneci's literally faultless performance occurred during the un-even bars segment of the women's all-round competition. Unusually self-possessed for a fourteen-year-old, she couldn't see what all the fuss was about. 'I've had nineteen tens in my career,' she revealed at a press conference. 'It's nothing new.' Comaneci ended the Games with seven perfect scores, Nellie Kim of the USSR with two. The pony-tailed Romanian had already wowed the gymnastic world at the 1975 European Championships, winning every event except the floor exercise.

Being the first Olympic gymnast to achieve perfection multiplied the pressure on her. At fifteen, after the Romanian sports establishment had forced her stop training under Béla Károlyi, her coach and mentor,

Comaneci apparently drank bleach, a protest that was enough to persuade the government to allow her to train with Károlyi again. In 1981, however, he defected, and in November 1989, just weeks before the overthrow of the Ceausescu regime, Comaneci followed suit. Her escape was facilitated by Constantin Panait, a Romanian roofer living in Florida, whose price appeared to be that he should thereafter manage her affairs and never let her out of his presence. Comaneci soon extricated herself from Panait's clutches: an old friend who had been a rugby coach in Romania intervened and invited her to live with his family in Montreal.

In 1996, Comaneci married the American Bart Conner, who had won two gymnastics golds at the 1984 Olympics. Today, the most famous gymnast in history runs a training facility in Oklahoma with her American husband. It's name? The Bart Conner Gymnastics Academy.

The pre-tournament favourite for the all-round women's gold at MOSCOW 1980 was YELENA MUKHINA (USSR), who had beaten Comaneci and Kim to the World Championship title two years before. Two weeks before the opening ceremony, she broke her spine during floor practice and was paralysed from the waist down. Mukhina had seen the tragedy coming. Already unhappy at having been rushed back into training after breaking a leg in 1979, she had expressed grave misgivings at her coaches' insistence that she incorporate a 'Thomas salto' into her floor routine. It was a mistimed attempt at this 1¾ somersault with 1½ twists that left her quadriplegic.

In Mukhina's absence, the competition came down to a head-to-head between YELENA DAVYDOVA of the Soviet Union and COMANECI. The Romanian seemed to have done enough to win with a near-perfect performance on the beam, but after a furious debate lasting 28 minutes, the judges gave her a score of 9.85, leaving her 0.05 points behind Davydova. Comaneci nevertheless took two golds and two silvers, while Nellie Kim again won a couple of golds.

AMERICAN GYMNASTS exploited the Eastern European boycott of LOS ANGELES 1984 by winning five gold medals, including the men's team and women's all-round titles. The latter was secured by MARY LOU RETTON in the only way possible – by scoring a 10 on the vault. Los Angeles also saw the first Olympic appearance of

CHINESE gymnasts (they won five titles), and the debut of RHYTHMIC GYMNASTICS, which was surprisingly won by LORI FUNG of Canada, who had only managed 23rd place at the preceding year's World Championship. At the following Olympics, the rhythmic gold went to MARINA LOBACH of the USSR, who received a perfect score for each routine. During the club exercise, she was saved by her pianist, who increased the pace to ensure she finished in the allotted time.

The gymnastic star of the Barcelona Games was VITALY SCHERBO of BELARUS, who won six of the eight titles available to men, including four in a single day. Away from the swimming pool, no Olympian has won as many gold medals at one Games. By 1994, Scherbo had claimed world titles in every discipline, a unique achievement that arguably makes him the greatest male gymnast of all time. As Scherbo's triumph emphasised, the collapse of the Soviet Union had done little to harm the fortunes of the former nation's gymnasts – the one-off UNIFIED TEAM carried away four other golds.

At Atlanta in 1996, KERRI STRUG of the USA did an imitation of Shun Fujimoto, performing her second vault in the artistic team event after badly damaging her ankle in her first. Her score of 9.712 helped the so-called Magnificent Seven to the women's team title. But overall the Americans had to play third fiddle to the Ukrainians and Russians, who won four and three titles respectively.

The Sydney Games saw the Olympic debut of the MEN'S AND WOMEN'S TRAMPOLINE: both were won by RUSSIANS, as were the two rhythmic titles. CHINA won the men's artistic team event and ROMANIA the women's. The latter came top of the artistic medal table at Athens 2004 by winning four of the six women's events, but the performance of the Games came from PAUL HAMM of the USA, who recovered from a fall on the vault to win gold in the men's all-round competition by 0.012 points, the closest margin in the history of Olympic gymnastics.

CHINESE gymnasts were the dominant force at BEIJING 2008, winning all but one title in the men's artistic division, plus two golds in the women's events and both the trampoline titles. As was by now customary, Russia claimed both rhythmic golds.

HANDBALL

28 JULY–12 AUG 2012

OLYMPIC PARK HANDBALL ARENA
PRELIMINARIES AND WOMEN'S QUARTER-FINALS

OLYMPIC PARK BASKETBALL ARENA
MEN'S QUARTER-FINALS PLUS ALL SEMIS AND FINALS

Athletes: 336 | **Golds up for grabs:** 2

OLYMPIC PRESENCE

MEN: DEMONSTRATION SPORT 1936 (AS FIELD HANDBALL), full medal sport 1972–present. Women: since 1976.

OLYMPIC FORMAT

THERE ARE TWELVE TEAMS IN EACH COMPETITION. IN THE preliminary phase they are divided into two groups of six, each nation playing all the others in its group. The four best teams in each group qualify for the knock-out stages.

CONTENDERS:

DENMARK, NORWAY, SOUTH KOREA AND RUSSIA ARE THE favourites for the women's gold, which is the big one in the eyes of many handball-playing countries. The main contenders for the men's competition are Germany, France, Croatia, Sweden and Spain.

PAST CHAMPIONS:

USSR/RUSSIA: 6 | YUGOSLAVIA: 3 | DENMARK: 3

WHY WATCH HANDBALL?

FOR BRITISH FANS AT LEAST, ONE REASON TO WATCH THE handball in London is its sheer novelty value. Like basketball and soccer, handball is fast-paced and skilful. As with basketball, it's a sport well suited to giants with ball-handling talent, while football fans will find the object of the game – propelling a ball into a netted goal – reassuringly familiar.

One of the more surprising aspects of handball is the degree of BODY CONTACT that is permitted. Body checking is perfectly legal provided the defender is directly between the attacking player and the goal. Another unusual aspect of the game is the absence of midfield players. Matches are END-TO-END affairs, with teams either attacking or defending.

Recently, the sport has gone PROFESSIONAL, raising the stakes and adding to the intensity. Alongside burgeoning commercialism, handball has acquired celebrity players, dubious officials and raucous (and occasionally violent) fans.

HANDBALL AT THE MOVIES

Oddly, handball has spawned a double bill of hit movies: *Machan*, directed by *Full Monty* producer Uberto Pasolini, and *Forever the Moment*, which topped the box office charts in South Korea following the country's silver medal in the women's tournament at Athens 2004.

Based on a true story, *Machan* concerns a posse of happy-go-lucky Sinhalese would-be-emigrants to Germany, who fail to get visas but then find a magazine on the beach inviting entries to a Bavarian handball tournament. Undeterred by the sport's non-existence in Sri Lanka, they form a squad and after a few knockbacks

FOREVER THE MOMENT, PROBABLY THE BEST KOREAN HANDBALL MOVIE EVER MADE

make it to Germany. Having initially planned to leg it from the airport, they get swept up in the tournament and can't resist playing a couple of matches first ...

Forever the Moment, similarly based on real life, celebrates the brief period when the entire South Korean nation found itself gripped by an Olympic sport about which it normally doesn't give a stuff. A cobbled-to-gether team of inexperienced youngsters, veterans pulled out of retirement and a sacked coach who decides to stay on as a player fights its way to the final in Athens, where it nearly, *nearly* pulls off a dramatic upset. The fact that the heroes fail to win makes a refreshing change but viewers are left with a feelgood glow all the same.

THE STORY OF HANDBALL

IT WASN'T QUITE HANDBALL AS WE KNOW IT, BUT THE ancient Greeks certainly liked to chuck a ball around. If this account in Homer's *Odyssey* is anything to go by, they did it in a celestial and rather elegant manner:

> *They took at once in their hands the lovely ball*
> *Which Polybos, with cunning art, had woven from purple wool.*
> *One cast this up to heaven to reach the sparkling clouds,*
> *Bent hard back; the other then sprang high up in the air*
> *And caught it nimbly, ere his foot touched ground again.*

Alexander the Great was known to enjoy SPHAIRISTERION, a Greek ball court game named after the boxing room in a classical gym-nasium, and the ROMANS played ball in their baths and spas. Team games involving the throwing of balls continued through the Dark Ages. There are medieval accounts of ladies of the court tossing around ribbon-wrapped balls and cushions, and British knights were so partial to a form of handball that Kings Edward II and Henry VIII banned it for the detrimental effect it was having on archery practice. Intriguingly, given Denmark's pre-eminence in the modern sport, the INUIT of Greenland were also known to be fans, with records of their matches dating back to 1793.

ANCIENT GREEK SPOT THE (HAND)BALL COMPETITION

MODERN HANDBALL emerged in the 1890s in two parallel forms. CZECH teachers created and set down the rules of HAZENA, a seven-a-side game played on an indoor court. Meanwhile in Denmark, where football had been banned in schools due to too many broken legs and windows, a PE teacher called HOLGER NEILSEN, who had won fencing and shooting medals at the Athens Games, created HAANDBOL. An instant hit, it spread throughout Scandinavia, and its rules form the basis of the modern game.

The game further developed in *fin de siècle* Germany, where the gymnastic movement was a serious business, training minds and bodies for a powerful and regimented nation. The intransigent, ultra-nationalist proponents of gymnastics never reconciled themselves to ball games, but for those who did, KONRAD KOCH came up with RAFFBALLSPIEL. This later evolved into TORBALL, a game for the women's branch of the gym, not unlike the Scandinavian version of handball. In the 1920s, CARL SCHELENZ, a German PE professor, decided the game needed to be more masculine and revised the rules, creating an eleven-a-side sport to be played outside on a football field, with body checking allowed for the first time.

While Scandinavians and central Europeans continued to prefer the indoor version, the Germans began to organise international matches in the new format. Given the opportunity to put on a demonstration sport at the 1936 BERLIN OLYMPICS, the regime opted for outdoor handball. Predictably, the Germans walked the competition, beating Austria 10-6 in the final in front of 100,000 rain-drenched spectators to win the first and only FIELD HANDBALL gold medal.

GAME ON: HANDBALL BASICS

THE OBJECT OF HANDBALL IS TO PUT THE BALL IN YOUR OPPO-
nents' net more often than they put it into yours. A match consists
of TWO 30-MINUTE HALVES separated by a 15-minute interval. If
the scores are level at the end of regulation time and a definitive
outcome is required, up to two five-minute periods of EXTRA TIME
are played. If the scores are still level at this point, a PENALTY SHOOT-
OUT takes place,.

Olympic handball is played on courts 40m long by 20m wide,
with 3m-wide goals pleasingly striped in the manner of barbers'
poles. The GOAL AREAS are bounded to the front by lines 6m from
the centre of the goals, and to the sides by quarter circles. FREE
THROW LINES curve across the court 9m from the goals, while PEN-
ALTY THROW LINES are 7m from the goals.

Each team has seven players: six outfielders and one goalkeeper.
Seven SUBSTITUTES are allowed per side. Players can be changed at
any time during a match and as often as the coach wishes. Each side
is allowed a one minute TIME OUT period in each half but must be
in possession of the ball when it is called.

Matches are officiated by TWO REFEREES, who direct the action using various hand signals. The one denoting a two-minute
suspension, for example, looks very like an earthy Anglo-Saxon
gesture meaning 'go away'. The refs have equal authority, which
you might think would be a recipe for paralysis. In fact, there are
set protocols. If they have different opinions about how an infrac-
tion should be punished, the more severe option must be taken. If
the refs cannot agree about a straight either-or, for instance which
team should be awarded possession after the ball goes out of play,
the matter is referred to the COURT JUDGE.

···································· **FOUR KEY RULES** ····································

NO KICKING: Handball is hands only, though goalkeepers can use
    their lower legs or feet to move the ball. The keeper is also the
    only player allowed to stand within the goal area.
THREE STEPS TO HEAVEN: Players can take up to three steps with
    the ball, after which you must pass or dribble (by bouncing it).

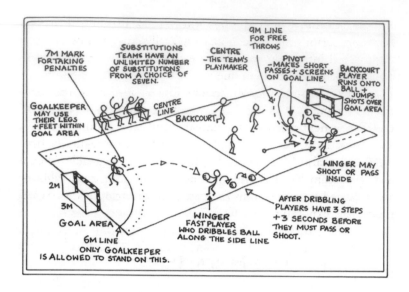

Once you stop moving you have three seconds to pass or shoot. If you jump before shooting you must let go of the ball before you land.

IN AND OUT OF PLAY: If the ball goes out of play along the sides of the court, the team that didn't touch it last is awarded a throw-in. If it goes out behind the goal line, the attacking team is awarded a corner throw if the ball was last touched by a defender; the defending team is awarded a goal throw if it was last touched by an attacker. In other words, it's just like soccer.

GETTING THE BALL BACK : Players can steal the ball by slapping it out of an opponents' hands and are allowed to disrupt their opponents by body checking, provided they approach them directly from the front. They may not, however, snatch the ball, use their hands to hold or check an opponent, or go in for tripping or any other rough stuff.

·················· **CRIMES AND MISDEMEANOURS** ··················

IF ANY OF THE ABOVE RULES ARE BROKEN, THE OPPOSING team is awarded a FREE THROW from the spot where the foul was committed. If the infringement occurred between the free throw and penalty throw lines, the free throw is taken from the former. For more serious misdemeanours, especially crossing into or playing the ball into your goal area, the official can award a PENALTY THROW taken from the 7m line.

A player's first reasonably serious foul or display of unsportsmanlike conduct gives rise to a warning, indicated by a YELLOW CARD. The next offence of a similar magnitude is punished by a TWO-MINUTE SUSPENSION. A player who has not previously been warned can also be suspended if they commit a suitable offence and their team has accumulated three warnings in total. Fighting and repeated or very serious fouls are punished by RED CARDS and permanent expulsion.

THE FINER POINTS

A BIG SLICE OF GOAL PIE

NEARLY ALL OF THE ACTION OCCURS AROUND THE GOAL AREAS, so expect a lot of goals – most games finish somewhere in the region of 28-24. Following a game is partly about sensing the momentum of scoring and the balance of opportunities taken and missed over time, rather than the impact of any one goal.

Handball is a sport loaded against goalkeepers, with big nets, small balls and players as little as 6m away when throwing. Nevertheless, keepers do make saves – and often spectacular ones.

THE ARTS OF DEFENCE AND ATTACK

TAKE A LOOK AT THE DEFENDERS – HOW ARE THEY ORGANISing themselves? Most start with a 6-0 formation with all the outfield players close to their goal area line, moving forwards and backwards to engage the opposition as the ball moves among them. More aggressive teams will use a 5-1 or even a 4-2 formation in which one or two players consistently stand further out trying to disrupt the attack and force a mistake.

Given that you can't use brute force to get round a defender, what can you do? Look for feints, swerves, high leaps and sudden body checks as ways of gaining an inch of space from which to pass or shoot. Players close to their opponents' goal will also try spin-shots that bounce around defenders and goalkeepers.

HANDBALL GOES TO THE OLYMPICS

AFTER THE SECOND WORLD WAR, GERMANY WAS TEMPORARILY excluded from the international community and consequently lost control of international handball. The new centre of power was DENMARK. The IHF (International Handball Federation) was created in Copenhagen in 1946 and though the outdoor Germanic game hung on for a decade, the indoor game, now known as TEAM or OLYMPIC HANDBALL, became the international standard. Not that anyone outside of continental Europe was taking much notice. The Anglo-Saxon world and Latin America were indifferent to handball and it was virtually unknown in Africa and Asia. Even in its heartlands, the culture of handball was unassuming and non-commercial.

Nevertheless, by the 1970s the sport had become sufficiently international to warrant inclusion in the Olympics. A men's competition was introduced at the 1972 Games and a women's followed at Montreal in 1976. For the next twenty years, both events were dominated by Warsaw Pact nations, whose state-sponsored athletes consistently outperformed the amateurs of the West.

Since then, things have been stirring in the world of handball. The sport has turned professional, with TV contracts worth tens and sometimes hundreds of millions of pounds. The men's game is closely followed in GERMANY, FRANCE, SPAIN and GREECE, while the women's version has become the sporting phenomenon of the last decade in DENMARK and NORWAY. The Women's World Handball Championship gets higher TV ratings in Denmark than any sporting event bar the football World Cup. The Posh and Becks of Norway are the celebrity couple GRO HAMMERSENG and KATJA NYBERG, stalwarts of the women's handball team. This westward shift in power, led by the all-conquering Danish women's team (Olympic champions in 2000 and 2004), was confirmed at the Beijing Games, with FRANCE taking the men's gold and NORWAY the women's.

DENMARK'S RIKKE SKOV 'MAKES HERSELF BIG' IN THE 2004 WOMEN'S FINAL

Handball's journey from northern European amateurism to global commercialism has not been smooth. In Greece and Egypt, where the sport has become immensely popular, the ULTRAS culture of the football stadium has reached the handball court. Games between Olympiakos and Panathinaikos in Athens are accompanied by crude chants and regularly descend into punch-ups. In Egypt, the Cairo derby between Al Ahly and Zamalek has had to be abandoned after crowd disturbances and a 2010 encounter was preceded by street riots and attacks by Zamalek fans on the Al Ahly club complex.

The arrival of so much money in handball is also having a corrosive impact. Rumours of MATCH-FIXING and BRIBERY abound in the upper echelons of the game. A qualifying match for the 2008 Olympics between Kuwait and South Korea was so blatantly misrefereed by the Jordanian officials that it had to be replayed, the IOC having threatened to drop handball from the Games if it was not.

HOCKEY

29 JULY–11 AUGUST 2012

HOCKEY CENTRE, OLYMPIC PARK

Athletes: 384 | Golds up for grabs: 2

OLYMPIC PRESENCE

MEN: 1908, 1920, 1928–PRESENT; WOMEN SINCE 1980.

OLYMPIC FORMAT

THERE ARE TWELVE TEAMS IN BOTH THE MEN'S AND THE women's events, divided into two qualifying groups, with the top two from each group going through to the semi-finals. Lower-ranked teams play a series of classification matches.

CONTENDERS:

THE DUTCH, GERMANS AND AUSTRALIANS LOOK SET TO field the strongest teams, with decent challenges to be expected from Argentina, Spain and the much improved British men's and women's teams.

PAST CHAMPIONS:

INDIA: 8 | HOLLAND: 4 | AUSTRALIA: 4

WHY WATCH HOCKEY?

ONE COULD DO WORSE THAN ATTEND TO THE WORDS OF Lord Lyttelton, the old Etonian Under-Secretary of State for War and the Colonies in the 1840s. A lifelong hockey fanatic, he explained his love of the sport in the *Eton College Magazine*: 'It is a game in which, as in poetry, mediocrity is not tolerable: indeed, a bad game at hockey is one of the most stupid sights ... but, on the other hand, when it is played, as at Eton, with a considerable degree of dexterity, we think it one of the most elegant and gentlemanlike exercises, being susceptible of very graceful attitudes and requiring great speed of foot.'

The best part of two hundred years later, hockey is recognisably the same game that Lyttelton gushed over, and at the Olympics it will be played with more dexterity, speed and elegance than was ever managed in early Victorian England. Olympic hockey offers the flow and teamwork of football, combined with skilled stick play and drilled, small-ball precision. It's also very physical. Struck correctly, a hockey ball can travel at 100mph, and in the modern era the fitness of players produces a game of relentless ebb and flow. Don't expect mediocrity; do expect poetry.

THE STORY OF HOCKEY

THE URGE TO SWIPE THE NEAREST OBJECT WITH A STICK and send it soaring into the air or scuttling along the ground is surely universal. From North America to Africa and East Asia, hockey has been invented and reinvented a dozen times, but the version that is now the global standard has its roots in Western Europe.

Europeans have been devising their own versions of the sport for over a millennium, most enthusiastically on the continent's Celtic fringe, where the Irish variant became HURLING. During the Peasants' Revolt of 1381, hurley sticks were the weapons of choice for many of the rural poor who marched on London; in the aftermath of the uprising, Richard II attempted to shore up his rule by ordering the burning of every last hurley stick in the realm. However, the game was too much a part of rural life across the British Isles and Ireland to be eradicated.

Like many other rural games, hockey was fashioned into a proto-sport in nineteenth-century public schools, and in the 1860s the first hockey club was formed at BLACKHEATH in southeast London. Here, the local rugby club developed a variant of 'Union Hockey' which pitted two rampaging fifteen-man teams against each other, belting a small leather cube – more hacky-sack than hockey ball – with one-handed sticks.

On the other side of London, the more genteel members of TEDDINGTON CRICKET CLUB were looking for a winter game. Adapting their flat-rolled cricket pitch and cricket balls, they devised an eleven-a-side version of hockey which forms the basis of the modern sport, with dribbling, passing, running and positional play. In 1875, Teddington joined forces with four other south London clubs to create the HOCKEY ASSOCIATION. This body set down the first written rules of hockey, introducing the scoring circle and banning high swinging, tripping and charging.

By the early 1890s there were hundreds of clubs across Britain and there were calls for leagues, cups and proper contests. The conservative Hockey Association promptly outlawed them all, to the delight of the editor of *Hockey*: 'Such a vital decision has undoubtedly saved hockey from disaster and being sacrificed upon the altar of popular, but ruinous competition.' The edict saved hockey for the upper classes in Britain, but not for long.

GAME ON: HOCKEY BASICS

HOCKEY IS AN ELEVEN-A-SIDE GAME IN WHICH EVERYONE, goalkeepers included, must carry a wooden stick at all times. The J-shaped sticks are all RIGHT-HANDED, which is tough on the lefties. One face is flat, the other rounded. Using the flat side only, the players must pass, push and flick a small hard plastic ball up the field and try to put it in their opponents' net.

The FIVE KEY RULES are: no using your LEGS OR FEET to move the ball (though unintentional deflections are overlooked); no CARRYING OR HANDLING the ball; GOALKEEPERS (of whom more below) may use their limbs and hands inside the defence zone around their goal; there is NO OFFSIDE, so the play is stretched right across the field; you can SCORE only from a shot taken inside the SCORING CIRCLE.

Tackling is allowed and encouraged. Players may use their sticks to intercept and take the ball from opponents.

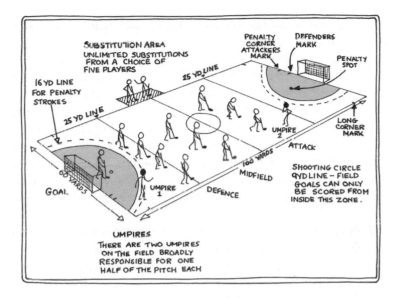

SUBSTITUTION AREA
UNLIMITED SUBSTITUTIONS
FROM A CHOICE OF
FIVE PLAYERS

PENALTY
CORNER
ATTACKERS
MARK

DEFENDERS
MARK

PENALTY
SPOT

25 YD LINE

16 YD LINE
FOR PENALTY
STROKES

25 YD LINE

LONG
CORNER
MARK

UMPIRE
2

ATTACK

100 YARDS

SHOOTING CIRCLE
9YD LINE – FIELD
GOALS CAN ONLY
BE SCORED FROM
INSIDE THIS ZONE.

MIDFIELD

60 YARDS

GOAL

UMPIRE
1

DEFENCE

UMPIRES
THERE ARE TWO UMPIRES
ON THE FIELD BROADLY
RESPONSIBLE FOR ONE
HALF OF THE PITCH EACH

·········· FOULS, PENALTIES AND SET PIECES ··········

A FOUL IS CALLED IF A PLAYER DOES THE FOLLOWING: PLAYS the ball with the ROUNDED SIDE of the stick; plays the ball in a DANGEROUS way (too high or at an opponent); uses any part of the BODY other than the stick to move the ball; RAISES THE STICK in an intimidating way; CHARGES, SHOVES OR TRAPS an opponent; deliberately OBSTRUCTS the movement of the ball or another player; hits, hooks or holds an OPPONENT'S STICK, or plays any part in the game WITHOUT HOLDING THE STICK.

The consequence of committing a foul depends on where the offence occurs. Outside the shooting zone, the other team gets a FREE HIT from where the misdemeanour was committed. The opponents must retreat 5m. Foul inside the shooting zone or commit an intentional foul in your own 25 yard area and the other team is awarded a PENALTY CORNER. Defenders who deliberately put the ball out of play behind their goals also concede penalty corners.

The most egregious sin is to commit a FOUL INSIDE THE SHOOTING CIRCLE against a player in possession who is deemed to have a chance on goal. This is punished by the award of a PENALTY STROKE or FLICK, taken from a spot 7 yards in front of goal.

The Finer Points

FORMATIONS

Although high-level hockey is a fluid game, with no formal positions apart from the goalkeeper, most teams have a basic shape with three lines of players – defence, midfield and forward line. Australian teams of the modern era favour an attacking 2-3-5 formation. More cautious sides play 4-4-2 or 4-3-3, often with a SWEEPER behind the back line as an insurance policy.

SPECIAL DUTIES

Like many sports, hockey has acquired a specialised division of labour. Players are not just midfielders, but will be defensive or attacking midfielders with specific roles and duties. Some defenders have a licence to move up the field, others will sit back.

STICK WORK

The speed, dexterity and creativity of top-class stick work are joys to behold. Players at Olympic level have a variety of tricks and moves to evade opponents when dribbling, or to extract themselves from tight marking.

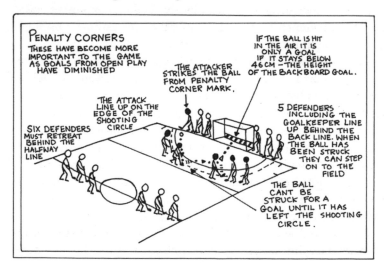

HOCKEY IS A LOW-SCORING SPORT — MANY MATCHES WILL BE won by just one or two goals. Some will be scored from open play but plenty will come from PENALTY CORNERS. It is harder to score from these than from penalties, but easier than from free hits or shots under pressure. Players will actively look to draw fouls which result in penalty corners.

HOCKEY GOES TO THE OLYMPICS

THE ORGANISERS OF THE 1900 PARIS OLYMPICS ASKED THE British Hockey Association if they would care to field a team, but were politely declined on the grounds that there would be no international opponents to play. St Louis in 1904 didn't even bother to ask. However, despite the insularity of the Hockey Association, the sport had made its way to the elite athletic clubs of the USA and continental Europe and, at the instigation of the French, a hockey tournament was played at LONDON 1908. The British presence, contrary to usual Olympic practice, was split into the four home nations, in order to make up the numbers with the French and Germans. England won. Absent again in 1912, hockey returned at ANTWERP 1920 — another small affair, won by the English, despite a fiendish ploy by the French team, who invited them to an immense dinner party the night before in the hope of slowing them down.

In the early 1920s the IOC insisted that to qualify for the Games, a sport had to have an international federation with whom they could do business. The Hockey Association in London, which retained copyright over the game's rules, remained aloof and uninterested, so hockey was off the menu at the 1924 Games. Finally, a small group of European nations formed an international federation, the FIH, with the tacit permission but not the involvement of the Hockey Association. This was enough to get hockey back into the Games at AMSTERDAM in 1928, where it was the INDIANS not the Europeans who turned out to be the masters of the sport.

Hockey had arrived in India via officers of the British army, who were playing at the Calcutta Club as early as 1885. The game quickly spread to the British, Indian and Anglo-Indian ranks, and was enthusiastically taken up by members of the Indian urban elite working for the imperial administration. By the beginning of the First World War, there were several teams sponsored by army regiments or by the Indian railways, telegraphs and customs departments. A network of provincial teams and competitions had also been established.

The Indians swept all before them in Amsterdam, winning every game without conceding a goal. They also provided hockey with its first global star, in the person of leading scorer DHYAN CHAND. They won again at Los Angeles in 1932, thrashing the hosts 25-1 with a team described in the local press as '. . . like a typhoon out of the east. They trampled under their feet and all but shoved out of the Olympic stadium the eleven players representing the USA.' In 1936, the Indian team arrived in Berlin with a huge burden of expectation on their shoulders. Seen as representatives of the simmering nationalist unrest at home, they underlined the feeling by saluting the Indian Congress flag in the dressing room before meeting the hosts in the final. The Germans held them to 1-1 in the first half, but were swept aside in the second as India won its third gold in a row, 8-1.

The subcontinent's domination of the sport survived partition and independence, with India winning its fourth gold in London in 1948, beating Pakistan 1-0 in the final. This amazing streak was sustained at the next two Games. PAKISTAN finally broke the Indian stranglehold in Rome in 1960, a victory celebrated by delirious crowds in Lahore and other Pakistani cities. India won again in 1964 and Pakistan in 1968, but the great turning point in global hockey came in Munich in 1972, when WEST GERMANY beat Pakistan 1-0 to win Europe's first gold in more than half a century. The losers did not take it well. The Pakistani players were so incensed by the refereeing of the game that on the final whistle they doused the Belgian president of the FIH with a bucket of water. Then they refused to wear their medals or face the flags during the medal ceremony. All members of the team were barred from the Olympics as a result, but they miraculously received pardons and reappeared at the 1976 Games.

THE LOST WORLD OF INDIAN HOCKEY

When Indian hockey ruled the world from the 1930s to the end of the 1950s, the game was at least the equal of cricket in the nation's affections. While cricket brought great pride and honour to India, it could hardly compete with hockey's six Olympic golds. In another universe, hockey would have become India's national sport, with all the razzmatazz of today's IPL Twenty20 cricket league. The introduction of synthetic turf as the international norm certainly hurt the south Asian nations, but political conflict and corruption in India's hockey federation has played an equally significant role in the country's declining competitiveness, allowing the sport to be marginalised by the juggernaut of cricket.

The hit Bollywood movie of 2007, *Chak de India*, provides a taste of what Indian hockey might have been, as well as an indication of the abiding popular affection for the sport. Shah Ruk Kahn stars as a former captain of the national hockey team, disgraced by defeat to Pakistan, ostracised from the sport and forced from his ancestral home. Redemption comes seven years later, when Khan welds the fractious members of the national women's team into a side that wins an Olympic gold.

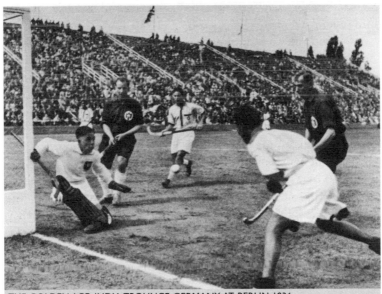

THE GOLDEN AGE: INDIA TROUNCE GERMANY AT BERLIN 1936

'WHERE WERE THE GERMANS?' THE OLYMPIC MEN'S FINAL, SEOUL, 1988

The Pakistanis, however, returned to a changed hockey universe. The competition at Montreal was played on SYNTHETIC TURF, as have been all subsequent Olympic tournaments. The south Asian nations, unable and unwilling to spend money on the new pitches, have lagged behind ever since. The 1976 final was played between rising stars from the Antipodes, AUSTRALIA claiming gold at New Zealand's expense. The hockey at Moscow 1980 was distorted by the absence of the many leading nations who boycotted the Games in protest at the Soviet invasion of Afghanistan. A scratch team of Soviet-sponsored ZIMBABWEANS won the women's tournament, while India had a last hurrah in the men's.

Since then, the golds in both men's and women's hockey have been divided amongst the DUTCH, GERMANS and AUSTRALIANS, with two notable exceptions. The SPANISH women won miraculously in Barcelona in 1992 and in 1988 GREAT BRITAIN's men slew the giants of West Germany by three goals to one. The occasion was bejewelled by the unashamedly partisan TV commentary of the BBC's Barry Davies. 'Where were the Germans?' he asked after one British goal, ' . . . but frankly, who cares?'

JUDO

28 JULY–3 AUGUST 2012

EXCEL ARENA

Athletes: 336 | Golds up for grabs: 14

OLYMPIC PRESENCE

MEN 1964 & 1972–PRESENT; WOMEN 1992–PRESENT.

OLYMPIC FORMAT

SEVEN WEIGHT CATEGORIES FOR BOTH MEN AND WOMEN.

CONTENDERS:

AT BEIJING 2008, JAPAN WAS THE STRONGEST JUDO NATION but CHINA'S WOMEN were very successful. Competition will be coming from the SOUTH KOREANS, the stars of MONGOLIA, GEORGIA and AZERBAIJAN, and the best European nations, especially the FRENCH, GERMANS and DUTCH. In the men's heavyweight and open divisions, look out for Japan's DAIKI KAMIKAWA and the French Guadeloupian TEDDY RINER. MASAE UENO (Japan) will be going for her third consecutive Olympic gold in the women's under 70kg.

PAST CHAMPIONS:

JAPAN: 35 | FRANCE: 10 | SOUTH KOREA: 9

WHY WATCH JUDO?

IN THE *KOJIKI*, AN EIGHTH-CENTURY CHRONICLE THAT GATHered the foundation myths of the Japanese people, the god Takemikazuchi fights a divine wrestler called Takeminakata for control of the earth, winning the islands for the sun goddess and her descendants – the people of Japan. Literally translated as 'the gentle way', Judo is a ritualised duel that may be seen as a manifestation of the Japanese soul. It is the embodiment of a profound tradition of self-discipline and self-improvement, while also being one of the purest expressions of sport as ruthless competition, hence its global popularity.

Judo bouts are sometimes tactical and wary, with each contestant – or judoka – searching for a micro-advantage. Some are bruising and apparently unstructured tussles. Some are drawn-out battles of fitness as much as of technique. And some are over in a moment's flurry of jackets and limbs – so you need to concentrate on the action right from the start.

The Story of Judo

In medieval Japan unarmed combat was widely practised among the warrior elites, but it was always seen as second best to the real business of killing with weapons. That said, a whole school of armoured wrestling was devised for samurai who, dismounted and unarmed, still wished to fight on.

In 1603 the Tokugawa shogunate began its long rule over Japan. Sidelining the emperor, the dynasty created a centralised state that was powerful enough to defeat and then disarm the samurai clans who had spent much of the previous five hundred years terrorising the country. In this new context, martial values were maintained largely by the practice of unarmed combat systems or Jujitsu – best translated as 'the gentle technique' or 'the technique of pliancy'. What had previously been the poor cousin of swordsmanship flourished in a hundred different schools: in some it was infused with an aesthetic that privileged the beauty of a fighter's movements; in others it served to train new generations of thugs and enforcers.

The shogunate lasted until 1868, when the old order was overturned. The Meiji restoration returned symbolic power to the emperor, while keeping real executive power with a core of modernisers, who embarked on half a century of systematic industrialisation, reverse-engineering western institutions for a Japanese context. Sport was part of that wave of change, and the Japanese embraced the newly imported games of baseball, athletics and basketball as emblems of modernity.

It was in this milieu that JIGORO KANO, born in 1860, grew up. A key figure in the educational establishment and intimately acquainted with the West, Kano was simultaneously a moderniser and a traditionalist. In the evenings he liked to spar and fight, old style. From the age of seventeen, he attended the leading jujitsu schools in Tokyo and systematically collated the fragmented fighting systems that had survived from the Tokugawa era. However, the crude and often violent teaching methods fell short of the spiritual, aesthetic and moral dimensions that Kano believed a modernised Japanese martial art should possess. In 1882 he founded his own school in a corner of the Eshishoji temple in Tokyo. It did not teach jujitsu, it taught JUDO; not the gentle technique, but the gentle way, which represented a journey of moral, personal and social progress.

Excising brute force and lethal techniques, judo focused on three forms of combat: THROWING (*nage waza*), and the concomitant skills of FALLING AND LANDING; GROUNDWORK (*newaza*), which

JIGORO KANO, THE MASTER OF THE GENTLE WAY, THROWS AN OPPONENT

consisted of PINNING HOLDS, STRANGLE HOLDS and JOINT LOCKS; and STRIKING (*atemi waza*). Judo would forge 'noble and vigorous characters' who, imbued with the values of self-perfection, mutual welfare and maximum efficiency, would be perfectly equipped for the social complexity of the new Japan. Its style of fighting – always seeking to turn an opponent's strengths and weaknesses against him, applying minimum force for maximum results, favouring technique and style over size and power – chimed with the ethos of Meiji Japan, a rising power in a world of giants.

Within a few years judo was on the curriculum at Japan's teacher-training institutes, police and naval academies, and its most prestigious universities. By the eve of the First World War it had become a central element of secondary school education, and was widely taught in the armed forces. For Kano, judo was a DISCIPLINE rather than a competitive sport or an adjunct of nationalist ideology. But after the invasion of China in 1937 and Kano's death the following year, judo became inevitably aligned with the imperialist ideology of Japanese fascism. Consequently it was banned by the US occupation authorities in 1946, along with all other martial arts. When judo was finally allowed to re-emerge publicly in 1951 it was as a sport rather than a martial philosophy.

The following year the INTERNATIONAL JUDO FEDERATION (IJF) was created, with seventeen founding national associations, signalling an end to Japan's automatic role as the heartland of the sport. The new judo nations were primarily European. JUJITSU had been popular in Britain and France since the early years of the twentieth century ('Jujitsu is everything! The streets, the newspapers and magazines, the theatres, the music halls – they all sound the triumphant clarion of this almost magic world,' proclaimed *Le Sport Universel Illustré* in 1906), and after the First World War a plethora of judo clubs – many led by Kano's students – sprang up in ENGLAND, FRANCE, GERMANY and the LOW COUNTRIES.

Meanwhile, in the SOVIET UNION, VICTOR OSHCHEPKOV, another of Kano's students, was commissioned with jujitsu expert Viktor Spirindov to devise a self-defence system for the Red Army. He created something that blended elements of the many different combat sports of the new Soviet republics with the core dynamics of judo. In 1937, though, Oshchepkov fell victim to the great purges and his name was obliterated from the official records, along with all references to the foreign and imperialistic influence of judo on the Red Army's SAMBO self-defence system. Closely aligned to judo, SAMBO followed its own independent path for the next two decades, but after Stalin's death a generation of Soviet *judoka* emerged, bringing a level of disciplined but high energy aggression to the sport that no other nation had achieved.

GAME ON: JUDO BASICS

THE PLAYING SPACE

JUDO BOUTS ARE CONDUCTED ON A TATAMI, BASED ON THE traditional Japanese domestic floor mat but now made of foam and covered in vinyl. The tatami must be scrupulously clean - in the event that blood is inadvertently spilt during a fight, the contest will be stopped and a maniacal cleaning process will follow. The contest area is a bounded inner square at least 8m by 8m and no larger than 10m by 10m. BOUTS last for five minutes for men and four for women. If no one is ahead at the end of 'regular time', the contest continues on a 'first to score wins' basis.

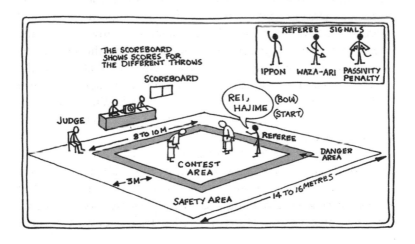

NEW KIT

THE DIFFICULTY OF DISTINGUISHING WHITE-CLAD JUDOKA IN action has led, at the insistence of the IJF, to the introduction of contrasting coloured suits, a move bitterly opposed by the All Japan Judo Federation. Japanese competitions continue to be conducted in all-white JUDOGI, with one contestant wearing a red belt.

HOW TO WIN A BOUT

KANO ENVISAGED JUST ONE WAY OF WINNING A BOUT – AN IPPON, scored from a throw that puts the opponent directly on to his back, or from a long hold or submission. For Kano this system aligned judo with the all-or-nothing peril of real combat. However, the demands of sporting competition and TV schedules have meant that endless bouts without *ippons* could not be tolerated, hence the introduction of lesser scores for imperfect throws – the WAZA-ARI and the YUKO – which function as tiebreakers.

IPPON is scored for a 30-second pin, a throw direct onto the back or a submission in a lock or choke hold. An *ippon* scores one full point and ends the match.

WAZA-ARI is scored for a throw not directly onto the back or of insufficient power to qualify as an *ippon* and for holds of twenty seconds. When two *waza-ari* are awarded in the same match they make an *ippon* and the match ends.

YUKO is scored for a throw of inferior quality to a *waza-ari*. One *waza-ari* beats any number of *yukos*.

If a bout ends in a draw, the contestants effectively fight a second bout, only this time the first to register any kind of score wins. If neither scores, the result is decided by HANTEI – a vote by the referee and two corner judges.

PENALTIES

A JUDOKA IS PENALISED FOR INACTIVITY, THE USE OF ILLEGAL moves, and standing outside the mat area. The first penalty received is a warning, the second is a *yuko* awarded to the opponent. A third penalty is scored as a *waza-ari* and a fourth – called HANSOKU-MAKE – constitutes an *ippon*. *Hansoku-make* can also be awarded for a very serious incident of dissent or rule-breaking.

THE FINER POINTS

THE PROCESSION

THE COMPETITORS' PROGRESS TO THE MAT IS ALWAYS WORTH watching: each *judoka* is flanked by an official and his or her coach, rather like a condemned prisoner en route to the firing squad. The warm-up routines can be idiosyncratic and instructive. Expect much ear-rubbing to stimulate adrenaline, plus sumo-esque squats to maximise suppleness. Competitors are called to the edge of the mat, then to their marks, where they must bow, before the call to engage (*Hajime!*).

THE BATTLE OF GRIPS

MOST BOUTS BEGIN WITH A STRUGGLE FOR THE BEST GRIP AS a prelude to a throw. British champion Neil Adams says that in the initial EXCHANGE OF GRIPS 'volumes of subtle tactical information are picked up ... in just a few seconds'. Note also how *judoka* on the defensive move, bend and use counter attacks to free themselves

LOOKING GOOD ON THE DANCEFLOOR

JUDOKA CONSTANTLY MOVE THEIR FEET AND SHIFT THEIR weight in response to the smallest change in their opponent's position and stance. Look closely and you'll see that the interlocking footwork of the contestants is suggestive of a dance.

JUDO GOES TO THE OLYMPICS

WHILE JUDO'S OWN WORLD CHAMPIONSHIPS ARE CENTRAL to the sport, its broader cultural history has been written most clearly at the Olympics. The inclusion of judo as an official sport at the 1964 TOKYO Games made it the first Olympic sport that had been formalised and codified outside the West. The Games themselves were emblematic of Japan's return to the international community as an economic superpower shorn of its of aggressive militarism. Rather than epitomising Japan's uniqueness and superiority, Judo

DUTCH COURAGE: ANTON GEESINK WINNING THE MEN'S OPEN
GOLD AT TOKYO 1964

appeared in the guise of a gift to the world – albeit one that the Japanese expected to win.

They certainly put on a show. A large corner of the gardens of the Imperial Palace was turned into a building site as the NIPPON BUDOKAN, a 15,000-seat octagonal temple to judo, was built – easily the largest purpose-built arena ever constructed for the sport. In the presence of the emperor, Japan took the first three gold medals, but for the fourth event, the OPEN WEIGHT final, the emperor stayed home, afraid perhaps of the humiliation of defeat.

The open weight was for the Japanese the most important judo medal, for in Kano's conception of judo mere body mass should never prevail over technique. As Japan's champion, AKIO KAMINAGA, faced the gigantic Dutchman ANTON GEESINK, parliament was closed and companies put TVs on factory floors so that the workers could watch the contest. They were to be disappointed: in an imperious display, Geesink ground his opponent down before trapping him in an unbreakable hold. Dutch spectators leapt to their feet and were about to invade the mat when Geesink stopped them – a gesture that made him a hero in Japan.

Though absent from the Games in Mexico City, judo has been a constant presence since Munich 1972. Japan continues to be the strongest nation, but the drug-fuelled winning machine of EAST GERMANY was a strong presence in the 1980s, and the FRENCH, AUSTRIANS and DUTCH have produced their fair share of champions too. From outside Europe, *judoka* from BRAZIL, SOUTH KOREA and most recently CHINA have all won gold. Perhaps the most intriguing force in modern judo are CUBA'S WOMEN, who have won several medals over the last twenty years.

YAMASHITA: LAST OF THE OLD GUARD?

If Kaminaga's defeat was the low point of Japanese judo at the Olympics, the gold medal won in 1984 by YASUHIRO YAMASHITA has been the pinnacle. Yamashita was the most popular and revered *judoka* in post-war Japan, both for his fighting prowess and for his demeanour and style. Brought to a judo club as an overweight and difficult child, he was soon recognised as a prodigy. Relentlessly focused and a very quick learner, he made rapid progress to the peak of the sport: from 1977 to 1984 he did not lose a single bout. He was meticulous – he studied his opponents in minute detail on video – and had the soul of a warrior. As he said: 'If they could see on my face what I feel in my heart, no one would ever fight me.' Yet in public he remained true to the dignified humility of Kano's idealised *judoka*.

Japan's boycott of the 1980 Moscow Games deprived Yamashita of a medal. At the 1984 LA Games, he was favourite to win the last open weight contest, and duly won his first two bouts with ease. But in the second, against the German Arthur Schnabel, he left the mat limping, having torn a muscle in his right ankle. Despite the pain and his restricted movement he swept a French opponent aside in his third bout and faced the Egyptian Mohamed Ali Rashwan in the final. Rashwan went straight for the damaged leg but Yamashita, seemingly oblivious to the pain, countered with a foot sweep, threw his man and pinned him down for the gold.

MODERN PENTATHLON

11–12 AUGUST 2012

HANDBALL ARENA, OLYMPIC PARK (FENCING)

AQUATICS CENTRE, OLYMPIC PARK (SWIMMING)

GREENWICH PARK
(RIDING, COMBINED RUNNING AND SHOOTING)

Athletes: 72 | Golds up for grabs: 2

-------------------------------- **OLYMPIC PRESENCE** --------------------------------

MEN 1912–PRESENT; WOMEN 2000–PRESENT.

-------------------------------- **OLYMPIC FORMAT** --------------------------------

THE PENTATHLON KICKS OFF WITH A ROUND-ROBIN ÉPÉE FENCING tournament, and continues with a 200m FREESTYLE SWIM, followed by SHOW JUMPING and a combined RUN/SHOOT, in which the competitors take five shots at a fixed target, run 1000m, then repeat the procedure twice.

-------------------------------- **CONTENDERS:** --------------------------------

EAST AND CENTRAL EUROPEANS HAVE DOMINATED OLYMPIC modern pentathlon, along with Sweden, which tops the medal table and can be expected to do so again. Britain's HEATHER FELL has a shout in the women's competition, having taken silver behind Germany's LENA SCHÖNEBORN in Beijing. ALEKSANDER LESUN and SERGEY KARYAKIN of Russia will be among the favourites for the men's contest.

-------------------------------- **PAST CHAMPIONS:** --------------------------------

SWEDEN: 9 | HUNGARY: 9 | USSR/RUSSIA: 8

WHY WATCH MODERN PENTATHLON?

IMAGINE A NINETEENTH-CENTURY SOLDIER TRAPPED BEHIND enemy lines, cornered in an island castle. He has to fight his way out with his sword before swimming across the lake and grabbing the nearest available horse. After galloping the animal to exhaustion, he'd have to abandon his mount and start running across the countryside. Every now and again he might need to fire off a few rounds at the enemy, but eventually he'd escape and return home to a hero's welcome.

This is the kind of scenario BARON DE COUBERTIN, father of the modern Games, had in mind when he devised the only sport specifically created for the Olympics. It's hard not to love an event based on a proto-Bond fantasy: pentathlon is anachronistic, but the old-fashioned strangeness is a major part of its charm. In some ways the modern pentathlon's presence in the Olympics is like The Boomtown Rats' slot at Live Aid in 1985. Nobody can really begrudge the organiser a place at his own party but does his creation deserve to be there on merit? The jury is out as far as the modern pentathlon is concerned.

THE STORY OF MODERN PENTATHLON

AT THE FOURTEENTH SESSION OF THE IOC IN BUDAPEST IN 1911, Baron de Coubertin reported that 'the Holy Ghost of sport illuminated my colleagues and they accepted a competition to which I attach great importance'. Just as the organisers of the ancient Games had used the original pentathlon as both a training for war and as an alternative to it, De Coubertin wanted the MODERN PENTATHLON to improve the world by getting the world's soldiers involved in friendly competition. He believed that the sport would test 'a man's moral qualities as much as his physical resources and skills, producing thereby the ideal, complete athlete'. It's just as well he never met Boris Onishchenko of whom more below.

Not surprisingly, given its origins, the history of the modern pentathlon is closely intertwined with that of the Olympics. Prior to the formation of the UIPM (Union Internationale de Pentathlon Moderne) in 1948, the sport was administered directly by the IOC.

GAME ON: MODERN PENTATHLON BASICS

THE STRUCTURE OF THE PENTATHLON AND THE DETAILS OF the events that comprise it have changed several times over the years. For London, the men's and women's events will both take place on a single day. The scoring system is based on a set of standard times and performances; a total score of 5000 points is considered 'par'.

FENCING

IN THE OPENING DISCIPLINE, EVERY COMPETITOR HAS ONE sixty-second fencing bout with each of the others. The swords used are épées (see 'Fencing') and the bouts are sudden death, i.e. the first dueller to score a hit wins. If neither fencer wins the bout in the allotted time, both register a defeat.

An Olympic pentathlete who wins 70 per cent of his or her fencing matches (in other words 25 out of 35 bouts), earns 1000 points. Deviations from that total are rewarded/punished to the tune of 24 points for every bout.

SWIMMING

SWIMMING IS CONSIDERED THE HARDEST DISCIPLINE FOR athletes to improve in substantially if they come late to the sport. As a result, many top pentathletes have a swimming background. Men and women both compete in 200M FREESTYLE RACES, with the heats seeded according to personal best times. For both sexes, completing the course in 2min 30sec earns 1000 points. Deviations are punished/rewarded at the rate of 4 points for every third of a second.

RIDING

FOR THE SHOW JUMPING, CONTESTANTS ARE ALLOTTED horses in a draw made shortly before the event begins, the idea being to test their ability to master an unfamiliar beast. The athletes then have twenty minutes to ride their new equestrian partners in a practice arena. The COURSE itself must include twelve obstacles, one of which must be a double and one a triple jump. The fences may be up to 1.2m in height and at least five of them have to be.

POINTS are awarded on the basis of a standard time for completion of the course, which varies according to its distance. A rider who achieves a clear round within the time limit earns 1200 points. Each additional second incurs a PENALTY of 4 points. If a competitor fails to complete the course within twice the standard time, he or she must stop riding, as must any rider who has fallen twice. They are then deducted 100 points for every obstacle they failed to negotiate.

Other penalties include 20 points for each fault (knocking down part of an obstacle) and 40 points for every refusal to jump. If a horse baulks twice at the same jump, the rider must move on to the next one.

COMBINED EVENT

IN 2008, THE UIPM COMBINED THE SHOOTING AND RUNNING disciplines into a new event, which closes each competition. It has a staggered start, the athletes being handicapped on the basis of the scores they have accumulated in the preceding events.

The race begins with a RUN OF ABOUT 20M to a SHOOTING RANGE, where each pentathlete has seventy seconds to hit five 59.5mm targets from a distance of 10m with an AIR PISTOL (or laser version). There is no limit to the number of shots competitors can fire within the time limit but they must keep their pistols in contact with the shooting table throughout the reloading procedure. They must also leave them in a safe position, i.e. open, unloaded and pointing at the target area. Each infringement of these rules results in a TIME PENALTY of ten seconds. These are paid on the spot: guilty parties are held back from continuing the event until they have done their time.

If athletes manage to hit all five targets within the allotted time, they can immediately set off on the first of three 1000m RUNS. If they fail to hit one or more of the targets, they have to wait until seventy seconds have elapsed before they can start running. There are no other penalties for missed targets – if you don't hit all five, you might as well miss the lot.

The shooting procedure is repeated after the first and second 1000m runs. The third run ends at the finishing line. As a result of the handicapping system, the FIRST TO CROSS is the winner of the entire competition.

THE FINER POINTS

MANY SPORTS ARE BETTER WATCHED LIVE THAN ON TV AND the modern pentathlon is a prime example. The tension builds throughout the day, creating a buzz around the last event that it is impossible to feel if you haven't watched the drama unfold in real time.

For some spectators, the modern pentathlon can suffer from a problem afflicting all multi-disciplinary sports: there are better performers of each of the individual elements elsewhere. But with this sport, you have to think cumulatively. If you can find time to watch only a couple of the disciplines, make them the RIDING and the COMBINED EVENT. The first can be especially dramatic, with some competitors scuppering their chances by ploughing into obstacles and others setting themselves up with immaculate rounds. The run/shoot provides an element of novelty as well as a satisfactory denouement.

MODERN PENTATHLON
GOES TO THE OLYMPICS

THE MODERN PENTATHLON MADE ITS DEBUT AT THE STOCKHOLM GAMES in 1912. The SWEDES took to the new sport in a big way, filling six of the first seven places in the inaugural competition and going on to win eight of the first nine Olympic titles. Future US General GEORGE PATTON came fifth in 1912, let down, ironically, by his shooting. He came 21st in that leg, though he claimed that he had been wrongly penalised for missing a target when, in fact, his bullet had passed through an existing hole. This demonstrated the initiative that would serve him well in wartime, but nobody believed him.

Before the shooting event at the 1932 Games, Sweden's JOHAN OXENSTIERNA decided to fire off a few practice rounds in the woods. He was accosted by an LAPD officer, who threatened to arrest him. Oxenstierna insisted that he was about to take part in an Olympic competition; the policeman, though suspicious, eventually relented, and Oxenstierna won the gold.

At Helsinki 1952, LARS HALL, a carpenter from Gothenburg, become the first non-military winner of the modern pentathlon, and struck lucky in the equestrian competition: after the horse he ini-

WILLIAM GRUT SHOOTS HIS WAY TO GOLD, LONDON 1948

tially drew turned out to be lame, he was matched up with the best show jumper in Finland. The Helsinki Games also saw the introduction of a TEAM COMPETITION, which endured until Barcelona.

The pentathlon competition at the 1968 Games in Mexico was marred by an incident involving West Germany's HANS-JÜRGEN TODT, who became so frustrated with the refusal of his horse to jump one of the obstacles that he attacked the animal and had to be dragged away by teammates. At the same Games, Sweden's HANS-GUNNAR LILJENWALL became the first athlete to fail an Olympic drugs test; he claimed he'd had a couple of beers to steady his nerves ahead of the shooting. At the next Olympics, in Munich, fourteen pentathletes were discovered to have taken TRANQUILISERS ahead of the shooting contest. The drugs in question, Librium and Valium, were banned by the UIPM but not by the IOC, whose verdict trumped that of the sport's governing body.

The pentathlon at Montreal in 1976 got off to a poor start when CAPTAIN ORBEN GREENWALD of the USA was court-martialled for insubordination by his own team manager, Lieutenant-Colonel Donald Johnson. Things went from bad to worse when Red Army Major BORIS ONISHCHENKO was discovered to have cheated in the team competition. The Soviet Union was disqualified, paving the way for Great Britain's JEREMY FOX, ROBERT NIGHTINGALE and ADRIAN PARKER to win the gold.

NOT SO ONISHCHENKO

B ORIS ONISHCHENKO went into the 1976 Montreal Games as a much respected modern pentathlete, having won team gold and an individual silver at the previous Games, and an individual silver four years before. By the time he left, the Soviet volleyball team had threatened to throw him out of a window if they ever came across him in the Olympic village.

The episode that shattered Onishchenko's reputation occurred during the USSR team's fencing contest against Great Britain. British captain Jeremy Fox had sensed something fishy when the Ukrainian registered a hit against his team mate Adrian Parker without appearing to have touched him. When the same thing happened to Fox, he protested. While the

THE SOCK OF SHAME: BORIS ONISCHENKO JUST AFTER HIS DISQUALIFICATION AT MONTREAL 1976

officials inspected his épée, Onishchenko continued to fence – remarkably well – with a substitute weapon. He won his duel with Fox but shortly afterwards it was announced that he had been disqualified.

It transpired that Onishchenko had equipped his sword with a hidden circuit breaker that allowed him to register a hit at the push of a button. The incident would have been embarrassing for any sport, but the modern pentathlon's connection with notions of military honour made it especially so. Onishchenko was whisked away from the Games and never seen outside the USSR again.

The organisers of the modern pentathlon at Los Angeles in 1984 took two important steps to restore the sport's reputation. To combat the problem of doping, they decided to move the shooting – the most common occasion for pill-popping – to a slot a few hours before the running competition. No one wanted to be tranquillised before a run, so the measure proved very effective. The second big decision was to stagger competitors' starting times in the final event, the cross-country, on the basis of their cumulative scores going into the race. The athlete who first crossed the line would win the gold medal, a move that undoubtedly improved the pentathlon as a spectacle.

In 1992 the UIPM decided to tinker with the formula again by moving the riding to the end of the team and the individual competitions. The logic was that this portion of the pentathlon was subject to wilder score swings than the other disciplines, so bad showings in the riding could knock participants out of contention for the remainder of the competition. It therefore made sense to hold the event at the end, maintaining the suspense for longer. The individual final did indeed produce a dramatic reversal – Russia's EDUARD ZENOVKA went into the final round 106 points ahead of Poland's ARKADIUSZ SKRZYPASZEK and finished it 212 behind – but the sport's authorities voted to return to the previous structure at the following Games.

The modern pentathlon at Atlanta was enlivened by the Swedish-American actor DOLPH LUNDGREN landing the role of non-competing US team leader. This was of limited relevance as the team competition had been dropped from the Games after Barcelona, but Lundgren's presence did much to raise the profile of the event. Two years earlier, he had starred in a universally panned film called *Pentathlon*, as an East German gold medallist escaping the clutches of a sadistic trainer, played by David Soul.

A WOMEN'S MODERN PENTATHLON competition was added to the Olympic menu at Sydney 2000, with Great Britain's STEPHANIE COOK taking the gold medal ahead of Emily de Riel of the USA. Hungary's ZSUZSANNA VÖRÖS and Germany's LENA SCHÖNEBORN have won the two subsequent Olympic titles.

The most significant recent development in modern pentathlon has been the UIPM's creation of a COMBINED RUNNING AND SHOOTING EVENT, which will be making its Olympic debut at London 2012. It remains to be seen whether the change will be enough to counter the many critics of its Olympic status, who argue that it's too esoteric a sport, and isn't well suited to television. The sport's finances aren't in great shape either: being a modern pentathlete is an expensive business, and national funding has diminished substantially since the demise of the team event. But the modern pentathlon survived a vote on its Olympic future in 2005 and its inclusion is guaranteed as far as the London Games at least.

ROWING

28 JULY–4 AUGUST 2012

ETON DORNEY ROWING CENTRE

Athletes: 550 | Golds up for grabs: 14

OLYMPIC PRESENCE

MEN'S 1900–PRESENT; WOMEN'S FROM 1976.

OLYMPIC FORMAT

FOURTEEN EVENTS ARE HELD OVER SIX DAYS (8 MEN'S, 6 WOMEN'S), in classes organised by number of rowers (SINGLES, PAIRS, FOURS and EIGHTS) and types of rowing (SCULLS and SWEEPS).

CONTENDERS:

IN MEN'S ROWING THE MEDALLISTS ARE LIKELY TO COME from NORTH AMERICA, AUSTRALASIA and NORTHERN EUROPE, with the GERMANS and BRITISH looking particularly strong. In the women's events the strongest crews tend to come from the USA, NETHERLANDS, CHINA, ROMANIA and BRITAIN.

PAST CHAMPIONS:

EAST GERMANY: 33 | USA: 31 | GREAT BRITAIN: 24

WHY WATCH ROWING?

IN 1996, ON WINNING HIS FOURTH CONSECUTIVE GOLD, AN exhausted STEVE REDGRAVE told the world that if anyone saw him near a rowing boat again they should shoot him. Rowing is a sport that demands a colossal amount of training, and an ability to endure immense physical pain. Rowers FACE BACKWARDS during a race, so a tactical and psychological advantage is gained by being in front;

consequently they must start with an EXPLOSIVE SPRINT that necessarily floods the body with lactic acid, which in turn means that the muscles are burning through the whole race.

Yet despite all this, Redgrave came back and won his fifth gold medal in the coxless fours at Sydney in 2000. What brought him back? A shot at making Olympic history? Or was it the adrenaline rush of making these lightweight boats fly through the water, of working in telepathic harmony with a team of superlative athletes?

THE STORY OF ROWING

ROWING BEGAN WHEN SOMEBODY WORKED OUT YOU GOT more bang for your buck if you moved a paddle on a fixed fulcrum rather than just dabbing at the water. It worked even better if you could corral a large number of people to row in time, and for longer and harder than they would otherwise choose. Thus the battleships of antiquity, from Egypt to Phoenicia, and Greece to Rome, were invariably rowed by banks of chained slaves. For over two millennia, maritime empires stuck with slave rowers where they could, though the Vikings rowed their own long boats in a spirit of commando imperialism. The BATTLE OF LÉPANTO in 1571, at which the combined forces of Spain, Venice and the papacy defeated the fleet of Ottoman Empire, was the last great naval engagement fought by rowing boats: oar power thereafter was the preserve of the domestic waters of rivers, harbours and canals.

Rowing's transition to an ORGANISED SPORT began in seventeenth century England. The Thames thronged with oarsmen and rowing boats, and the quays were thick with gentlemen itching for a wager. The first regular ROWING RACE was established by the Georgian actor and comedian THOMAS DOGGETT. On a late-night journey from the West End to his home in the City, he had difficulty in persuading any ferryman to row him through the stormy weather. One finally agreed and got Doggett home, and in his honour Doggett established in 1715 an annual race on the Thames for ferrymen, for which a badge and coat where offered as prizes. The craze for rowing races grew to the point where Joseph Strutt,

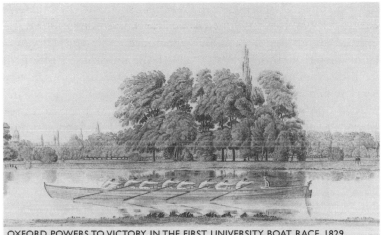

OXFORD POWERS TO VICTORY IN THE FIRST UNIVERSITY BOAT RACE, 1829

the great chronicler of Georgian sport, could report in 1801, that, 'when a rowing match takes place near London, if the weather be fine, it is astonishing to see what crowds of people assemble themselves on the banks of the Thames as spectators, and the river itself is nearly covered with wherries, pleasure boats and barges, decorated with flags and streamers and sometimes accompanied by bands of music.'

Through the nineteenth century the British public's appetite for rowing races grew, but in two almost entirely separate social spheres. On the one hand was PROFESSIONAL RACING, which flourished in London and on the Tyne. On the other was a world of elite amateur rowing clubs such as the LEANDER, which developed as rowing became a central element of the culture of Thames-side public schools like Eton and Westminster. Schoolboys took their enthusiasm to university and by the 1820s rowing races had begun in Oxford and Cambridge. The first OXBRIDGE BOAT RACE was held in 1829, with considerable wagers at stake; by 1845 it had, like the Derby, become an unofficial national holiday, with huge crowds packing the banks of the Thames.

The brief life of rowing as a commercial spectacle was finished by the late nineteenth century. In part the sport was driven from England's rivers by the ships of the industrial revolution and the arrival of steam power. However, an additional assault came from the elite rowing establishment, who from the 1850s onwards prosecuted an ever more fearsome war against professionals, excluding them from all of the major rowing events. The definition of PROFESSIONALISM, originally confined to just watermen, was extended to anyone who was a tradesman, artisan or labourer. The result, inevitably, was a decline in the competitiveness of British rowing. By the late nineteenth century the sport had spread widely across NORTH AMERICA, AUSTRALIA and NORTHERN EUROPE and by the time rowing reached the Olympics in 1900, Britain's early lead was waning.

GAME ON: ROWING BASICS

ROWING RACES COME IN MANY FORMATS, BUT AT THE Olympics the competition is simple. In all events, up to eight boats race side-by-side in LANES, over a dead straight 2000M COURSE. The current race length was first tried in Stockholm in 1912 but became the norm only in 1952. WOMEN'S RACES, first held over 1000m, were lengthened to 2000m in 1988. Early Games saw head-to-head match racing but the side-by-side format became standard in 1956.

All Olympic competitions combine HEATS, a REPECHAGE (second-chance round) and FINALS. If enough crews are entered there may be semi-finals too.

Boats are allowed one FALSE START; any more and you are out. A RESTART is called if a boat suffers a mechanical failure, such as an oar splitting, before it has travelled 100m. This occurred in the repechage round of the men's eights at the 1984 Games, when an oar on the French boat broke and was subsequently found to have been tampered with. The LANES, though marked by buoys, are optional. Crews can take any course they like as long as they don't interfere with others.

················ **OLYMPIC ROWING CLASSES** ················

ROWING TAKES TWO FORMS: SCULLING, IN WHICH THE rower has two oars, and SWEEPING, in which the rower has just one oar, held with both hands.

SCULLS are raced with one, two or four rowers, called SINGLES, DOUBLES and QUADS. SWEEPS are raced with two, four or eight rowers, called PAIRS, FOURS and EIGHTS. In eights, a coxswain or COX sits at the back of the boat, steers the craft and directs the crew's stroke rate. In STRAIGHT or COXLESS craft, the boat is directed by the STEERSMAN, a rower who has the rudder cable attached to a shoe.

Men compete in all of these boats, with an additional category of LIGHTWEIGHT men (no one heavier than 70kg) in the coxless fours. Women compete in all boats except the coxless fours and have a lightweight event (no one heavier than 55kg) in the double sculls.

Sculls go faster than sweep boats with the same number of rowers, and the more rowers a boat has the faster it will be. Men's eights are capable of speeds up to 25kmh.

These are the CLASSES:

SINGLE SCULL. *Length: 8.2m; Minimum weight: 14kg. Events: men and women.* The SINGLE − or the SKIFF, as it is known in Europe − is the only individual event in rowing. There's nowhere to hide.

DOUBLE SCULL. *Length: 10.4m; Minimum weight: 27kg. Events: men, women and lightweight women.* Like all pair events in rowing, double sculls seem to favour partnerships made up of different kinds of rowers: POWER ROWERS are often combined with more TECHNICAL athletes. Personal chemistry between the pair is crucial.

QUAD SCULL. *Length: 13.4m; Minimum weight: 52kg. Events: men and women.* Eight blades and four rowers makes for the fastest boats after the eights. Great precision and team work are required to keep time and avoid blade clashes.

PAIR OR COXLESS PAIR. *Length: 10.4m; Minimum weight: 27kg. Events: men and women.* The coxless pair is technically among the most demanding of boats, responding poorly to any indiscriminate use of power. Balance, stability and elegance are the watch words.

FOUR OR COXLESS FOUR. *Length: 13.4m; Minimum weight: 50kg. Events: men, lightweight men.* The same balance of power and technique is required to get the best from this boat, but with four rowers the level of complexity is even higher. The crew spend more time rowing at maximum stroke rate than in any other class.

EIGHT. *Length: 19m; Minimum weight: 96kg. Events: men and women.* Considered by many the premier regatta format – and the only coxed event at the Olympics – the eights is an unbelievably demanding competition with rowers close to four-minute mile pace and constantly on the verge of a lactic acid burn-out.

THE FINER POINTS

································· **THE ROWING STROKE** ·································

EACH STROKE CONSISTS OF FOUR ELEMENTS: THE CATCH, IN which the oar is lowered into the water; the DRIVE, in which the oar is pulled through the water as the rower slides back in their seat, driving the boat forward; the EXTRACTION, where the oar is lifted out of the water, and the SLIDE or RECOVERY, which returns the rower to his or her original position. After the extraction, the rower FEATHERS the oar (rotates it through 90 degrees) to minimise air

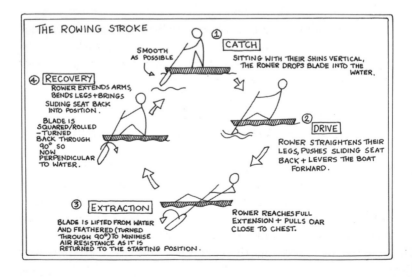

resistance during the recovery. At the end of the slide, they SQUARE the blade, twisting it back into a sideways-on position before dropping the end into the water for the next catch.

It is crucial to remember that rowers sit on SLIDING SEATS, which allow them to contract and expand their bodies during the stroke sequence to maximise leverage.

·· **RACE TACTICS** ··

IN RUNNING RACES ATHLETES OFTEN CHOOSE TO HANG BACK, gaining advantage from monitoring their opponents. In rowing, where you face backwards, you want to be OUT FRONT from the start, so you can see and cover any attack.

Nearly all crews will row fastest in the FIRST 500M of the race at a stroke rate of around 45–48 a minute. For the MIDDLE 1000M they drop down to around 35 strokes a minute and then pick the pace up again in the LAST 500M.

The explosive effort required to get the boat up to 48 stokes a minute means that rowing is a sport of STRATEGIC PHYSIOLOGY. The opening 500m burns more oxygen than any athlete can take in: consequently they will experience the LACTIC ACID BUILD-UP and MUSCLE PAIN that comes with anaerobic respiration.

Rowers have to decide how much lactic acid they can tolerate and carry throughout the race, balancing the advantage of being ahead early on against the risk of complete fatigue due to lactate accumulation. Towards the finish the rate of energy consumption increases again as does the production of lactic acid. If they time it correctly, the FINAL STROKE of the race is the last they are able to pull.

ROWING GOES TO THE OLYMPICS

CANCELLED DUE TO BAD WEATHER AT THE INAUGURAL modern Olympics in 1896 (as were the sailing events), rowing made its debut at the PARIS GAMES of 1900, in predictably chaotic fashion. Disagreements over the rules saw two final runs for the men's coxless fours, with two different boats awarded gold medals. In the men's coxed pairs, the Dutch team ditched their portly cox after the semi-final and employed a more slender Parisian youth instead. They duly won the title.

ST LOUIS 1904 was a near walkover for the home nation, as only a Canadian eight showed up from outside the USA, winning a silver medal. The oddball 1906 INTERCALATED GAMES saw a suitably eccentric rowing programme, including the six-man and seventeen-man naval rowing boats, the larger of which provided GREECE's first and only rowing gold.

The BRITISH teams won all the golds at LONDON in 1908, when the regatta was held in HENLEY. In the inter-war era the British haul declined, despite the best efforts of JACK BERESFORD, who won rowing medals at five consecutive Games (1920–36), including three golds. SWISS and ITALIAN teams won Olympic titles during this period, but the USA was the leading rowing nation, with JOHN B. KELLY their leading rower. The son of an Irish immigrant, Kelly learnt his rowing while working as a bricklayer, and was excluded from competing at the prestigious Henley Royal Regatta because of his status as an artisan. Undaunted, he went on to win two golds at the 1920 Antwerp Games and a third in 1924. His son JACK would win a bronze rowing medal at the 1956 Games, while his daughter GRACE would wind up as Princess Grace of Monaco. A more conventional Harvard eight of the era, winners of the gold in 1924, included BENJAMIN SPOCK, the future child care guru.

MASTERS OF THE RIVERVERSE: THE USA'S ROWING AND RULING ELITES

CAMERON AND TYLER WINKLEVOSS are best known as the Harvard graduates who received $65 million from Mark Zuckerberg, the founder of Facebook, in a lawsuit that tried to resolve who owned and who invented which bit of the ubiquitous social media site. But they are also top-class sportsmen: while at college they were the engine room of a Harvard men's eight that won the US national championship and finished sixth at the world cup in 2006. The twins went on to compete in the coxless pair at Beijing in 2008, finishing 6th.

The Winklevosses are just the latest in a long line of blue bloods in American rowing. Both Yale and Harvard have supplied gold-winning eights to the US team. Other competitive rowers from America's ruling and celebrity elites include Secretary of State DEAN ACHESON (Yale), AVERILL HARRIMAN (Yale), ADMIRAL

STATUS UPDATE: THE WINKLEVOSS TWINS AFLOAT

CHESTER NIMITZ (Navy), the actors GREGORY PECK (Cal-Berkeley) and VINCENT PRICE (Yale), PRESIDENT TEDDY ROOSEVELT (Harvard) and astronaut ALAN B. SHEPARD (Navy).

A change in the balance of power became clear in 1936, when the GERMANS won five of the seven events, but in the post-war era the dominance of northern Europe (SWITZERLAND, GERMANY and SCANDINAVIA) and the ANGOLOPHONE nations (USA, CANADA, GREAT BRITAIN and AUSTRALIA) began to weaken. Up against a rigidly amateur or college-based framework in the West, the new state professionals of EAST GERMANY and the SOVIET UNION became increasingly successful. VYACHESLAV IVANOV won three consecutive gold medals in the single scull (1956–64) with his blistering turn of speed. East Germany peaked at the Moscow Olympics in 1980, where they won eleven of the fourteen rowing titles on offer.

Since the break-up of the Soviet Bloc the rowing fortunes of Eastern Europe have declined, with the exception of the women's teams from ROMANIA: no rower has won more medals than ELISABETA LIPA, who has claimed five golds (1984, and 1992–2004) in three different classes. KATERIN DORON of Germany runs her close, though: she won four straight golds between 1992 and 2004 and only just missed out on a fifth at Beijing.

SHOOT ME NOW: HAVING FORESWORN ROWING FOUR YEARS EARLIER, STEVE REDGRAVE WINS A FIFTH GOLD IN THE MEN'S COXLESS FOUR, SYDNEY 2000

In MEN'S ROWING the dominant figure has been Britain's STEVE REDGRAVE, the only rower to win five gold medals at consecutive Olympics (1984–2000). MATHEW PINSENT, his team mate for three of those golds, went on to win a fourth himself in 2004, in a coxless four. Together they have helped trigger a considerable revival in British rowing.

AUSTRALIA'S 'OARSOME FOURSOME' (originally NICK GREEN, JAMES TOMKINS, MIKE MCKAY and SAM PATTEN; Patten was replaced by ANDREW COOPER in 1991–92 and he by DREW GINN in 1995), won the men's coxless fours in 1992 and 1996, and brought a dash of populism to a sport which has remained rather narrowly based. It was only in 2004 that the first black African rower, Kenya's IBRAHIM GITHAIGA, took part in an Olympic rowing regatta.

SAILING

28 JULY–11 AUGUST, 2012

WEYMOUTH AND PORTLAND

Athletes: 380 | Golds up for grabs: 10

OLYMPIC PRESENCE

MEN AND WOMEN SINCE 1900.

OLYMPIC FORMAT

THERE ARE TEN EVENTS IN 2012, FOUR FOR MEN, FOUR FOR WOMEN and two events OPEN TO ALL; different yacht classes are used for each. Men and women have their own events in the WIND-SURFING, LASER and 470 CLASS. Men alone compete in the STAR CLASS, women in the ELLIOTT 6M CLASS. The open events are in the FINN and 49ER CLASSES.

CONTENDERS:

AT BEIJING 2008 BRITAIN WAS THE TOP SAILING NATION with four gold medals out of eleven. In 2012 Britons will be challenging in almost every class. Other notable crews include the Dutch pair LISA WESTERHOF AND LOBKE BERKHOUT, who are the women's 470 world champions; MAT BELCHER AND MALCOLM PAGE, the Australian men's 470 world champions; and the Spaniard BLANCA MANCHÓN, a favourite for the women's windsurfing.

PAST CHAMPIONS:

GREAT BRITAIN: 24 | USA: 19 | NORWAY: 17

Why Watch Sailing?

Once the preserve of aristocrats and millionaires, Olympic sailing has become a somewhat more open and democratic sport in recent decades: standardised equipment has reduced the costs of participation, and since its Olympic debut in 1900 the sport has been open to women as well as men. Nonetheless, sailing retains much of the élan and glamour of its high-society origins, while offering a complex and compelling spectacle, combining TACTICAL SOPHISTICATION and ATHLETICISM with the unpredictability of WIND AND WAVE. What it does not offer is a decent experience for the live viewer: in 2012, as usual, the races will be so far from the shore that television will provide the best seat in the house.

The Story of Sailing

The word yacht derives from the Dutch word *JAGHTE*, itself derived from the verb *jagen,* to hunt or pursue. In the seventeenth century the NETHERLANDS was arguably the leading maritime nation in the world, with fleets of advanced sailing ships criss-crossing the oceans for both trade and war. One of the ways in which the Dutch spent their new-found wealth was by messing about in boats at home: the wealthy delighted in building sumptuously fitted *jaghte* for gentle cruises, parties, parades and mock battles. They did not, however, race them.

An injection of competitive spirit was introduced, as ever, by the BRITISH. CHARLES II was in exile in the Netherlands when the monarchy was restored in 1660, and he returned to London in a yacht gifted to him by the Prince of Orange. Charles was entranced by his new toy, as was his younger brother, the DUKE OF YORK. Back home, each commissioned a version of the ship, and named it after his wife. The two vessels were raced against each other in October 1661, and the British ARISTOCRACY soon followed suit, racing their yachts on rivers and down the coast, for honour, pleasure and − above all − wagers.

The first properly organised YACHT-RACING CLUB was established in London in 1815 as the Yacht Club, which with the patronage of George IV became the ROYAL YACHT CLUB in 1820. Six years later the Club held its first regatta at COWES on the Isle of Wight, which established itself as the premier festival in the sailing calendar.

For much of the late nineteenth and early twentieth century, the sport's most public face was racing between very large ocean-going yachts. In 1851 the Royal Yacht Squadron announced a race around the Isle of Wight, for which a silver trophy – the RYS £100 Cup – was offered as a prize. The New York schooner *America* won the race, and the cup was donated to the New York Yacht Club as 'a perpetual challenge cup'. The trophy, now known as the AMERICAS CUP, has remained the most prestigious prize in yacht racing, but SMALL-CRAFT RACING began to gather pace in the late nineteenth century and it was this form of the sport that went to the Olympics.

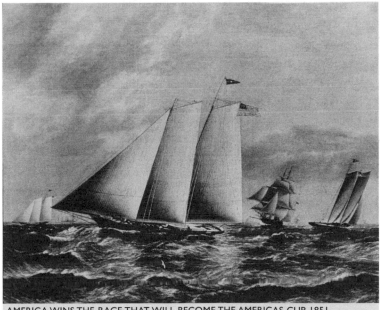

AMERICA WINS THE RACE THAT WILL BECOME THE AMERICAS CUP, 1851

GAME ON: SAILING BASICS

.... **COMPETITION RACING** ....

THERE ARE TWO FORMS OF SAILING RACE: MATCH RACING and FLEET RACING. Match racing is simple: two boats race head-to-head, with competitors trying to outmanoeuvre each other and force their opponents into rule violations and penalties. Fleet racing involves more than two boats, usually many more, and generally consists of more than one race. POINTS are awarded according to race position (the higher the position the lower the score) and are accumulated over a series of races. The boat with the lowest total wins.

At the Olympics, after many years of varying formats, a more uniform system is now in place. The WOMEN'S ELLIOTT 6M CLASS will be a MATCH RACE event. All other competitions begin with an OPENING SERIES of FLEET RACES (ten in all classes except the 49ers, who have to do fifteen). The vagaries of wind and current being what they are, crews are allowed to discard their worst score after five races and their two worst after nine. The top ten boats then

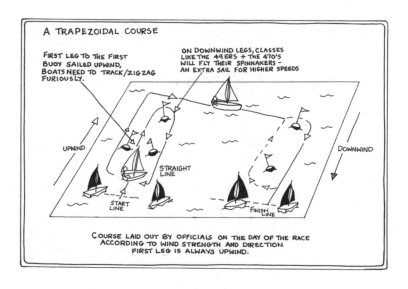

A TRAPEZOIDAL COURSE

FIRST LEG TO THE FIRST
BUOY SAILED UPWIND,
BOATS NEED TO TRACK/ZIGZAG
FURIOUSLY.

ON DOWNWIND LEGS, CLASSES
LIKE THE 49ERS + THE 470'S
WILL FLY THEIR SPINNAKERS –
AN EXTRA SAIL FOR HIGHER SPEEDS

UPWIND

STRAIGHT
LINE

DOWNWIND

START
LINE

FINISH
LINE

COURSE LAID OUT BY OFFICIALS ON THE DAY OF THE RACE
ACCORDING TO WIND STRENGTH AND DIRECTION
FIRST LEG IS ALWAYS UPWIND.

go into a final MEDAL RACE on a shorter course. Double points are awarded for positions in this race and these are added to the open ing series scores to determine the winners.

Two different types of course are used: TRAPEZOIDAL and WIND-WARD RETURN. Their precise location and orientation will depend on the prevailing patterns of wind and current on race day.

The trapezoidal course has a separate start and finish line and three points around which boats must turn to complete the four-leg course. The windward return course is simply a two-leg affair but orientated so that the first leg is a leeward sail against the wind (called a BEAT) and the second leg a sail with the wind (called a RUN). When boats are sailing neither with nor against the wind, the leg is called a REACH.

THE LAW OF THE SEA

THE RULE BOOK OF INTERNATIONAL SAILING IS LONG AND complex. A century of fearsome competition has produced a vast case history of wrangles over what constitutes a RIGHT OF WAY when two boats want to occupy the same space or path. Broadly speaking, when the boats are on OPPOSITE TACKS (angles to the

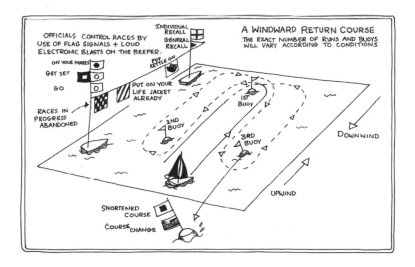

wind) the onus is on the PORT-TACKING BOAT (lying to the left of the wind) to stay clear. When two boats on the SAME TACK overlap or sit side to side, the boat CLOSER TO THE WIND must stay clear of the other boat.

Sailing remains a highly self-regulated sport in which, like golf, competitors are expected to declare their mistakes and violations. If competitors think they have committed a VIOLATION they can avoid disqualification by performing a voluntary 360 turn in the water (some formats specify double turns or 720s). However, in the case of a really serious breach of the rules, boats are expected to retire. Injured parties may protest after a race to a panel of FIVE JUDGES, which can disqualify perpetrators.

···························· **OLYMPIC SAILING CLASSES** ····························

YACHTING WAS ONCE ALL ABOUT HOW BIG A BOAT YOU could afford and how much you could spend on technology. In its survey of the 1920 Olympic competitions, *Yachting World* asked: 'Are they intended to be a test of seamanship or a test of Yachts? Or both?' While ocean-going racing retains elements of both, Olympic sailing is now focused on seamanship, as the degree of variation between boats has diminished to the point where Olympic events are raced with virtually identical equipment. At London 2012, seven different classes will be used across the ten events – a WINDSURFING BOARD, two KEELBOATS and four variants on the DINGHY. Dinghies have movable centreboards that can be taken up into the boats; keelboats have fixed ones.

470 (DINGHY). *Crew: 2; Events: men and women; Olympic debut 1976. Designer: André Cornu (France).* Exactly what it says on the tin: the light and manoeuvrable 470 is 470cm long. The two crew members are usually little and large: a lightweight skipper who steers, and a heavyweight second crew member who hangs outside the boat in a trapeze to balance it on sharp turns and in high winds.

LASER (DINGHY). *Crew: 1; Events: men and women; Olympic debut 1996. Designer: Bruce Kirby (Canada).* Since making its Olympic debut in 1996, the laser has become the most popular one-person sailing boat in the world. Women will race the LASER RADIAL, which has

TEAM GB EXPERIMENTS WITH NEW TECHNIQUE FOR PAUL GOODISON, LASER CLASS VICTOR IN BEIJING

a reduced sail area and a shorter mast, making it easier for light sailors to sail in heavy winds.

RS:X (WINDSURF BOARD). *Crew: 1; Events: men and women; Olympic debut 2008. Designer: Jean Bouldorres and Robert Straj.* The RS:X was introduced at the 2008 Olympics, replacing the Mistral class windsurfing board. While former Olympic-class sailboards were all the classic long board shape, the RS:X is a compromise between traditional longboards and the wider formula racing boards not used at the Olympics.

STAR (KEELBOAT) *Crew: 1; Events: men; Olympic debut 1932. Designer: Francis Sweisguth (USA).* The Star class boats were introduced at the 1932 Los Angeles Games and have been raced at every Olympics since.

ELLIOTT 6M (KEELBOAT). *Crew: 3; Events: women; Olympic debut 2012. Designer: Greg Elliott (New Zealand).* The Elliott 6m makes its debut at London 2012, having been selected for its robustness in match racing.

49ER (DINGHY). *Crew: 2; Events: open; Olympic debut 2000. Designer: Julian Bethwaite (Australia).* The 49er is the fastest craft in the Games, but speed comes at the price of instability, so both crew members need to get outside of the craft in a double trapeze to balance it.

FINN (DINGHY). *Crew: 1; Events: open; Olympic debut 1952. Designer: Richard Sarby (Sweden).* In 1949 Richard Sarby, a Swedish polymath who combined marine engineering with hairdressing, designed the Finn, a single-handed dinghy considered to be the purest athletic experience in sailing. Getting the best from its large sail area and heavy boom requires a lot of strength. Introduced in 1952, the Finn is basically unchanged from its original design.

THE FINER POINTS

ON THE START LINE

SAILING BOATS DON'T BEGIN A RACE FROM A STANDING START; they are already in motion. Timing your run to the starting line is a crucial element of the sport. If crews go too fast or too early and cross the line before the beginning of the race they are sent back to start again. However, if a crew plays it too cautiously they will begin the race behind bolder boats and at a lower speed.

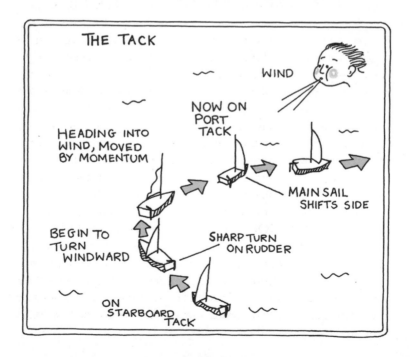

THE TACK

WIND

NOW ON PORT TACK

HEADING INTO WIND, MOVED BY MOMENTUM

MAIN SAIL SHIFTS SIDE

BEGIN TO TURN WINDWARD

SHARP TURN ON RUDDER

ON STARBOARD TACK

TACKING AND JIBING

TACKING IS THE MOST BASIC MANOEUVRE IN SAILING. WHEN a boat is sailing into the wind, it must chart a ZIG-ZAG COURSE to use the wind's energy to move it forward. Boats accomplish this by shifting the direction of the BOW (the front of the craft) and altering the position of the MAINSAIL. JIBING is a similar manoeuvre used by boats that are sailing with the wind or downwind; it involves turning the STERN (the back of the boat).

KEEP AN EYE ON THE NUMBERS

APART FROM MATCH RACING CLASSES, WHICH ARE HEAD TO head, first to the line occasions, Olympic sailing events are won on a CUMULATIVE POINTS basis, with extra points awarded for the final race. Keep an eye on the boats' points totals before the race. A crew might only need to come in fourth or fifth to win a gold medal.

SAILING GOES TO THE OLYMPICS

FOR ITS FIRST THREE DECADES AT THE GAMES, THE EVENT that was known as yachting until 1996 was characterised by a prevalence of upper-class participants and an element of chaos, as it lacked an international sporting body, agreed rules or defined boat classes.

A sailing event was planned for the inaugural Olympics in ATHENS in 1896, but the weather in the Bay of Piraeus made racing impossible. Things picked up in PARIS in 1900, but only marginally. There were two separate courses: on the Seine at Meulan, for smaller boats; and on the coast at Le Havre, for larger vessels. In contrast to the values of amateur sportsmanship that De Coubertin and the IOC had hoped to showcase at the Games, the sailing events were contested with considerable prize money at stake, and SKULDUGGERY duly ensued – two boats were disqualified for using means of propulsion other than sail. High society was well represented in the 1–2 Tonne class, with ÉDOUARD ALPHONSE JAMES DE ROTHSCHILD losing out to his Swiss rival, COUNT HERMANN DE POURTALÈS.

St Louis, 1500 miles inland, passed on the sport in 1904, and in 1908 LONDON outsourced the sailing to Ryde and Hunters Quay on the Clyde in Scotland. Britain monopolised the medals, as not a single foreign team competed. A boat owned by CONSTANCE EDWINA CORNWALLIS WEST, Duchess of Westminster, came third in the 8m class, thus making the duchess the first woman to win a medal in sailing; how active a role she played in the event is debatable.

By 1936, when Kiel hosted the sailing events for the BERLIN GAMES, the sport had acquired standardised rules, classes and equipment, yet it hadn't lost much of its aristocratic air: CROWN PRINCE OLAF OF NORWAY (the future Olav V), who won a gold in 1928, was the first member of a royal household to compete in Olympic sailing; his son HARALD (Harald V – the current king) has competed in three Olympic regattas, and members of the SPANISH, GREEK and THAI royal families have also represented their countries in the sailing events.

The dominant figure in post-war Olympic sailing was the Dane PAUL ELVSTRØM, who won gold medals at four consecutive Games

GOLD ALREADY! MISTRAL WINDSURFER GAL FRIDMAN WINS ISRAEL'S FIRST EVER OLYMPIC TITLE, ATHENS 2004

in the Finn class (1948–60). Elvstrøm came out of retirement to sail with his daughter TRINE in 1984 in the Tornado class and finished fourth. Four years later, at the age of sixty, he competed in his eighth Olympics and finished 15th. Tenacious and skilled, he brought new levels of innovation and experiment to the design of racing boats, inventing new rigs, sails, bailers and training techniques. In 1996 he was voted 'Danish Sportsman of the Century'. Separate women's events were established in 1988, the year of Elvstrøm's last appearance.

Over the last two decades sailing has become an ever more professionalised and technocratic sport. It has also become more open, with champions emerging from a host of newer sailing nations. In 1992, on home waters, SPAIN won four gold medals. HONG KONG claimed its very first Olympic gold medal when LEE LAI SHAN won the women's windsurfing at the Atlanta Games. GAL FRIDMAN did the same for Israel in the men's windsurfing in 2004. AUSTRIA, an entirely land-locked nation, won two sailing gold medals in the now discontinued Tornado class.

YIN JIAN won CHINA's first sailing gold in the women's WIND-SURFING at Beijing 2008, while Brazilians ROBERT SCHEIDT, TORBEN GRAEL and MARCELO FERREIRA have four golds between them. The leading sailor of the era, though, is Britain's BEN AINSLIE. The son of a round-the-world racer, he started sailing at the age of four and began competing at ten. A silver medal at Atlanta 1996 has been followed by a gold at each of the last three Games.

SHOOTING

OLYMPIC PRESENCE

MEN'S EVENTS: 1896–PRESENT, EXCEPT 1904 AND 1928. WOMEN'S SHOOTING arrived in 1984. Up until Barcelona 1992, men and women competed together.

OLYMPIC FORMAT

THERE ARE FIVE COMPETITIONS WITH EACH OF THREE TYPES of gun – RIFLE, PISTOL and SHOTGUN. Pistol and rifle competitors shoot at small FIXED TARGETS. In the shotgun events competitors shoot at CLAY PIGEONS flying through the air. There are five events for both sexes (10M AIR PISTOL, 10M AIR RIFLE, 50M RIFLE THREE PO-SITIONS, TRAP and SKEET), four events for just men (25M RAPID FIRE PISTOL, 50M PISTOL, 50M RIFLE PRONE and DOUBLE TRAP) and one event for just women (25M PISTOL).

CONTENDERS:

IN BEIJING, FIVE OUT OF FIFTEEN GOLDS WENT TO THE CHINESE, who remain the strongest shooting nation. In recent World Championships the AMERICANS and RUSSIANS have shown strength and a number of new shooters have come on the scene, including Italian NICCOLO CAMPRIANO in the 10m air rifle and the rising star of Indian women's shooting, TEJASWINI SAWANT.

PAST CHAMPIONS:

USA: 50 | SOVIET UNION/RUSSIA: 23 | CHINA: 19

Why Watch Shooting?

When the opening ceremony has been and gone, and we finally get down to the sport, the first medal that will be won in London will be in shooting. The excruciating tension of the final rounds, in which the margins for error are minuscule, will provide a compelling start to the Games, if Beijing is anything to go by. Shooting had the opening spot in 2008 too, and the gigantic weight of expectations generated by more than a billion Chinese fell on the shoulders of their star Du Li in the women's 10m air rifle. Wilting under pressure, she lost out to the Czech shooter Katerina Emmons, who equalled the world record with a perfect 400 in the qualifying round. A few days later, to the roar of the hugely partisan home crowd, Du Li recovered from a poor start to pip Emmons for the gold in the 50m rifle, three positions, competition.

It might seem unlikely that a sport that is all about intense self-absorption, static posture and micro-movements of the trigger finger could generate this kind of fervour in a live crowd or amongst a television audience, but over the last decade, efforts have been made to make shooting more spectator-friendly. Crowds are no longer expected to maintain a rigid silence – indeed, in Beijing they were extremely partisan and raucous. Clay pigeons now explode in puffs of purple smoke when hit. Big screens and shoot-offs have been introduced to make the event more exciting, and tiny cameras are now placed on competitors' guns. Be patient. Imagine what is going on behind the shooter's sunglasses and blinkers. Let the competition unfold and the margins of error diminish. Enjoy the tension, for the pressure on spectators and competitors alike can be deliciously unbearable.

The Story of Shooting

Shooting as a target sport has its roots in Central Europe. There are records of arquebus competitions sponsored by the municipal authorities in Geneva as early as the 1450s. From the middle of the sixteenth century the leading edge of European rifle technology was in SWITZERLAND and GERMANY where they made guns that could shoot straight over a reasonable range – a basic precondition of target shooting. Across the Alps, in ITALY and FRANCE shooting competitions were held on religious holidays.

In nineteenth-century Europe – especially in SCANDINAVIA, GERMANY, FRANCE and SERBIA – shooting was fostered by gymnastic clubs, where the sport was encouraged in a spirit of nationalistic, militarised self-defence. In Switzerland, shooting became compulsory for schoolboys between the ages of sixteen and nineteen and a lifelong commitment to a citizens' army meant shooting skills were widespread, while in France and Italy rifle skills were honed by legions of rural small bird hunters. Meanwhile, in Britain and the USA, National Rifle Associations were established in the middle of the century with the dual intention of promoting shooting sports and raising the level of military marksmanship. In BRITAIN they signally failed in the latter task. After the South African War of 1899–1902 had exposed the disastrous state of shooting in the ranks of the army, the government supported the creation of civilian rifle clubs, providing them with free ammunition, in addition to subsidising rifles for members of the NRA.

While COMPETITIVE RIFLE AND PISTOL SHOOTING evolved primarily in a military milieu the SHOTGUN as a sporting event has its roots in the hunting of birds in Britain and the United States. Shooting grouse and pheasants is a seasonal activity and in the mid-nineteenth century there emerged a niche for a sport that could simulate the game shoot without the game. Initial efforts included glass-ball shooting (as featured in Buffalo Bill's Wild West shows), in which catapults – or traps – fired glass balls stuffed with bird feathers straight up into the air. Alongside live pigeon shooting, this simulated form of hunting formed a staple of marathon competitions between professional shooters like CAPTAIN ADAM H. BOGARDUS and DOC CARVER.

However much the glass ball was refined (it was coloured, covered in ridges, filled with flour, explosives and shredded newspaper), it could not simulate the flight of a bird. Inventors experimented with pitch and concrete variants, wooden balls, tin pigeons and brass globes filled with charcoal, but all proved disappointing. In 1880

American GEORGE LIGOWSKY patented a compressed clay disc for shooting. Initially known as MUD SAUCERS, Ligowsky's targets swept the competition aside and quickly came to be known as CLAY PIGEONS. While their flight was just what was required, the early clays were almost impossible to break, and though a hit could be heard – the pigeon would ring like a bell when struck - it could only be registered once the pigeon had been found. They were superseded by more fragile targets made of limestone and pitch which fragmented on being hit. When these were combined with the new mechanised traps the sport acquired its modern technological form.

GAME ON: SHOOTING BASICS

IN RIFLE AND PISTOL COMPETITIONS, SHOOTERS AIM AT A fixed circular target divided into rings, with the centre circle worth 10 POINTS. The format is similar for all rifle and pistol events. In the qualifying rounds, shooters have a limited amount of time to fire their SIGHTING SHOTS and a fixed number of COMPETITION SHOTS. The top shooters then progress to a final round, where the inner zone of the target is itself subdivided into concentric rings so scores from 10.1.to 10.9 are possible rather than just 10. The scores from this round are added to those of the qualifying round to determine the winners. In the event of a tie, a SHOOT-OFF is held – a sudden death, shot-by-shot competition. Both disciplines have events for guns firing bullets and air-powered guns firing smaller pellets.

SHOTGUN EVENTS use a similar format but competitors are shooting at flying targets released from traps, which is an either-or business. Each shot scores either a hit or a miss. The guns are double-barreled and fire sprays of pellets.

RIFLE

50M THREE POSITIONS

IN THE MEN'S EVENT THE COMPETITORS FIRE FORTY SHOTS IN A limited time in each of the three positions: STANDING, KNEELING and PRONE (lying down). In the women's event competitors take twenty shots in each position in the qualifying round. In both competitions, the top eight go into the final where they have ten standing shots at the target. The target they are aiming at is just over 15cm in diameter and the ten-point ring at the centre a minuscule 1.4cm across.

50M PRONE

A MEN'S EVENT IN WHICH SIXTY SHOTS ARE FIRED IN THE qualifying round and ten in the final.

10M AIR RIFLE

MALE COMPETITORS SHOOT SIXTY TIMES IN THE OPENING round; WOMEN FORTY TIMES. In both competitions, the top eight go into the final for the usual 10 shots. The target for this event is even smaller, just 4.5 cm in diameter with a bulls eye of 0.5cm diameter. That is really very small – smaller than a 5p piece!

PISTOL

50M PISTOL

A MEN'S EVENT IN WHICH SHOOTERS HAVE 120 MINUTES TO fire sixty shots at a target that's 5cm across and 50m away.

25M RAPID FIRE

A MEN'S EVENT IN WHICH SHOOTERS FIRE SIX ROUNDS OF five shots, within time limits (4, 6 or 8 seconds). There are five different targets, slightly larger than those used in free pistol shooting. In one of the series of shots all five targets must be aimed at.

25M PISTOL

A WOMEN'S EVENT THAT COMBINES FREE AND RAPID FIRE shooting. The qualification round consists of thirty free shots and thirty rapid fire shots. The final round is just rapid fire.

10M AIR PISTOL

MEN HAVE 105 MINUTES FOR SIXTY SHOTS, WOMEN 75 MINUTES for forty. The final eight in each competition fire a further 10 shots each.

Shotgun

TRAP

Competitors move round five shooting stations, taking two shots at a single target at each. Men shoot five circuits (25 targets), women three (15 targets). The top six progress to the final, in which they shoot at the same number of targets as in the first round but this time have only one pop at each.

SKEET

Competitors move round eight shooting stations and take it in turn to fire at two targets, one thrown from a high position and one from a low position, with a random gap of zero to three seconds between their release. The first target mimics an on-coming bird approaching swiftly overhead, while the path of the second approximates to the flight of a grouse launching itself from the heather.

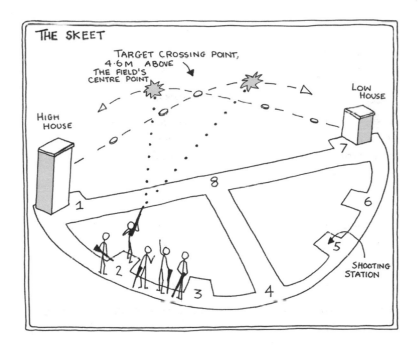

DOUBLE TRAP

THIS EVENT IS CONTESTED ONLY BY MEN; THE WOMEN'S version was dropped from the Olympic programme after 2004. Shooters fire one shot at each of two targets released simultaneously on set paths. They rotate through five shooting stations, firing thirty shots from each. Six finalists shoot an extra round of fifty shots and add their score to the qualifying round score to determine the winner.

THE FINER POINTS

WHAT TO WATCH

ONE OF THE BEST EVENTS FOR SPECTATORS IS THE SHOTGUN, in which you get a nice swing of the arm as the shooters track the clays out of the traps and pleasing puffs of purple smoke when the targets shatter. The RAPID FIRE PISTOL competitions have a manic intensity, particularly the rounds in which shooters are firing at more than one target.

SHOOTING'S NEW DRESS CODE

CLOTHING HAS BECOME A CONTENTIOUS ISSUE IN SHOOTING. Because thick apparel might offer some additional support or absorb more recoil than thinner material, the authorities have introduced stringent and unbelievably detailed rules on the thickness and stiffness of competitors' clothing – and that includes undergarments. All shooters face the possibility of CLOTHES TESTING at the 2012 Games.

SHOOTING GOES TO THE OLYMPICS

SHOOTING APPEARED AT THE INAUGURAL MODERN GAMES IN 1896 with five events, and it proved to be enormously popular: the 200m army rifle attracted one hundred and sixty contestants, under the personal supervision of the Greek CROWN PRINCE NICHOLAS. The pistol shooting was dominated by two brothers from Harvard,

A YOUTHFUL OSCAR SWAHN (BEARDED) AT STOCKHOLM 1912, EIGHT YEARS BEFORE BECOMING THE OLDEST EVER OLYMPIC MEDALLIST

JOHN AND SUMNER PAINE, whose weapons were far superior to those of their opponents. John won the Military Pistol and Sumner took the silver, while John fraternally withdrew from the free pistol competition leaving the field clear for Sumner to bag the gold. It saved his bacon. In 1901 Sumner was charged with assault after firing four shots at his daughter's music teacher who he had found at home with his wife in a compromising position. The case was dropped when it was argued that his marksmanship would have allowed him to hit the music teacher with ease had be really wanted to.

LIVE PIGEON SHOOTING came and went with the PARIS OLYMPICS of 1900: nearly three hundred pigeons were killed in the course of the event, leaving blood and feathers all over the participants, officials and spectators. Thankfully, such slaughter is no longer a feature of the Olympics. Rather more regretfully, the DUELLING PISTOL competition – in which the targets were mannequins dressed in frock coats, with bullseyes on the throat – made its last appearance in 1912.

Shooting was absent from the 1904 Games, having been displaced by archery, but it returned at LONDON 1908 with a vengeance: more than two hundred competitors took part in fifteen events, with TRAP SHOOTING included for the first time. The sport has been a feature of every Games bar 1928, when the IOC decided to get strict about its AMATEURISM rules – most leading shooters of the time were winning prize money in tournaments.

Because shooting requires mental and physical composure rather than athleticism, its list of Olympic champions is rather more diverse than that of other sports. At ANTWERP 1920 the Swede OSCAR SWAHN, a gold medallist at the two previous Olympics, won a team silver in the RUNNING DEER contest and at the age of 72 became the Olympics' OLDEST MEDALLIST. (The deer, by the way, were moving targets made of cardboard; the event has, alas, been lost from the Olympic programme.) At the other end of the scale, at Atlanta in 1996 the American KIM RHODE became the youngest shooting medallist when she won the double trap at the age of seventeen.

In 1924 LT SIDNEY HINDS helped the USA to the gold in the team rifle with a perfect score that was achieved after he had been wounded by an accidental discharge. Even more remarkable was the Hungarian KÁROLY TAKÁCS. By the mid-1930s he had become a top-class pistol shooter, but he was unable to compete in the 1936 Berlin Games because the event was open only to commissioned officers and he was a mere sergeant. Worse, in 1938 his right hand was maimed in a grenade accident. Undaunted, he learnt to shoot with his left hand, and went on to take gold in the rapid fire pistol competition in both 1948 and 1952. French world champion FRANCK DUMOULIN showed similar pluck: he broke his arm in a motorcycle accident in 1999 but came back to win a gold in the 10m air pistol in 2000.

2004 provided Olympic shooting's first love match. KATERINA KURKOVA, who won a bronze in the 10m air rifle, became romantically linked to American shooter MATTHEW EMMONS. Emmons provided the Games' big hard-luck story. Leading in the men's 50m rifle, triple position, he hit the bullseye with his last shot but had fired across the shooting lanes into an opponent's target; he scored zero for that shot, and so lost out on a medal. The pair married in 2007 and both returned to the Beijing Games in 2008. Kurkova (now Emmons) won the first gold medal of the Games. Matthew

'I DID WHAT?' – MATTHEW EMMONS LEARNS HE'S SHOT THE WRONG TARGET AT ATHENS 2004

once again lost a winning position on the last shot and finished with silver.

The silver and bronze medallists in the WOMEN'S AIR PISTOL in Beijing were Russia's NATALIA PODERINA and Georgia's NINO SALUKVADZE, who embraced on the podium and called for their warring nations to desist. At the same Games, 61-year-old Latvian shooter AFANASIJS KUZMINS became the first athlete to appear in eight Games, while ABHINAV BINDRA won India's first ever individual gold medal in the 10m air rifle; the nation rewarded him with heaps of cash and a lifetime pass on Indian railways. In a final narrative twist, North Korean shooter KIM JONG-SU, who had won silver in the men's 50m pistol and a bronze in the 10m air pistol, was stripped of his medals after testing positive for the beta-blocker propranolol.

SWIMMING

28 JULY–4 AUGUST 2012

AQUATICS CENTRE, OLYMPIC PARK

Athletes: 850 | Golds up for grabs: 34

·········· **OLYMPIC PRESENCE** ··········

MEN, 1896–PRESENT; WOMEN, 1912–PRESENT

·········· **OLYMPIC FORMAT** ··········

MEN AND WOMEN BOTH CONTEST FOURTEEN INDIVIDUAL races and three team relay races.

·········· **CONTENDERS:** ··········

AMERICANS AND AUSTRALIANS WON EIGHTEEN GOLD MEDALS at Beijing, though American MICHAEL PHELPS, who has been out of sorts, will be hard pressed to retain his eight titles. Britain's double gold medallist, REBECCA ADDLINGTON (400m and 800m freestyle) will be locked in a duel with Italian world champion FEDERICA PELLEGRINI, while Japan's KOSUKE KITAJIMA, king of men's breaststroke, will be aiming for a third double gold in a row. Brazilian CESAR CIELO FILHO is defending the men's 50m freestyle after time out for failing a drugs test.

·········· **PAST CHAMPIONS:** ··········

USA: 214 | AUSTRALIA: 56 | EAST GERMANY: 38

WHY WATCH SWIMMING?

SWIMMING IS AN ELEMENTAL AND SENSUAL EXPERIENCE THAT'S known to almost every culture. Swimming and ceremonial bathing were celebrated in the art of ancient Egypt and Assyria, and inscribed in the military training manuals of the Romans, the Japanese samurai and the knights of medieval Europe. In classical Greece, where races were held in honour of the god Dionysius, swimming was considered to be on a par with literacy – indeed, the fundamentals of education were 'the alphabet and swimming'.

In its modern super-conditioned and competitive forms, swimming is a rather different beast, demanding of its athletes immense cardiovascular reserves and muscular power combined with supple grace and perfect technique. A top-class swimmer has to master the art of extreme but relaxed effort – if you start fighting the water, speed and power are lost. As the great American coach WILLIAM BACHRACH once remarked 'You can't do anything violently or suddenly in water, it even takes time for a stone to sink.'

THE STORY OF SWIMMING

WITH THE SELF-ASSURANCE CHARACTERISTIC OF THE AGE, A Victorian treatise on swimming could open: 'There is no instance of any foreigner, civilised or uncivilised, whose achievements in the water surpass those of the British.' The modern craze for swimming had begun in GEORGIAN ENGLAND, when the aristocracy discovered the benefits and pleasures of sea bathing. Once public swimming had become acceptable, it wasn't long before races were being held on the Thames, off the Kent coast and across Portsmouth harbour. A small circuit of professional swimmers, known as 'the professors', found an audience for feats of endurance, exhibitions of diving stunts, fancy swimming, and races in lakes, rivers and ponds.

In 1828 the world's first MUNICIPAL SWIMMING POOL was opened in Liverpool. Although private pools had been in existence in Britain for the previous fifty years, the municipal version was to provide the infrastructural backbone of the sport, a spine greatly stiffened by the passage of the 1846 Baths and Washhouses Act. This law was passed in an effort to raise the level of urban hygiene by encouraging local authorities to build laundries and bathhouses for the poor. Large plunge pools – the most economical way of cleansing the masses – provided space for swimming as well as washing. Those of a more refined sensibility could use the first class pools, in which the water was changed more regularly.

A British SWIMMING SOCIETY, formed in 1837, organised races in the Serpentine and embarked on a programme of instruction. Its successors attempted to organise the sport on a more orderly basis and the rule book established by the BRITISH AMATEUR SWIMMING ASSOCIATION (founded 1869) set out the principles on which international and Olympic swimming are nowadays based.

While competitive swimming took off in Europe's elite ATHLETIC CLUBS AND SCHOOLS from the mid-nineteenth century, the popular expansion of the sport came in the 1880s. Pools became widespread and water quality improved. In 1875 one CAPTAIN WEBB became the first man to swim the English Channel, becoming a global celebrity and lending swimming an air of heroic manliness. Thirty years later, the Australian film star ANNETTE KELLERMAN's (unsuccessful) attempts to do the same helped bring women into the swimming mainstream and ensure that swimming was the FIRST REGULAR WOMEN'S SPORT at the Olympic Games.

GAME ON: SWIMMING BASICS

FOR FREESTYLE THERE ARE FIVE RACES – 50M, 100M, 200M, 400M and 1500M (800M for women). All the other strokes are raced over 100M and 200M. In 2008 the first 10KM MARATHON was contested. Swum in open water, the 2012 competition will be held in the Serpentine Lake in Hyde Park.

······································ **BREASTSTROKE** ·······································

BREASTSTROKE IS A TWO-PART STROKE: A FROG-LIKE KICK OF the legs is followed by an arm movement sweeping the water behind the swimmer. The oldest of the four racing strokes, it was often depicted and described in ancient art and literature, and was practised with the swimmer's head out of the water. Over the years swimmers have increased their speed by keeping the HEAD SUBMERGED as much as possible.

BRITAIN'S LUCY MORTON WINNING GOLD IN THE WOMEN'S 200M
BREASTSTROKE, PARIS 1924

At the 1956 Olympics Japanese gold medallist MASARU FURU-KAWA swam entire lengths without surfacing. While this raised speeds it also led to oxygen deprivation and health concerns. Under modern rules, the head must break the surface on every full stroke, although the swimmer is allowed just one stroke underwater after turning.

100M BREASTSTROKE | MEN: 58.91, KOSUKE KITAJIMA (JAPAN) BEIJING 2008. WOMEN: 1:05.17, LEISEL JONES (AUSTRALIA) BEIJING 2008.
200M BREASTSTROKE | MEN: 2:07.64, KOSUKE KITAJIMA (JAPAN) BEIJING 2008. WOMEN: 2:20.22, REBECCA SONI (USA) BEIJING 2008.

BUTTERFLY

IN THE 1930S AMERICAN BREASTSTROKE SWIMMERS AT THE University of Iowa began to experiment with a new action in which the arms were brought through the air together, over the head and into the water, rather than being pushed through the water. This was combined with a newly invented dolphin or fin–tail kick. First seen at the 1936 Olympics, the butterfly stroke proved faster than traditional breaststroke within two years, and in 1952 it was codified as a separate event.

100M BUTTERFLY | MEN: 50.58 MICHAEL PHELPS (USA) BEIJING 2008.
WOMEN: 56.61 INGE DE BRUJIN (NETHERLANDS) SYDNEY 2000.
200M BUTTERFLY | MEN: 1:52.03, MICHAEL PHELPS (USA) BEIJING 2008.
WOMEN: 2:04.18, LIU ZIGE (CHINA) BEIJING 2008.

-------------------------------- **BACKSTROKE** --------------------------------

BACKSTROKE BEGAN LIFE AS A VERY GENTEEL AFFAIR WITH BOTH
hands brought up and over the head simultaneously and then pulled
through the water to propel the swimmer. But at the 1912 Olympics
American backstroker HARRY HEBB powered the competition aside
with the straight-armed, alternate arm stroke that is still used today.

In the 1930s Australian swimmers worked out that a BENT ARM
under water was better than a straight arm. At the 1988 Seoul Games
the Japanese swimmer DIACHI SUZUKI and the American DAVID
'BLAST-OFF' BERKOFF blew their competition away by swimming
up to 30m under water using a butterfly kick. The technique was
promptly banned. Today, underwater backstroke swimming is restricted to 15m after turning.

100M BACKSTROKE | MEN: 52.54, AARON PEIRSOL (USA) BEIJING 2008.
WOMEN: 58.77 , KIRSTY COVENTRY (ZIMBABWE) BEIJING 2008.
200M BACKSTROKE | MEN: 1:53.94, RYAN LOCHTE (USA) BEIJING 2008.
WOMEN: 2:05.24, KIRSTY COVENTRY (ZIMBABWE) BEIJING 2008.

-------------------------------- **FREESTYLE (CRAWL)** --------------------------------

ANY KIND OF STROKE IS ALLOWED IN FREESTYLE RACES –
you could use sidestroke or doggy paddle if you chose – but as
FRONT CRAWL is the fastest stroke that's what everyone uses. As
with backstroke, 15m of underwater swimming is allowed per
length in Olympic freestyle racing.

Widely practised in the PACIFIC and SOUTH AMERICA, it was first
seen in Britain in 1848 when an ex-army officer and impresario
called Rankin brought a troupe of OJIBWA INDIANS to London. In
Holborn Baths two of their number – THE FLYING GULL and TO-
BACCO – took on one of the London swimming 'Professors', a Mr
Harold Kenworthy. After giving a long display in the water, in which
The Times saw them 'lash the water violently with their arms like the

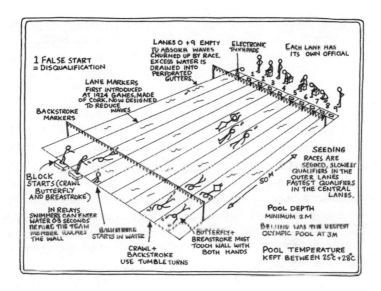

1 FALSE START = DISQUALIFICATION

LANES 0 +9 EMPTY TO ABSORB WAVES CHURNED UP BY RACE. EXCESS WATER IS DRAINED INTO PERFORATED GUTTERS.

ELECTRONIC TOUCH PADS

EACH LANE HAS ITS OWN OFFICIAL

LANE MARKERS FIRST INTRODUCED AT 1924 GAMES, MADE OF CORK. NOW DESIGNED TO REDUCE WAVES

BACKSTROKE MARKERS

BLOCK STARTS (CRAWL BUTTERFLY AND BREASTSTROKE)

IN RELAYS SWIMMERS CAN ENTER WATER 0-3 SECONDS BEFORE THE TEAM MEMBER TOUCHES THE WALL

BACKSTROKE STARTS IN WATER

CRAWL + BACKSTROKE USE TUMBLE TURNS

BUTTERFLY + BREASTSTROKE MUST TOUCH WALL WITH BOTH HANDS

SEEDING RACES ARE SEEDED, SLOWEST QUALIFIERS IN THE OUTER LANES FASTEST QUALIFIERS IN THE CENTRAL LANES.

POOL DEPTH MINIMUM 2M BEIJING WAS THE DEEPEST OLYMPIC POOL AT 3M

POOL TEMPERATURE KEPT BETWEEN 25°C + 28°C

sails of a windmill', the Americans were soundly beaten by the fresher Kenworthy, doing the breaststroke. Disconcerted by the inelegance of the crawl, the British persisted with breaststroke, and it fell to the Americans to modernise the technique. CHARLES DANIELS, American gold medallist at the 1904 Games, was an early exemplar, and at the 1912 Olympics the Hawaiian swimmer DUKE KAHANMOKU introduced the world to the six-kicks-a-cycle technique, in which the kick starts from the hips, producing more power.

50M FREESTYLE | MEN: 21.30, CESAR CIELO FILHO (BRAZIL) BEIJING 2008. WOMEN: 24.06, BRITTA STEFFEN (GERMANY) BEIJING 2008.

100M FREESTYLE | MEN: 47.05, EAMON SULLIVAN (AUSTRALIA) BEIJING 2008. WOMEN: 53.12, BRITTA STEFFEN (GERMANY) BEIJING 2008.

200M FREESTYLE | MEN: 1:42.96, MICHAEL PHELPS (USA) BEIJING 2008. WOMEN: 1:54.82 , FEDERICA PELLEGRINI (ITALY) BEIJING 2008.

400M FREESTYLE | MEN: 3:40.59, IAN THORPE (AUSTRALIA) SYDNEY 2000. WOMEN: 4:02.19, FEDERICA PELLEGRINI (ITALY) BEIJING 2008.

800M FREESTYLE | WOMEN: 8:14.10, REBECCA ADDLINGTON (GREAT BRITAIN) BEIJING 2008.

1500M FREESTYLE | MEN: 14:38.92, GRANT HACKETT (AUSTRALIA) BEIJING 2008.

MARK SPITZ OVERCOMING 'TACHE DRAG' IN THE 200M BUTTERFLY AT MUNICH 72

MEDLEYS & RELAYS

THERE ARE TWO INDIVIDUAL MEDLEY EVENTS, THE 200M AND 400m, in which each swimmer must swim four sequences of 50m or 100m in the following order: BUTTERFLY, BREASTSTROKE, BACKSTROKE, FREESTYLE.

Finally, there are the TEAM RELAY RACES in which swimmers take it in turns to compete. These races are the 4 x 100M FREESTYLE, the 4 x 200M FREESTYLE and the 4 x 100M MEDLEY, in which each of the four members of the team swims a different stroke in the same order as the individual medley.

200M INDIVIDUAL MEDLEY | MEN: 1:54.23, MICHAEL PHELPS (USA) BEIJING 2008. WOMEN: 2:08.45, STEPHANIE RICE (AUSTRALIA) BEIJING 2008.
400M INDIVIDUAL MEDLEY | MEN: 4:03.84, MICHAEL PHELPS (USA) BEIJING 2008. WOMEN: 4:29.45, STEPHANIE RICE (AUSTRALIA) BEIJING 2008.
4 x 100M FREESTYLE RELAY | MEN: 3:08.24, USA, BEIJING 2008. WOMEN: 3:08.24, NETHERLANDS, BEIJING 2008.

4 x 200M FREESTYLE RELAY | MEN: 6:58.56, USA,
BEIJING 2008. WOMEN: 7:44.31, AUSTRALIA, BEIJING 2008.
4 x 100M MEDLEY RELAY   MEN: 3:29.34, USA, BEIJING 2008.
WOMEN: 3:52.69, AUSTRALIA, BEIJING 2008.

THE FINER POINTS

SUITED AND BOOTED

IN RECENT YEARS, OLYMPIC AND WORLD SWIMMING RECORDS
have fallen like nine pins. Twenty-five world record times were set
at BEIJING 2008 and another forty-three at the 2009 World Championships.

While technique, nutrition and training have undoubtedly
played a part in this, the consensus was that NEW BODY SUITS and
POOL TECHNOLOGIES had introduced a step change into the sport.
The all-body polyurethane suits – which can change a swimmer's
body shape and seriously REDUCE DRAG – proved so controversial that FINA (the sport's governing body) banned them in 2010.
Comparing performances in Beijing with London 2012 will be an
interesting exercise, and a guide to just how significant this short-
lived swimsuit technology has been.

A HISTORY OF SWIMMING KIT

PRE-NINETEENTH CENTURY Medieval knights and samurai warriors had to
learn to paddle in their armour, but the BIRTHDAY SUIT was the kit of
choice for most swimmers.

EARLY TWENTIETH CENTURY Knitted WOOLLEN ONE-PIECE SUITS were the
norm. They preserved modesty but were incredibly heavy and hard
to swim in.

1924 SILK SUITS make their debut at the Paris Olympics.

1956 Men's NYLON SWIM BRIEFS arrive at Melbourne. The Australian men
are the first known Olympic competitors to shave their bodies. This
has a minor impact on drag, but a psychological validity.

1976 At Montreal swimmers are for the first time allowed to use GOGGLES. Persian divers had been using tortoiseshell examples three thousand years earlier. The first modern version of goggles was created in the 1930s by Guy Gilpatrick, who tried to waterproof a pair of aviator goggles with window putty.

1980s NYLON/LYCRA becomes the material of choice. Men's long trunks (or JAMMERS) are introduced.

2004 All-in-one BODY SUITS make their Olympic debut at the Athens Games.

2010 FINA bans polyurethane body suits.

PANTS OF POWER: GERMANY'S EMIL RAUSCH, DOUBLE GOLD MEDALLIST AT ST LOUIS 1904

·· **TACTICS** ··

SWIMMING SPRINTS REQUIRE EXPLOSIVE STARTS, ABSOLUTE concentration and almost flat-out effort for much of the race. The longer events are tactically more complex: some competitors like to lead from the front, others prefer to conserve energy and reel in the front runners.

The MEDLEYS, where each swimmer will be stronger at certain strokes than others, are often more eventful than single-stroke events, with competitors able to build and lose large leads.

In all these disciplines the smoothness and speed of TURNS are crucial – and watch how much power and speed a swimmer can get into the UNDERWATER GLIDES AND STROKES permitted at the beginning of each length.

SWIMMING GOES TO THE OLYMPICS

THEY WANTED A POOL BUT MONEY WAS TIGHT, SO THE ORGANIS-ers of the first modern Olympics held four races in the frigid waters of the BAY OF ZEA, south of Athens. 20,000 spectators saw Hungarian ALFRED HAJOS, whose father had drowned in the Danube when he was a child, win two gold medals. It sounded tough out there. Hajos remembered, 'The icy water almost cut into our stomachs ... My will to live completely overcame my desire to win. I cut through the water with a powerful determination and only became calm when the boats came back in my direction and began to fish out the numbed competitors who were giving up the struggle.'

The murky waters of the RIVER SEINE provided the setting for two brilliant but one-off races at PARIS 1900. In the UNDERWATER RACE contestants swam submerged for up to 60m, and were awarded two points for each metre swum, and one point for each second that they stayed under water. Frenchman CHARLES DEVANDEVILLE took the gold. Curiously the Danish bronze medallist PETER LYKKEBERG actually swam for nearly thirty seconds longer than DeVandeville, but did not travel as far, as he went in a circle. Meantime, in the AQUATIC OBSTACLE RACE, competitors had to climb a pole, scramble over a row of boats and then swim (against the river's currents) under a second row of boats. The winner, FREDERICK LANE of Australia, received a 50-pound bronze horse instead of a gold medal. In the more conventional events, the star of the Games was JOHN JARVIS, described as 'fat all over . . . his breasts fall like a woman's, but he has powerful shoulders and tremendous thighs'.

In the bacteria-infested boating lake of the ST LOUIS GAMES of 1904, the 50-yard freestyle race came down to a contest between the American J. SCOTT LEARY and the Hungarian ZOLTAN HAMAY. Hamay appeared to lead from start to finish, but American judges stationed some distance from the finishing line claimed he'd stopped swimming short of the line. Leary then got out of the water and complained that the Hungarian had obstructed him. The debate soon degenerated into a brawl involving both athletes and officials, and was only resolved by all parties agreeing to a swim-off. After two nervy false starts, Hamay got his gold.

The 1908 London Games saw the first tailor-made OLYMPIC POOL, which was 100 yards long and placed inside the athletics track in the White City Stadium. It was the first and last Games at which Britain topped the swimming medals table. At Stockholm in 1912 SARAH 'FANNY' DURAC won a gold for Australia, while the British women won the relay. The Austrian team, which won the relay bronze, was entirely JEWISH. In Vienna, and all over Central Europe, swimming had become a defining feature of a modern, muscular *mitteleuropa* Judaism, countering the stereotypes of the unathletic Jew who was too timid to get in the water.

In the inter-war years, AMERICAN SWIMMING began its rise to global domination, driven by a combination of well-funded university programmes and a craze for all forms of aquatic sports and entertainments in the beach metropolis of Southern California. The swimming star of the 1920 Antwerp Games was the Hawaiian DUKE KAHANMOKU, best known for his pioneering role in the development and popularisation of surfing. At Antwerp he added to the gold and silver he had won in Stockholm in 1912 with two golds, powered by his innovative freestyle flutter kick. He took silver at the 1924 Paris Games before launching into parallel careers as surfer, Hollywood actor and sheriff of Honolulu. He lost out in Paris to JOHNNY WEISSMULLER who won three titles that year and a further two in Amsterdam 1928, before himself heading off to Hollywood.

The next swimming powerhouse was JAPAN. The Japanese had first competed in Olympic swimming in 1920, disastrously; schooled in the nineteenth-century tradition of SAMURAI SWIMMING, they were utterly uncompetitive. There was a furious reaction at home, and the modernisers soon prevailed, with pioneering photographic stroke-analysis combined with the iron discipline of the warrior life at the Lake Hamman training complex.

By 1932 the Japanese were ready: they won five out of the six men's events and all three medals in the 100m backstroke. Their coach argued there was something more than technique at work, arguing 'our swimmers are imbued with the national spirit . . . and what superiority we have can be attributed to this'. At Berlin the men won another three medals and HIDEKO MAEHATA, in the 200m breaststroke, became the first Japanese woman to win a swimming gold. Japan was excluded from the first post-war Games in 1948, which meant that the great HIRONOSHIN FURUHASHI – the fastest swimmer on the planet – was unable to compete.

HOLLYWOOD'S OLYMPIC TARZANS

THE RACING DIVE WAS NEVER HIS STRONG SUIT: OLYMPIC CHAMPION JOHNNY WEISSMULLER IN *TARZAN FINDS A SON* (1939)

Many actors have played Edgar Rice Burroughs' 'King of the Jungle' on TV and in the cinema, but in the classic black-and-white era Tarzan was defined by four American Olympians, two of them swimmers.

JOHNNY WEISSMULLER, who won five swimming gold medals in 1924 and 1928, got his break as Tarzan in 1932 and kept the part until 1948. As well as his Tarzan water dives, he invented the ullulations that defined the movie version of the character.

BUSTER CRABBE, who won a swimming bronze medal in 1928 and a gold in 1932, was cast as Tarzan in 1933 by a competing studio. A twelve-movie run was planned but Crabbe jumped ship and got himself cast as Flash Gordon and later as Buck Rogers.

HERMANN BRIX, silver medallist in the shot put in 1928, was poised to be cast as Tarzan but broke his shoulder and lost the gig to Weissmuller. He got a second chance in 1935, cast in *The New Adventures of Tarzan*, from which a second film – *Tarzan and the Green Goddess* – was spun off in 1938. He then changed his name to Bill Bennet and did a couple of decades of character roles.

GLEN MORRIS, who took gold in the decathlon in 1932, made *Tarzan's Revenge* in 1938. His acting was rightly lambasted and he swiftly moved into insurance sales.

After their annihilation in 1932, the Americans improved at Berlin 1936 and would have done even better if gold medal prospect ELEANOR HOLM had not been kicked out of the squad for drunken misbehaviour during the Atlantic crossing. After the war, however, the USA swept everyone aside, winning eight out of eleven gold medals in 1948, and ten out of twelve in 1952. A rare non-American champion was JEAN BOITEAUX, whose victory in the 400m freestyle prompted his overwrought father to leap into the pool fully clothed.

Throughout the 1950s, 1960s and early 1970s America ruled the swimming world, challenged only occasionally by Australia. MARK SPITZ's seven golds at the Munich Olympics was both a personal triumph and a measure of American supremacy. But the 1970s witnessed the rise of EAST GERMAN swimming, and in just two drug-fuelled decades of top-level competition they accumulated 38 golds in the pool. The women's team was particularly strong: in Montreal in 1976 KORNELIA ENDER won eight medals, four of them gold, while in Seoul in 1988 KIRSTIN OTTO won six gold medals.

Since the demise of European communism, the USA has resumed its place as the most powerful presence in swimming, albeit with consistent challenges from AUSTRALIA, CHINA and the NETHERLANDS — and, in recent years, a much improved BRITISH team. Chinese women's swimming was particularly strong for a while, but has suffered greatly from the much stricter doping tests that are now in operation.

GOLDRUSH: 10 GREAT OLYMPIC SWIMMERS

TEN OF THE GREATS – IN ORDER OF APPEARANCE.

1. CHARLES DANIELS, USA (GOLD 5, SILVER 1, BRONZE 2)

The leading swimmer of his era, Daniels was a well-heeled banker who loved to swim and was pretty damn good at golf, too. He went to three consecutive Games – 1904, 1906, 1908 – and won gold medals at all of them, having been the first Olympic swimmer to perfect the powerful six-beat kick.

2. DAWN FRASER, AUSTRALIA (GOLD 4, SILVER 4)

Fraser, too, won golds at three consecutive Games (1956, 1960 and 1964) and was the first woman to go under one minute in the 100m freestyle. Her career was cut short after she stole an Olympic flag from outside the emperor's palace at the 1964 Tokyo Games. The emperor forgave her – and gave her the flag – but the Australian swimming authorities froze her out.

3. MARK SPITZ, USA (GOLD 9, SILVER 1, BRONZE 1)

A rising star at Mexico 1968 where he won two gold medals, Spitz arrived in Munich in 1972 with a luxuriant drag-inducing coiffure and epoch defining moustache. He blew the field away, retired at 22, and rode the emerging sports sponsorship celebrity nexus all the way to a very comfortable retirement. He was a dentist, too.

4. KORNELIA ENDER, EAST GERMANY (GOLD 4, SILVER 4)

At just thirteen years of age Ender won three team silvers at the Munich Games in 1972. Four steroid boosted years later she swept the competition and won four golds and a silver.

5. DARA TORRES, USA (GOLD 4, SILVER 4, BRONZE 4)

Torres had won four golds, a silver and four bronzes between 1984 and 2000. However, her most amazing performance came at the 2008 Games in Beijing where, at the age of 41, she was the first women over forty to swim at the Olympics. She won two silvers in the relays and an individual silver in the 50m freestyle, which she lost by just 0.01 of a second.

6. KRISZTINA EGERSZEGI, HUNGARY (GOLD 5, SILVER 1)

Egerszegi is Hungary's greatest swimmer and a national hero. She was immortalised in popular culture by commentator Tamás Vitray who roared her home to gold in Seoul in 1988, shouting 'Come on Mouse, come on little girl.'

7. GARY HALL JR, USA (GOLD 6, SILVER 3, BRONZE 2)

Modern swimming's brashest personality, Hall won six golds at three Olympic Games with a trademark boxing robe and a shadow boxing routine before races. Mid-career, in 1998, he was banned from competition for a year for smoking marijuana and since retiring has saved his sister from a shark attack – Hall punched the fish in the head until it gave in.

8. AMY VAN DYKEN, USA (GOLD 6)
Van Dyken won four golds at Atlanta in 1996 and two in Sydney in 2000 – not bad for an asthmatic who took up swimming to strengthen her lungs.

9. IAN THORPE, AUSTRALIA (GOLD 5, SILVER 3, BRONZE 1).
The 'Thorpedo' won three golds at Sydney 2000 and two more in Athens in 2004 – and there would almost certainly have been a sixth medal if he hadn't fallen off his starting blocks and been disqualified in a heat of the 400m freestyle. Massively popular in Australia and across Asia, he retired from swimming in 2006 to devote more time to his sponsors Armani, but he is threatening a comeback in 2012.

10. MICHAEL PHELPS, USA
(GOLD 14, BRONZE 2)
The 'Baltimore Bullet' is without question the greatest swimmer ever. He has won sixteen medals at just two Olympic Games. At Beijing in 2008 he won eight golds, seven of them with world record times. His capacious breakfasts, required to fuel his gruelling training schedule, have received almost as much coverage as his drag on a bong at a college frat house party. Stoner blogs around the world marvelled at his drawing strength.

THE BALTIMORE BULLET: MICHAEL PHELPS AT ATHENS 2004

SYNCHRONISED SWIMMING

5–9 AUGUST, 2012

AQUATICS CENTRE, OLYMPIC PARK

Athletes: 104 | **Golds up for grabs:** 2

OLYMPIC PRESENCE

EXHIBITION SPORT 1952 AND AT FOUR OTHER GAMES. FULL medal event since 1984.

OLYMPIC FORMAT

SYNCHRONISED SWIMMING LAUNCHED AS A SOLO AND A duet event in 1984, became just a team event in 1996, and in 2000 reverted to the original format. Like rhythmic gymnastics, synchronised swimming is a WOMEN-ONLY Olympic sport.

CONTENDERS:

IN BOTH EVENTS THE RUSSIANS ARE THE SWIMMERS TO BEAT. Usual challengers include CANADA, USA, JAPAN and FRANCE, and you can expect serious performances from SPAIN, CHINA and AUSTRALIA.

PAST CHAMPIONS:

RUSSIA: 6 | USA: 5 | CANADA: 3

Why Watch Synchronised Swimming?

Benjamin Franklin was extraordinary: inventor, scientist, man of letters, signatory to the American Declaration of Independence, US Post Master General, and ambassador to France. In his spare time he was a keen swimmer and at one point contemplated becoming a swimming coach. Fortunately for American public life he concentrated his energies on more elevated occupations, but his contribution to aquatic pursuits was significant, which is why he's now a member of the International Swimming Hall of Fame. He re-engineered the swimming flipper, carried out an early form of kite water-skiing, and in 1726, in London, he gave the first recorded exhibition of 'ornamental swimming'.

'At the request of the company, I stripped and leaped in the river, and swam from near Chelsea to Blackfriars, performing on the way many feats of activity, both upon and under water, that surprised and pleased those to whom they were novelties. I had from a child been ever delighted with this exercise, had studied and practised all Thevenot's motions and positions, added some of my own, aiming at graceful and easy as well as useful. All these I took occasion of exhibiting to the company, and was much flattered by their admiration.'

For the next two hundred years or so we find occasional references to swimmers performing water ballet and other such forms of aquatic art, but swimming as a sport has long been about speed rather than grace. Synchronised swimming, the direct descendant of these activities, appeared on the Olympics stage at Los Angeles 1984 – and then only for women. In fact, men have only very recently begun to compete in the sport and do not yet have an Olympic event.

Derision is often heaped upon the sport for its cheesy aesthetics and its reliance on subjective scoring, but neither of these aspects should dissuade you from taking a look: synchronised swimming is a mercilessly demanding form of competition, requiring immense core strength, great agility, perfect timing and huge lungs. Yes, it's sequin-heavy and the grins are unnervingly fixed, but that's to be expected in an event that's a cousin to the Hollywood musical. And who, in their heart, doesn't love a song and dance act?

The Synchronised Swimming story

THE STORY OF SYNCHRONISED SWIMMING REALLY BEGINS
with ANNETTE KELLERMAN – 'The Venus of the South Seas', as she
was sometimes known. Born to a middle-class family in New
South Wales, in 1887, Kellerman was a teenage swimming sensation. She broke records for sprints and distance swims as well as
taking her first steps in vaudeville, performing as a MERMAID in
a glass fish tank at the Melbourne Aquarium in 1903. Her fame
and notoriety grew when she made three attempts to become the
first women to swim the English Channel. Though unsuccessful,
her heroic efforts brought immense coverage for both her and her
revolutionary one-piece bathing suit.

She headed for America next, and in 1907 performed in a
large glass tank at the New York Hippodrome. Her appearance on
a Massachusetts beach in her one-piece swimming attire led to
her arrest for indecency – just one of several such incidents in
Kellerman's lifelong campaign to democratise aquatic sports (and
costumes) for women. Inevitably Hollywood came calling and

MAKING MATTERS WORSE: ANNETTE KELLERMAN IS ARRESTED FOR INDECENT
EXPOSURE, MASSACHUSETTS 1910

in 1911 Kellerman debuted in her first movie, rather predictably entitled *The Mermaid*. Further aquatic adventures followed in *Neptune's Daughter* (1914) and *A Daughter of the Gods* (1916), the first movie with a million-dollar budget.

Hollywood's enthusiasm for water ballet dried up in the mid-1920s, but the style of AQUATIC GYMNASTICS pioneered and popularised by Kellerman found a new home in women's swimming clubs across North America. Swimming coach KATHERINE CURTIS, who first experimented with combining aquatic routines with music while a student at the University of Wisconsin, founded a WATER BALLET CLUB at the University of Chicago in 1923. In 1939 the city held the first recorded water ballet competition, between the Chicago Teachers' College (coached by Curtis) and Wright Junior College.

If American colleges and amateur sports clubs provided the places where this form of swimming could develop as a sport, it was Hollywood and vaudeville that defined its aesthetic and increased its popularity. In 1934, sixty of Curtis's students performed as the 'MODERN MERMAIDS' at the Chicago World's Fair. The event announcer, Olympic swimming gold medallist Norman Ross, used the phrase 'SYNCHRONISED SWIMMING' to describe it, thereby coining the name under which that sport would be accepted as a competitive event by the American Athletic Union in 1941.

The rave reviews for the Chicago show encouraged vaudeville entrepreneur BILLY ROSE to stage *Aquacade* at the Great Lakes Exhibition in 1937. Success there prompted Rose to go for broke with a much more extravagant version of the show at the 1939 New York World's Fair. Held in a specially built 11,000-seat outdoor amphitheatre, with the accompaniment of a full orchestra, *Aquacade* starred Olympic swimming gold medallists JOHNNY WEISSMULLER and ELEANOR HOLM, plus a cast of hundreds. The performance combined formation swimming, comic clowning on the high board and synchronised diving – and it went down a storm. When the show transferred to San Francisco the following year, Holm was replaced by a new star: ESTHER WILLIAMS.

Williams had been a top level competitive swimmer, but with no Olympics to go to in 1940, *Aquacade* seemed like the best gig

MILLION DOLLAR MERMAID: ESTHER WILLIAMS STARRING IN THE EPONYMOUS MOVIE, 1952

going. MGM scouts were impressed and signed her up, casting her in romantic comedies, frothy musicals and lightweight dramas, inevitably with a swimming subplot. In 1952 Williams starred in the defining movie of the aqua-musical genre, *Million Dollar Mermaid*, a super-hydrated Technicolor pageant perfectly attuned to its subject – it was a biopic of Annette Kellerman. Choreographed by Busby Berkeley, Williams cavorted against a backdrop of water slides, surfers and river nymphs, defining for ever the image of the artistic swimmer: effortless, despite the enormous difficulty of what she was doing, and flawlessly made-up, with a preference for gold lamé, tiaras and cherry-red lipstick. The public loved the movie, and flocked to Esther's follow-ups, like the following year's *Dangerous When Wet*.

Williams retired in the early 1960s and a decade passed before the baton of theatrical synchronised swimming was taken up again, by choreographer Charlie Phillips. In the mid-1970s Phillips formed a troupe called THE KROFTETTES who peaked in popularity when they danced with Miss Piggy in *The Great Muppet Caper*, ensuring that another generation of young American women would come into the sport.

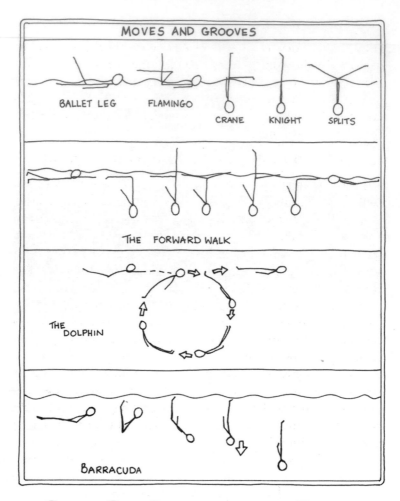

GAME ON: SYNCHRONISED BASICS

SYNCHRONISED SWIMMING IS A FORM OF COMPETITIVE DANCE, in which the swimmers must move in time with each other and the music, performing a variety of strokes, twists, turns and lifts. Participants may not touch the bottom of the three-metre-deep pool and must keep themselves aloft with a combination of SCULLS (small hand movements) and EGGBEATER STROKES (made with the legs).

########## **SHALL WE DANCE? COMPETITIVE FORMATS** ##########

THE OLYMPIC COMPETITIONS ARE BETWEEN PAIRS OF DANCERS (duets) and eight-women teams. In both events, participants perform a TECHNICAL ROUTINE and a FREE ROUTINE, each around four minutes long. The technical competition involves a set series of moves and lifts, whereas in the free competition the choreography is created by the swimmers.

########## **ART AND INDUSTRY: JUDGING AND SCORING** ##########

EACH ROUTINE IS SCORED BY TEN JUDGES. FIVE JUDGES GRADE the technical qualities and five the artistic qualities. Technical criteria include the DEGREE OF SYNCHRONISATION, the PRECISION OF MOVEMENT and the DIFFICULTY OF THE ROUTINE. ARTISTIC CRITERIA, although voluminously detailed in the regulations, remain at best a grey area: points are scored for — among other things — flair, creativity and feel for the music.

After the five judges have given their scores, the highest and lowest are discounted and the three remaining scores are averaged. The FINAL SCORE for each routine is calculated by multiplying the technical score by six and the artistic score by four, with the results added to give a maximum of 100. A team or duo's total for the competition is determined by adding the scores for the two routines together, with the free routine counting for more than the technical one (they are multiplied by 0.65 and 0.35 respectively). Anyone still with us?

THE FINER POINTS

######## **JUST FOR SHOW: DECKWORK** ########

ROUTINES BEGIN ON THE POOL SIDE WITH ELABORATE WAVING and diving — this is called DECKWORK and it does not have to be synchronised. Great as it is, the judges are instructed not to include deckwork in their scoring.

LOOK MA, NO GOGGLES

THE ONLY EQUIPMENT ALLOWED, APART FROM SWIMSUITS and gelatine (to keep the hair in place), are nose clips: amazingly, synchronised swimmers manage their complex manoeuvres underwater without the aid of goggles.

MOVES AND GROOVES

THERE ARE THREE MAIN COMPONENTS TO ANY SYNCHRONISED swimming routine: positions, movements and lifts. POSITIONS or postures generally involve competitors sticking their legs in the air in some way. Judges will be looking for precision of movement and the synchronicity of the team. MOVEMENTS are structured series of positions that move the athletes forward, like the WALK, or allow them to descend gracefully, like the BARRACUDA. Underwater speakers help athletes keep time with the music and with each other.

The most dramatic elements of the sport are the LIFTS. All of them have one designated BASE – the member of the team on which the lift is built - plus a FLYER, a lighter member who is lifted up on the back of the base. The rest of the team are the PUSHERS, who swim around the base and lift the flyer up out of the water. Flyers are increasingly likely to perform acrobatic dismounts at the end of lifts.

SYNCHRONISED SWIMMING
GOES TO THE OLYMPICS

IT'S BEEN A LONG HAUL FOR SYNCHRONISED SWIMMING: FIVE Olympic exhibition performances, starting with HELSINKI 1952, and a global tour by the US synchronised swimming team in 1960 to promote the sport finally paid off with its full medal debut at the 1984 LOS ANGELES GAMES. At the next three Olympics the USA and CANADA won all the solo and duet events. ATLANTA 1996 was the high point for the US team: performing on home soil, they won the gold medal with a series of perfect scores.

This long period of North American dominance was broken in SYDNEY 2000, where the RUSSIANS took both golds. They have held on to them ever since, exploiting the nation's strong

THE WORLD TURNED UPSIDE DOWN: RUSSIA'S WOMEN AT SYDNEY 2000

background in artistic disciplines such as ballet and acrobatics. They also introduced new HYBRID FIGURES and HIGHER LIFTS, performing at speeds that no one knew were possible.

Trailing in the Russians' wake, other nations have been scrambling for the minor medals, resorting to the most extraordinary themes and costumes. The trend was initiated by the JAPANESE at the 1995 World Championship with a routine entitled 're-enactment of the Kobe earthquake'. The FRENCH team at the 1996 Games did a lot of damage to the sport's reputation when they planned a performance on the theme of the HOLOCAUST. Dressed in black bathing suits, team members were to goose-step to the side of the pool before re-enacting, in the water, the arrival of Jewish women in the death camps, the selection by Nazi doctors and the final march to the gas chambers. In the end, after much protest, they thought again.

The USA duo at Athens 2004 mined GREEK MYTHOLOGY for inspiration, appearing in swimsuits adorned with sequinned snakes and performing movements that were meant to suggest the Medusa. In 2008, the SPANISH duet team took things a stage further, working for months to perfect a swimsuit with built-in fairy lights, batteries and circuit breakers. Unfortunately, the sports ruling body deemed them unacceptable.

TABLE TENNIS

28 JULY–8 AUGUST 2012

EXCEL ARENA

Athletes: 172 | Golds up for grabs: 4

OLYMPIC PRESENCE

BECAME AN OLYMPIC SPORT IN 1988.

OLYMPIC FORMAT

STRAIGHT KNOCK-OUT TOURNAMENTS FOR MEN'S AND WOMEN'S SINGLES and TEAMS, seeded according to ITTF World Rankings. In the team competitions (which replaced the doubles event after Athens 1988) teams of three players play between them four singles matches and one doubles match per round.

CONTENDERS:

THE CHINESE WILL CONSIDER ANYTHING LESS THAN A CLEAN sweep of the gold medals a failure. The ranking tables show why: the top five women and four of the five top men are Chinese. The one exception is Germany's Timo Boll, currently the second ranked male.

PAST CHAMPIONS:

CHINA: 20 | SOUTH KOREA: 3 | SWEDEN: 1

WHY WATCH TABLE TENNIS?

AT THE ELITE LEVEL, TABLE TENNIS HAS THE SPEED AND INTENSITY of a martial art. It has become so fast, in fact, with balls flying around at over 70mph, that it is hard to follow for the uninitiated. But the pace is precisely what makes it so thrilling.

Despite its bewildering speed, top-class table tennis is a game of great subtlety. It is all about sending your opponent the wrong way, mentally as well as physically, and to do this you need plenty of TRICKS in the locker. Among these are DISGUISE, a knack for SECOND-GUESSING and a facility for suddenly CHANGING TACTICS mid-point. QUICK FOOTWORK is also essential. The most important element, however, is SPIN – both delivering it and reading and utilising your opponent's. The best players can seemingly make the ball defy the laws of physics.

The sport has also acquired a small but intriguing place in global POPULAR CULTURE. The cheapness of its basic equipment and the relatively small space required for the table has made it a staple of youth clubs everywhere and a favourite of groups as diverse as Premiership footballers and the Zen warrior monks of contemporary Tokyo. Table tennis has even made its impact on cinema, featuring notably in *Forrest Gump* and the cult Japanese movie *Ping Pong*.

THE STORY OF TABLE TENNIS

'PING PONG'S COMING HOME!' QUIPPED LONDON MAYOR BORIS JOHNSON after taking possession of the Olympic flag at the end of the Beijing Games. The genius of his remark was that it managed to be cheekily flattering to his hosts, yet true. Table tennis was indeed born on the dining tables of Victorian Britain but it is in East Asia that it has found its spiritual home, as China's domination of the 2008 competition had just confirmed.

According to table tennis lore, the sport was invented by a group of BRITISH OFFICERS in India (or possibly South Africa) in 1881. Looking for after-dinner entertainment, they carved a champagne cork into a ball and started hitting it over a net made of cigar-box lids. They brought the game back home to England, where it proved a big hit among the upper classes. At this stage, the embryonic sport went by such splendid onomatopoeic names as 'WHIFF WAFF' and 'FLIM FLAM', and was frequently played with a golf ball.

In 1891 JOHN JACQUES of London introduced a game called GOSSIMA, played with long-handled racquets that had drum-like

SPIN DOCTOR: FIDEL CASTRO PLAYING BARE CHEST PING PONG, 1963

heads of stretched parchment, but a general problem with such early forms of table tennis was the poor quality of the projectiles. This was resolved in 1900 by the introduction of HOLLOW CEL-LULOID BALLS, which bounced predictably, offered the possibility of spin, and sped the game up dramatically. Sensing the beginning of a full-blown craze, John Jacques reintroduced Gossima as 'PING PONG'. The firm also moved quickly to trademark the name – by now the standard term for the sport – and sold the American rights to PARKER BROTHERS. Henceforth, competitors in any event that described itself as 'ping pong' were legally obliged to use Jacques/ Parker equipment.

This restriction might have strangled the sport in its infancy had not a group of free-spirited enthusiasts decided to form an association based on the generic name 'TABLE TENNIS'. The Table Tennis Association, formed in England in 1901, just four days before the establishment of the rival Ping Pong Association, is the direct ancestor of the ITTF (International Table Tennis Federation), the body that governs the sport today.

Although it remained popular in parts of Eastern Europe, where it had penetrated during the 'ping pong' days, the initial craze for table tennis quickly burned out elsewhere. But by the early 1920s a revival was underway, particularly in Britain, where the laws of the game were codified. This organisational effort was spearheaded by a colourful aristocrat named IVOR MONTAGU, who was the prime mover behind the establishment of the ITTF in 1926. The first World Championships were held during the same year. All the medals went to HUNGARIANS, who would go on to dominate the championships for most of the pre-war period, with VIKTOR BARNA and MARIA MEDNYANSZKY each collecting five singles titles. A young FRED PERRY, of future lawn tennis and shirt fame, was the only non-Hungarian to win one of the first nine men's World Championships.

The period between 1926 and 1952 is often described as the 'HARD BAT' ERA, because bats then consisted simply of thin sheets of pimpled rubber stuck on to plywood blades. They offered little scope for spin and lacked spring, making the sport considerably slower than it is today. The route to victory was guile, with players working relentlessly to manoeuvre their opponents out of position. RALLIES could be interminable – one at the 1936 World Championships lasted over two hours. Nevertheless, there are those who still hanker after this simpler, purer form of the game, as witnessed by a recent rise in the number of 'old school' hard bat clubs in the USA and Western Europe.

Everything changed in 1952. At that year's World Championships, HIROJI SATOH of JAPAN blew away all-comers with a bat that, in the words of one commentator, resembled a handheld mattress. Featuring a thick layer of SPONGE between the blade and the pimpled rubber surface, it enabled Satoh to hit shots with speed

THE WEIGH-IN: TABLE TENNIS BALLS MUST TIP THE SCALES AT 2.7G

and spin that his opponents could only dream of. His victory in the tournament triggered a technological arms race in which ever more sophisticated combination bats were developed, transforming the sport for ever.

Satoh's triumph was also significant for ushering in an era of ASIAN SUPREMACY that has continued ever since, aside from a brief period in the late 1980s and early 1990s. The dominant force, however, would not be Japan but CHINA. Ominously for the rest of the table tennis world, MAO ZEDONG had recently declared *pinpang qiu* the national sport. It was an idiosyncratic choice – table tennis had made little impact on China prior to the Communist Revolution – but an inspired one. The game required little space or expensive equipment and its emphasis on quick reflexes and nimble movement fitted the Chinese psyche perfectly. The sport was also ruled by an organisation that, almost uniquely among global bodies of the era, was prepared to admit the People's Republic into its ranks. It therefore offered a rare opportunity for Chinese sporting success on the world stage.

Once Mao had his heart set on table tennis glory, concrete tables were constructed everywhere from collective farms to suburban railway stations. The effort paid off. In 1959, a mere six years after

China's admission to the ITTF, RONG GUOTUAN won the World Championship, becoming the first Chinese national to hold such a title in any sport. The country went table tennis crazy.

Chinese dominance might have continued unabated had not Mao decided to unleash the chaos of the Cultural Revolution. Missing the 1967 and 1969 World Championships was the least of the worries of the nation's top players during this period, in which three of them were hounded into suicide by the Red Guards. Nevertheless, when it suited Mao's political interests to rehabilitate the sport after a six-year hiatus, the top Chinese players were able to pick up more or less where they had left off.

PING PONG DIPLOMACY

As the 1960s drew to a close, China and the USA had many reasons for wanting to cosy up. China had been devastated economically by the Cultural Revolution and the Mao regime was desperate that it, rather than the exiled government in Taiwan, should be recognised by the international community. US President Richard Nixon, meanwhile, badly needed China onside for his planned withdrawal from Vietnam. He also recognised that closer relations with Beijing would strengthen his hand in negotiations with the Soviets. The problem was that neither side could admit to wanting a rapprochement without losing face. What was needed was a 'chance encounter' which could be exploited to pave the way for future discussions. Opportunities were limited – the two superpowers had broken off diplomatic relations in 1949 and contact of any kind between Chinese and American citizens was extremely rare – but there was one international body to which both nations still belonged: the International Table Tennis Federation.

And so it was that the chance encounter took place at the World Championships in Nagoya, Japan. On 4 April 1971, nineteen-year-old GLENN COWAN, a member of the US team with hippyish tendencies, found himself stranded after a training session and jumped on to the People's Republic team bus to grab a lift. Initially, the Chinese players were as dumbfounded as if a Martian had appeared in their midst. There were several minutes of awkward silence but eventually the team captain

PIGGY IN THE MIDDLE: ZHOU ENLAI AND RICHARD NIXON OUTMANOEUVRING
TAIWANESE LEADER CHIANG KAI SHEK THROUGH 'PING PONG DIPLOMACY'

Zhuang Zedong walked up to Cowan with an interpreter and presented him with a silk painting of the Huangshan Mountains. Cowan rummaged around in his bag for a suitable gift but all he could find was a comb, so he promised to reciprocate with something more appropriate the next day (a 'Let It Be' T-shirt, as it transpired).

By the time the coach pulled into its destination, the world's media had assembled to cover this seminal moment in Sino-American relations. One journalist asked Cowan whether he would like to visit China. 'Of course,' the athlete replied. From then on, things moved remarkably quickly. Within two days, Mao had ordered the Chinese team to invite their American counterparts to Beijing. Less than a week after the bus incident, the US table tennis team crossed from Hong Kong to the Chinese mainland to commence a week-long tour. Four days later, the US government lifted a twenty-year trade embargo on China and in February 1972 Richard Nixon paid his historic visit to Beijing. The Great Thaw had begun.

Well, that's the story, at least. It later transpired that Premier Zhou Enlai had raised the possibility of inviting the US to compete in China at a high level meeting held seventeen days before the World Championships began.

But in 1989, the unthinkable happened. In the team event final at the World Championships in Dortmund, China was thrashed 5-0 by SWEDEN. The coaches knew that what was holding the country's table tennis back was the same force that was paralysing so much of national life – the omnipresent influence of Chairman Mao – but to say so in public was unthinkable.

In the 1950s, Mao had approved a COACHING MANUAL that had taken on the status of a holy document. Unquestioned adherence to its doctrines, particularly its insistence on the use of the 'distinctively Chinese' PENHOLD GRIP which only allowed one side of the bat to be used, had stultified the nation's table tennis. But at the start of the 1990s DENG XIAOPING began to put into practice his famous remark that 'It doesn't matter whether the cat is black or white as long as it catches mice.' Suddenly the doors were opened to reform in all areas of Chinese life, ping pong included.

Leading players like WANG LIQUIN abandoned the sacred grip and the diminutive DENG YAPING occupied the number one spot in the women's world rankings for the first eight years of the 1990s using a Western 'SHAKEHAND' GRIP. She was later voted the greatest female Chinese athlete of the twentieth century. Meanwhile, LIU GUOLIANG developed a swivel-wristed variant of the penhold that allowed him to use both sides of the bat, thus removing the one great weakness of the traditional grip. By the time table tennis was established as an Olympic event, the top Chinese players were catching mice again with astonishing regularity.

GAME ON: TABLE TENNIS BASICS

FORMAT

OLYMPIC TABLE TENNIS IS A KNOCK-OUT TOURNAMENT, with each nation permitted to enter up to three men and three women, with a maximum of two in each of the singles events.

SINGLES MATCHES are the BEST OF SEVEN GAMES, TEAM MATCHES the BEST OF FIVE. A TEAM CONTEST consists of two singles matches followed by a DOUBLES MATCH, followed if necessary by up to two more singles matches until one team has chalked up three victories.

RULES

EACH POINT BEGINS WITH A SERVICE AND ENDS WHEN A player fails to make a legitimate return. When a player SERVES, the ball must bounce once on each side of the net; all other shots during a rally must land on the opponent's side only. As in lawn tennis, if a service clips the net but lands in play it is counted as a 'LET' and the point is replayed, whereas if a shot clips the net during a rally play continues regardless. There is also a DEUCE SYSTEM, which kicks in when both players are one point away from what would normally be a winning score. Thereafter, the first player to draw two points ahead wins the game. Unlike in lawn tennis, volleys are not allowed and servers get only one attempt per point (barring 'lets').

For most of the history of the sport 21 POINTS were required to win a game but in 2001 the ITTF made the seismic decision to reduce the figure to 11, with SERVICE TO ALTERNATE EVERY 2 RATHER THAN 5 POINTS. The consensus is that the changes have heightened the tension and drama in a sport which already had plenty of both.

A less well known aspect of the scoring system is the so called 'EXPEDITE' RULE. If a game is unfinished after ten minutes and both players have fewer than 9 points, service alternates for the remainder of the match and a receiver who makes thirteen good returns in a rally automatically wins the point.

EQUIPMENT

AMERICANS KNOW THEM AS 'PADDLES', IN EUROPE THE WORD is 'bat' and the official ITTF terminology is 'RACKET'. Whatever they are called, in the quest for more spin and speed the devices used to hit table tennis balls have evolved dramatically since Hiroji Satoh first used his sponge-filled instrument in 1952.

The modern table tennis bat is rather like a sandwich. The core structure, known as the blade, must be 85 per cent wood, but the remaining 15 per cent gives plenty of scope for the use of other materials: carbon fibre, for example, stiffens a blade and gives it a bigger 'SWEET SPOT'. The 'filling' consists of a layer of sponge on either side of the blade, which can be thick, thin, hard or soft according to player preference. The outer layers of the sandwich are formed by two thin pimpled sheets of rubber. Depending on the precise petrochemical formula used in their manufacture, rubbers can impart varying degrees of spin and speed. They are usually adhered to the sponge layers with their smooth sides outward but 'PIMPLES-OUT' RUBBERS are sometimes employed by players who specialise in neutralising their opponent's spin or turning it against them.

It is perfectly legitimate, indeed normal, for players to use bats with completely different characteristics on each side. To help players 'read' their opponents' shots, however, one of a bat's surfaces must be BLACK and the other RED.

One aspect of bat technology which competitors in London will have to do without is SPEED GLUE, a volatile adhesive previously applied by many players to the underside of their top-sheets to make them springier and faster. Following a couple of incidents in which spectators were rendered unconscious by toxic vapours emanating from recently treated bats, the IOC outlawed its use after the Beijing Games.

The BALLS used in table tennis are made of celluloid and filled with gas. They must bounce at least 23cm when dropped on to the table from a height of precisely 30.5cm. After the Sydney Games in 2000, the ITTF increased the diameter of regulation balls from 38 to 40mm, partly to make them more visible to television audiences and partly to slow the action down a notch.

EYES ON THE PRIZE: DENG YAPING, CHINA'S FEMALE ATHLETE OF THE 20TH CENTURY

Other key pieces of equipment include the TABLE, which must be 2.74m (9ft) long, 1.525 m (5ft) wide and topped by a smooth, low-friction coating; the net is 15.25cm (6in) high; and PLAYERS' CLOTHING must not be white, as this would make the ball difficult to see.

THE FINER POINTS

HOLDS

THERE ARE TWO BASIC WAYS OF HOLDING A TABLE TENNIS bat. The PENHOLD GRIP, beloved of players from China and north Asia, involves wrapping the thumb and index finger around the handle with their tips touching the front of the bat while the remaining fingers support its back. Penhold grip players were restricted to using just one side of the racket until the 1990s, when the Chinese developed the REVERSE PENHOLD BACKHAND. The SHAKEHAND GRIP, as its name implies, involves a player holding the bat as if he or she were shaking a hand. Traditionally the hold of choice of EUROPEAN and SOUTH ASIAN players, it has been growing in popularity worldwide as it makes backhand shots much easier to deliver than the penhold.

SERVICE

AS IN TENNIS, THE SERVER HAS A SIGNIFICANT ADVANTAGE AS he or she can dictate the initial 'shape' of a rally. The HIGH SERVE, initiated by the server tossing the ball up to four metres in the air, has become standard among top-class players. The ball gathers speed on its descent, enabling it to take more spin from the bat when the two connect. Serves are usually given heavy SIDE SPIN but on occasion a NO-SPIN SERVE can be thrown into the mix to catch an opponent off-guard.

SPIN

SPIN IS CRUCIAL. TOPSPIN, EXECUTED THROUGH AN UPWARD movement of the bat, causes the ball to dip then leap forward when

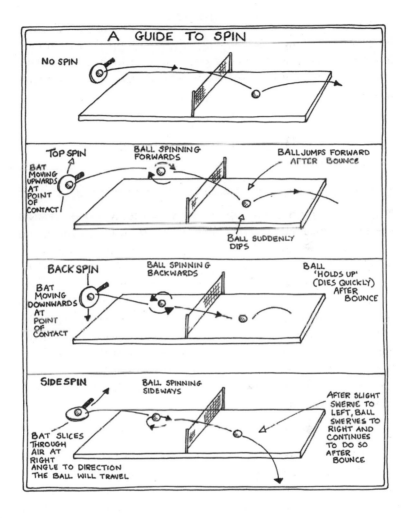

A GUIDE TO SPIN

NO SPIN

TOP SPIN — BAT MOVING UPWARDS AT POINT OF CONTACT — BALL SPINNING FORWARDS — BALL JUMPS FORWARD AFTER BOUNCE — BALL SUDDENLY DIPS

BACK SPIN — BAT MOVING DOWNWARDS AT POINT OF CONTACT — BALL SPINNING BACKWARDS — BALL 'HOLDS UP' (DIES QUICKLY) AFTER BOUNCE

SIDE SPIN — BALL SPINNING SIDEWAYS — AFTER SLIGHT SWERVE TO LEFT, BALL SWERVES TO RIGHT AND CONTINUES TO DO SO AFTER BOUNCE — BAT SLICES THROUGH AIR AT RIGHT ANGLE TO DIRECTION THE BALL WILL TRAVEL

it hits the opponent's side of the table. By contrast, BACKSPIN shots, generated by a downward chopping motion, 'hold up' when they strike the table. SIDESPIN, imparted with a slicing action, causes the ball to move in the opposite direction to the original slice. To add to the devilment, sidespin is frequently applied in combination with top- or backspin.

---------------------------- **FOOTWORK** ----------------------------

THE ROLE OF FOOTWORK IS EASY TO MISS WITH SO MUCH action going on above the table, but take a look beneath. The nimbleness required at this level is astonishing.

---------------------------- **PLAYING STYLES** ----------------------------

ALTHOUGH TOP PLAYERS VARY THEIR STYLE ACCORDING TO circumstance, they tend to have a 'default setting'. They are usually categorised in terms of aggression and can generally be divided into those who play to win and those who play not to lose. Fortunately, defensive play can be every bit as thrilling to watch as all-out attack. As with many one-on-one sports, the most thrilling matches often involve players with contrasting styles.

TABLE TENNIS GOES TO THE OLYMPICS

DESPITE THE GLOBAL POPULARITY OF TABLE TENNIS, IT DID not feature in the Games until 1988. This was largely down to ITTF founder IVOR MONTAGU, who ruled the sport for over forty years. (He also produced several Hitchcock movies, worked as *The Observer*'s first film critic and allegedly spied for the Soviet Union.) Montagu was resolutely opposed to table tennis becoming an Olympic sport on the grounds that he already ran a perfectly good World Championship.

A further obstacle was the issue of PROFESSIONALISM. As early as 1935, the ITTF had erased the distinction between professional and amateur players in its constitution, setting it at odds with the IOC's insistence on amateurism. It fell to Montagu's successor, H. Roy Evans, to make the necessary amendments to the ITTF's constitution in 1979. Two years later, the IOC voted to admit table tennis into the Olympic fold. Ironically, by the time the sport made its debut at the Seoul Games, the 'amateurs only' clause had been dropped from the IOC charter.

Four events were scheduled at SEOUL: MEN'S and WOMEN'S SINGLES and DOUBLES. To no one's astonishment, CHINA captured gold in the women's singles and men's doubles, as they would go on to do at every subsequent Olympics featuring those events. (Men's doubles was discontinued after 2004.) Rather more surprising were victories for SOUTH KOREA in both the other events.

Further evidence that Chinese table tennis had allowed itself to be caught napping was provided by the country's thrashing by SWEDEN at the 1989 World Championships. The presence of this new kid on the ping pong block was confirmed at Barcelona in 1992 when the great Swede JAN OVE WALDNER collected Olympic gold playing a dazzling close-to-the-table game. Often described as the Mozart of the sport, Waldner is as big a celebrity in China as in his native country. He owns a restaurant in Beijing called the W Bar and has acquired the affectionate Chinese nickname Lao Wan ('the evergreen tree').

These humiliations, combined with a new openness to foreign influences, finally spurred the Chinese coaches into amending their game. They dropped their insistence on the unreconstructed penhold grip and dispatched the top players' training partners to study the playing styles of the best Europeans. The new approach has certainly paid off: aside from South Korean RYU SEUNG-MIN's victory in the men's singles in 2004, Chinese players have won every Olympic gold medal since Barcelona.

TAEKWONDO

8–11 AUGUST 2012

EXCEL ARENA

Athletes: 128 | Golds up for grabs: 8

.... **OLYMPIC PRESENCE** ....

DEMONSTRATION SPORT 1988, 1992; FULL OLYMPIC SPORT since 2000.

.... **OLYMPIC FORMAT** ....

FOUR WEIGHT DIVISIONS FOR MEN (58KG, 58–68KG, 68–80kg, 80kg+) and women (49kg, 49–57kg, 57–67kg, 67kg+). All events are KNOCK-OUT CONTESTS, with eight contestants in each competition seeded on the basis of WTF rankings; others are subject to a random draw. The two BRONZE MEDALS awarded in each weight division go to the winners of a pair of REPECHAGE TOURNAMENTS, one contested by everyone who lost to the first finalist during the main phase of the competition, the other by those who lost to the second.

.... **CONTENDERS:** ....

THE SOUTH KOREANS ARE EXPECTED TO DOMINATE – AFTER all, *taekwondo* is their national sport – but they won't have things entirely their own way. In the 2011 World Championships, the country's men lost out to IRAN. Their female compatriots did come out on top in the women's division, but only by way of a strange accounting system. CHINA and FRANCE won more gold medals.

.... **PAST CHAMPIONS:** ....

S. KOREA: 9 | CHINA: 4 | USA, TAIWAN, MEXICO, IRAN: 2

WHY WATCH TAEKWONDO?

TAEKWONDO IS ONE OF THE MOST POPULAR MARTIAL ARTS, and one of the fastest growing: it has been around for less than sixty years but there are already an estimated 60m practitioners, including the American action movie actor CHUCK NORRIS and *Buffy the Vampire Slayer* star SARAH MICHELLE GELLAR, both of whom are black belts. If you like your sport aggressive, taekwondo could be right up your street. It is spectacular, lightning-quick and brutal – which is why contestants wear head and body protectors. Yet, with its graceful movements and super-high kicks, it also has a balletic quality. These elements combine to form what can seem like a video game transmuted into reality.

Aside from its inherent attractions, taekwondo offers a fascinating way in to the culture of KOREA – the history of the sport is intimately entwined with that of the nations. Don't expect to see momentous clashes between NORTH and SOUTH though: the North Koreans practise taekwondo in a form slightly different from the version sanctioned by the IOC.

THE STORY OF TAEKWONDO

ALTHOUGH THE ANCIENT FIGHTING ARTS OF THE KOREAN peninsula undoubtedly fed into the development of taekwondo, the sport is essentially a modern invention, amalgamating elements of Japanese karate and Chinese kung fu. It came into existence formally on 11 April 1955, when the masters of several South Korean *kwan* (martial art schools) agreed to merge their styles into a new, unified discipline, to be known as TAE SOO DO. Two years later, at the instigation of GENERAL CHOE HONG HI, the name was changed to TAEKWONDO to foster a sense of continuity with TAEKKYEON, a martial art developed during the first half of the first millennium.

Although little is known about its precise techniques during this era, *taekkyeon* was a subset of SUBAK, a leg-oriented fighting system that emerged in Goguryeo, one of the three kingdoms that shared the Korean peninsula from 57BC to 668. The smallest of these was Silla, which was subject to regular raids by Japanese pirates. When the Sillans approached the Goguryeons for help with this problem, part of the aid package was training a few Sillan warriors in *taekkyeon*. This elite group, which also studied Confucian philosophy and Buddhist ethics, became known as the *Hwarang* ('flowering of manhood'). As they travelled around the Korean peninsula, they brought *taekkyeon* with them.

In 936, the three kingdoms were united under Goryeo, the successor state to Goguryeo, from which the name Korea is derived. With relative peace, the status of *taekkyeon* and related disciplines declined, and by the close of the nineteenth century they had all but disappeared. But interest was rekindled following the Japanese invasion of Korea in 1909. The occupiers tried to suppress all aspects of the nation's culture, including its martial arts, which naturally increased their appeal to the natives. In remote Buddhist temples, small groups of nationalistic Koreans kept the flame of *taekkyeon* alive.

ALEXANDROS NIKOLAIDIS LANDS A NICE 3-POINTER IN THE 2008 MEN'S HEAVYWEIGHT FINAL

In 1943 the Japanese officially introduced karate, judo and kung fu to Korea as aspects of military training for conscripted locals: thus, by the time Korea was liberated in 1945, all the ingredients were in place for the new hybrid of TAEKWONDO to blossom. The crucial role of Choi Hong Hi in formulating the rules of taekwondo and popularising the sport is covered below, as is the acrimonious split between its ruling bodies. Another key moment in the development of what was soon to become taekwondo was a demonstration in front of President Syngman Rhee in 1952, during which a master named TAE HI NAM broke thirteen roof tiles with a single blow. Rhee was sufficiently impressed to order that all Korean troops should receive training in the evolving martial art.

The growth of taekwondo during the few decades of its existence has been phenomenal: by 1974 there were around six hundred ITF trained instructors distributed across the globe. But it was the newly formed WTF, which held its first WORLD CHAMPIONSHIP in Seoul the previous year, which was to take its version of the sport into the Olympic Games, thanks to some intense South Korean lobbying. Today the organisation encompasses 197 national unions.

THE DISOWNED FATHER OF TAEKWONDO

GENERAL CHOI HONG HI developed taekwondo, gave the sport its name and was the force behind its global spread. Yet today the sport's governing body can scarcely bring itself to mention his name.

Born in what is now North Korea in 1918, Choi Hong Hi studied calligraphy under a tutor called Han Il Dong, a master of *taekkyeon*, an ancient Korean form of foot fighting. When his pupil showed interest, Han Il Dong taught it to him, despite its being banned by the country's Japanese occupiers.

During the war, Choi was imprisoned by the Japanese for attempting to avoid conscription, and during this time created a hybrid of *taekkyeon* and karate. After his release, he joined the newly established Korean army and began teaching his method. On the outbreak of the Korean War in 1950, he formed a crack regiment on the island of Cheju, which marched under a flag displaying his clenched hand over a map of Korea.

The 'Fist Division' provided taekwondo instructors for the whole South Korean army and Choi was promoted to the rank of major general. His star continued to rise and he demonstrated the new martial art in the Far East and America. But the coming to power of General Park Chung Hee in 1961 presented Choi with a major problem; back in the 1940s he had been a member of a military panel that had sentenced the General to death.

GENERAL CHOI HONG HI SEEMS UNHAPPY WITH HIS EASEL

Choi had no option but to leave the army, though for a time he continued to live and teach in South Korea, founding the INTERNATIONAL TAEKWONDO FEDERATION (ITF) in 1966. But life under the Park regime became increasingly intolerable and in 1972 he went into exile in Canada, taking the ITF with him. The South Korean government promptly set up a rival body, the WORLD TAEKWONDO FEDERATION (WTF), and set its intelligence unit on Choi. Told that his son and daughter, who had stayed in South Korea, would be executed if he didn't return home, he responded with the line: 'I chose taekwondo over my son' (his daughter doesn't appear to have got a mention).

If Choi was no longer a pin-up in Seoul, his reputation there took a nose dive when he introduced taekwondo to North Korea in 1980. He eventually moved to Pyongyang, where he died in 2002.

GAME ON: TAEKWONDO BASICS

AS WITH MOST ORIENTAL MARTIAL ARTS, TAEKWONDO IS A philosophy of life as much as a method of fighting: the extreme concentration required to smash through a stack of wooden boards is an aspect of the mental discipline that will lead one to the truth. But competitive taekwondo requires measurable criteria of success, as well as certain measures to prevent serious injury. Olympic taekwondo is therefore confined to SPARRING (GYEORUGI), a form of constrained combat in which points are awarded for striking various points of the opponent's body. Other elements of taekwondo include self-defence, breaking boards and tiles, and POOMSAE – set movements based on imaginary contests against multiple attackers.

Taekwondo means 'the way of the foot and the fist', and that in a nutshell is what the sport is about. Contestants are allowed to strike each other only with their feet and the leading part of their closed hands. The LEG is the primary weapon, which is logical as it is the longer and more powerful limb. The FISTS are of secondary importance – although they are invaluable for blocking, strikes with them score fewer points. In boxing parlance, hand-strikes are the jabs, while the kicks are the hooks and uppercuts.

THE FORM OF THE BOUT

OLYMPIC TAEKWONDO BOUTS ARE HELD ON A SQUARE measuring 8 x 8m, with a 2m margin which is not a part of the fighting area. The fighters begin facing each other, standing on starting positions 1m from the centre of the mat. They return to these positions at the beginning of each round. After they have bowed to each other, the referee calls out 'SHI-JAK' and the fighting begins.

Bouts consist of three TWO-MINUTE ROUNDS separated by ONE-MINUTE REST PERIODS. If the scores are level at the end of the final round, the bout goes into sudden death – the first combatant to score a point wins the match. If no victor has emerged after two minutes, the officials choose a winner on the basis of aggression shown in the sudden death round.

According to WTF literature, for a blow to score a point the judges must deem it to have been executed 'accurately and powerfully'. Glancing or half-hearted contact does not count.

OFFICIALS

A SINGLE REFEREE CONTROLS EACH BOUT AND KEEPS IT FLOWING. In the normal course of events, referees do not award points. This is the job of the four CORNER JUDGES, whose main task is to score shots to the head (body strikes are recorded electronically). If, however, the judges fail to reach a majority decision about the award or deduction of a point(s), the referee has the casting vote.

EQUIPMENT

TAEKWONDO IS PRACTICED IN A TRADITIONAL UNIFORM known as a DOBOK, with a protective jacket called a HOGU worn over the top. At the Olympics and other major competitions, *hogu* are fitted with SENSORS that automatically register hits to the parts of the torso that must be struck to earn points (the front and the sides). This development has relieved the judges of a major burden, but the new technology won't altogether put a stop to controversy: it has been argued that the sensors are too sensitive, and cannot distinguish between a legitimate strike and a part of the wearer's body hitting the hogu in a counter-reaction to a successful block. KICKS TO THE HEAD are scored solely by the judges.

Contestants wear plenty of SAFETY EQUIPMENT. If they didn't, few bouts would last long. In addition to their blue or red *hogu*, they sport head and hand protectors, groin, forearm and shin guards and gum-shields.

SCORING

PUNCHES TO THE HEAD ARE FORBIDDEN BUT KICKS TO IT ARE positively encouraged by the award of up to 4 points.

Points are scored as follows:

KICK OR PUNCH to the *hogu* – 1 point
KICK to the *hogu* involving a partial turn of the assailant's body – 2 points
KICK to the face or side of the head – 3 points
KICK to the head or face involving a full spinning turn – 4 points

SOME KICKS AND A PUNCH		
EXTENDED LEG KICK TO FACE	KICK TO SIDE /RIBS	BODY PUNCH

TURNING KICK — (CRESCENT)		
FIGHTER SPINS ROUND, AT ONE STAGE TURNING HIS BACK ON OPPONENT	AS HE SPINS HE PRIMES HIS KICKING LEG.	BEFORE EXTENDING IT TO MAKE CONTACT WITH THE SIDE OF OPPONENT'S HEAD

To WIN A BOUT ahead of the end of the third round, a fighter must achieve a LEAD OF 12 POINTS, though this rule doesn't apply during the first round. In the event of a KNOCKDOWN, the referee counts to ten – in Korean. As in boxing, there is a mandatory eight count. If a fighter fails to get up in time, or if the referee deems them to be in no state to continue, their opponent wins.

······························ **PENALTIES AND WARNINGS** ······························

FOR EVERY TWO WARNINGS (KYONG–GO) A FIGHTER RECEIVES, HE is punished with a ONE-POINT DEDUCTION (GAM-JUM). If a fighter accumulates FOUR POINT DEDUCTIONS he forfeits the bout. Warnings are issued for the following offences: attacking below the waist; inadvertently striking an opponent's face with the hand; both feet going over the boundary of the fighting area; feigning injury; avoiding combat; turning the back to an opponent except in the course of executing a spinning kick; holding, pushing, butting or kneeing.

MORE SERIOUS OFFENCES such as attacking a fallen opponent or deliberately striking them in the face are punished with an instant *gam-jum*.

The Finer Points

Competitive taekwondo requires mastery of a wide range of kicks, punches, blocks and dodges. A selection is shown in the diagram.

The contestants in Olympic taekwondo go at each other hammer and tongs from the word go, because aggression is rewarded. The kicks and punches are so attention grabbing that it's easy to miss the blocks and dodges, but avoiding being hit is just as important as hitting: developing an eye for this aspect of taekwondo will greatly enhance your enjoyment of the sport.

Taekwondo Goes to the Olympics

The opening ceremony at the 1988 Seoul Games was a pretty emphatic pitch for taekwondo's elevation to the ranks of full Olympic sports: several hundred white-clad South Koreans performed a perfectly co-ordinated taekwondo routine, accompanied by spine-tingling sound effects on the stadium PA. The crowd went wild. South Korea went on to win nine of the sixteen demonstration events.

It wasn't until 2000, however, that taekwondo made its FULL OLYMPIC DEBUT. South Koreans won three of the eight golds on offer in Sydney, but the diversity of the nationalities of the other medallists (GREEK, CUBAN, AUSTRALIAN and CHINESE) was equally striking. In Athens four years later, CHINA and TAIWAN tied with KOREA, taking two titles each. The South Koreans were back on form in Beijing, winning half of the titles on offer, but the main talking point of the event was Cuban fighter ÁNGEL MATOS, the men's middleweight champion at Sydney, who kicked the referee in the face after being disqualified for exceeding a time limit. Matos was banned for life; Fidel Castro expressed his 'total solidarity' with the fighter.

More consequential for the future of the sport was the quarter-final between SARAH STEVENSON (GB) and CHEN ZHONG (China). Four seconds before the end, with the Chinese fighter leading 1-0,

YOU CANNOT BE SERIOUS! SARAH STEVENSON REACTS IN DISBELIEF TO HER
APPARENT DEFEAT IN BEIJING

Stevenson landed a clear match-winning kick on her opponent's face. Unaccountably, two of the four corner judges failed to register the strike, as did the referee, who had the authority to cast the deciding vote. As a result, Zhong was awarded the fight. After vigorous protests from the British team, the judges watched a video replay and reversed their decision, to the fury of the Chinese crowd. Following this incident, the adoption of replay technology was just a matter of time.

TENNIS

28 JULY–5 AUGUST, 2012

ALL ENGLAND CLUB, WIMBLEDON

Athletes: 172 | Golds up for grabs: 5

OLYMPIC PRESENCE

1896–1924; 1988–PRESENT.

OLYMPIC FORMAT

THE FIVE EVENTS ARE MEN'S AND WOMEN'S SINGLES, MEN'S and WOMEN'S DOUBLES and MIXED DOUBLES, which is making its first Olympic appearance since 1924. All competitions have a knock-out structure, with players and pairs SEEDED according to ITF rankings. All matches are the BEST OF THREE SETS, except the men's singles final, which is the best of five.

CONTENDERS:

THE LIST OF 2012 FAVOURITES WILL BE MUCH THE SAME AS for the regular Wimbledon tournament, held just three weeks earlier, adjusted according to how they actually perform there. Grass specialists will obviously have an advantage. The chances of team GB repeating its clean sweep of gold medals the last time Wimbledon hosted Olympic tennis in 1908 are zero, though ANDY MURRAY will have a shot at the men's singles title, which RAFA NADAL will be defending. There will definitely be a new women's singles champion, as ELENA DEMENTIEVA, who won the title at Beijing, has retired.

PAST CHAMPIONS:

USA: 17 | GREAT BRITAIN: 16 | FRANCE: 5

WHY WATCH TENNIS?

TENNIS IS A SPLENDID SPECTATOR SPORT: FAST, INTENSE AND intimate. You can get to know the competitors surprisingly well during the course of a match, or at least have the illusion of doing so, as the TV cameras pick up every emotion flickering across their faces. But you know this already. The question is therefore not so much why you should watch the sport as why you should watch the Olympic version.

Twenty years ago, this would have been a tricky question to answer. When tennis was reintroduced as an Olympic sport in 1988, few of the world's top performers were interested: the tournament had no prestige, fell right in the midst of an already packed season, and there was no prize money. But the decision of the sport's governing bodies to start awarding RANKING POINTS for Olympic tennis – to men from 2000 and women from 2004 – transformed its relevance to hard-bitten pros, who have come to appreciate that a gold medal looks nice in the trophy cabinet. Barring injury, most of the big fish will be there in 2012.

Admittedly, there is still some doubt as to whether tennis really belongs in the Olympics. A gold medal should be a pinnacle of an athlete's career, but no tennis player would rather win an Olympic title than a GRAND SLAM. Nevertheless, the competition in London will be fierce and provide a welcome additional fix for those who haven't been satiated by Wimbledon, just three weeks earlier. It will also be fascinating to see whether the same players can prevail in both.

THE STORY OF TENNIS

LAWN TENNIS IS OFTEN ASSUMED TO HAVE DESCENDED FROM REAL or ROYAL TENNIS, an indoor game involving a droopy net and asymmetrical racquets, played by Henry VIII. In fact, the two sports have little in common, although both ultimately derive from *jeu de paume*, a game played in medieval France using bare hands (*paume* = 'palm') rather than racquets. However, LAWN TENNIS was created chiefly by Major Walter Wingfield of Llanelidan, for the amusement of his summer guests. A hybrid of several pre-existing games, his invention went by the name of SPHAIRISTIKÈ (from the ancient Greek for 'playing ball'), was played on a court shaped like an hourglass, and in 1874 was deemed original enough to earn a patent.

The game swiftly morphed into LAWN TENNIS. Indeed, the world's first 'tennis club' had been founded in Leamington Spa two years before the patent, and within months of the patent a court had been laid in NEW YORK. In BRITAIN, Oscar Wilde became a devotee, and in 1878 women's colleges at Oxford and Cambridge began organising doubles competitions.

Four years after Wingfield's patent, the ALL ENGLAND CROQUET CLUB in WIMBLEDON held its first MEN'S TOURNAMENT. A WOMEN'S TOURNAMENT followed in 1884. The entrants initially played in voluminous bustle dresses, but in 1887 a teenager named LOTTIE DOD took the title wearing shortish skirts, in defiance of Victorian convention. (Twenty-one years later she won an Olympic silver medal for archery.)

Other centres of the new sport began to organise national championships of their own. England was followed by the USA in 1881, FRANCE a decade later and AUSTRALIA in 1905. These tournaments, collectively known as the GRAND SLAMS, became the heart of the international tennis circuit and remain so today. The other key ingredient in the development of the game was the establishment in 1900 of the DAVIS CUP, an annual competition for men's national teams; the women's equivalent, the FEDERATION (NOW FED) CUP, arrived 63 years later.

The British dominated the sport until the 1920s, when the pendulum bifurcated towards AMERICA and FRANCE. The latter's so called 'Four Musketeers', featuring RENÉ LACOSTE of crocodile fame, won twenty singles and twenty-three doubles Grand Slam titles between them in the men's division, while the great SUZANNE LENGLEN lost only two sets in seven years.

The winners' lists from the Davis and Federation Cups show clearly how power has shifted over the years. Prior to 1975, the men's championship was invariably held by one of the Grand Slam nations, usually either the USA or AUSTRALIA (the British dropped off the radar after 1936 and France went almost sixty years

'LA DIVINE' SUZANNE LENGLEN, WHO LOST JUST TWO SETS IN SEVEN YEARS

without a win after 1932). Since then, new countries have entered the fray, with SWEDEN, GERMANY, RUSSIA and SPAIN successively challenging the supremacy of the old guard. The women's game has followed a similar pattern: AMERICA and AUSTRALIA dominated the picture in the 1960s and 1970s, but a power shift towards Eastern and Central Europe began in the 1980s. Williams sisters aside, it has continued ever since.

GAME ON: TENNIS BASICS

THE COURT

TENNIS IS PLAYED ON A RECTANGULAR COURT 78FT (23.77M) long, divided by a net 3ft high at its centre. The WIDTH of the playing area is 27ft (8.23m) in singles matches and 36ft (11m) in doubles, hence the TRAMLINES on either side of the court. Balls other than services hit into these tramlines are deemed 'in' in doubles matches but 'out' in singles matches.

··· **SCORING** ···

WHOEVER INVENTED THE SCORING SYSTEM IN TENNIS WAS equal parts genius and lunatic. There seems no obvious logic at work, yet the system is devised in such a way that a match can remain tense and in the balance right to the death. Indeed a single point can prove a player's undoing or salvation, turning a whole match.

There are three fundamental units: points, games and sets.

A GAME is made up of several exchanges ('POINTS'), all beginning with services delivered by the same player. Each point ends either with a 'double fault' (failure to deliver a valid serve in two attempts) or with a player failing to make a legitimate return. The game is won by the first player or doubles pair to ACCUMULATE 4 POINTS, with the proviso that they must be at least 2 points ahead of their opponents. If the score reaches 3 points all, it is described as 'deuce', and the game continues until one player wins it by drawing 2 points ahead.

Except it's not that simple. Tennis scoring does not operate on a single-point system: instead, a player earns 15 points for the first exchange they win during a game, another 15 for the second and 10 for the third. A score of nil is describe as 'love', a term derived from the French *oeuf* (egg), a suitably zero-shaped object. The server's score is always announced first, so a typical progression might be 0-15, 15 all, 30-15, 40-15, game to the server. If 40–40 (DEUCE) is reached and a player draws one point ahead, they are described as having 'advantage'.

A SET is made up of several games, with the service changing sides after each one. The first player to win 6 games wins the set, provided they are at least 2 games ahead of their opponent. If the score reaches 5 games all, a player can win the set by winning the next two games, but if it reaches 6-6, the players enter a TIE-BREAK. Thankfully at this point the accounting system reverts to normal. The first player or pair to reach 7 points wins the set, provided there is a 2-point lead; if the score reaches 6-6, play continues until one player has a 2-point lead. (In the final set of an Olympic mixed doubles match, the target is 10 points rather than 7; the 2-point rule applies.) The player whose turn it was to serve in the set serves the first point of the tie-break; his or her opponent serves the next two points and after that the serve rotates after every two points.

Olympic tennis matches are the best of THREE SETS, with the exception of the MEN'S SINGLES FINAL, which is, as per tradition, the BEST OF FIVE.

PLAY

PLAY BEGINS WITH ONE PLAYER SERVING THE BALL FROM BEHIND the baseline on the right-hand side of his or her end of the court. For a service to count, it must land in the box diagonally opposite the server, who changes sides after each point. Servers get two chances to deliver a legitimate serve per point. If they fail, they register a DOUBLE FAULT and the point goes to the opponent. If the ball clips the net en route to landing in the correct box, a LET is played and the service is retaken with no penalty. If the receiver fails to get his or her racquet to a winning serve, it is known as an ACE.

If a legitimate service is returned, a RALLY ensues, with the players alternately hitting the ball over the net until one of them loses the point by committing a fault, either by missing a ball that lands in the court, or by hitting it into the net or out of bounds. If a shot ends with the ball clipping any part of a boundary line, it is deemed valid.

EQUIPMENT

PLAYERS IN THE FIRST OLYMPIC INCARNATION OF TENNIS used RACQUETS made of laminated wood, with animal gut strings forming a head with a surface area of around 65 square inches. Today, racquets are typically made of carbon fibre mixed with fibreglass and all manner of high tech substances. They have much larger heads than their predecessors (up to 137 square inches) and far bigger 'SWEET SPOTS' – the part of the striking surface that delivers maximum power and control. Strings are now synthetic.

The BALLS used in tennis are made of felt-covered vulcanised rubber. They rapidly lose their bounce and 'nap' (fluffy coating), once released from the pressurised cans in which they are stored and knocked around the court, and start behaving oddly. For this reason, they are changed frequently during the course of a match.

The All England Club usually insists that PLAYERS WEAR WHITE but has agreed to relax its rules for the 2012 Olympics. Expect a riot of sartorial colour.

······························· **EVOLUTION OF THE RULES** ·····························

THE RULES OF TENNIS HAVE CHANGED LITTLE SINCE THE 1890s. Between 1908 and 1961, players were required to keep one foot on the ground when serving. TIE-BREAKS were instituted during the 1970s and latterly the sport has introduced a points challenge system, based on 'Hawk Eye' technology: players can call for a video-based review of an official's decision any time they like, although they lose this right for the remainder of any set in which they have made three invalid challenges. They do, however, get another 'life' in the event of a tie-break.

THE FINER POINTS

GRASS COURT TENNIS IS FASTER THAN TENNIS PLAYED ON clay or hard courts. Expect lots of ACES, particularly in the men's competitions. If you are lucky enough to attend a match, relish the opportunity to see the action from a different angle to the one invariably used in television coverage. You don't appreciate how FAST the game is until you see it live. Watch how the players try to manoeuvre their opponents into positions where wide expanses of court open up, allowing them to deliver killer shots.

You'll appreciate, too, the diverse playing styles of the competitors. SERVE-VOLLEYERS typically rush to the net after serving, trying to narrow the angle of possibility for their opponents' returns. BASELINE PLAYERS only approach the net when they have to, for instance when retrieving a drop shot.

For those only accustomed to watching Grand Slam tournaments, the THREE-SET FORMAT of the men's singles and doubles will be a novelty. The effect is to reduce the margin for error. Losing a set is far more serious than in five set matches, where a player who falls far behind in one may choose to kiss it goodbye and conserve his energy for the next one.

Tennis Goes to the Olympics

Tennis was one of the nine sports that featured in the 1896 Games in Athens, and the men's singles title was won by an Irishman named John Boland, representing 'The United Kingdom of Great Britain and Ireland'. Not having expected to participate in the competition (he was drafted in by a Greek friend who was a member of the organising committee), Boland played in heeled shoes with leather soles.

In 1900, Charlotte Chattie Cooper of the UK defeated Hélène Prevost of France in the women's singles final, becoming the first female to win an Olympic title – her gender having been forbidden to compete in the ancient Games.

Americans won all the tennis medals in St Louis in 1904, which is hardly surprising as there was only one foreign entrant. British players won gold in all six tennis events at the subsequent Games in London – but this time there weren't any Americans. There was just one American in 1912, when medals were divided fairly equally between France, Britain and South Africa, and none again when France and Great Britain split the golds at Antwerp in 1920. But the USA was back with a vengeance four years later, winning all five titles.

GOLDEN SLAM FOR THE GOLDEN GIRL: STEFFI GRAF ADDS THE OLYMPIC TITLE TO HER 1988 GRAND SLAM

At this point, the issue of PROFESSIONALISM ruined Olympic tennis. The International Lawn Tennis Federation, formed in 1913, banned any player who turned pro from the competitions under its control, which included the Olympic Games. It was, however, fighting a lost cause. In 1926 the promoter C.C. Pyle lured SU-ZANNE LENGLEN and American star VINNIE RICHARDS, double Olympic gold medallist in Amsterdam two years earlier, to join his lucrative travelling tour. Within a few years the 'PRO SLAMS' established in the USA (1927), France (1930) and England (1934) had effectively replaced the old Grand ones. Deprived of its stars, tennis was always likely to fade out of the Olympic programme, and after the 1924 Games it did.

In 1968, the ILTF finally bowed to the pressure and admitted professionals to its tournaments. The IOC eventually followed suit in the 1980s, and tennis reappeared at the SEOUL GAMES, after an absence of 64 years. The men's singles title was won by Czecho-slovakia's MILOSLAV MEČIŘ, the women's by STEFFI GRAF, whose victory secured her a unique 'Golden Slam' – all four Grand Slam titles plus an Olympic gold in the same year.

The tennis tournaments at the next few Games were marked by the inconsistent attendance of the world's best players – the top five men in the world all participated in the men's singles in BARCELONA but only three of the top ten pitched up in ATLANTA – and some surprising results, notably when Switzerland's MARC ROSSET pipped the likes of Pete Sampras and Boris Becker to the gold in 1992. The growing status of Olympic tennis and the intro-duction of ranking points for participation have gone some way to solving the attendance problem but the tournaments have contin-ued to throw up the occasional unexpected champion. NICOLÁS MASSÚ anyone? The Chilean won both the men's singles and dou-bles titles in 2004.

TRIATHLON

4 & 7 AUGUST 2012

HYDE PARK

Athletes: 110 | Golds up for grabs: 2

.... **OLYMPIC PRESENCE** ....

SINCE 2000.

.... **OLYMPIC FORMAT** ....

1500M SWIM FOLLOWED BY 40KM BICYCLE RACE, THEN 10KM RUN.

.... **CONTENDERS:** ....

AUSTRALIA, NEW ZEALAND, CANADA AND GERMANY OCCUPY the first four places in the all-time Olympic medals table, followed by Switzerland and Austria. Although it evidently helps to come from a mountainous country, the UK's Alistair Brownlee is the favourite for the men's triathlon in London.

.... **PAST CHAMPIONS:** ....

AUSTRALIA, NEW ZEALAND, CANADA, GERMANY, SWITZER-LAND and AUSTRIA: 1 MEDAL EACH.

WHY WATCH TRIATHLON?

ONE OF THE FASTEST-GROWING SPORTS IN THE WORLD, triathlon is a mightily punishing endurance event: the cumulative effects of its three disciplines – swimming, cycling, running – are gruelling in the extreme, and success hinges on an athlete's ability to overcome levels of pain that would bring ordinary mortals to a halt. To put the event into perspective, the world's best times for the INDIVIDUAL COMPONENTS of the triathlon give a cumulative time of a little over 1hr 20min. Given that a triathlete has to do the three events back-to-back, swimming in cold water outdoors rather than in a warm indoor pool, and running and cycling on tarmac rather than on a springy athletics track and the sleek boards of a velodrome, it's amazing that Canada's SIMON WHITFIELD took only 1:48:24 to complete the fastest triathlon on record when winning the men's gold in Sydney.

As a spectacle, triathlon offers all the pleasures of its constituent disciplines plus some that are uniquely its own. The changeovers are particularly gripping. Watching a competitor zero in on a bicycle racked among 54 similar machines is always impressive and there is the tantalising possibility of an athlete coming to grief while changing out of a wetsuit.

THE STORY OF TRIATHLON

MULTI-SPORT RACES OF VARYING DEGREES OF FORMALITY HAVE been around for a long time. For example an event called LES TROIS SPORTS has been held at Joinville-le-Pont in France since 1902. It originally featured running, cycling and canoeing, but by 1920 the canoeing had been replaced by a swim across the Marne River. It was in the USA, however, amid the 1970s craze for jogging, that the form of triathlon contested at the Olympics took shape. In fact, the triathlon is one of the few Olympic sports with an identifiable date of birth. It came into existence in California on 25 September 1974, heralded by an announcement in the San Diego Track Club newsletter.

The event was the brainchild of JACK JOHNSTONE, a 38-year-old who had taken to jogging three years earlier to rein in his expanding waistline. An enthusiastic but mediocre runner, he had grown accustomed to finishing way down the field in road races. He had, however, been an excellent swimmer in his youth, so when he heard about an event called the DAVID PAIN BIRTHDAY BIATHLON, which consisted of a 4.5 mile run followed by a quarter-mile swim, he thought 'this could be the event for me'.

Encouraged by finishing in the top ten in the 1974 version, Johnstone decided to stage a race with a longer swimming section. Then he learnt that DON SHANAHAN, a fellow member of the San Diego Track Club, was also planning a multi-sport race, and the two joined forces. When Johnstone caved in to Shanahan's insistence on a cycling component, the format for the newly christened triathlon was established. Forty-six men and women took part in the inaugural race. Johnstone came sixth and everyone went out for a pizza.

IRON MEN AND WOMEN

The Mission Bay Triathlon started the fire but the event that really drew the world's attention to the infant sport was conceived by the man who finished 22nd in that race. In 1977, US Navy Commander JOHN COLLINS was attending the awards ceremony for the Oahu Perimeter Relay in Hawaii when he overheard members of the Waikiki Swim Club and the Mid-Pacific Road Runners debating whether swimmers or runners were the fitter athletes. He chimed in that according to an article he'd read in *Sports Illustrated*, the Belgian cyclist Eddie Merckx had the highest maximum oxygen uptake ever recorded, so perhaps cyclists were fitter than either group.

To settle the argument, he devised the mother of all triathlons, consisting of a 2.4 mile swim followed by a 112-mile bike race and a full marathon. 'Whoever wins, we'll call him the Ironman,' Collins announced. On 18 February 1978, GORDON HALLER, now a Denver-based computer consultant, became the first man to earn that accolade, completing the course in a shade under 11hr 47min. He might have gone quicker had he not popped into a hotel for a shower after the swimming leg. But his performance would still have looked lame compared to those of the Ironpersons of today. The male record now stands at 8:4:8, the female at 8:54:2.

As the sport evolved, the happy-go-lucky spirit of the early days was inevitably supplanted by a more professional and scientific approach. One of the symptoms – mega-events like the Ironman notwithstanding – was the standardisation of the 1500M/40KM/10KM FORMAT, which was developed in the mid-1980s for the US TRIATHLON SERIES. Another was the emergence of techniques and training regimes specifically tailored to the triathlon, as opposed to borrowed from its constituent disciplines. TRANSITIONING (changing equipment and clothes between stages as rapidly as possible) became a particular focus of training, as did the quest for maximally efficient balance between expenditure and conservation of energy at every point in the race.

A major debate that has coloured the first four decades of the triathlon has been the legitimacy or otherwise of DRAFTING, the practice of SLIPSTREAMING during the cycling and swimming phases to save energy. This would have been anathema to the earliest triathletes. The sport is now divided into draft-legal and draft-illegal events, with the Olympic triathlon falling into the first category.

In 1989, the INTERNATIONAL TRIATHLON UNION was established in Avignon, France. Aside from organising an annual World

ALL CHANGE PLEASE: THE SWIMMING TO CYCLING TRANSITION ZONE AT SYDNEY 2000

Championship, which was first held that year, its specific goal was to get the sport on the Olympic agenda. The ITU took just five years to accomplish its aim. The sport was awarded full medal status at the 1994 IOC Congress in Paris and scheduled to make its debut at Sydney 2000.

GAME ON: TRIATHLON BASICS

SWIMMING

OLYMPIC TRIATHLON RACES BEGIN WITH THE COMPETITORS diving en masse off a pontoon or on-shore launching platform. During the swimming section, athletes may use any stroke they like but it will be headline news if anyone opts for other than front crawl. They can take a breather by treading water, floating or holding on to a marker buoy but it's a bad sign if they do. Swimming caps must be worn at all times. If the water temperature exceeds 20°C the wearing of WETSUITS is forbidden; if it is below 14°C they are mandatory.

CYCLING

AFTER EMERGING FROM THE WATER, ATHLETES ENTER THE first transition zone, where they remove their wetsuits and put on their cycling shoes, which may be placed on their bicycles in advance. Before removing their bikes from the racks, they must put on CYCLING HELMETS and fasten them properly. Failure to do so leads to disqualification, as does removing a helmet at any point before racking the bike in the second transition zone, unless stationary and doing something desperate like repairing a puncture.

RUNNING

ATHLETES MUST DISMOUNT WHEN THEY REACH A LINE JUST ahead of the second transition zone. Here they will find their running shoes placed as close to their personal racks as possible. Having racked their bikes, removed their helmets and changed their footwear (in that order), they can set off.

The Finer Points

PACING

Be aware that athletes will be pacing themselves until the final stages of race: if they cycle like a time-trialler they're not going to make it to the finish line.

SIGHTING

In the swimming section, watch out for competitors 'sighting'. This is where they raise their heads above water to look for course markers, using modified strokes that allow them to do so with minimal expenditure of energy and loss of speed.

DRAFTING

In the swimming section, and still more during the cycling, look out for athletes drafting – slipstreaming the competitors just ahead of them.

TRANSITIONING

Pay close attention to transitions. Top triathletes can perform them very smoothly but they can also come a cropper. Many a triathlon has been lost by a tangle with a wetsuit or the clumsy placement of a bicycle in its rack.

Triathlon Goes to the Olympics

The inaugural Olympic triathlons were held in the photogenic environs of the Sydney Opera House. The women went first, with Switzerland's Brigitte McMahon pipping the local favourite Michellie Jones in a sprint finish. The men's champion was Simon Whitfield of Canada.

At Athens in 2004, the women's race again went to an athlete with a British-sounding name from an alpine nation. Austria's Kate Allen had been in 28th place after the cycling and her victory was a dramatic illustration of the importance of keeping something

TRIATHLETES EMERGING FROM THE WAVES AT ATHENS 2004

in reserve for the 10km run. The men's title was won by New Zealand's HAMISH CARTER, who finished just under eight seconds ahead of his compatriot BEVAN DOCHERTY.

The reigning women's Olympic champion, Australia's EMMA SNOWSILL, won the Beijing event by an astounding margin of 66 seconds. Victory in the men's race went to the German champion JAN FRODENO, who passed Whitfield in the last 100 metres, leaving hot favourite Javier Gómez in fourth. The event – due to Whitfield's presence – attracted Canada's biggest television audience of the Games.

VOLLEYBALL

INDOOR: 28 JULY–12 AUGUST 2012

EARLS COURT

BEACH: 28 JULY–9 AUGUST 2012

HORSE GUARDS PARADE

Athletes: 288 (INDOOR), 96 (BEACH) | **Golds up for grabs:** 4

OLYMPIC PRESENCE

INDOOR: DEMONSTRATION SPORT 1924; FULL MEDAL SPORT since 1964. BEACH VOLLEYBALL since 1996.

OLYMPIC FORMAT

IN INDOOR VOLLEYBALL TWELVE NATIONS COMPETE IN GROUPS to produce eight qualifiers for the knock-out rounds. On THE BEACH twenty-four nations compete in groups to produce sixteen qualifiers for the knock-out rounds

CONTENDERS:

IN THE MEN'S VOLLEYBALL THE USA, BRAZIL AND RUSSIA are the main players, but the ITALIANS and the DUTCH are competitive. In the women's volleyball it's JAPAN, CHINA, CUBA and BRAZIL that everyone else will have to worry about. In the beach version, the big guns are the USA, AUSTRALIA and BRAZIL.

PAST CHAMPIONS:

INDOOR USSR: 7 | JAPAN: 3 | USA: 3 | BRAZIL: 3
BEACH USA: 5 | BRAZIL: 2 | AUSTRALIA: 1

WHY WATCH VOLLEYBALL?

VOLLEYBALL HAS A SPLIT PERSONALITY. ITS INDOOR VERSION, with SIX-A-SIDE teams, began as a wholesome sporting recreation for paunchy MASSACHUSETTS CHRISTIAN BUSINESSMEN and until very recently revelled in its honourable amateurism. BEACH VOLLEYBALL is, by contrast, a hedonistic, flamboyant and acrobatic variant, born on the beaches of HAWAII and CALIFORNIA. It spent its early years in the company of beauty pageants, and entered the world of globalised TV sport as a fiesta of hot bodies, tiny swimsuits and garish commercialism.

In reaction, indoor volleyball is now trying to sex itself up, introducing new rules and skimpier outfits to make the game faster and more television-friendly, while beach volleyball finds itself battling the constant accusation that it is not a serious sport. Neither version should worry: both are intensely athletic, tactically sophisticated and absorbingly competitive.

THE STORY OF VOLLEYBALL

LIKE BASKETBALL, ITS MUSCULAR CHRISTIAN COUSIN, VOLLEYball began life as a project for YMCA physical educators in MASSACHUSETTS. Basketball, first codified in 1891 by James Naismith at the SPRINGFIELD YMCA, was designed to provide recreation in the organisation's underused gyms. But not everyone could cope with the game's physicality, least of all the kind of slow-moving businessmen that came to William G. Morgan's classes in Holyoke.

Morgan experimented with a number of options for a new sport played with bare hands and a ball. He liked the idea of a court divided by a high net, as in badminton, and after experimenting with a basketball (too heavy) and a basketball bladder (too light) he got the sports goods manufacturer Spalding to create a ball that was just right. Basic rules for batting the ball back and forth were drawn up, and a demonstration game of what was initially known as MINTONETTE was played at the YMCA conference of

1895. A member of that first audience, Professor Alfred T. Halstead, suggested that the sport be known as VOLLEYBALL.

In 1897 the rules were refined, and subsequently, through the YMCA's network of gyms, the sport spread to countries such as Canada, Cuba, Japan, Mexico, South America, China and India. The game really took off in the PHILIPPINES, where players were the first to perfect the attacking SET-AND-SPIKE routine, which they showcased at the 1913 Far Eastern Games.

In AMERICA itself the game became a craze, as colleges and the army introduced the sport into the curriculum. The US Overseas Expeditionary Force, stationed in Europe after the First World War, distributed 160,000 volleyballs to the public and played the game in front of huge crowds at the 1919 INTER-ALLIED GAMES in Paris – a mini-Olympics for the allied armies. Steadily spreading into Central and Eastern Europe, volleyball became a popular minority sport in the inter-war era. Its rise continued after the Second World War and in 1947 an international governing body, the FIVB, was founded. The first volleyball World Championships were held in Prague in 1949.

The precise origins of BEACH VOLLEYBALL are disputed: some say it originated with surfers on WAIKIKI BEACH near Honolulu, in the 1910s; others trace it to SANTA MONICA, California, in the following decade. Either way, it was only a matter of time before volleyball hit the beach: playing on sand, the most arduous aspects of the game – falling and rolling on the court – became part of the fun. Southern California was the place where the sport really stuck and evolved into its established TWO-A-SIDE format. Initially played on family outings, beach volleyball grew more popular through the 1930s as Californians flocked to the shore for exercise and fun. The scene became big enough to support organised tournaments after the Second World War and Pepsi, alert to the game's close association with beach culture, started sponsoring it in 1948.

For the next two decades beach volleyball hovered between sport and showbiz. Proper competitions were organised in California but they were invariably paired with beauty pageants, bathing-suit contests and musical entertainments. MARILYN

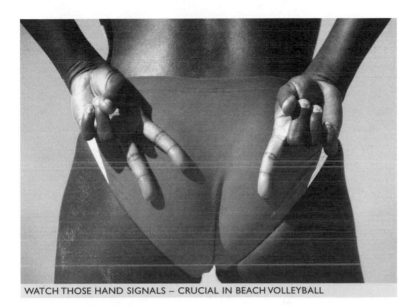

WATCH THOSE HAND SIGNALS – CRUCIAL IN BEACH VOLLEYBALL

MONROE and JFK both thought the sport cool enough to be photographed in the audience. By the 1970s beach volleyball had turned professional in the USA, was spreading to the other major beach cultures of the world – notably BRAZIL and AUSTRALIA – and was attracting so much attention and money that the FIVB, much to the displeasure of the old guard, took the sport under its wing in 1986. The move was one of many controversial acts by the Mexican FIVB president, Rubén Acosta, a relentless commercialiser whose methods led to his investigation by the IOC ethics committee. Acosta quit the FIVB in 2008 and his place was taken by a reformer.

GAME ON: VOLLEYBALL BASICS

INDOOR VOLLEYBALL

INDOOR VOLLEYBALL IS PLAYED SIX-A-SIDE WITH A HIGH NET dividing the court. Teams hit the ball back and forth over the net until one side grounds the ball in the opponents' half or puts

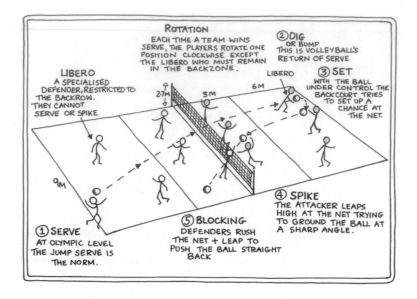

it out of play or into the net. Players may use any part of their bodies above the waist to hit the ball, but may not hold it. Any individual may touch the ball only ONCE before it goes back over the net, but the team as a whole is allowed THREE HITS before the ball is returned.

DIG, SET, SPIKE!

PLAY BEGINS WITH A SERVE FROM THE BACK LINE. THE receiving side will look to DIG THE BALL (cushion and control it with their forearms), then play a SET UP, putting the ball into a position where it can be struck hard and downwards over the net – a shot known as the SPIKE. Whenever possible a team will try to BLOCK the ball as soon as it comes over the net so it drops straight back the other side and is hard to return. Players must not TOUCH THE NET at any time.

SERVING UP

SERVICE ROTATES AMONG THE PLAYERS OF THE TEAM, EACH player continuing to serve until their team loses the point. Each time the side wins back the serve the players ROTATE clockwise around the court, consequently the best defensive players must sometimes play attack and vice versa. Serves may be UNDERARM or OVERARM, but at Olympic level most players will throw the ball high, leap and attempt an overarm jump serve.

THE SPECIAL ONE

THE LIBERO IS A SPECIALISED POSITION. THE PLAYER MUST wear different kit from the rest of the team, can play only in the back row, and is not allowed to serve or spike the ball. The libero is usually a defensive specialist, who receives serve and cushions attacks from the back of the court

POINTS, SET, MATCH.

POINTS ARE SCORED ON EVERY RALLY, WITH THE WINNER OF the point taking the next serve. SETS are won by the first team to 25, provided they are 2 points clear. If they aren't, play continues until one side pulls 2 points ahead. MATCHES are the best of five sets. The fifth set is played to 15 points.

SUBSTITUTIONS

SUBSTITUTIONS CAN BE MADE AT THE START OF A SET OR during a time out. A maximum of six changes can be made per set. Each team has twelve members.

BEACH VOLLEYBALL

THE BEACH RULES ARE THE SAME AS FOR INDOOR VOLLEYBALL except that the game is played TWO-A-SIDE, with no fixed player positions and no substitutions. The court is fractionally smaller and is played on SAND which must be at least 40cm deep; the ball is slightly bigger and pumped to a lower pressure; a BLOCK counts as one of the three hits; and games are the best of THREE SETS – in the first two the winner is the first to reach 21 by 2 clear points (or to pull 2 points ahead), while in the third set it is the first to reach 15.

THE FINER POINTS

SERVICE WITH A SMILE

LOOK OUT FOR TOP-SPIN SERVES, WHICH ARE HIT WITH THE wrist and drop sharply once they cross the net, and FLOATS, in which the ball is given no spin and has a very unpredictable flight.

DEFENSIVE TACTICS

ALTHOUGH TEAMS USUALLY PLACE THREE PLAYERS AT THE BACK of the court to receive serve, they sometimes use just two, leaving the third player free to occupy a better position for setting the ball.

Many teams will gamble on where a return is going to cross the net. Team members will jump high at the net before the ball is released by the opposition. When it works the effect is devastating. Watch for blockers who reach over the net to play the ball sharply down, thus instantly turning defence into attack.

ATTACKING TACTICS

LOOK FOR THE TANDEM ATTACK, WHERE TWO PLAYERS AP-proach the ball at the net simultaneously, forcing defenders to choose which of the two to block and giving the attackers the

chance to play the ball to an unmarked hitter. A similar play is the CROSSOVER, in which the two attackers run on crossing diagonals. The PISTON move has two attackers at the net, one behind the other, again forcing the defender to follow the movement of one of them, potentially leaving the other with an open shot.

ON THE BEACH

IN BEACH VOLLEYBALL KEEP AN EYE ON THE SIGNALS PLAYERS are making behind their backs, indicating what kind of serve or defensive play they want their teammates to make.

VOLLEYBALL GOES TO THE OLYMPICS

VOLLEYBALL'S FIRST MOMENT IN THE OLYMPIC LIMELIGHT MAY have been its finest. Seventy per cent of the Japanese population watched the opening ceremony of the 1964 TOKYO OLYMPICS and nearly all of them turned on again for the hosts' most celebrated sporting triumph, the WOMEN'S VOLLEYBALL FINAL. It was an epic battle between the tall, powerful squad from the Soviet Union and the shorter, lighter but indefatigable Japanese team. The latter had begun life in 1953 when DAIMATSU HIROFUMI, a manager at the Nichibo Spinning Mills near Osaka, started up a women's

'THE WITCHES OF THE ORIENT' GIVE COACH DAIMATSU HIROBUMI THE BUMPS AFTER WINNING THE 1964 WOMEN'S FINAL

volleyball programme. An ex-soldier, the harshness of his methods was legendary and his team trained after work for six hours a day. But it worked, and Japan – in effect the Nichibo team – arrived at the Olympics as defending World Champions. The final went

BRAZIL'S WOMEN ATTEMPT A TRIPLE BLOCK, BEIJING 2008

all the way to a fifth set, and the Soviet team, having pulled level, threatened to take the game at the death, but the Japanese held their nerve, took back the serve and won.

Though Olympic volleyball has never quite matched this moment of high emotion, the women's game has continued to provide the sport's biggest stories. The victory of the CHINESE women's team at the 1984 LOS ANGELES Games, the first in which China had competed, was acclaimed at home as a huge triumph for the nation. LANG PING, the team's star, acquired heroic status and earned the soubriquet 'iron hammer'. A trio of golds for the CUBAN women (in 1992, 1996 and 2000) was followed by the brilliant recovery of the Chinese women in the 2004 Olympic final against the Russians, a victory met with euphoria by a Chinese population that was now glued to its television sets. The women's volleyball was duly one of the hottest tickets at BEIJING 2008, where the competition was made all the spicier by the presence of Lang Ping as coach of the US women's team. They took the silver ahead of China, with the gold going to BRAZIL.

In the MEN'S GAME the Olympics were dominated by the SOVIET UNION and EASTERN EUROPEAN nations until the 1980s. Since then the USA (1984, 1988 and 2008) and BRAZIL (1992, 2004), both benefiting from the decline of communist volleyball and the rise of the professional game, have won golds, as have the DUTCH (1996) and the YUGOSLAVS (2000).

Since volleyball first arrived at the Olympics in 1964, it has become faster and more acrobatic. Yet outside of Japan and China it has not been able to attract the kinds of audience and TV ratings that a game played so widely might be expected to attract. On and off the court, volleyball remains bound to its amateur roots, with strict forms of etiquette applied to player behaviour. Bad language, for example, is regularly punished and over-emotional displays are frowned upon.

BEACH VOLLEYBALL offers much of what the traditional game has lacked. When it debuted at the 1996 ATLANTA OLYMPICS, it was the third event to sell out – though cynics suggested that was as much down to the bikinis and well-toned flesh on display as the sporting experience. Indeed, in 1999 the FIVB rewrote the sport's sartorial rules, insisting on the two-piece bikini kit for women (with a maximum size for the bottom half) and making more revealing kit compulsory for men, too. The beach discipline has proved enormously popular at every Olympics since.

WATER POLO

29 JULY–12 AUGUST 2012

WATER POLO ARENA, OLYMPIC PARK

Athletes: 260 | Golds up for grabs: 2

OLYMPIC PRESENCE

MEN SINCE 1900; WOMEN SINCE 2000.

OLYMPIC FORMAT

BOTH MEN AND WOMEN'S TEAMS PLAY IN PRELIMINARY GROUPS and the top eight progress to the quarter-finals.

CURRENT CONTENDERS:

IN THE MEN'S TOURNAMENT THE ESTABLISHED NATIONS ARE ITALY, HUNGARY, RUSSIA, SERBIA and CROATIA – though the USA are contenders too. In the women's tournament, AUSTRALIA and the NETHERLANDS will field strong teams, as will the AMERICANS and ITALIANS.

PAST CHAMPIONS:

HUNGARY: 9 | ITALY: 4 | GREAT BRITAIN: 4

WHY WATCH WATER POLO?

'FISTS FLEW AND BLOOD FLOWED,' RAN THE HEADLINE IN THE *New York Times* on 6 December 1956. You might have been expecting a boxing report and in a way you would have been right, but the *Times* was actually reviewing Hungary's 4-0 victory over the Soviet Union in the water polo competition at the Melbourne Olympics. By far the most famous moment in the sport's history, it was also the biggest ever Olympic brawl.

The swimming caps with huge ear protectors worn by water polo players wouldn't look out of place on a rugby field and they wear two pairs of trunks for a reason. Ears get mauled, trunks get ripped and these are among the least of the shenanigans that go on in this furious form of aquatic handball. It is insanely demanding. Players must constantly tread water, beating out furious eggbeater patterns of strokes with their legs, lift themselves up out of the water when necessary and then switch to lung-burning sprints as the play moves from end to end

Dominated in modern times by Hungary, Russia, Italy, Yugoslavia and its descendant states, water polo is invariably played at a momentous emotional and physical pitch, with players, coaches and fans given to outbreaks of volcanic temper. What the sport lacks in elegance it more than makes up for in tempestuousness and titanic competitiveness.

THE STORY OF WATER POLO

THE PRECISE ORIGINS OF WATER POLO ARE NOT CLEAR. SOME sources trace it back to members of the British Army of the Raj attempting an aquatic version of the horse-bound form of polo, but it seems more likely to have been developed for a lark by young men in Britain swimming in lakes and the first generation of Victorian municipal baths.

Players took their cues from rugby and football, attempting to score goals with much fighting, rucking, ducking and punching along the way. Early variants included scoring by placing the ball on a buoy or at the end of the pool, and goalies standing outside the water and only jumping in when their goals were threatened.

A measure of rationality, if not civility, was introduced to the melee by Scottish pioneer William Wilson, whose 1877 rules for the game of 'water football' forbade the tackling of players not in possession of the ball. The first organised competition, the London Water Polo League, was established in 1888 and two years later Scotland beat England 4-0 in the sport's international debut. Interestingly, the Scottish players' preference for collective

VICTORIAN GENTLEMEN EXPERIMENT WITH AQUATIC FORMS OF POLO

passing over the English taste for individual dribbling mirrored the nations' contemporary approaches to football.

In the years before the First World War, young, often college-educated men were introduced to the game in the cities of continental Europe and North America. The Italians were particularly keen, despite a Milanese paper describing the game in 1890 as being 'like football but more tiring and difficult, requiring energy and strength beyond the ordinary'. The sport also proved immediately popular in France, Belgium, the United States and, above all, in Hungary and Yugoslavia.

Controlled by FINA since 1930, the game has been steadily re-fined to speed up play and try to get players to concentrate on the ball rather than the man or woman. The Hungarians were the first to use the dry pass, in which the ball moves from hand to hand rather than the receiver picking it up out of the water. This was the basis of their long era of superiority either side of the Second World War.

Leather balls, which absorbed water and got slower and heavier as the game progressed, were replaced by rubber coated versions during the 1930s. As with basketball, which was suffering from low-scoring and over-physical play, shot clocks were introduced in the 1950s. Henceforward, a team had 45 seconds (now down to 35) to attempt a shot on goal before possession passed to the opposition. Similarly, accumulated fouls and violent play were increasingly punished, ultimately leading to players being excluded for short periods of the game. It is in these situations, with one side a player down, that most goals are scored.

GAME ON: WATER POLO BASICS

WATER POLO IS A GAME OF ATTACK, DEFENCE AND TRANSITION. When a team has the ball it moves it by dribbling, passing and hopefully shooting on goal. When a team loses possession, it blocks, tackles and tries to snatch the ball back. Whenever it changes hands there is an almighty sprint by both sides from one end of the pool to the other.

THE POOL must be at least two metres deep and players are not allowed to touch the bottom, which means that they must

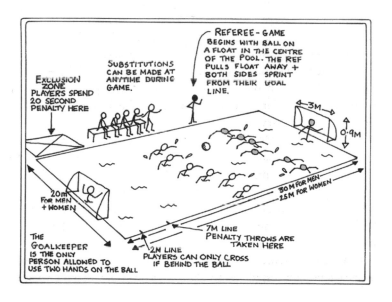

constantly tread water, including during STOPPAGES. There are a lot of these in most games, which despite being scheduled for just 28 minutes of play can last over an hour. The MAIN NO-NOS are taking the ball underwater, tackling a player without the ball and using two hands to hold the ball (unless you are a goalkeeper). When a FOUL is called against a team it concedes possession to the opposition. If it commits a foul inside its own 5-metre line, the opponents get a PENALTY THROW on goal.

DANGEROUS, VIOLENT AND UNSPORTSMANLIKE PLAY, of which there is plenty, results in an exclusion foul being called and a 20-SECOND PENALTY imposed on the guilty party. Examples include splashing water in an opponent's face, and holding or sinking them. Brutal play, such as kicking or punching with malicious intent, leads to permanent exclusion, with substitution only allowed after four minutes.

ATTACK AND DEFENSE

DRIVER - A PLAYER CAPABLE OF SUDDEN SHOT COMES TOWARDS GOAL.

ATTACKING PLAYERS POSITIONED ON THE POST

TWO METRE MAN

PLAYERS ON WING CAN PASS BACK TO THE CENTRE OR TAKE A SHOT.

THE FINER POINTS

WATCHING THE ATTACK

FOR MUCH OF THE TIME, BOTH TEAMS CLUSTER AROUND ONE of the goals. The key player to look for is the 2-METRE or 'HOLE'

MAN positioned in the centre, and the defender whose job it is to guard him. As well as absorbing a lot of fouls, the 2-metre man is the pivot of most attacking moves, passing the ball along to team-mates along the semi-circular perimeter of the 2-metre line.

Some of the best SKILLS in the game can be seen when attacking players find an angle around the defence, using a body feint, a sudden leap or a flick of the wrist to change direction.

································ **WATCHING THE DEFENCE** ································

DEFENDERS look to block their opponent's paths to goal and to contest and block passes and shots. They can also tackle players with the ball and attempt to steal it from their grasp.

The best defenders play the ball not the man and concentrate on turning possession over. However, there is a lot of aggressive body contact, especially underwater. Look out for illegal grapples, punches, elbowing and GROIN GRABBING.

WATER POLO GOES TO THE OLYMPICS

THE FIRST OLYMPIC WATER POLO TOURNAMENT TOOK PLACE IN the River Seine in 1900 and was contested by clubs from Brussels, Lille and Manchester. The Osborne Swimming Club from Manchester took gold for Great Britain, which went on to win another three titles (1908, 1912 and 1920) before disappearing from the world of competitive water polo altogether. Britain last qualified for an Olympic tournament in 1956, where it finished seventh of eight.

The 1904 Games saw all the medals go the USA, but as all three teams were American this was scarcely surprising. A team from Germany had made the journey to St Louis but found itself at odds with the American officials, who decided that a goal could only be scored by holding the ball in the net and deemed a partially deflated volleyball perfectly adequate for the competition. The Germans, who were accustomed to different rules and better equipment, derided this 'softball water polo' and refused to compete. Maybe they knew something the Americans didn't. Due to the players' long immersion in the bacteria-ridden lake, four of the American participants were dead within a year from typhoid.

In 1932 the Hungarians, who had taken the silver medal in 1928, crossed the Atlantic by liner, practising in a tiny onboard pool, and made for Los Angeles. Their victory was the first of the country's nine subsequent gold medals. Since then, all but one Olympic tournament has been won by Hungary, Italy, Yugoslavia, the Soviet Union or descendent states of the last two.

Hungary's victory in 1932 established the new global water polo aristocracy but the future tone of the sport was set at the same tournament by the Brazilians. They almost failed to make the Games at all, the government having initially responded to a collapse of the world coffee market by refusing to fund the trip to LA. Then, in a stroke of administrative genius, it decided that there was a way to send an Olympic squad to America after all, accompanied by a fifty-strong marine band and 25 tonnes of coffee. Squad members would serve as crew and sell the coffee en route, to cover their expenses.

Things didn't quite work out. An attempt to pass the ship off as a military vessel to get free passage through the Panama Canal was rumbled by the Panamanian authorities despite the presence of two rusty cannons on board. And coffee sales were so poor that on arriving in the USA, the athletes could only muster $24 between them, enough to send just 24 representatives ashore paying the $1 immigration tax each. Fortunately for the water polo team, its members were among them. While the rest of the squad headed for Portland and Seattle on a coffee selling mission, they travelled to Los Angeles and wrote themselves into Olympic history at the conclusion of their first round 7-3 defeat by the Germans. Incensed by what they perceived as the Hungarian referee's bias, they finished the game with a polite cheer for their opponents and a mass attack on the judges' stand, eventually halted by the LAPD.

And so it has gone on. The greatest Olympic punch-up of them all took place at the 1956 Hungary-USSR semi-final (see opposite page) but it has not been without rivals. There was a bitter Russia-Hungary rematch at the 2000 Olympics, and women's water polo, which belatedly debuted at the same Games with swimsuit ripping, punching and all, has shown that the boys have no monopoly on this roughhouse of a sport.

HUNGARY v. USSR
AT THE 1956 OLYMPICS

The Melbourne Olympics were played in the shadow of the Hungarian revolution and the recent invasion of the country by the Soviet Army. As luck would have it, the Hungarian and Soviet water polo teams shared a boat for the journey to Australia – and the fighting began on board. Once in Australia, the large expatriate Hungarian community in Melbourne made sure that the Hungarian team were well aware of their feelings – and when the two teams met in their final group game, nearly 5,000 Hungarian Australians came along to watch.

The Hungarians went into the game intending to wind up their opponents. It didn't take much to get them going. The second minute of the game saw one Soviet player grip his Hungarian opponent in a hammer lock, whereupon he was excluded, to a hail of cat calls. This set things up nicely. Early in the second half, with the Hungarians leading 2-0, Boris Markarov delivered a haymaker punch to the eye of Hungary's Belvari. All hell broke loose; the pool was engulfed in fighting and the ball all but forgotten. In the final minutes of the game, a Russian hit Hungarian Ervin Zador so hard that he split his brow, opening a wound that bled profusely into the water. The crowd spilled out of the stands and on to the tiles around the pool, screaming at the Soviets and forcing the police to intervene.

Hungary held on to win 4-0. Afterwards Zador made clear what had been at stake: 'We felt we were playing not just for ourselves but for our whole country.' Several members of the Hungarian team defected and stayed in Australia.

ERVIN ZADOR AFTER THAT PUNCH

HELLO BOYS! THE SINGAPOREAN GOVERNMENT WASN'T BEST PLEASED WITH THIS SARTORIAL COCK-UP

There is fun to be had, too, for fashion spotters. At the 2010 Asian Games, Singapore's male players were sharply criticised by their government for their undignified swim suits. Designed by the team themselves, the trunks, like the national flag, were red with five white stars and a white crescent. Unintentionally or not, the crescent was positioned directly over the players' groins.

WEIGHTLIFTING

28 JULY–7 AUGUST 2012

EXCEL ARENA, LONDON

Athletes: 260 | **Golds up for grabs:** 15

OLYMPIC PRESENCE

1896, 1904, 1920–PRESENT

OLYMPIC FORMAT

ATHLETES IN ALL WEIGHT CATEGORIES PERFORM TWO LIFTS: the snatch, in which they raise the bar over their heads in one movement, and the clean-and-jerk, in which they do it in two. The maximum weights a competitor lifts in each are added together to give his or her total.

CURRENT CONTENDERS:

GREECE, TURKEY, RUSSIA, BULGARIA AND CHINA ARE THE leading nations in men's weightlifting. Asian lifters, Chinese in particular, are likely to dominate the women's competition.

PAST CHAMPIONS:

USSR: 39 | CHINA: 24 | USA: 16 | BULGARIA: 12

WHY WATCH WEIGHTLIFTING?

IF THE 100 METRES IS THE PUREST TEST OF THE *CITIUS* ('faster') portion of the Olympic motto, and the high jump and pole vault of the *altius* ('higher'), the *fortius* ('stronger') bit unquestionably belongs to Weightlifting. The sport provides some of the best theatre at the Games. It may have a drug record to rival the Tour de France but there are few Olympic sights as exhilarating

FREDERICK WINTERS, SILVER
MEDALLIST IN THE ALL-ROUND
DUMBBELL EVENT, ST LOUIS 1904

as an athlete psyching himself up to an almost unbearable pitch before hoisting three times his body weight over his head.

The mechanics of the sport favour short, squat athletes who don't have to hoist the weight as far as their longer-limbed peers. The ultimate example was JOE DI PIETRO of the USA, who won bantamweight gold in 1948. Standing just 4ft 10in, he had arms so short he could barely raise the bar above his head.

Aside from the need for SHORT ARMS and BRUTE STRENGTH, the sport is intensely PSYCHOLOGI-CAL: if a lifter doesn't believe they can lift a weight, they haven't a chance. Conversely, if they convince themselves that they can, they may well prove correct. Meanwhile, the fact that competitors can only attempt THREE LIFTS in each discipline allows them to play fearsome mind games with their opponents. The most common is to select an intimidating STARTING WEIGHT. Of course this policy can backfire – it isn't un-heard of for a weightlifter to make the initial bar so heavy that they fail to register a single lift.

THE STORY OF WEIGHTLIFTING

HUMANS HAVE DOUBTLESS BEEN COMPARING STRENGTH BY lifting heavy objects since we developed opposable thumbs. The earliest historical record of the practice, however, is a mural of men exercising with weights (possibly sacks of sand) in the ANCIENT EGYPTIAN tomb of the Beni Hassan, c. 3500BC. Weightlifting was an important aspect of military training in several parts of the ancient world, notably in CHINA, where two distinct forms of contest evolved during the first millennium BC. The first was QIAO GUAN, which involved grabbing one end of a heavy door bar and lifting it with one hand. Popular among court warriors, by the Tang Dynasty (618–907AD) it had become part of the examination for admission to the army, with the door bar replaced by tailor-made weights. The other format, KANG DING, entailed the lifting of massive two-handled cooking pots or *dings*. During the Han Dynasty (206BC–220AD), Kang Ding developed into a fully fledged professional sport.

Weightlifting was also big in ANCIENT GREECE, both as a conditioning activity for soldiers and as a demonstration of machismo. A red sandstone block weighing 143kg displayed at the archaeological museum at OLYMPIA bears the inscription 'Bybon son of Phola lifted me over his head with one hand'. Meanwhile, Bybon's contemporary Milo of Croton, the sixth-century BC superman who we will meet again in the Wrestling chapter, is the first lifter recorded as using a progressive system of resistance training. He acquired a male calf, lifted it every day and continued to do so until it had grown into a bull. When he could no longer shift it, he ate it.

The ROMANS inherited the Greeks' penchant for weightlifting but during the Dark and Middle Ages the focus of activity shifted to the CELTIC and SCANDINAVIAN fringes of Europe. Here the sport took the form of elemental battles between man and nature in the shape of enormous rocks. To get work on a fishing vessel in Iceland, a candidate had to be able to hoist a 104kg boulder called a *hálfsterkur* ('half strength') onto a hip-height ledge. The full strength version *(fullsterkur)* weighed 155kg. The SCOTS also used LIFTING STONES as male initiation devices. Known as *clach cuid fir* ('manhood stones'), they included such legendary lumps of mineral as the McGlashen Stones and the Blue Stones of Old Dailly.

Weightlifting in its modern form grew out of a mania for all things classical that swept through Europe and the USA during the eighteenth and nineteenth centuries. One aspect of this was a renewed interest in physical training, which led aristocratic young men to join GYMNASIUMS and universities to add PE to their curricula. The phenomenon that really glamorised weightlifting, however, was the CIRCUS STRONGMAN. People on both sides of the

Atlantic flocked to watch big moustachioed men break chains, lift horses and pick up cannons.

One of the most influential members of this colourful gang was the German LOUIS ATTILA, born Ludwig Durlacher in 1844. Following a spell in partnership with Valerie the Female Gladiator, he introduced all kinds of innovations to weightlifting, including the invention of the SHOT-LOADED GLOBE BARBELL. This device, which allowed the weight of a single piece of equipment to be varied precisely, spelled the end for the old fashioned dumbbell (originally a shaft with a pair of clapperless bells at either end). People – including crowned heads of state – began to solicit Attila's advice on strength and fitness training, and around 1887 he opened his first gym in Brussels. After running a similar institution in London, in 1893 he founded the wildly successful Attila's Athletic Studio and School of Physical Culture in New York. Among his students were the boxing champion James J. Corbett and, astonishingly for the era, several women.

Other developments that helped transform weightlifting from sideshow attraction to sport included the DISC LOADING SYSTEM of weights, introduced by M. M. PELLETIER MONNIER in the 1880s, and, in the 1920s, CHARLES RIGOULOT's pioneering use of a LONG, SPRINGY BAR, which he employed to break the clean-and-jerk world record. Meanwhile, training became increasingly scientific. In 1906, the nine-stone W. A. PULLUM founded the first weightlifting school that emphasised technique over strength. Six years later, he vindicated his methods by becoming the first Briton to lift twice his bodyweight.

VASILY 'THE BODY' ALEXEYEV IN ACTION IN MOSCOW IN 1980

The final pieces in the jigsaw were the establishment in 1920 of a global governing body for the sport, the INTERNATIONAL WEIGHT-LIFTING FEDERATION, and the emergence of competitions for women. The first women's event was held in the USA in 1947.

GAME ON: WEIGHTLIFTING BASICS

FORMAT

MEN COMPETE IN EIGHT BODYWEIGHT CATEGORIES (56KG, 62KG, 69kg, 77kg, 85kg, 94kg, 105kg, 105kg+) and women in seven (48kg, 53kg, 58kg, 63kg, 69kg, 75kg, 75kg+). 156 men and 104 women will take part in the weightlifting competitions in London. No nation may enter more than ten individuals in total or more than two in any one event.

RULES

COMPETITORS ARE REQUIRED TO REGISTER SUCCESSFUL LIFTS in both the SNATCH and the CLEAN-AND-JERK, which take place in that order. A maximum of THREE ATTEMPTS is allowed in each discipline, whether the lifts are successful or not. After being called to the platform, a competitor has one minute to commence their lift or two if they made the previous lift in the competition themselves. If they succeed in lifting a weight, it must be increased by at least 1kg for their next attempt (though they are usually increased in multiples of 2.5kg).

For a lift to be declared valid it must be performed in the CORRECT NUMBER OF MOVEMENTS – one in the snatch, two in the clean-and-jerk. Once the weight is above the head, the elbows must be locked, the legs brought together and the competitor must be in complete control for long enough for at least two of the three judges to register a GOOD LIFT.

They do this by pressing buttons which illuminate WHITE LIGHTS. NO-LIFTS are signalled by RED LIGHTS. A jury is on hand to vet the judges' decisions. If a lifter DROPS THE BAR before lowering it to waist height, the lift is technically invalid. If two competitors

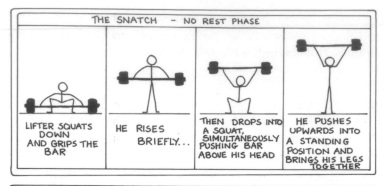

lift the SAME TOTAL WEIGHT during the competition, the one with the lower bodyweight is placed higher in the rankings.

TECHNIQUE

THE STANDARD WAY OF GRIPPING THE BAR IS KNOWN AS THE HOOK. The thumb is wrapped around the bar and the first and second fingers are placed tightly over it. The SNATCH is the more difficult of the two disciplines as the lifter must judge precisely when to position their body under the rising bar for the decisive upwards push. Too early and the bar will come down on to their chest. Too late and it will fall behind, quite possibly dislocating the lifter's shoulders in the process.

Lifters generally place their hands less far apart on the bar for the CLEAN-AND-JERK than for the snatch. Having completed the first movement (bringing the bar to shoulder height), the lifter drops into a squat position before simultaneously straightening the legs and powering upwards with their arms.

EQUIPMENT

LIFTING TAKES PLACE ON A 4X4M WOODEN PLATFORM COATED with a non-slip surface. The DISC WEIGHTS, which are fastened in place with a 2.5kg collar at each end, are colour-coded from black (2.5kg) to red (25kg).

Competitors wear one-piece LEOTARDS, with or without T-shirts underneath. They are allowed to wear SUPPORT BELTS, GLOVES, KNEE BANDAGES and CAPS. Lifters are allowed to CHALK THEIR HANDS to improve their grips and tend to do so copiously. They are also permitted to use ammonium carbonate SMELLING SALTS to render themselves suitably pugnacious.

THE FINER POINTS

PSYCHING UP

ONE OF THE PLEASURES OF WATCHING THE SPORT IS TRYING to guess whether or not a lifter is going to succeed at a particular weight on the basis of their conduct immediately prior to the attempt. Pay attention to the way a lifter chalks their hands and to their facial expressions and body language. Do they betray nervousness or suggest self-belief? And does the vibe change during the maximum of sixty seconds they have between mounting the platform and attempting the lift?

Some lifters have highly distinctive ways of getting themselves into the zone. The Iranian Kurd MOHAMMAD NASIRI, who won the bantamweight gold in Mexico, used to pray for thirty seconds, then turn to the bar and shout 'Ya Ali!' in homage to the first leader of the Shiites. Japan's TAKASHI ICHIBA, who came fourth in the same class in 1984, performed a back-flip before each attempt. Other lifters more or less beat themselves up to get their adrenaline pumping.

················ **ELBOWS, EXPLOSIONS AND EXECUTION** ················

WHEN THE MOMENT OF TRUTH COMES, TRY TO GAUGE THE EXPLOSIVITY of the lift or the lack of it. This is a pretty good guide to how much the lifter may have left in the tank. SPEED OF EXECUTION is essential to successful weightlifting as it minimises the expenditure of energy. Watch out for whether the elbows lock and the legs come together in the last phase of the lift. If they don't, it ought to be declared invalid. Allow yourself to get swept up by the emotions of the crowd. Weightlifting fans are a vocal lot so don't be shy about yelling at the telly.

THE INSIDE DOPE ON WEIGHTLIFTING

O f the ninety-nine humans (there have also been a few horses) busted for doping offences at the Games between 1968 and 2008, thirty-eight were weightlifters, the first two testing positive in 1972.

The use of performance-enhancing substances in sport is as old as sport. Athletes at the ancient Games used to pep themselves up by eating lizard meat, nineteenth-century bike-racers sometimes ingested nitroglycerine to dilate their blood vessels, and the winner of the 1904 marathon was boosted by a shot of strychnine and a glass of brandy. But weightlifting, being all about explosiveness and muscle development – attributes which the illicit administration of drugs can profoundly improve – has been particularly vulnerable to interference from the laboratories.

The key figure in the evolution of doping in the modern era was the American DR JOHN ZIEGLER. In 1954, he travelled to Vienna with the US weightlifting team, where he fell into conversation with a Soviet trainer. Lubricated by a few drinks, the Russian revealed that 'his boys' had been routinely receiving TESTOSTERONE injections since the mid-1940s. When Ziegler got back to the States, he dosed himself, the great Bob Hoffman and two lifters with the hormone but was unhappy with the side effects.

His dissatisfaction led him to work with the Ciba Pharmaceutical Group to develop an oral ANABOLIC STEROID (a class of drugs that mimic the effects of testosterone) called Dianabol, which hit the market in 1960. Ziegler administered the drug to the entire US weightlifting squad at that year's Olympics – entirely legally, it should be pointed out, as the IOC didn't formally ban performance-enhancing drugs until 1967 – but they were still resoundingly beaten by the Soviets. When Ziegler discovered that some of his lifters had damaged their livers by taking twenty times the recommended dose of Dianabol, he abandoned his experiments. 'I lost interest in fooling with IQs of that calibre,' he would later state. But the damage had been done.

Lowlights in the subsequent history of drug abuse and Olympic weightlifting have included the disqualification of the Bulgarian IZABELA DRAGNEVA shortly after winning the first ever women's weightlifting gold in Sydney, eleven out of thirteen members of the GREEK SQUAD testing positive ahead of Beijing, and the withdrawal of the entire BULGARIAN TEAM from the same Games after similarly dismal test results in the run-in.

The doping record has naturally been acutely embarrassing for the IWF and the IOC. Unfortunately, there is only so much they can do about it. They can and have devised ever more sophisticated testing procedures but this has only led to an arms race with the shady men in white-coats, who have simply developed cleverer ways of avoiding detection. In recent years, the authorities have also twice given the sport a clean slate by changing the weight divisions (ahead of the Atlanta and Sydney Games), thus rendering all previous records obsolete. But they are up against a classic herd mentality, with lifters not unreasonably thinking that if they don't use drugs they'll lose out to those who do.

WEIGHTLIFTING GOES TO THE OLYMPICS

WEIGHTLIFTING FEATURED IN THE INAUGURAL MODERN Games in Athens but it was a very different animal from the contemporary sport. For one thing, it was deemed a track and field event. For another, there were no weight classes (which remained the case until ANTWERP 1920). Instead, there were just two events, open to all. LAUNCESTON ELLIOT of Great Britain took gold in the ONE-HAND LIFT but had to settle for silver in the TWO-HAND-ED equivalent. He lifted the same weight (111.5kg) as the winner, Denmark's VIGGO JENSEN, but was adjudged to have done so with less style. Clearly a sporting polymath, Jensen also won a couple of shooting medals and came fourth in the rope climb.

The sport was absent from the 1900 Games but reappeared at ST LOUIS. Again there were just two events, this time the two-hand lift and an ALL ROUND DUMBBELL CONTEST, which featured a bewildering nine different lifts. The fields were rather thin – a mere five athletes took part, four of whom won medals – which may explain why there was no weightlifting at the London or Stockholm Games of 1908 and 1912. But the sport made a comeback at ANTWERP in 1920 and has remained on the Olympic menu ever since.

There was still some tinkering around with the formula to be done, however. One-handed lifts continued to feature until LOS ANGELES 1932, when the competition switched to a THREE-LIFT FORMAT (snatch, clean-and-jerk and press, which involved hoisting the bar to the shoulders and waiting two seconds before raising it above the head with arm power alone), which endured until the press was dropped in 1972.

During the Olympic era, different regions of the world have dominated the sport in turn. If the 1920s belonged to ITALY, FRANCE and CENTRAL EUROPE, the 1930s and 1940s were bossed by EGYPT and the USA. A large part of America's success during this period can be attributed to BOB HOFFMAN of York, Pennsylvania, who recruited promising European immigrants to work in his oil burner business and trained them up in his gym. The dramatic decline of the USA's weightlifting fortunes after the Second World War coincided with the ascendancy of the SOVIET BLOC, whose lifters claimed the lion's share of Olympic medals between 1950 and the fall of the Berlin Wall. Latterly, things have come nicely full circle, with the nations with the longest weightlifting pedigree – CHINA plus GREECE, TURKEY and BULGARIA – again ruling the roost.

SULEYMANOGLU: THE POCKET HERCULES

The featherweight Naim Suleymanoglu is not just the greatest Olympic weightlifter of all time – on a pound for pound basis, he is one of the strongest men ever to have lived. Heaven knows what he would have achieved if he hadn't puffed his way through fifty fags a day, 'to find my inner peace,' as he memorably put it.

THE INCOMPARABLE NAIM SULEYMANOGLU ABOUT TO LIFT THE EQUIVALENT
OF THREE-PLUS CHERYL COLES OVER HIS HEAD

Born in 1967 in Pitchar, Bulgaria, to a diminutive family of ethnic Turks (his father, a zinc miner, was 5ft tall, his mother, a hothouse worker, 4ft 7in), Suleimanov – as he was originally called – was prodigiously strong from an early age. In his first international competition at the age of fourteen, he came within 2.5kg of the adult world record for combined lifts. The following year he went one better, breaking the first of 46 WORLD RECORDS he would claim during his career. He would have been a shoo-in for gold at the LA Olympics had Bulgaria not joined the Eastern Bloc's boycott.

The mid-1980s was a turbulent period for Bulgaria's ethnic Turks, with mosques forcibly closed and the speaking of Turkish banned. Suleimanov was tempted to defect while at a training camp in Melbourne in 1985 but told his would-be helpers that he would only do so if the government in Sofia tried to force him to take a non-Islamic name. As soon as he got back to Bulgaria, his passport was confiscated and reissued in the name of NAUM SHALAMANOV.

When he returned to Melbourne for the 1986 World Championship, he slipped his minders at a formal banquet, went to the Turkish consulate and asked for asylum. A few days later he was flown to Turkey in President Turgut Ozal's private jet; he kissed the tarmac on arrival, securing his status as a national hero. When the Bulgarian government later permitted over 300,000 ethnic Turks to leave the country as a direct result of the publicity generated by Suleimanov's defection, he ascended to near deity.

Olympic rules stipulated that an athlete who changed nationality had to wait three years before competing in international tournaments, unless he obtained a waiver from his old nation. The Turkish government happily coughed up $1m to the Bulgarians to obtain such a document in time for Suleymanoglu (as he re-spelled his name in Turkish style) to compete in the Seoul Games. It was money well spent. The little man cruised to gold, breaking world records in two of his three lifts in each discipline. His best lifts in both the snatch and the clean-and-jerk exceeded those racked up by Paul Anderson in winning the super-heavyweight gold in Melbourne 32 years earlier. Anderson had tipped the scales at 303 pounds; Suleymanoglu weighed a mere 132.

Having initially intended to retire after the 1988 Games, Suleymanoglu was persuaded to think again by a crowd of a million which assembled at Ankara airport to greet him on his return. He went on to win featherweight golds at Barcelona and Atlanta.

WRESTLING

5-12 AUGUS 2012

EXCEL ARENA

Athletes: 344 | Golds up for grabs: 18

-------------------------- **OLYMPIC PRESENCE** --------------------------

MEN 1896 AND 1904–PRESENT; WOMEN SINCE 2004.

-------------------------- **OLYMPIC FORMAT** --------------------------

TWO STYLES: GRECO-ROMAN, IN WHICH HOLDS BENEATH the waist are forbidden, and FREESTYLE, in which they are allowed. WOMEN only compete in freestyle at the Olympics.

-------------------------- **CURRENT CONTENDERS:** --------------------------

THE TOP-RANKED NATIONS ARE RUSSIA, FRANCE, ARMENIA and CUBA in the Greco-Roman events; AZERBAIJAN, IRAN, RUSSIA and KAZAKHSTAN in the men's freestyle; and CHINA, CANADA, JAPAN and UKRAINE in the women's freestyle.

-------------------------- **PAST CHAMPIONS:** --------------------------

USA: 46 | USSR: 28 | JAPAN: 19 | TURKEY: 16

WHY WATCH WRESTLING?

SEOUL, 1988. WITH THIRTY SECONDS TO GO IN THE FINAL OF the Greco-Roman super-heavyweight competition, RANGEL GEROVSKI, a twenty-stone Bulgarian, has a seemingly unassailable three-point lead over his Russian opponent, ALEKSANDR KARELIN. Suddenly, the giant Siberian pulls Gerovski over his knee; then, without releasing his grip, he hoists himself to his feet while turning his adversary upside down, flings himself backwards, twisting as he falls, and slams the Bulgarian shoulders-first on to the ground. Gold is secured in an instant. Welcome to Olympic wrestling.

Olympic wrestling may come across as a somewhat colourless affair to the unenlightened, particularly those brought up on the slapstick theatre of WWE or Mexican *Lucha Libre*. A bout, it must be admitted, can look rather like two blokes just rolling around in an undignified manner. But it only appears that way because the competitors are so good at neutralising each other. Put a body builder on the mat and he'd be flying out of the ring in seconds.

Wrestling may not be the most aesthetically pleasing event at the Games but it is certainly among the most primal, as befits what is perhaps the most ancient sport of all. The high percentage of flesh-to-flesh contact ensures that the strength and guile of the protagonists are tested in the most direct way possible. And the nations which dominate the sport make a refreshing change from the usual suspects: wrestling is huge in Central and Western Asia, and countries ending in '-STAN' regularly feature in the medal tables.

The Story of Wrestling

Variations of wrestling are found among the Inuit, the Maori and pretty much everyone in between, a universality that suggests that the sport has a deep place in the human psyche.

The importance of wrestling in prehistoric times is indicated by its presence in the mythologies of several cultures. In the book of Genesis, Jacob wrestles a mysterious stranger in an all-night bout which ends only when the adversary touches 'the hollow' of Jacob's thigh, wrenching his hip out of joint. (This is clearly seen by the author(s) as foul play, suggesting that the contest was Greco-Roman in essence.)

According to Shinto legend, divine ownership of the Japanese archipelago was decided by the victory of the thunder god Take-mikazuchi in a wrestling contest on a beach in Izumo (see Judo chapter). And in Greek myth, Zeus took on the old Titan deities with his fellow Olympian gods and out-grappled his father Kronos for possession of the Universe.

BAS RELIEF OF ANCIENT GREEK WRESTLING

By the time the first city-based empires were established, wrestling had developed into a formalised sport. SUMERIAN wall carvings from 3000BC depict refereed contests accompanied by music. The EGYPTIANS, for their part, elevated the sport into a science. Of the six HOLDS depicted in the tomb of Ptahhotep (c. 2300BC), five are still used by Olympic athletes.

Wrestling appears to have made its OLYMPIC DEBUT in 708BC, and it remained an integral part of the ancient Games for the remainder of their existence, both in its own right and as part of the not-at-all-modern pentathlon.

The ancient Greeks had two main styles of wrestling: KALO PALE (ground wrestling), somewhat reminiscent of modern FREE-STYLE, in which a bout was ended by one participant's submission; and ORTHIA PALE (upright wrestling), which appears to have been the dominant form and was closer to modern GRECO-ROMAN wrestling. It was conducted in a standing position and consisted of five rounds, each ending when one of the contestants was thrown to the floor. There were no time limits and no separate weight divisions. The naked participants wrestled on bare earth, which could become a sea of mud in wet weather. They arrived in the arena coated with olive oil (rather like modern Turkish oil wrestlers) and heavily dusted with powder.

By the Middle Ages, there were hundreds of folk wrestling styles in existence, ranging from Icelandic GLIMA, in which contestants wear special leather harnesses to provide gripping points, to formats such as CUMBERLAND WRESTLING, in which the action commences with the combatants locked in a bear hug.

During the late nineteenth century, two forms of wrestling evolved into internationally recognised professional sports. The first, known as FLAT HAND or FRENCH CLASSICAL WRESTLING, in which holds beneath the waist were banned, had been developed during the 1840s by a former Napoleonic soldier named JEAN BROYASSE (or 'Exbroyat' as he styled himself, as a professional strongman). By the end of the century, the style had become extremely popular in France, Italy and the Austro-Hungarian and Russian empires.

In the English-speaking world, however, the dominant wrestling style was CATCH-AS-CATCH-CAN, in which, as the name implies, competitors were allowed to perform holds with and to almost any part of the body. Catch-as-catch-can was a well-established fairground attraction in the UK and USA, and was also adopted by universities throughout America.

By the eve of the sport's Olympic debut, flat-handed wrestling had evolved into the GRECO-ROMAN discipline and catch-as-catch-can into FREESTYLE.

GAME ON: WRESTLING BASICS

IN GRECO-ROMAN WRESTLING IT IS FORBIDDEN TO GRASP the opponent below the beltline or to use the legs 'actively' to perform any action. In FREESTYLE the first rule doesn't apply, and legs can be used aggressively, though it is not permitted to lock them scissor-style around an opponent's head, neck or body. That aside, the rules are broadly the same for each form.

Freestyle is the more dynamic form of wrestling, with the competitors spending a lot of time circling each other looking for an opportunity to dive in. Greco-Roman wrestling is more obviously a matter of brute strength, but in both styles the maintenance of balance is essential: at times the action may appear to have frozen, but the wrestlers are always probing for small losses of equilibrium.

Wrestlers are NOT ALLOWED to talk during a bout. Neither may they pull each other's hair, pinch, bite, head-butt, attack genitals, hold an opponent's singlet, grab the sole of his foot or generally do anything 'with the intention of torturing the opponent', as the rule book puts it. Double Nelsons are strictly forbidden in women's wrestling.

THE MAT

THE ACTION TAKES PLACE ON A CIRCULAR MAT 9M IN DIAMeter. The outer 1m of this area is known as the RED ZONE. Its function is to alert the wrestlers and officials that the action has moved to the margin of the legitimate wrestling area.

The region beyond the red zone is a 1.5m strip called the PROTECTION AREA. If a wrestler places a foot in the protection area, the bout is stopped, a point is awarded to his opponent and wrestling resumes in the centre of the mat.

In the middle of the central wrestling area is the CENTRAL CIRCLE, which is 1m in diameter. Aside from forming the area of the mat where wrestling commences or recommences after a break, the central circle determines how the wrestlers are to disport themselves during curious set pieces called ORDERED HOLDS, of which more later.

DRESS CODE

EACH MALE COMPETITOR MUST BE CLOSELY SHAVEN OR HAVE a BEARD of several months' growth. Moustaches, which are very popular in some of the sport's dominant nations, are not mentioned in the official rules. Competitors wear either BLUE OR RED SINGLETS made of nylon or Lycra. The use of light, metal-free KNEE PADS is permitted. Women are not allowed to wear under-wired bras. Wrestlers are not permitted to apply greasy or sticky substances to their bodies. They must have CLOTH HANDKERCHIEFS with them at all times, to wipe away any escaped bodily fluids. Fingernails must be cut very short.

THE OFFICIALS

EACH BOUT IS OFFICIATED BY A REFEREE, A MAT CHAIRMAN and a JUDGE. The referee controls the action on the mat, using voice and whistle, and indicates the scoring of points with hand signals. The judge keeps tally of the score and acts as a second pair of eyes, alerting the ref if he feels he has missed something important. The mat chairman acts as arbiter in the event of a disagreement between referee and judge, and keeps time.

···················· STRUCTURE OF THE TOURNAMENT ····················

THERE ARE SEVEN WEIGHT CLASSES, RANGING FROM 50KG upwards. Rather marvellously, there is now a MAXIMUM WEIGHT LIMIT for Olympic wrestlers of 120kg.

The competition for each weight division takes place on a SINGLE DAY. The first part of the contest is a series of knock-out rounds, delivering two finalists. The second is contested by everyone who was beaten by either of the finalists earlier in the competition. They are divided into two groups according to which finalist they lost to. Each group then has a mini-tournament, with the winners claiming the two bronze medals awarded.

···················· HOW A BOUT IS WON ····················

THE RULES AND SCORING SYSTEMS OF OLYMPIC WRESTLING change with infuriating frequency, but a grasp of the following principles should allow you to appreciate what is going on.

If one wrestler manages to PIN THE OTHER'S SHOULDERS to the ground long enough for the referee to determine that they are indeed pinned, a FALL is scored and they win the bout immediately. A wrestler also wins a bout if their opponent is DISQUALIFIED, either through incurring three cautions or, in cases of egregious brutality, through instant dismissal.

In all other cases, a bout is the BEST OF THREE ROUNDS. These can be won in three ways. The first is TECHNICAL SUPERIORITY, in which one wrestler goes so far ahead in a round that they are declared its winner before two minutes have elapsed. The second is simply for a wrestler to SCORE MORE POINTS during its duration than their opponent.

The final way of winning a round, if the scores are level, is to be AWARDED IT. In GRECO-ROMAN ROUNDS, the judges use complex criteria based on cautions, high scoring manoeuvres and so forth. In FREESTYLE, if neither wrestler scores a technical point during the thirty-second round extension, the one who pulled the short straw in the draw for the ordered hold (see p.362–63) is automatically awarded the round.

················· **HOW POINTS ARE SCORED** ·················

THE USUAL WAY TO WIN A ROUND IS THE ACCUMULATION OF POINTS. These can be scored in a variety of ways, which will make more sense once you have grasped the definition of the DANGER POSITION. A wrestler is said to be in this undesirable state when the line of their back or shoulders forms an angle of less than ninety degrees to the mat while they are using their upper body to avoid the indignity of a fall.

That established, here are the chief moves and points:

TAKEDOWN A takedown involves gaining control over an opponent from a neutral position, i.e. when the taker-down is on his feet.

A FIVE-POINT takedown involves a throw of GRAND AMPLITUDE which places the opponent in a direct and immediate danger position.

THREE POINTS are awarded for a grand amplitude throw that does not bring the opponent into a direct and immediate danger position, or for a SHORT AMPLITUDE throw which does. ONE POINT is awarded for a short amplitude takedown which does not put the opponent in the danger position.

REVERSAL A wrestler who gains control over their opponent immediately after being in the reverse position (i.e. in the opponent's control) is awarded ONE POINT.

EXPOSURE A wrestler is said to be exposed when they are in the danger position but not via a throw. TWO POINTS are awarded whenever a wrestler exposes their opponent's back to the mat, whether it is pinned or not. An EXTRA POINT is earned if a wrestler keeps their opponent in an exposed position for five continuous seconds.

PENALTIES If a wrestler takes a time out due to injury, their opponent is awarded ONE POINT unless the injured combatant is bleeding. Infractions such as fleeing the mat, openly refusing contact, using an illegal hold or striking an opponent result in the award of ONE OR TWO POINTS to the other wrestler, depending on the severity of the offence. The guilty party also receives a CAUTION; three strikes and you're out.

OUT-OF-BOUNDS If a wrestler puts a foot in the protection area, the match is stopped and ONE POINT is awarded to their opponent. Wrestling then resumes in the centre of the mat.

THE FINER POINTS

················ **GRECO-ROMAN BOUTS: THE PAR TERRE** ················

IN GRECO-ROMAN WRESTLING, ROUNDS ARE NOMINALLY TWO minutes long, but if one wrestler achieves technical superiority the round ends immediately. The combatants begin each round in a standing position and spend sixty seconds trying to take each other down. Then something rather odd happens: a PAR TERRE session. The wrestler who is behind at this stage – or, if the scores are level, the one who loses the toss of a two-coloured disc – kneels in the centre circle, with his hands on the floor; the other wrestler approaches him from the side, placing one knee on the ground if he

TWO WRESTLERS GRAPPLING AT THE 1936 BERLIN OLYMPICS

so desires, and wraps his arms around his opponent's waist, linking his hands.

The combatants are now said to be in the ORDERED HOLD or CLINCH POSITION. The wrestler on top then executes what is known as an UPSIDE-DOWN BELT HOLD. As the thirty second period unfolds, both wrestlers may get to their feet. At the end of the thirty seconds the wrestlers swap positions, with the one who had the advantage in the first *par terre* session assuming the disadvantaged kneeling position in the second. If the wrestler who began a *par terre* session with the advantage fails to score a technical point during his thirty seconds, his opponent is awarded a technical point.

The usual structure of a Greco-Roman round does not apply if one of the wrestlers is in the DANGER POSITION either at the end of the first minute (in which case both *par terre* sessions are cancelled) or at the end of the first *par terre* session, in which case the second one is cancelled.

·· **FREESTYLE BOUTS** ··

A STANDARD FREESTYLE ROUND IS ALSO TWO MINUTES LONG and ends prematurely if one wrestler achieves technical superiority. If the score is 0-0 after two minutes, the action is extended for up to thirty seconds with the wrestlers in an ORDERED HOLD position, also known as THE CLINCH. Advantage in this situation is determined by the toss of a disc.

The freestyle ordered hold is not the same as the Greco-Roman: the contestant who loses the toss must place one leg in the middle of the centre circle (the leg is determined by his opponent) and the other outside the circle. The wrestler with the ADVANTAGE then grabs the leg inside the circle with both arms, placing his head on the outside of his opponent's thigh. The wrestler with the DISADVANTAGE must place both hands on the shoulders of his adversary. When the referee is happy with this complex arrangement of limbs, he blows his whistle and action commences. The first point scored ends the round and determines its winner. If the wrestler with the advantage fails to score a point, one is awarded to his opponent.

Wrestling Goes to the Olympics

When Baron de Coubertin and his cronies were drawing up the list of events for the first modern Olympics, wrestling was a shoo-in, as it had featured in the ancient Games. The difficulty was deciding which form of the sport to go for.

In the end, the organisers of the Athens Games went for the French version of the sport – now styled Greco-Roman wrestling – partly because of its supposed resemblance to the ancient Olympian version and partly because it had an established World Championship. Unfortunately, as the British and Americans did not recognise the French rules, the top performers were absent from the 1896 Olympics. So too, because of De Coubertin's allergy to professionalism, were most of the big names in European flat hand wrestling. There was one unlimited weight class in the Athens Games, with the gold medal going to the 5ft 4in Carl Schuhmann of Germany, who also distinguished himself by winning three gymnastics golds.

Perhaps as a result of the poor turnout at Athens, wrestling did not feature in the 1900 Games and when it returned at St Louis in 1904, it was in the American-friendly freestyle format. US athletes won golds in all seven weight divisions.

1908 was the first year in which both disciplines were featured at the Olympics, but all the wrestling events at Stockholm in 1912 were Greco-Roman, with the Finns and Swedes taking the four gold medals awarded. Because bouts could be ended only by a fall, disqualification or withdrawal, they were often lengthy. The most notable contest at Stockholm was an eleven-hour middleweight marathon between the Estonian Max Klein and Finland's Alfred Asikainen. Klein eventually prevailed but was too exhausted to compete in the final, so gold went to Sweden's Claes Johanson by default. The unsatisfactory nature of interminable contests of this kind led to the introduction of time limits and a scoring system at the Paris Games in 1924.

Since Antwerp 1920, every Olympic Games has featured both freestyle and Greco-Roman events. Highlights have included

US WRESTLING TEAM *PAR TERRE* AHEAD OF THE 1932 GAMES

Sweden's IVAR JOHANSSON winning the freestyle middleweight gold in 1932, then shedding 5kg in a sauna to allow him to win the Greco-Roman welterweight title 24 hours later, and the USSR's AVTANDIL KORIDZE whispering something in Bulgarian DIMITRO STOYANOV's ear a minute before the end of a 1960 semi-final that instantly persuaded Stoyanov to roll over and submit to a fall. American JEFF BLATNICK's victory in the Greco-Roman super-heavyweight competition at LA 1984, two years after being diagnosed with Hodgkin's disease and having his appendix and spleen removed, was perhaps the most inspiring story in Olympic wrestling history.

In 2004, Olympic wrestling took the long overdue decision to introduce a WOMEN'S FREESTYLE COMPETITION (female Greco-Roman wrestling has yet to appear). The Central Asian nations have dominated this less, thus far, than the men's events. Of the eight golds contested, JAPAN have won four, CHINA two and the UKRAINE and CANADA one each.

ALEKSANDR KARELIN

The greatest Olympic Greco-Roman wrestler of modern times, Siberian-born ALEKSANDR KARELIN won gold at the 1988 Olympics (with the outrageous takedown described in this chapter's introduction) and then didn't lose another bout until Sydney 2000. Some dubbed him 'The Experiment', hinting that – though Karelin passed any number of doping tests – his awesome record might have had its roots in the laboratory. To his detractors, Karelin had a ready answer: 'I train every day of my life as they have never trained a day in theirs.' A softly spoken man with a penchant for opera, the mighty Karelin once took delivery of a 400lb refrigerator and lugged it up the stairs to his eighth-floor apartment. He has been a member of the Russian parliament since 1999.

THE EXPERIMENT: ALEKSANDR KARELIN HALF WAY THROUGH A GRAND AMPLITUDE THROW AT ATLANTA 96

MEDALS CEREMONIES

THE OFFICIAL OLYMPIC LINE IS THAT IT IS MORE IMPORTANT to participate than to win. This is not a sentiment endorsed by the MEDALS CEREMONIES. The athletes on the podium have worked unbelievably hard to get there and their governments have paid millions of pounds to share in the glory. As a consequence, the Ceremonies are invariably occasions of intense emotion, both for the happy winners and the occasionally sour losers. Viewers may find themselves welling up, too.

MEDAL CEREMONY BASICS

MEDALLISTS MUST BE DRESSED IN OFFICIAL NATIONAL TEAM uniforms and are not allowed to display political affiliations or make statements of any kind during the ceremony. They enter the stage together and then climb on to the podium with the winner on the highest tier in the centre, the silver medallist on their right and the bronze medallist on their left. The MEDALS are awarded in reverse order (bronze first, gold last) by a member of the IOC, accompanied by volunteers from the host city bearing the now obligatory Olympic BOUQUETS. Then the NATIONAL ANTHEM of the winner is played while the flags of all three medallists' nations are raised, with the winner's elevated above the others. The anthems are now pre-recorded.

The MEDALS themselves must be a minimum of 6cm in diameter and 3mm thick. Despite the different denominations, they are all largely made of silver, but the golds have to be coated with at least 6 grams of the metal. The medals for London 2012 are the biggest to date, 85mm in diameter and weighing in at 400g (nearly a pound).

The Medal Ceremony Story

Winners at the ancient Games were presented with olive wreaths harvested by boys with golden sickles. They were then expected to make sacrifices to the gods who had supported them. When the Games revived at Athens 1896, the victors were presented with crowns of Olive branches, certificates of victory and silver medals, while the runners–up got Laurel crowns and bronzes. Third placed athletes got nowt. In keeping with the gentlemanly aura, Olympians received their awards in evening dress, at the closing ceremony rather than after each individual competition.

Things acquired a more familiar shape at London 1908, with the medal ceremonies held on the same days as the competitions and Gold, silver and bronze medals awarded to first, second and third place. It was at LA 1932, however, that many of the features we now associate most closely with the Ceremony were introduced: the three tiered podium, the raising of the national flags of the medallists and the playing of the winners' national anthems.

The average medal ceremony is graced by trembling lips and a great deal of handshaking, but on occasion the script gets altered. The IOC has never quite recovered from the Black power salutes made on the podium by American sprinters Tommie Smith and John Carlos in 1968. Other notable breaches of decorum have included the US basketball team's no-show in 1972, the body builder poses stuck by the USA 4 x 100m gold medallists at Sydney 2000, and Greco-Roman wrestler Ara Abrahamian tearing off his consolation bronze in disgust at Beijing 2008.

There have been heart-warming moments too. At LA 1984, the Yugoslav Anton Josipovic, newly crowned light heavyweight boxing champion, hauled bronze medallist Evander Holyfield up on to the winner's rostrum in acknowledgement that he had only lost his semi-final due to a ludicrous refereeing decision. Even more poignant was the ceremony for the 10m air pistol in Beijing, which ended with Georgia's Nino Salukvadze and Russia's Natalia Paderina embracing and calling for an end to the fighting between their nations.

THE CLOSING CEREMONY

12 AUGUST 2012

OLYMPIC STADIUM

Athletes: All 12,000 are invited but many will have gone home.

OLYMPIC PRESENCE

THE 1896 ATHENS GAMES ENDED WITH A SPLENDID MIX OF marching bands, medals, victory laps and laurels, and with the exception of PARIS 1900 some kind of show has been staged ever since. It acquired something close to its settled form with the introduction of the Olympic flag in 1920.

OLYMPIC FORMAT

THE IOC STIPULATES A PROGRAMME OF SPEECHES, FLAGS AND ANTHEMS, but there is plenty of room for the hosts to indulge in all kinds of artistic interpretation.

CONTENDERS

LONDON IS THE STAR OF THE SHOW BUT, AS IS NOW TRADI-tional, the next Olympic host city, RIO DE JANEIRO, will be given a ten minute slot to do its thing.

WHY WATCH THE CLOSING CEREMONY?

HOW DO YOU BRING THE CURTAIN DOWN ON THE GREATEST show on Earth? After two weeks of intense immersion in sporting competition, tens of thousands of athletes, officials and spectators can't just push off home and put the kettle on. What is needed at this stage is a party. A chance to reflect on what has happened, look forward to what is to come and affirm that we are all good friends really, despite our nations having devoted the preceding fortnight to trying to beat the crap out of each other. Throw in a few solemn rituals and pompous speeches and everyone will be primed to do it again in four years' time.

Armchair viewers can also do with a rite of passage to ease themselves back to normal life. So draw up a chair and watch the show. Share in the feel-good factor as the world's athletes MARCH TOGETHER unsegregated by nationality. Get a foretaste of the flavour of the next Games during the HANDOVER CEREMONY. And keep an eye out for the unexpected. Whether it's a streaker or a visit from a flying saucer, the closing ceremony has a habit of coming up with something memorable.

THE CHINESE PROVIDE LONDON WITH AN EASY ACT TO FOLLOW

CLOSING CEREMONY BASICS

THE OPENING MOMENTS OF THE CLOSING CEREMONY ARE unpredictable. In the past clocks have chimed, stilt walkers have performed, fireworks have gone off and spaceships have landed. For London 2012 – which will be produced, like the opening ceremony, by Danny Boyle – we can probably expect a fanfare of trumpets somewhere in the opening mix, the appearance of mascots and a countdown. 'God Save the Queen' and the Union

Jack could get an early cameo, or could be saved for the handover ceremony later. And there will be music. Probably not the kind of music you will buy later on CD.

THE MARCH OF THE ATHLETES

THE MAIN BUSINESS KICKS OFF WITH A PARADE OF EVERY competing nation's flag and name board. Compared to the opening ceremony this is mercifully brisk. The flag bearers and placard holders will then go and line up somewhere, probably near the OLYMPIC FLAG. Then the athletes will show up in a great unstructured crowd. Note how well policed they are, though Mexico 1968 was memorable for some unscripted sprints by Nigerian athletes who broke out to embrace the crowd.

THE MARATHON MEDALS

EARLIER IN THE DAY THE MEN'S MARATHON WILL HAVE BEEN run, the competitors crossing the finishing line in the Olympic Stadium. Its medal ceremony will feature somewhere in the mix. If you have watched a fraction of the 10,000 hours plus of sporting action over the previous fortnight, this can be your medal ceremony too. Relive those late nights when you caught up on the early rounds of the volleyball. Feel righteous in your endurance of the very real pain of the early rounds of the 50m rifle; pat yourself on the back for those hours you put in watching weightlifting and water polo.

FLAGS AND SPEECHES

NOW TAKE A DEEP BREATH, WE'VE GOT TO GET THROUGH the FLAGS, ANTHEMS and SPEECHES bit. There may well be more fanfares at this point, plus other specially commissioned musical concoctions. Atlanta, for example, took the opportunity to pay tribute to the athletes with a tune called 'Faster Higher Stronger', followed by Gloria Estefan belting out 'Reach'.

Next up is the lowering of the GREEK FLAG and the playing of the GREEK NATIONAL ANTHEM. Then there will be lots of introductions in various languages before LORD COE, chief cheese of the Local Organising Committee, gets his slot. There will be an awful lot of thank yous, possibly hints of relief and a touch of valediction. Finally, the president of the IOC, Jacques Rogge, will say:

> I declare the Games of the Thirtieth Olympiad closed and, in accordance with tradition, I call upon the youth of the world to assemble four years from now in Rio de Janeiro to celebrate the Games of the Thirty-First Olympiad.

This is the president's chance to pass judgement. Rogge's predecessor Juan Antonio Samaranch got himself stuck on an escalator of superlatives, pronouncing every Games he attended, 'the best ever Olympics' – a comment he pointedly withheld from Atlanta 1996. Rogge has made it clear that he will never use this phrase, describing Beijing as just 'truly exceptional'.

THE HANDOVER

SPEECHES DONE, THE NEW HOST NATION'S FLAG WILL BE RAISED and its NATIONAL ANTHEM played: at London 2012, this will be Brazil. Then the Olympic flag comes down, to another round of the Olympic anthem (see The Opening Ceremony, p.12), and London will pass the baton to the representatives of RIO 2016. The floor is now theirs for about ten minutes. At Beijing 2008, the London delegation parked a red double-decker bus at one end of the stadium, out of which emerged Leona Lewis, Jimmy Page and David Beckham to the riff of 'Whole Lotta Love'. The world was suitably underwhelmed. Expect more from the BRAZILIANS at London 2012, including a good dose of scantily clad samba.

LIGHTS OUT!

THE FINAL CEREMONIAL ACT IS THE EXTINGUISHING OF THE Olympic flame. Simple as this task might seem, past producers have managed to make a remarkable business of it. The compulsory programme now complete, the ceremony will move on to the music. Hopefully the athletes will be breaking ranks to dance and the crowd will be out of its seats.

THE CLOSING CEREMONY STORY

THE ANCIENT OLYMPICS CLOSED WITH OATH TAKING, VENER-
ating and feasting. The closing ceremony of the first modern
Olympiad didn't stretch to feasting and was delayed by torren-
tial rain for a day but ATHENS 1896 did sign off with fanfares and
odes, silver medals for the champions and a victory parade for all
the medallists led by Spyridon Louis, winner of the marathon. The
King of Greece (the Danish-born George I) declared the Games
closed and left the stadium to the strains of the Greek national
anthem.

At ANTWERP 1920 the Olympic flag had made its appearance
at the opening ceremony, so symmetry dictated that the Games
ended with its lowering. This ritual, which would become the central feature of the closing ceremony, was given suitable grandeur by
a booming fusillade from the Belgian army's artillery and a cantata
sung by a massed choir. Next time around, at PARIS 1924, they
raised the flags and sung the anthems of France (as current hosts)
and the Netherlands (the next hosts) and handed the Olympic flag
over to the latter. The Greeks, who had wanted to be hosts every
time, had to be satisfied with having their flag raised and anthem
sung at this HANDOVER CEREMONY.

The big full stop to the Games, the EXTINGUISHING OF THE
OLYMPIC FLAME, was introduced in a low-key way in 1928 (when
the flame first appeared). But it was at BERLIN 1936 that lighting
and extinguishing of the Olympic cauldron became fixed and dramatic features of the Games.

The immediate post-war Games were rather low key affairs,
closing, as our man T.S. Eliot would have put it, not with a bang
but a whimper. LONDON 1948 featured music from the Band of
the Guards and a column of boy scouts carrying wooden name
placards. King George VI and Queen Elizabeth sent a representative as they had already quit town for Balmoral and the start of
the grouse shooting season. Most of the athletes had also already
gone home. But at Melbourne 1956 there was a bit more spirit to
the occasion, and the last key element – the athletes entering the
stadium together without national groupings – debuted. It came

about as the result of an anonymous suggestion – by, it turned out, a seventeen-year-old Chinese-Australian, John Ian Wing.

The ceremony in ROME 1960 was illuminated by the crowd simultaneously lighting thousands of paper torches, not a trick likely to get past the fire safety committee at LONDON 2012. The Games then concluded with a giant FIREWORK DISPLAY. Unfortunately, hot sparks descended from the sky and fell on the dry grass of the Monte Marino hill, where thousands of people had gathered to watch the displays. Ten people were injured in the ensuing fires and stampedes.

Controversies continued in the next two closing ceremonies. At MUNICH 1972 a light-hearted concoction of Bavarian kitsch cast an odd note after the earlier assassinations of eleven Israeli athletes. Then at MONTREAL 1976 the organisers got themselves in a dreadful pickle over how to represent Canada's First Nation peoples. The show included the creation of a tepee village in the centre of the stadium, from which Canadian Indians in traditional

MICHAEL LEDUC REVIVES THE ANCIENT GREEK TRADITION OF EXERCISING IN THE NUDE, MONTREAL 76

dress were meant to dispense necklaces and feathered headbands to the athletes and the crowd. Although the intention was to honour Canada's First Nation, the organisers bodged things by recruiting a Montreal troupe, made-up and dressed as native Canadians, to dance to *La Danse Sauvage*. The bare faced cheek of the display was best answered by Michael Leduc, who stripped off in the stands and headed into the arena to cavort amongst the performers. The Mounties let the world rediscover the ancient Olympic love of the naked male body for three minutes before moving in.

The Olympic dance routines had got going, predictably, at MEXICO 68, where a supersized mariachi band arrived in the midst of the athletes to whip up a frenzy. This was all a bit too undignified and worryingly spontaneous for the IOC and the organisers of Munich and Montreal, who tried to keep athlete numbers and spirits down. But at least the Canadians' pseudo-Indian dances were recognition that the Games needed something more upbeat to go out on than sombre rituals, hymns and anthems.

In a clumsy, gargantuan way, MOSCOW 1980 was another step in the right direction. Once the flags and the speeches were done it was show time, albeit in a form calculated to float the boat of the octogenarian politburo of the Soviet Communist Party. The massed bands of various wings of the Soviet military were given a stomping outing, thousands of rhythmic gymnasts whirled their ribbons in formation and giant Russian dolls waddled their way around the field. Then a huge Misha – the Games' ursine mascot with its implausible fixed smile – came to say goodbye, clutching a bunch of balloons. A card stunt from the stands displayed Misha crying, then everyone cried as the balloons pulled the bear away from the sea of tearful Slavic schmaltz and up into the night sky.

The logic of the Cold War demanded that LOS ANGELES 1984 show the communist world how it should be done. Where Moscow had to make do with coloured cardboard squares, LA could hand out 100,000 electric torches for the crowd to light. Then in a live pastiche of every Hollywood alien UFO flick, a flying saucer came to hover above the stadium. At last, we had a proper Olympics party. Indeed a disco, spearheaded by the figure of LIONEL RICHIE.

PARTY, KARAMU, FIESTA, FOREVER ...

Since LA 1984, no Olympic closing ceremony can be complete without a performance from a leading figure or two from the world of popular music, and a playlist that people can dance to. What now seems obvious was once a mystery, and it fell to the king of Californian soul schmooze, Lionel Richie, to show us the way. From the moment he appeared in his blue sequinned track suit and tight white slacks, Lionel oozed class and confidence. As befits the man who brought us 'Easy Like Sunday Morning', Lionel brought laid-back charm and mellow grooves to an occasion previously notable for its tight-arsed aesthetic. A stadium-sized, neon-lit dance floor pulsated around him as he thanked the crowd and sang an Olympic length version of 'All Night Long' – the late-disco classic spiced with salsa rhythms and a horn section of gilded smoothness.

After working the crowd Lionel ascended onto a pulsating multi-coloured Olympic podium while more than 400 break dancers took to the floor. Mummified figures span round on their heads; ladies in red leather miniskirts struck a sequence of robotic poses. Lionel's injunction to the world? 'Party, Karamu, Fiesta, Forever'. The closing ceremony would never be the same again.

BARCELONA 1992 was big on pageantry, planetary balloons and fire dancing. Placido Domingo, Jose Carreras and that well-known Spaniard Sarah Brightman all sang beautifully, while FREDDIE MERCURY provided the Games' best-known theme tune. More hits followed at ATLANTA 1996, which shrugged off its critics (commercial crassness ... and a bomb attack on the Centennial Olympic park that killed two people and injured over 100), as everyone took their cue from President BILL CLINTON. He was smiling like a Cheshire cat as Boyz II Men did their a capella take on the 'Star Spangled Banner', alongside an A-list that included Little Richard, Stevie Wonder, Gloria Estefan, Tito Puente and BB King. To top it all, REVEREND AL GREEN, pastor to the global soul, delivered an epic version of 'Take Me to the River' backed by The Pointer Sisters.

SYDNEY 2000 presented the nation's cultural crown jewels: supermodel Elle McPherson, comedian Paul Hogan (AKA Crocodile

Dundee), golfer Greg Norman and, of course, Kylie Minogue. The set mixed up Kylie's super camp version of 'Dancing Queen' with thumping Oz rock from John Paul Young and INXS, before going out with a sentimental sing-song of 'Waltzing Matilda' by folk legend Slim Dusty.

It is just as well that the Greeks invented satire, for they can hardly blame the rest of us for retrospectively reading the closing ceremony of ATHENS 2004 as a biting commentary on the nation's tragic borrowing binge. The opening music, perhaps addressed to the gods of the derivative and bond markets, was entitled 'May the Dances Last for Ever'. How prescient that the Games were closed by young girl extinguishing the Olympic cauldron with a single breath. Job done, Greece got down to the party with an unrelentingly domestic line up of old chanteuses, melancholy crooners, pop playboys in testosterone overdrive and mass bouzouki madness.

BEIJING 2008 was acrobat-heavy but musically rather light and while no one could accuse the Chinese of skimping, there was no way they could top their own opening ceremony. Still they threw in a gigantic orange human tower, representing the eternal Olympic flame, thousands of drummers, bell dancers and the best of East Asian pop. Beijing let us know in no uncertain terms that China is the rising power of this world, though the pop stars on offer may just have revealed its Achilles heel.

APPENDIX 1:
DISCONTINUED OLYMPIC SPORTS

GETTING INTO THE CLUB IS ONE THING, STAYING THERE IS another. A whole raft of sports have appeared at one or two Olympics and then dropped off the radar. Here's the story of the late-lamented, in order of first appearance.

TUG OF WAR

1900, 1904, 1908, 1912, 1920

THE ABSENCE OF TUG OF WAR SINCE 1920 has deprived the Games of some of sport's juiciest potential match-ups. Imagine the tension surrounding a Cold War contest between the USA and USSR or East and West Germany, or North and South Korea. Alas. it was not to be, and there is no sign of the IOC seeking to reintroduce the sport.

The object of tug of war is to pull the other team six feet forward from its initial position. If this hadn't occurred within five minutes, the team that had forced the other to advance was declared the winner, even if they had only managed to pull them forward an inch. At the Olympics, the number of team members varied from five at the St Louis Games to eight at subsequent tournaments.

Olympic tug of war notched up two notable firsts. In 1900, France's

THE LATE AND MUCH LAMENTED TUG OF WAR, STOCKHOLM 1912

CONSTANTIN HENRIQUEZ DE ZUBIERA became the first black man to compete in the Games. Eight years later, the tournament was the subject of the first Olympic FOOTWEAR CONTROVERSY. The Liverpool police team pulled their US opponents over the line within seconds, leading the US to protest that they had been aided by illegal steel spiked boots. The coppers rebutted the claim, stating that they had been wearing standard issue police footwear. The US team withdrew in disgust, leaving the Scousers to lose to their Scotland Yard colleagues in the final.

CRICKET

1900

CRICKET'S UMBILICAL RELATIONSHIP with the British Empire made it an odd bedfellow for the universalistic Olympic movement. The sport had been scheduled as part of the 1896 Games but no one signed up to play. Cricket made its one and only Olympic appearance in the chaos that was the 1900 Paris Games.

A single twelve-a-side match was held over two days between a side notionally representing GREAT BRITAIN (actually the Devon & Somerset Wanderers CC) and one notionally representing FRANCE (comprising expatriate Brits in Paris). The match was played at the Vincennes velodrome, where the banked cycling track made an unusual boundary marker. The expats were thumped: Great Britain scored 117 and 145 for 5 declared, against France's pitiful 78 and 26 all out.

LACROSSE

1904, 1908

LACROSSE, WHICH IS SIMILAR TO hockey but played with sticks with nets that can be used to catch and throw the ball, has its roots among French colonialists in Montreal in the early nineteenth century. They adapted a family of games played by the indigenous people with sticks that they thought resembled bishops' crooks ('la crosse' is a bishop's crook in French). By the 1880s lacrosse had spread across CANADA and touring teams took the game to BRITAIN and the USA. It would later spread to Australia and New Zealand but failed to penetrate beyond the Anglophone world.

Lacrosse has been on the official Olympic programme twice. In 1904, two Canadian teams played a local team from St Louis. The Shamrocks of Winnipeg – virtually a professional outfit – won the gold medal; the players on the other Canadian squad were all Mohawks. Lacrosse returned to the Olympics as an exhibition sport in 1928, 1932 and 1948 but has not been seen since, although a recent surge in popularity in Asia and Europe may yet lead to a miraculous recall.

CROQUET, ROQUE

1900, 1904

FIRST PLAYED IN IRELAND IN THE 1830s (or, according to another theory, derived from the French game of *paille maille*), CROQUET took off on the manicured lawns of upper-class Britain, not least because men and women could play it together, providing some relief from the stuffy etiquette of the times. Aristocrats and haute-bourgeoisie with big lawns followed suit in France and North America.

According to the official report on the Paris 1900 Games, 'M. André Despres, civil engineer by profession and the legislator of croquet, lavished the most enlightened and devoted care on the tournament. Baron Gourgaud provided him with a sand court built specially for the occasion, not without expense, in a pretty corner of the Cercle du Bois de Boulogne. The best players in Paris competed there.'

Although it was a strictly French affair, the croquet competition did feature the first WOMEN OLYMPIANS in any sport, listed in the press as MME. FILLEAUL BROHY, MLLE. MA-RIE OHNIER and MLLE. DESPRÈS. Unfortunately, the crowds for this landmark event were rather thin. A report stated: 'Spectators were not at all numerous; although I must mention an English lover of the game who made the journey from Nice to Paris ... unless I am very much mistaken, however, this gentleman was the only paying spectator.'

Croquet was back at ST LOUIS in 1904 but in a cut-price US-version called ROQUE, which was played on a hard surface with concrete borders. John Steinbeck described it in *Sweet Thursday*: 'Roque is a complicated kind of croquet, with narrow wickets and short-handled mallets. You play off the sidelines, like billiards. Very complicated, it

is. They say it develops character.' Not surprisingly the only entrants in the competition were American. The game never made it back to the Olympics but it remained popular for another thirty years, boosted during the Depression of the 1930s when large numbers of pitches were built as public works projects. By the 1960s the American game had pretty much disappeared.

RAQUET SPORTS

1900 (PELOTA), 1908 (JEU DE PAUME & RACQUETS)

RACQUET SPORTS HAVE STRUGGLED to make it onto the Olympic roster. Badminton only arrived in 1992; Tennis was absent from 1924 to 1988; while SQUASH has never been played. The minority sports of BASQUE PELOTA, JEU DE PAUME (or REAL TEN-NIS) and RACQUETS all got their one and only shot in 1900–08.

In PELOTA, the high-speed game of the French and Spanish Basque regions, players catch and throw a ball against a wall using curved baskets or similar implements. In real tennis, the predecessor of the lawn version, players strike the ball over a net on an irregular and asymmetrical court, while racquets is a faster, fiercer predecessor of squash, played on a bigger court with a hard ball.

If pelota's appeal has been restricted to a single region, real tennis and racquets have been the preserve of a single class – the upper echelons of Britain, America and (in the case of jeu de paume) France. The RACQUETS competition in 1908 was played among a small group of public school and Oxbridge graduates. The REAL TENNIS competition that year was won by American tycoon JAY GOULD II, grandson of one of the great railroad barons. None of these sports seem likely to return, though pelota was an exhibition sport in 1924, 1968 and 1992.

MOTOR BOATING

1908

THE 1908 MOTOR BOATING COMPETITION was the Olympic movement's only dalliance with motorised sport. It was not a success. Nine races in three classes of boat were planned, each race consisting of five laps of an eight-mile course off Southampton. Because of bad weather, six out of the nine races were cancelled and

speeds in the other three were pitiful, averaging around 20mph. Given the location of the course and the awful weather, virtually no one could see the action anyway.

POLO, BIKE POLO

1900, 1908, 1920, 1924, 1936 (POLO), 1908 (BIKE POLO)

POLO'S ARISTOCRATIC AND MILITARY connections got it into the early Olympics, but the same narrow social base and the cost of moving polo horses around the globe led to its departure after the Second World War. BRITAIN, the early victors, soon had to give way to the sport's new superpower, ARGENTINA. In 1936, in the last polo match to be played at the Olympics, more than 75,000 people saw Argentina win the gold medal by whipping Great Britain 11-0.

BICYCLE POLO WOWING THE BRITISH PUBLIC IN 1908

A rather more democratic sport, BIKE POLO was invented in 1891 by Richard McCready, the owner and editor of *Irish Cycling* magazine, and was played in North America, Europe and the British Isles in the years before the First World War. It made a lone appearance as a demonstration game on grass at the 1908 Olympics when Ireland beat Germany 3-1. It has yet to make an Olympic comeback, though its modern hard court three-a-side form is now recognised by the International Cycling Union and is gaining in popularity.

BASEBALL, SOFTBALL

1992–2008 (BASEBALL), 1996, 2000–08 (SOFTBALL)

BASEBALL AND SOFTBALL HAVE HAD a strange relationship with the Olympic Games. BASEBALL was played no fewer than eight times as a demonstration event before it finally became an official sport in 1992. SOFTBALL followed suit eight years later. But after Beijing both sports were removed from the Olympics.

The reasons behind the expulsions, the first since polo was axed in the 1930s, remain opaque. Certainly there was pressure to trim the size of the Olympic programme, but no sooner were baseball and softball fired than they were replaced by golf and rugby union. By contrast, modern pentathlon, which barely exists outside of the Olympics, was reprieved.

Most likely, the demise of Olympic baseball is due to the professional game's rather casual attitude to drug-taking and (in contrast to basketball) the US professional league's unwillingness to release its leading players mid-season. Consequently US interest in the Olympic competition was slim. CUBA, by contrast, revelled in the event, winning three gold medals in what is its national sport.

The fate of Softball, which was an Olympic sport for women only, was hitched to that of its big ugly brother, though the sport did itself no favours by producing phenomenally one-sided competitions. The US women, three times gold medallists, outscored their opponents 51-1 over three Games.

APPENDIX 2:
THE 26 PREVIOUS OLYMPIC GAMES

THE SUMMER OLYMPICS HAVE COME A LONG WAY SINCE 241 amateur gentlemen sportsmen took to the field in Athens in 1896. Having not just survived but flourished in the two face of two World Wars and a Cold one, they have grown into mighty big beasts ... so big (and corporate) that we're not even allowed to reproduce the Olympic rings, flame or – alas – the strange array of mascots.

ATHENS 1896

NATIONS 14 | COMPETITORS 241
SPORTS 9 | EVENTS 43

On a shoestring budget, BARON DE COUBERTIN mobilised enough good will to realise his dream of re-suscitating the ancient Olympics in modern form. The highlight, at least for the host nation, was local water-carrier SPYRIDON LOUIS winning the marathon.

PARIS 1900

NATIONS 24 | COMPETITORS 997
SPORTS 18 | EVENTS 95

Effectively a sideshow to the simultaneous *Exposition Universelle*, the Paris Olympics was hideously disorganised. Tennis player CHARLOTTE COOPER became the first woman to win an Olympic title. ALVIN KRAENZLEIN (USA) was both hero and villain, winning four athletics events but duping a rival into giving him a clean run at the long jump.

ST LOUIS 1904

NATIONS 12 | COMPETITORS 651
SPORTS 17 | EVENTS 91

The Games were this time tacked on to the World's Fair and, to test the hosts' bizarre racial ideas, featured 'anthropology days' in which ethnic groups working at the Fair competed both in Olympic sports and in disciplines deemed 'primitive' like mud throwing and tree climbing. RAY EWRY (USA) won all the standing jump events (as he had in 1900 and would do again in 1908).

LONDON 1908

NATIONS 22 | COMPETITORS 2008
SPORTS 22 | EVENTS 110

The London Games were originally destined for Rome but the Italians spent the money on a relief fund following an eruption of Mount Vesuvius. Britain rode to the rescue, put on a splendid show and won more golds than the rest of the world put together – a feat it has not come close to approaching since. Italian waiter DORANDO PIETRI, the plucky but disqualified winner of the marathon, became the darling of the home nation.

STOCKHOLM 1912

NATIONS 28 | COMPETITORS 2407
SPORTS 14 | EVENTS 102

The Swedes finally produced a modern Olympics that wasn't a poor relation to a bigger show. At Baron de Coubertin's insistence, they also introduced ARTISTIC COMPETITIONS, which would remain as incongruous counterparts to the sports up until 1952. The good Baron himself, using a pseudonym, won a literature gold medal for a poem entitled 'Ode to Sport'. JIM THORPE (USA) was the star of the sporting show, winning the pentathlon and decathlon.

ANTWERP 1920

NATIONS 29 | COMPETITORS 2627
SPORTS 22 | EVENTS 154

Belgium's pay-off for becoming the First World War's principal battlefield was the 1920 Games. The IOC left it to the hosts to send out invites and, not surprisingly, Germany, Austria, Hungary and Turkey were not on the guest list. The OLYMPIC RINGS, FLAG and ATHLETE'S OATH got their first outings and OSCAR SWAHN won a

shooting gold medal for Sweden at the age of 72.

PARIS 1924

NATIONS 44 | COMPETITORS 3089
SPORTS 17 | EVENTS 126

This was an altogether better effort from the French than 1904. Paris 1924 was the first Games to boast a purpose-built Olympic village, the first broadcast live on radio and the first to feature the Olympic motto. On the sporting front, it belonged to 'Flying Finn' PAAVO NURMI (Finland), who won five middle and long distance running titles.

AMSTERDAM 1928

NATIONS 46 | COMPETITORS 2883
SPORTS 109 | EVENTS 109

The Amsterdam Games saw the arrival of the first Olympic FLAME, the Greeks leading the parade of nations and WOMEN finally allowed to compete in the athletics. A quarter of a million people applied for just 40,000 tickets to see URUGUAY beat Argentina in the FOOTBALL final, and the INDIAN MEN'S HOCKEY TEAM began a winning streak that wouldn't be ended until 1960

LOS ANGELES 1932

NATIONS 37 | COMPETITORS 1332
SPORTS 14 | EVENTS 117

It wasn't easy to get folk to come to LA in the midst of the Great Depression. The number of competitors plummeted but they should have made the trip – the stadiums were beautiful and the weather fabulous. The MEDAL CEREMONY as we know it made its debut and everything was condensed into just over two weeks. LA 1932 was a glimpse of the future. BABE DIDRIKSON (USA) was the belle of the ball – she qualified for all five women's athletic events, winning two golds and a silver.

BERLIN 1936

NATIONS 49 | COMPETITORS 3963
SPORTS 19 | EVENTS 129

When the IOC awarded the 1936 Games to Berlin, they had no idea that they were handing them to the Nazi party. Hitler was lukewarm about the prospect until Olympic administrator Carl Diem convinced him otherwise. Then his regime pulled out all the stops, treating the Games as a powerful propaganda exercise. JESSE OWENS (USA) hadn't read the script. He won the 100m, 200m, long jump and 4 x 100m relay.

LONDON 1948

NATIONS 59 | COMPETITORS 4104
SPORTS 17 | EVENTS 136

The world was in ruins, but the show had to go on. There was no Olympic village but plenty of room in converted schoolrooms and Nissan huts. Athletes were provided with soap but had to bring their own towels. FANNY BLANKERS-KOEN (Netherlands) won golds in the women's 100m, 200m, 80m hurdles and 4 x 100m.

HELSINKI 1952

NATIONS 69 | COMPETITORS 4955
SPORTS 17 | EVENTS 149

The Cold War had turned Hot, but Helsinki was open to all. The SOVIET UNION made its Olympic debut, the GERMANS and JAPANESE returned to the international fold, and the planet seemed to have recovered its sporting poise – more world records were broken at these Games than at any other. The greatest performer was EMILE ZÁTOPEK (Czechoslovakia), who won the 5000m, 10,000m and the marathon at his first attempt at the distance.

MELBOURNE 1956

NATIONS 72 | COMPETITORS 3314
SPORTS 17 | EVENTS 145

At one stage the Australians were so behind schedule that the IOC considered moving the Games, but they got their act together in the end. Referred to as the Friendly Games, Melbourne was nonetheless notable for fierce battles between SOVIET and HUNGARIAN athletes, who were competing against the backdrop of the Hungarian uprising. The Magyars prevailed in the men's water polo and LAZLO PAPP won a third straight boxing gold.

ROME 1960

NATIONS 83 | COMPETITORS 5338
SPORTS 17 | EVENTS 150

Utterly amateur and commercially unadorned, Rome represented a last blast for De Coubertain's vision. But change was in the air, with the first major Olympic doping scandal, and a squabble between Adidas and Puma over whose shoes would be worn by 100m gold medallist ARMIN HARY. The Games threw up two superstars: light heavyweight CASSIUS CLAY (USA), and barefooted marathon runner ABEBE BIKILA (Ethiopia), who became the first black African to win a gold medal.

TOKYO 1964

NATIONS 93 | COMPETITORS 5151
SPORTS 19 | EVENTS 163

Asia's first Olympic Games heralded Japan's post-war economic miracle and its return to the centre of the international community. These were the most expensive Games since Berlin, with the Japanese taking the opportunity to build highways, subways, a trans-Pacific telecom cable and new port facilities. To the delight of the home fans, 'The Witches of the East' won the women's volleyball, while LARYSA LATYNINA (USSR) collected her eighteenth Olympic gymnastics medal.

MEXICO CITY 1968

NATIONS 112 | COMPETITORS 5516
SPORTS 18 | EVENTS 172
MASCOT: PALOMA DE LUZ (DOVE)

The '68 Games were intended to showcase the modernisation of Mexico. It didn't look that way a few weeks before the opening ceremony, when protests were mercilessly repressed in the city streets and dozens of civilians were killed. IOC president Avery Brundage saw no reason to delay

and the Games went ahead. Dozens of world records were broken in the thin air of the capital – BOB BEAMON (USA) smashed the long jump record by more than half a metre. The popular hero was VERA ČÁSLAVSKÁ (Czechoslavakia), who won the Women's all-round gymnastics and snubbed the Soviet anthem.

MUNICH 1972

NATIONS 121 | COMPETITORS 7134
SPORTS 21 | EVENTS 195
MASCOT: WALDI THE DACHSHUND

West Germany went out of its way to ensure the Games were everything Berlin 1936 was not – transparent modern architecture was preferred to imperial bombast and officials were dressed in nursery colours. Tragically, the sport was overshadowed by the murder of 11 ISRAELI ATHLETES by the Palestinian Black September group. MARK SPITZ (USA) swam his way to seven gold medals and OLGA KORBUT (USSR) enchanted the planet in the women's gymnastics.

MONTREAL 1976

NATIONS 92 | COMPETITORS 6084
SPORTS 21 | EVENTS 198
MASCOT: AMIK THE BEAVER

Responding to fears over the costs of staging the Games, Montreal's Mayor Jean Drapeau claimed that 'the Olympics can no more have a deficit than a man can have a baby'. Montreal only cleared its Olympic debts in 2006. The headlines belonged to NADIA COMANECI (Romania), who scored the first perfect 10 in Olympic Gymnastics, then repeated the feat six times.

·········· **MOSCOW 1980** ··········

NATIONS 80 | COMPETITORS 5179
SPORTS 21 | EVENTS 203
MASCOT: MISHA THE BEAR CUB

The Cold War had lingered over every Games since the Soviet Union joined the party in 1952. Here it took centre stage. Moscow put on an extravaganza to demonstrate the sporting and economic power of communism but the intended audience didn't show up, as the USA decided to boycott the event following the Soviet invasion of Afghanistan. 'COVETT' (Sebastian Coe and Steve Ovett) won the men's middle distance titles for Great Britain and TEÓFILO STEVENSON (Cuba) became heavyweight boxing champion for the third time.

········· **LOS ANGELES 1984** ·········

NATIONS 140 | COMPETITORS 6829
SPORTS 21 | EVENTS 221
MASCOT: SAM THE BALD EAGLE

'Anything you can do, I can do better' should have been the theme tune of LA 84. While the communist nations staged a tit-for-tat boycott, La-La land mobilised its corporations and the magic of the movies. This was the first Olympic Games to make a profit, amidst a riot of sponsorship and Venice Beach glamour. CARL LEWIS (USA) secured immortality by repeating Jesse Owens' feat of forty-eight years earlier.

················ **SEOUL 1988** ················

NATIONS 160 | COMPETITORS 8391
Sports 23 | Events 237
MASCOTS: HODORI AND HOSUNI
(TIGER CUBS)

Perhaps the only Games that has fundamentally changed the course of the host nation's history, Seoul '88 was intended to glorify South Korea's economic miracle and authoritarian government. When massive pro democracy protests broke out in 1987, the rulers decided that political reform was better than a blood-stained Olympics. South Korea got the Games and a constitution. GREG LOUGANIS (USA) was one of the heroes, winning two golds after knocking himself out on a diving board. BEN JOHNSON (Canada) was the zero; he won the 100m in world record time, then failed a dope test.

········· **BARCELONA 1992** ·········

NATIONS 169 | COMPETITORS 9356
SPORTS 25 | EVENTS 257
MASCOT: KOBI THE SHEEPDOG

Barcelona's brilliant mix of operatic staging and urban rebranding convinced a hundred city mayors that hosting the Olympics was the way to get their cities redeveloped. The first post-Cold War Games saw a reunited GERMAN team, the return of SOUTH AFRICA, and the arrival a raft of nations that had left the Soviet Union. One of their representatives, VITALY SCHERBO of Belarus, won six out of eight men's gymnastics golds. JAN-OVE WALDNER (Sweden) broke Asia's table tennis monopoly.

ATLANTA 1996

NATIONS 197 | COMPETITORS 10,318
SPORTS 26 | EVENTS 271
MASCOT: IZZY, A CARTOON THING

The centenary Games were brash, commercial and not to everyone's taste. The sport was overshadowed by the bombing of the Centennial Olympic Park, which killed two people and injured over a hundred. IOC president Juan Antonio Samaranch famously declared every Games to have been 'the best ever' but was unable to roll out the cliché to describe Atlanta. The abiding sporting image was MICHAEL JOHNSON (USA) knocking a third of a second off the world 200m record and winning the 400m in his gold Nikes.

SYDNEY 2000

NATIONS 199 | COMPETITORS 10,651
SPORTS 28 | EVENTS 300
MASCOTS: OLLY (KOOKABURRA), SYD (PLATYPUS), MILLIE (ECHIDNA)

The Melbourne Games in 1956 had been a modest hurrah for Anglo-Australianism. Sydney 2000 belonged to the new nation, multicultural and supercharged with enthusiasm. The sporting and social legacies fell a long way short of the organisers' claims, but the Aussies sure knew how to party. Their pin-up girl was CATHY FREEMAN, who lit the Olympic flame then powered to victory in the women's 400m. STEVE REDGRAVE (Great Britian) won a rowing gold for the fifth consecutive Games.

ATHENS 2004

NATIONS 201 | COMPETITORS 10,625
SPORTS 28 | EVENTS 301
MASCOTS: ATHENA AND PHEVOS, PECULIARLY PHALLIC GREEK DOLLS.

These were the Games that broke the bank. Greece spent more per person than any nation before – about US$1500 per head. They threw a great party, but many of the magnificent buildings constructed for the occasion are now not merely empty, but rotting. The biggest surprise of the Games was the ARGENTINIAN MEN'S BASKETBALL team, which beat the supposedly unassailable USA in the semis en route to gold.

BEIJING 2008

NATIONS 204 | COMPETITORS 10,942
SPORTS 28 | EVENTS 302
MASCOTS: A FISH, GIANT PANDA, OLYMPIC FLAME, TIBETAN ANTELOPE AND SWALLOW.

What do you get for forty billon dollars? Answer: the biggest coming out party ever. On the back of the fastest industrial revolution in history, the hosts rebuilt Beijing and put on a gargantuan show that left no one in any doubt that China was back at the centre of world affairs. USAIN BOLT (Jamaica) broke the men's 100m and 200m records, seemingly without breaking sweat, and MICHAEL PHELPS (USA) went one better than Mark Spitz, winning eight golds in the pool.

INDEX

Italic numbers indicate photos;
SMALL CAPS are OLYMPIADS.

A

ABA (Amateur Boxing
  Association) 97, 99
Abrahamian, Ara 368
Abrahams, Harold 60
Acheson, Dean 237
Acosta, Rubén 327
Adams, Neil 217
Addlington, Rebecca 260,
  265
Agrippa, Camillo 151
Ainslie, Ben 249
Alenka, Virgilijus 54
Alexandra, Queen 16, 59
Alexeyev, Vasily *346*
Ali, Muhammad (previously
  Cassius Clay) 14, 95, 103,
  104–5, *104*, 107, *386*
All England Lawn Tennis
  and Croquet Club,
  Wimbledon 310, 314
All Japan Judo Federation
  216
Allen, Kate 322–23
Amateur Swimming Asso-
  ciation 132
American Athletic Union
  38, 278
Americas Cup 241, *241*
AMSTERDAM (1928) 270,
  271, 384;
  athletes' parade 17; boxing
  106; closing ceremony 373;
  gymnastics 187; hockey
  207, 208, 384; Olympic
  flame 17; women's athletics 60–61, *61*
Anderson, Paul 354
animal rights activists 148
ANTWERP (1920) 59, 106,
  146, 158, 187, 207, 244,
  270, 315, 351, 352, 364,
  373, 384;
  closing ceremony 373;
  cycling 127–28; football

168; Olympic logo 17;
  shooting 258, 384
Aquacade 278–79
archery 21–30
  bow parts 27; etiquette 26;
  history 23–24; Olympic
  formats 25; Olympic
  history 28–30; recurve
  bow 27; scoring 25
Argentina
  basketball 92, 388; boxing
  106; football 169; polo 381
Armstrong, Lance 130
Ashford, Evelyn 66
Asian games (2010) 342, *342*
Asikainen, Alfred 364
ATHENS (1896) 9, 16, 38, 47,
  105, *152*, 383
  athletics 58; closing
  ceremony 369, 373;
  cycling 127; gymnastics 186;
  medal ceremonies 368;
  rowing and sailing events
  cancelled 235, 247; swimming 269; weightlifting
  351; wrestling 364
ATHENS (2004) 22, 29, 44,
  49, 51, 55, 56, 57, 72, 92,
  146, *169*, 170, 194, 196,
  201, *248*, 249, 256, 268,
  274, *274*, 283, 306, 315,
  316, 322–23, 365, 388
  athletics 67; closing
  ceremony 377; diving 135;
  equestrianism 148, *148*;
  gymnastics 192; Olympic
  flame 13; opening
  ceremony 20, *20*; parade
  of nations 12, 20; shooting
  258, *259*; spending on the
  Games 388
ATHENS OLYMPIC INTER-
  NATIONAL EXHIBITION
  (1906) 16; athletes' parade
  11–12, 16–17, 19
athletics 31–70
  10 athletic greats 68–70;
  combined events 57;
  history 33–38; hurdling

48–49; jumping 50–52;
  Olympic history 58–67;
  race and athletics performance 42–44; running
  40–42, 44–47; throwing
  53–56; walking 56
ATLANTA (1996) *30*, 44, 45,
  51, 52, 70, 92, 117, 123,
  165, 169, *170*, *182*, 244,
  249, 258, 274, 282, 316,
  351, 354, *366*, 371, 388
  athletics 66; closing
  ceremony *376*; cycling
  130; modern pentathlon
  227–28; Olympic flame 14,
  105; synchronised swim-
  ming 283; volleyball 333
Attila, Louis (born Ludwig
  Durlacher) 346
Attila's Athletic Studio and
  School of Physical Culture,
  New York 346
Auffay (French cyclist) *127*
Austin, Charles 51
Australia
  athletics 67; rowing 238 ;
  swimming 260
Austria
  canoeing 118; sailing 249
Averoff, Georgios 16

B

Bachrach, William 261
backstroke 264
badminton 71–80
  games and matches 77;
  history 73–75; on ice 76;
  Olympics history 79–80;
  rallies 77; shuttlecock
  72–73
Badminton Association 74
Badminton House 74
Baker, Reginald 'Snowy'
  105–6
balance beam 174
Baldini, Ercole 128
Bale, Gareth 167
ball (in gymnastics) 184

BARCELONA (1992) 49, 72, *87*, 129, 169, 192, 210, 225, 297, 316, 354, 382, 387
archery 21–22; athletics 66; basketball 92; canoeing 117; closing ceremony 376; modern pentathlon 227, 228; Olympic anthem 12; Olympic flame 13, 21–22
Barkley, Charles 92
Barna, Viktor 287
Bart Conner Gymnastics Academy 191
baseball 382
basketball 81–92
fouling up 85; history 82–84; moving and dribbling 84–85; no goal hanging, no goaltending 86; Olympic history 89–92; scoring 84; shot clock 86; time in, time out 84
Basque pelota 380
beam 176, 178, *188*, 191
Beamon, Bob 52, 63–64, 386
Bear, Fred 29
Beck, Emil 159
Becker, Boris 316
Beckham, David 167, 372
BEIJING (2008) *41*, 46, 47, 49, 52, 55, 56, 72, *75*, 109, *124*, 131, 148, 161, 180, 183, 192, 201, 211, 220, 239, 245, 249, 251, 260, 263–67, 283, 285, 293, 308, 323, 332, *332*, 351, 382, 388
artistic programme 10, *11*, 20; athletics 67; basketball 92; boxing 93; closing ceremony 372, 377; cycling 130; fireworks 14, 15; medal ceremonies 368; miming 15–16; Olympic anthem 12; shooting 258–59; swimming 273, 274; taekwondo 300–301, *301*
Bekele, Kenenisa *43*, 47
Belcher, Mat 239
Belov, Sasha 90
Belvari, Antol 341
Beresford, Jack 236
Berkeley, Busby 279
Berkhout, Lobke 239
Berkoff, David 'Blast-Off' 264
BERLIN (1936) 89, 106, 196, 208, *362*, 381, 385

athletics 62; canoeing 118; closing ceremony 373; equestrianism 147; football 168; Jesse Owens' defiance 32, 385; Olympic flame 17–18; opening ceremony 18–19; sailing 248; swimming 263, 270, 272
Bethwaite, Julian 245
bike polo 381–82, *381*
Bikila, Abebe 63, 70, 386
Bindra, Abhinav 259
Bird, Larry 92
black athletes
first black African gold medallist 63; first black athlete to win an individual gold 60; first black female African Olympic gold medallist 62, 66
Black Power 64, *64*, 368
Black September 386
Blackheath hockey club, southeast London 203–4
Blankers-Koen, Fanny 62, 69, 104, 385
Blatnick, Jeff 365
Blatter, Sepp 7, 167
blood transfusions 128–29
Blue Stones of Old Dailly 345
Boardman, Chris 129
Bogardus, Captain Adam H. 252
Boiteaux, Jean 272
Boland, John 315
Bolin, Victor 15
Boll, Timo 284
Bolt, Usain 32, 40, 41, *41*, 42, 44, 67, 70, 388
Boltenstern, Gustaf 146
Boron, Katerin 237
Boston Marathon (1963) 70
Bouldorres, Jean 245
boxing 93–108
the Cubans 107–8; history 95–98; Muhammad Ali 104–5; Olympic history 105–7; prize (bare knuckle) fighting 95–97, 98–99; the ring and the seconds 99; safety and equipment 101; scoring 100–101; ways of winning 100; weight divisions 100; women boxers 93, 95, 98–99, *98*

Boyle, Danny 10, 370
Boyz II Men 376
Brabant, Tim 109
Braglia, Alberto 187
Braunschweiger, Alfred 136
Brazil
water polo 340
breaststroke 262–63, *263*
Brightman, Sarah 376
Britain – see Great Britain
British Amateur Swimming Association 262
British National Diving Championships 132
Brix, Hermann 271
Brohy, Filleaul 380
Broughton, Jack 96
Broughton's Rules 96
Brownlee, Alistair 317
Broyasse, Jean ('Exbroyat') 358
Brozov, Valeri 64
Brundage, Avery 386
Bryant, Kobe 92
Budd, Zola 65
Buffalo Bill (William Cody) 252
Buffalo German YMCA 89
Burroughs, Edgar Rice 271
butterfly 263, *266*
Buttrick, Barbara 99
Byun Jong-Il 108

C

Cagney, James 75
Cameroon: football 169
Campriano, Niccolo 250
Canadian Canoe Association 118
canoeing 109–19
the course 115; equipment 113, 114, 117; Eskimo roll 113, 116; history 110–12; Olympic history 118–19; scoring 115–16; slalom canoeing 109, 110, 111, 113, 115–17, *116*, 118, 119; sprint canoeing 109, 110, 111, 113, 114, 118–19
Carlos, John 64, *64*, 368
Carpenter-Phinney, Connie 129
Carreras, Jose 376
Carter, Hamish 323
Carver, Doc 252

Čásalavská, Vera 188–89, *188*, 386
Castiglione, Baldassare 151
Castro, Fidel 286, 306
catch-as-catch-can 348
Centennial Olympic Park, Atlanta bomb attack (1996) 376, 388
Chak de India (Bollywood film) 209
Chalibashvili, Sergei 132
Chambers, John Graham 96
Championnat du Cheval des Armes 141
Champlain, Samuel de 111
Chand, Dhyan 208
Chariots of Fire (film) 60
Charles II, King 240
Chateauvillard, Comte de 152
Chen Zhong 306–7
Chiang Kai Shek 290
Chicago World's Fair (1934) 278
China
  badminton 71, 72, 79, 80; boxing 93, 108; diving 131, 136, 138; gymnastics 191–92; shooting 250; table tennis 284, 288, 289, 291, 296–97; volleyball 332
Choe Hong Hi, General 299, 301–2, *302*
Christie, Linford 66
Chukarin, Viktor 188
Ciba Pharmaceutical Group 350
Cielo Filho, Cesar 260, 265
circus strongmen 345–46
Clarke, Ron 64
Clay, Cassius *see* Ali, Muhammad
clay pigeons 251, 253
Clinton, Bill 376
Closing Ceremony 10, 369–77
  extinguishing the Olympic flame 372, 373; flags and speeches 371–72; the handover 372, 373; history 373–77; marathon medals 371; march of the athletes 371
clubs 184
Coachman, Alice 62
Coe, Lord (Sebastian) 65, 371, 387
Collins, Doug 90

Collins, US Navy Commander John 319
Comaneci, Nadia 179, 182, 189, 190–91, *190*, 386
Conan Doyle, Arthur 59
Conner, Bart 191
Cook, Stephanie 228
Cook, Theodore 157
Cooper, Andrew 238
Cooper, Charlotte Chattie 315, 383
Corbett, James J. 346
Cornu, André 244
Cotswold Games 38
Coubertin, Baron Pierre de 7, 17, 221, 247, 364, 383, 384, 385
Coventry, Kirsty 264
Cowan, Glenn 289–90
Cowes regatta, Isle of Wight 241
Crabbe, Buster 271
Crawford, Joan 75
cricket 379
croquet 379–80
Cuba
  baseball 382; boxing 107–8; judo 219
Cumberland wrestling 357
Curtis, Katherine 278
Cuthbert, Betty 63
cycling 120–30
  BMX 125, 130; elimination race 125; the flying lap 124; history 121–23; individual pursuit 125; individual sprint 123; keirin 124; mountain bike 125, 130; Olympic history 127–30; the omnium 124; the points race 124; road racing 125; the scratch race 125; team pursuit 123–24; team sprint 123; the time trial 125;
Czechoslovakia
  gymnastics 187

D

Daley, John 106
Daly, Tom 131
Dangerous When Wet (film) 279
Daniels, Charles 265, 272
David Pain Birthday Biathlon 318–19

Davidson, Ken 76, *76*
Davies, Barry 210
Davis, Geena 29
Davis Cup 310
Davydova, Yelena 191
de Brujin, Inge 263
de la Hoya, Oscar 103
de Lima, Vanderlei 67
de Riel, Emily 228
decathlon 57
Decker, Mary 65
Dellinger, Bill 66
Delsarte, François 175
Dementieva, Elena 308
Deng Xiaoping 291
Deng Yaping 291, *293*
Denmark
  handball 200, *201*
Despres, André 380
Despres, Ville 380
Deutsche Turnerschaft 174
Devon & Somerset Wanderers CC 379
Dianabol 350, 351
diaulos 35
Dibaba, Tirunesh 47
Dick, Kerr's Ladies 163
Didrikson, Mildred 'Babe' (later Zaharias) 61, 68, *69*, 385
Diem, Carl 17, 18, 385
discontinued Olympic sports 378–82
discus 53–54, *54*, 63
diving 131–38
  basic dives 134–35; history 132–33; Olympic history 136–38; pinwheeling 133; platforms 133; rounds 133; scoring and judging 134; springboards 133
Docherty, Bevan 323
Dod, Lottie 310
Doggett, Thomas 230
Doggett's Coat and Badge Race 230
dolichos 35
Domingo, Placido 376
Dominican Republic
  boxing 93
Douglas, Johnny 106
dove release 14, *14*, 17, 18
Dragneva, Izabela 351
Drais, Baron Karl Friedrich von 121

Drapeau, Jean 386
dressage 140–44, 146
Du Li 251
Du Pietro, Joe 344
dumbbells 344, 346
Dumoulin, Franck 258
Duncan, Isadora 175
Durac, Sarah 'Fanny' 270

E

East Germany see GDR
Edward VII, King 16
Edwards, Jonathan 39
Egerszegi, Krisztina 273
Egypt: handball 201
El Guerrouj, Hicham 67
Elizabeth, Queen, the Queen
    Mother 76, 373
Elliot, Launceston 351
Elliott, Greg 245
Elvstrøm, Paul 248–49
Elvstrøm, Trine 249
Emmons (Kurkova), Katerina,
    251, 258
Emmons, Matthew 258, 259,
    259
Ender, Kornelia 272, 273
English Amateur Athletics
    Association 38
English Canoe Club 111
English Channel, swimming
    the 262, 277
English Football Association
    163, 166
English Ladies Football Asso-
    ciation 163
equestrianism 139–48
    dressage 140–44, 146; event-
    ing 140–44, 146; history
    140–41; Olympic history
    145–48; show jumping 141,
    142–43, 146
Estefan, Gloria 371, 376
eurhythmic system 175
European Championships
    (1975) 190
European Federation of
    Gymnastics 175
European Football Champion-
    ships 161
Evans, H. Roy 296
eventing 140–44, 146
Ewry, Ray (aka 'The Human
    Frog') 50, 58–59, 383

F

Fairbanks, Douglas, Jr 75, 147,
    149–50
Fairhall, Neroli 28
Far Eastern Games (1913) 326
Fédération Internationale de
    Boxe Olympique 97
Fédération Internationale de
    Football Association (FIFA)
    7, 161, 163, 166
Fédération Internationale de
    Gymnastique (FIG) 175,
    176, 179, 180, 182–83
Fédération Internationale
    de Natation (FINA) 267,
    268, 336
Fédération Internationale
    de Volleyball (FIVB) 326,
    327, 333
Federation (now Fed) Cup
    310
Fell, Heather 220
fencing 149–59
    electronic scoring 154; épée
    154, 155, 157; foil 154, 155,
    157; history 150–53; kit and
    injuries 156–57; in modern
    pentathlon 222; Olympic
    history 157–59; penalties
    153; sabre 154, 156, 157;
    team events 154
Ferreira, Marcelo 249
Fiedler, Joerg 149
Finland
    athletics 59, 60, 63
Finlay, Donald 61
firework displays 14, 15, 374
Fischer, Birgit 118
Fix, Oliver 117
Flameng, Leon 127
flat hand (French classical)
    wrestling 358
fleet racing 242
floor exercise 174, 176,
    177–78
Flying Gull, The (an Ojibwa
    Indian) 265
Flynn, Errol 29, 150
football 160–70
    competition format 165;
    extra time and penalty
    shoot-outs 165; Great
    Britain 161, 165, 166–67;
    history 161–63; offside

laws 164; Olympic history
    167–70; women's football
    161, 163, 166, 170
Foreman, George 103, 107
Forever the Moment (film) 194,
    194, 195
Forgie, Hugh 76
Fosbury, Dick 51, 51, 64
Fox, Jeremy 226, 227
Foxhunter 147
France
    boxing 106; equestrianism
    140–41; fencing 151–53,
    157, 158, 159; football 169;
    gymnastics 186
Francis, David Rowland 16
Franco, General 159
Franklin, Benjamin 276
Fraser, Dawn 273
Frazier, Joe 95, 103, 107
Fredriksson, Gert 118
Freeman, Cathy 14, 67, 388
freestyle (crawl) 265
freestyle wrestling 357, 358,
    360–61, 363, 364, 365
French Ministry of War
    152–53
Fridman, Gal 248, 249
Frodeno, Jan 323
Fu Mingxia 138
Fuchs, Gottfried 167
Fujimoto, Shun 189, 192
funeral games 34
Fung, Lori 192
Furuhashi, Hironoshin 271
Furukawa, Masaru 262

G

Gaiardoni, Sante 128
Galkina, Gulnara 46
Gallo, Rafael 117
GDR (East Germany)
    athletics 65; canoeing 118,
    119; rowing 237; swimming
    272; see also Germany; West
    Germany
Gebrselassie, Haile 47, 66
Geesink, Anton 218
Gellar, Michelle 299
George I, King of Greece 373
George VI, King 76, 373
Germany
    boxing 106; canoeing 109,
    118; equestrianism 141;

handball 196; *see also* GDR;
West Germany
Gerovski, Rangel 355–56
Gilpatrick, Guy 268
Ginn, Drew 238
Ginóbili, Manu 92
Githaiga, Ibrahim 238
glima 357
Goguryeo 299–300, 1300
Golden Gloves Tournament 97
Gómez, Javier 323
Goryeo 300
Gossima 285–86, 286
Gould, Jay, II 381
Gourgaud, Baron 380
Grael, Torben 249
Graf, Steffi 315, 316
Grand Olympic Festival
(Liverpool 1862-7) 38
Great Britain
boxing 106; cycling 120;
football 161, 165, 166–67;
hockey 210; rowing 236,
238, *238*; sailing 239;
swimming 270; tennis 308,
309–10; water polo 339
Great Lakes Exhibition (1937)
278
Great Muppet Caper, The (film)
279
Greco-Roman wrestling 357,
358, 360, 362–65
Greece
handball 201; marathon 58;
rowing 236
Greek flag 371
Greek national anthem 371
Green, Reverend Al 376
Green, Nick 238
Griffith-Joyner, Florence
(Flo-Jo) 32, 41, 42, 66
Grissone, Federico 140
Grut, William *225*
Gu Yong-Jo 107
Gulick, Luther 82–83
Gustav V, King of Sweden
17, 68
gymnastics 19, 171–92
age issue 179–80; artistic
172, 175, 176–83; beam
176, 178, *188*; clubs 184;
floor exercise 174, 176,
177–78; high bar 176, 181;
history 172–76; hoop 184;
Olympic history 186–89,

191–92; parallel bars 176,
181–82; pommel horse 172,
174, 176, 178–79; rings
176, 180–81; rhythmic 172,
175–76, 183–85, 192; ball
184; scoring 182–83, 185,
186, 190–91; uneven bars
176, 178; vault 176; ribbon
184; trampoline 172, 176,
185–86, 192

H

haandbol 196
Hackett, Grant 265
Hageborge, Otto 132
Haile Selassie, Emperor of
Ethiopia 70
Hajos, Alfred 269
Hall, Gary, Jr 273, 274
Hall, Lars 225
Haller, Gordon 319
Halstead, Professor Alfred
T. 326
Hamay, Zoltan 269
Hamm, Mia 170
Hamm, Paul 192
hammer 55–56
Hammerseng, Gro 200
Han Il Dong 301
handball 193–201
at the movies 194–95;
crimes and misdemeanours
198–99; four key rules
197–98; history 195–96;
Olympic history 200–201
Harald V, King of Norway 248
Harriman, Averill 237
Harrison, Kenny 52
Hartel, Lis *146*, 147
Hartono, Rudi 79
Harvard University 236, 237
Hary, Armin 63, 386
Hayes, Joanna 49
Hayes, Johnny 59
hazena 196
Hebb, Harry 264
Hellmann, Martina 54, *54*
HELSINKI (1952) 90, 187, 225,
245, 258, 272, 282, 385;
athletics 63, 69, *69*, 106,
385; equestrianism *146*, 147;
Olympic flame 11
Henley Royal regatta 236
Henry VIII, King 309

heptathlon 57
Heydrich, Reinhardt 159
Hicks, Thomas 59
high bar 176, 181
high jump 50–51, *51*, 64
Hill, Howard 29
Himmler, Heinrich 159
Hinds, Lt Sidney 258
Hirobumi, Daimatsu 331, *331*
Hitler, Adolf 68–69, 385
Hochschorner twins 109, *116*
hockey 202–10
fouls, penalties and set pieces
205; history 203–4; Indian
hockey 207–8, 209, *209*; key
rules 204; Olympic history
207–8, 210
Hockey Association 204, 207
Hoffman, Bob 350, 352
Hogan, Paul (aka Crocodile
Dundee) 376–77
Holm, Eleanor 272, 278
Holmes, Kelly 67
Holyfield, Evander 108, 368
Hong Kong: sailing 249
Hooker, Steven 52
hoop 184
hoplitodromos 36
horizontal bar 174
Howard de Walden, Lord 157
Hristov, Alexander 108
Hubbard, William DeHart 60
Huelamo, Jaime 128
Huish, Justin 29, *30*
Hungary
fencing 159; swimming
273; water polo 334, 336,
340–41, *341*
Hunter, CJ 67
hurdling 48–49
hurling 203

I

Ichiba, Takashi 349
Im Dong-Huyn *22*
India
hockey 207–8, 209, *209*,
384; shooting 259
Indonesia
badminton 72, 79
Indurain, Miguel 130
Inter Milan team 168
Inter-Allied Games (Paris,
1919) 326

'intercalcated Games' (1906) 16, 157, 236, 272
International Amateur Athletics Federation (IAAF) 38, 44, 54–55
International Amateur Boxing Association 97–98
International Badminton Federation (IBF) 79, 80
International Basketball Federation (FIBA) 89
International Boxing Association (AIBA) 99, 101
International Cycling Union 382
International Fencing Federation (FIE) 157, 159
International Handball Federation (IHF) 200
International Hockey Federation (FIH) 207
International Horse Show (Olympia, London) 141
International Judo Federation (IJF) 214, 216
International Lawn Tennis Federation 316
International Olympic Association 166
International Olympics Committee (IOC) 16, 68 ban on performance-enhancing drugs 350–51; and Closing Ceremony 369, 375; created (1894) 7; and cycling 128; equestrianism 146, 147; football 166, 169; handball 201; hockey 207; medal ceremonies 367, 368; modern pentathlon 222, 226; Olympic logo 17; President 12; professionals allowed to compete 92; role 7; sailing 247; shooting 258; table tennis 293, 296; taekwondo 299; tennis 316; triathlon 321; volleyball 327; women competitors 60
International Table Tennis Federation (ITTF) 287, 289, 292, 293, 296
International Taekwondo Federation (ITF) 301, 302
International Tennis Federation (ITF) 308

International Triathlon Union (ITU) 320–21
International Weightlifting Federation (IWF) 301, 347, 351
INXS 377
Ireland equestrianism 148
Isaacs, Harry 106
Isinbayeva, Yelena 52
Israel windsurfing 248
Italy fencing 151, 157, 158, 159; football 168
Ivanov, Vyacheslav 237

J

Jacques, John 285, 286
Jacques-Dalcroze, Émile 175
Jahn, Friedrich Ludwig 174
James, LeBron 92
Japan judo 211–12, 213–14, 218–19; samurai swimming 270
Jarvis, John 269
javelin 54–55
Jensen, Knut 128
Jensen, Viggo 351
jeu de paume 309, 380
Johanson, Claes 364
Johansson, Ivar 365
Johnson, Ben 66, 387
Johnson, Boris 285
Johnson, Lieutenant-Colonel Donald 226
Johnson, Magic 92
Johnson, Michael 44, 66, 67, 70, 388
Johnstone, Jack 318–19
Jones, Henry 71–72
Jones, Leisel 263
Jones, Marion 51, 67
Jones, Martha 98
Jones, Roy, Jr 103, 108
Jordan, Michael 87, 92
Josipovic, Anton 108
Joyner-Kersee, Jackie 52, 57
Juantorena, Alberto 44, 65
Jubilee 147
judo 211–19, 301 history 212–15; how to win a bout 216; new kit 216; Olympic history 217–19;

penalties 216; the playing space 215; Yamashita 219
jujitsu 212, 213, 214

K

Kahanmoku, Duke 265, 270
kalo pale (ground wrestling) 357
Kaltenbrun, Henry 127
Kamikawa, Daiki 211
Kaminaga, Akio 218, 219
Kang Ding 345
Kaniskina, Olga 56
Kano, Jigoro 213, 213, 214, 216, 218, 219
karate 299, 301
Karelin, Aleksandr 355–56, 366, 366
Kariuku, Julius 46
Karloff, Boris 75
Karlovic, Ivo 72
Károlyi, Béla 190–91
Karyakin, Sergey 220
Kato, Sawao 179, 189
Keino, Kip 64
Keleti, Agnes 179, 188
Keller, Jack 61
Kellerman, Annette 262, 277–78, 277, 279
Kelly, Grace (Princess Grace of Monaco) 236
Kelly, Jack 236
Kelly, John B. 236
Kennedy, John F. 327
Kenteris, Konstantinos 67
Kenworthy, Harold 265
Kenya boxing 108
Kharlan, Olga 149
Kim, Nellie 180, 189, 190, 191
Kim Jong-Su 259
Kim Su-Nyeong 30
Kim Won-Tak 13–14
King, BB 376
Kipchoge, Eliud 43
Kirby, Bruce 244
Kitajima, Kosuke 260, 263
Kittel, Patrik 148
Klein, Max 364
Koch, Konrad 196
Kolehmainen, Hannes 59
Korbut, Olga 173, 189, 386
Koridze, Avtandil 365
Korzeniowski, Robert 56

Kostantinidis, Aristidis 127
Kovacs (Hungarian judge) 158–59
Kraenzlein, Alvin 58, 383
Kratochvilova, Jarmila 60
Kroftettes, The 279
Kruminsh, Jan 90
kung fu 299, 301
Kurkova, Katerina 251, 258
Kusuma, Alan 72
Kutscher, Marco 148
Kuzmins, Afanasijs 259

L

Lacoste, René 310
lacrosse 379–80
lactic acid build-up 235
Lajoux (French judge) 158
Lane, Frank 58
Lane, Frederick 269
Lang Ping 332
Larsen, Poul-Erik Hoyer 80
Latynina, Larysa 104, 188
lawn tennis 309, 310
Leander rowing club 231
Leary, J. Scott 269
Leduc, Michael 374, 375
Lee Lai Shan 249
Lee Valley White Water Centre 115
Legendre, Robert 60
Lei Sheng 149
Lenglen, Suzanne 310, 311, 316
Leonard, Sugar Ray 95, 107
Leonidas of Rhodes 37
Lesun, Aleksander 220
Lever, Sir Ashton 23–24
Lewald, Dr 136
Lewis, Carl 51, 57, 65, 68, 70, 104, 387
Lewis, John 168
Lewis, Leona 372
lifting stones 345
Ligowsky, George 253
Liljenwall, Hans-Gunnar 225
Limbach, Nicolas 149
Lin Dan 72, 75
Lin Miaoke 15–16
Ling, Per Henrik 174
Lipa, Elisabeta 237
Little Richard 376
Litvinov, Sergey 56
Liu Guoliang 291

Liu Xiang 44, 49, 67
Llewelyn, Colonel Harry 147
Lobach, Marina 192
Lochte, Ryan 264
LONDON (1908) 9, 105–6, 127, 127, 167, 187, 207, 236, 257–58, 270, 272, 308, 315, 352, 379, 380, 381, 381–82
archery 28, 28; athletes' parade 16–17; athletics 59; marathon 47, 384; medal ceremonies 368; sailing 248
LONDON (1948) 89, 106, 146–47, 168, 225, 258, 385
athletics 62, 69; closing ceremony 373; Japan excluded 271; opening ceremony 18
London Prize Ring Rules 96
London Water Polo League 335
long jump 51–52, 63–64
Long, Luz 62
Lorz, Fred 59
LOS ANGELES (1932) 61, 68, 69, 106, 147, 168, 187, 208, 245, 270, 271, 380, 384
medal ceremonies 368, 384; Olympic flame 17; water polo 340; wrestling 365, 365
LOS ANGELES (1984) 29, 91, 108, 137, 169, 191, 219, 225, 227, 249, 276, 282, 332, 353, 387
archery 28; artistic programme 11; athletics 65, 387; closing ceremony 375–76; cycling 128–29; medal ceremony 368; Olympic oath 15; opening ceremony 19; Soviet-led boycott 65, 191, 387; wrestling 365
Louganis, Greg 137–38, 137, 387
Louis, Spyridon 58, 373, 383
Louisiana Purchase Centenary Exhibition 16
Lu Zige 263
Lunden, Leon de 17
Lundgren, Dolph 227–28
Lykkeberg, Peter 269
Lyttelton, Lord 202–3

M

McCready, Richard 382
McGlashen Stones 345
MacGregor, John 111–12
Macjan (film) 194–95
McKay, Mike 238
McMahon, Brigitte 322
McPherson, Elle 376
Maehata, Hideko 270–71
Manchón, Blanca 239
Mao Zedong 288–91
marathon 47, 371
Mariles, Humberto 147
Markarov, Boris 341
Marozzo, Achille 151
Martin, Miklos 341
Massú, Nicolás 316
match racing 242
Mathias, Bob 62
Matos, Ángel 306
Mauritzi, CF 132
Mbango, Françoise 52
Mečiř, Miloslav 316
Medal Ceremonies 367–68
Mednyanszky, Maria 287
MELBOURNE (1956) 90, 138, 144, 179, 188, 267, 273, 354, 385
athletics 63; closing ceremony 373–74; opening ceremony 18; water polo 334, 340–41, 341, 385
Menendez, Osleidys 55
Menkova, Oksana 56
Mennea, Pietro 70
Merckx, Eddie 319
Mercury, Freddie 376
Messi, Lionel 161
MEXICO CITY (1968) 52, 146, 208, 218, 273, 349, 371, 386
altitude problems 40, 63; athletics 40, 51, 51, 63–64; Black Power salutes 32, 64, 64; closing ceremony 375; diving 138; gymnastics 188–89, 188; modern pentathlon 225; opening ceremony 18
Meyfarth, Ulrike 64, 65
Michaux 121–22
Mid-Pacific Road Runners 319
Million Dollar Mermaid (film) 279, 279

Milo of Croton 345
Minogue, Kylie 377
Mintonette 325
Misáková, Eliska 187
Misha (Moscow 1980's mascot) 375
Mission Bay Triathlon 319
modern pentathlon 220–28
combined event 223–24, 228; fencing 222; history 221–22; Olympic history 224–26, 227–28; Onishchenko 226–27; riding 222–23; swimming 222
Mongolia
boxing 93
Monnier, M.M. Pelletier 346
Monroe, Marilyn 326–27
Montagu, Ivor 287, 296
Montenegro, Gilda 117
MONTREAL (1976) 29, 44, 64, 65, 90–91, 107, 128, 137, 179, 200, 208, 210, 244, 268, 272, 386–87
closing ceremony 374–75, 374; gymnastics 189, 190, 190, 386; modern pentathlon 226, 226; Olympic flame 14
Morgan, William G. 325
Morris, Glen 271
Morton, Lucy 263
MOSCOW (1980) 45, 49, 55, 108, 128, 179, 210, 237, 346, 387
artistic programme 10–11; closing ceremony 375; diving 138; fencing 156; gymnastics 191; Japan's boycott 219; opening ceremony 19; USA's boycott 65, 91, 137, 387
Moses, Edwin 15, 65
Mosley, Oswald 159
motor boating 381
Mukhina, Yelena 191
MUNICH (1972) 64, 107, 119, 128, 173, 189, 200, 218, 386
athletes' parade 19; basketball 90, 91, 368; closing ceremony 374; hockey 208; murder of Israeli athletes 386; Olympic anthem 12; opening ceremony 18–19; pentathletes and drugs 225–26; swimming 266, 272, 273

Munitionettes' Cup 163
Murray, Andy 308
Mussolini, Benito 159

N

Nadal, Rafael 308
Nadi, Aldo 158
Nadi, Nedo 158, 159
Naismith, James 83, 87, 89, 325
Nasiri, Mohammad 349
National Basketball Association (NBA) 81, 83, 84, 86, 90, 92
National Olympic Committees 7
National Rifle Associations (NRAs) 252
Neilsen, Holger 196
Nemeth, Imre 65
Nemeth, Miklos 65
Netherlands: gymnastics 187
New York World's Fair (1939) 278
Newall, Queenie 28, 28
Nicholas, Crown Prince of Greece 256
Nielsen, Sophus 167
Nigeria
football 169
Nightingale, Robert 226
Nikolaidis, Alexandros 300
Nimitz, Admiral Chester 237
Nippon Budokan, Tokyo 218
Nishi, Takeichi 147
Nissen, George 174
Nixon, Richard 289, 290, 290
Nordwig, Wolfgang 64
Norman, Greg 377
Norris, Chuck 299
North Korea
boxing 107; taekwondo 299
Norway
women's football 170
Noverre, I.G. 175
Nurmi, Paavo 14, 59, 60, 68, 70, 384
Nyberg, Katja 200

O

Oahu Perimeter Relay, Hawaii 319
O'Connor, Cian 148, 148
Oda, Mikio 60

Odlozil, Josef 189
Oerter, Al 63
Ogta, Yuki 149
Ohnier, Marie 380
Olav, Crown Prince, of Norway (Olaf V) 248
olive wreaths 37, 368
Olizarenko, Nadezhda 45
Olympiade de la République 38
Olympic anthem 12–13, 372
Olympic flag 13, 371, 372, 373, 384
Olympic flame 13–14, 17, 21–22, 372, 377, 385, 388
Olympic hymn 16
Olympic logo 17
Olympic motto 384–85
Olympic oath 15, 384
Olympic rings 17, 384
Olympics, ancient 34, 35–37
Onishchenko, Boris 221, 226–27, 226
Opening Ceremony 9–20
artistic programme 10–11; athletes' parade 11–12; compulsory programme 11–16; countdown to the Games 10; firework display 15; flying the flag 13; lighting of the cauldron 13–14; Olympic anthem 12–13; Olympic oath 15; release of doves 14; speeches 12
orthia pale (upright wrestling) 357
Osborne Swimming Club, Manchester 339
Oshchepkov, Victor 214–15
Ostermeyer, Micheline 62
Otto, Kirstin 272
Our Solo 139
Ovett, Steve 45–46, 65, 387
Owens, Jesse 32, 62, 62, 65, 68–69, 70, 385, 387
Oxbridge Boat Race 231, 231
Oxenstierna, Johan 225
Ozal, President Turgut 353

P

Pace, Darrell 29
Paderina, Natalia 368
Page, Jimmy 372
Page, Malcolm 239

Paine, John 257
Paine, Sumner 257
Pakistan: hockey 208
Palamas, Kostis 12
Panait, Constantin 191
pankration 35–36
Papp, Laszlo 103, 106, 385
parallel bars 174, 176, 181–82
PARIS (1900) 9, 145, 186, 207,
    247, 339, 364, 369, 378–82,
    383
    athletics 58; live pigeon
    shoot 17, 257; rowing
    235–36; swimming 269
PARIS (1924) 46, 60, 106, 118,
    162, 187, 258, 263, 267, 270,
    316, 364, 381, 384
    closing ceremony 373;
    diving 136–37; doors 17;
    fencing 158–59
Park Chung Hee, General 302
Park Kyung-Mo 30
Park Si-Hun 108
Park Sung-Hyun 30
Parker, Adrian 226
Parker Brothers 286
Pasolini, Uberto 194
Patten, Sam 238
Patterson, Floyd 102
Patton, General George
    224–25
Pearce, Stuart 167
Peck, Gregory 237
Peirsol, Aaron 264
Pellegrini, Federica 260, 265
Pendelton, Victoria 124
Peng, Bo 135
pentathlon 36
Pentathlon (film) 228
Pérec, Marie-José 44, 66, 67
Perez, Joaquin Capilla 138
Peris, Giancarlo 13
Perry, Fred 287
Persson, Gehnäll 146–47
Pettenella, Giovanni 123
Pezzo, Paola 129, 130
Pheidippides 47
Phelps, Michael 260, 263, 265,
    266, 274, 274, 388
Philippines
    volleyball 326
Phillips, Charlie 279
Piccini, Achille 168
Pickford, Mary 147
Pietri, Dorando 59, 384

Pietrzykowski, Zbigniew 105
pigeon shooting 17, 252, 257
Ping Pong Association 287
Pinsent, Mathew 238
pistol 254
Pleyer, Barbara Rotraut 18
Poage, George 58
Poderina, Natalia 259
Pointer Sisters, The 376
pole vault 52–53
polo 381
pommel horse 172, 174, 176,
    178–79
Portnov, Aleksandr 138
Pourtalès, Count Hermann
    de 247
Prevost, Hélène 315
Price, Vincent 237
'Pro Slams' 316
professionalism 316
Puente, Tito 376
Puica, Maricica 65
Puliti, Oreste 158–59
Pullum, W.A. 346
Pyle, C.C. 316

Q

Qiao Guan 345
Queen 22
Queensbury, Marquess of 96
Queensbury Rules 96–97

R

racquets 380
Radke, Lina 61, 61
raffballspiel 196
Rankin (impresario) 265
Rashwan, Mohamed Ali 219
Rausch, Emil 268
real tennis 309, 380
Rebollo, Antonio 21, 22
Redgrave, Steve 229, 230, 238,
    238, 388
Redmond, Derek 66
Redmond, Jim 66
Retton, Mar Lou 191
Rhee, Syngman 301
Rhode, Kim 258
ribbon 184
Rice, Stephanie 266
Richards, Vinnie 316
Richie, Lionel (revolutionary
    artist) 375, 376

Riefenstahl, Leni 131
rifle 253–54
Rigoulot, Charles 346
Riner, Teddy 211
rings 176, 180–81
RIO DE JANEIRO (2016) 369,
    372
Rodal, Vebjørn 45
Roddick, Andy 72
Rogers, Ginger 75
Rogge, Jacques 372
Romania
    rowing 237
Romanian Gymnastics
    Federation 180
ROME (1960) 18, 104, 138,
    188, 208, 273, 385
    athletics 63, 385; boxing 107,
    385; closing ceremony 374;
    cycling 128; equestrianism
    139–40; Olympic anthem
    12; Olympic flame 13;
    wrestling 365
Ronaldinho 161
Rong Guotuan 289
Rono, Henry 45
Roosevelt, Teddy 237
roque 379–80
Rose, Billy 278
Rose, Ralph 17
Rosen, Count Clarence von
    145
Ross, Norman 278
Rosset, Marc 316
Rothschild, Édouard Alphonse
    James de 247
rowing 229–38
    history 230–32; Olympic
    history 235–38; Olympic
    rowing classes 232–34;
    women's races 232
Royal Dublin Society 141
Royal Gymnastic Central
    Institute 174
royal (real) tennis 309
Royal Yacht Club 241
Royal Yacht Squadron 241
Roycroft, Bill 139–40
running 40–42, 44–47
Russell, Bill 90
Russia
    synchronised swimming 275,
    282–83, see also USSR
Ryu Seung-Min 297

S

sailing 239–49
  competition racing 242–43
  fleet racing 242; history
    240–41; jibing 247; law
    of the sea 243–44; match
    racing 242;
  Olympic history 247–49;
  Olympic sailing classes
    244–46; tacking 247
St Louis (1904) 9, 16, 89,
  132, 157, 186, 207, 236, 257,
  268, 315, *344*, 352, 364, 378,
  379, 383
  athletics 58–59; boxing 98,
    105; diving 136; swimming
    269, 272; water polo 340–41
Sakai, Yoshinori 14
Salukvadze, Nino 259, 368
Samaranch, Juan Antonio
  372, 388
Samaras, Spiros 12
SAMBO self-defence system
  215
Sampras, Pete 316
San Diego Track Club 318,
  319
Sandström, Bertil 146
Saneyev, ViKtor 65
Sarby, Richard 245–46
Satoh, Hiroji 287–88, 292
Savon, Felix 108
Sawant, Tejaswini 2
Scheidt, Robert 249
Scherbo, Vitaly *182*, 192, 387
Schilles (French cyclist) *127*
Schnabel, Arthur 219
Schöneborn, Lena 220, 228
Schuhmann, Carl 364
Schwazer, Alex 56
Scurry, Briana *169*, 170
Šebrie, Roman 57
Seoul (1988) 46, 49, 52, 55,
  56, 57, 91, 169, 180, 210,
  210, 249, 272, 273, 296, 354,
  366, 387
  artistic programme 11, 19;
    athletics 66; boxing 108;
    diving 137, 387; Olympic
    flame 13–14; parade of
    nations 12; release of doves
    14; taekwondo 306; tennis
    316
Shamrocks of Winnipeg 379

Shanahan, Don 319
Shatner, William 29
Sheldon, George 136
Shepard, Alan B. 237
Shevtsova, Lyudmilla 63
shooting 250–59
  history 251–53; in modern
    pentathlon 223–24; pistol
    254; rifle 253–54; shotgun
    255–56
shot put 55
shot-loaded globe barbell 346
shotguns 252, 254–55
show jumping 141, 142–43,
  146; in modern pentathlon
  222–23
Silivas, Daniela 180
Silla 300
Singapore: water polo 342,
  342
Skov, Rikke *201*
Skrzypaszek, Arkadiusz 227
Slesarenko, Yelena 51
Slim Dusty (David Gordon
  Kirkpatrick) 377
Slupianek, Ilona 55
Smirnov, Vladimir 156
Smith, Tommie 64, *64*, 368
Snowsill, Emma 323
softball 382
Sokol movement 174
Soni, Rebecca 263
Soul, David 228
South Africa
  boxing 106
South Korea
  archery 21, 23, 29–30;
    handball 194–95, *194*; table
    tennis 297; taekwondo
    298, 306
Soviet Communist Party 375
Soviet Union *see* USSR
Spain
  football 169; sailing 249
Spalding 325
sphairisterion 195
sphairistikè 310
Spinks, Leon 107
Spinks, Michael 107
Spinnler, Adolf 186
Spirindov, Viktor 214
Spitz, Mark 158, *266*, 272, 273,
  386, 388
Spock, Benjamin 236
Springfield YMCA 325

squash 380
stade 35
Stadler, Joseph 58
Stalin, Joseph 215
standard bearers 11, 17
Starley, John Kemp 122
steeplechase 46
Steffen, Britta 265
Steinbeck, John 380
Steiner, Karel 168
Stenquist, Henry 128
Stevenson, Sarah 306–7, *307*
Stevenson, Teófilo 107, 108,
  387
Stockholm (1912) 59, 106,
  128, 141, 167, *175*, 224, 264,
  270, 315, 352, 364, *378*, 384
  athletes' parade 17; eques-
    trianism 145–46; fencing
    157–58; shooting 257, *257*
Stockholm (1956)
  opening ceremony 18;
    equestrianism 148
Stoyanov, Dimitro 365
Straj, Robert 245
Strug, Kerri 192
Strutt, Joseph 230–31
subak 299
Suleymanoglu, Naim 352–54,
  353
Sullivan, Eamon 265
Susanti, Susi 72
Suzuki, Diachi 264
Swahn, Oscar *257*, 258, 384
Sweden
  equestrianism 145, 146–47;
    football 168; gymnastics
    187; modern pentathlon
    220, 224; table tennis 297;
    women's football 163
Swedish system 174
Sweisguth, Francis 245
swimming 260–74
  10 great Olympic swimmers
    272–74; backstroke 264;
    breaststroke 262–63, *263*;
    butterfly 263, *266*; freestyle
    (crawl) 265; history 261–62;
    history of swimming kit
    267–68, *268*; Hollywood's
    Olympic Tarzans 271; in
    modern pentathlon 222;
    Olympic history 269–72;
    sprints, medleys, relays
    266–67

Swimming Society (British) 262

Switzerland
canoeing 111; shooting 252

SYDNEY (2000) 47, 56, 92, 165, 169, 170, 192, 228, 245, 258, 263, 265, 274, 282, 283, 293, 306, 342, 351, 366, 388
athletics 67, 70; closing ceremony 376–77; cycling 130; formation horse troupe 11, 20; medal ceremony 368; miming 15; Olympic flame 13, 14, 388; rowing 230, 238, 388; triathlon 320, 321, 322

Sydney Symphony Orchestra 15

synchronised swimming 275–83
competitive formats 281; history 277–79; judging and scoring 281; Olympic history 282–83

Szabo, Gabriela 47

T

table tennis 284–97
equipment 288, 91; history 285–89, 291; Olympic history 296–97; ping pong diplomacy 289–90; rules 202

Table Tennis Association 287

Tae Hi Nam 301

tae soo do 299

taekkyeon 299, 300, 301

taekwondo 298–307
disowned father of taekwondo 301; equipment 304; the form of the bout 303–4; history 299–301; officials 304; Olympic history 306–7; penalties and warnings 305; scoring 304–5

Takács, Károly 258

Takhashi, Naoko 47

Teddington Cricket Club, Middlesex 204

tennis 308–16
the court 311; equipment 313–14; evolution of the rules 314; history 309–11; Olympic history 315–16; play 313; scoring 312–13

Thanou, Ekaterini 67

Thompson, Daley 57

Thorkildsen, Andreas 55

Thorpe, Ian 104, 265, 274

Thorpe, Jim 59, 68, 104, 384

Timmerman, Ulf 55

Tobacco (an Ojibwa Indian) 265

Tobian, Gary 138

Todt, Hans-Jürgen 225

TOKYO (1964) 150, 188, 208, 273, 386
athletics 63; cycling 123, 128; judo 217–18, 218; Olympic anthem 12; Olympic flag episode 273; Olympic flame 14; release of balloons 18; volleyball 331–32, 331

Tomkins, James 238

torball 196

Torres, Dara 273

Tour de France 120, 122, 127, 130, 343

Tourischeva, Ludmilla 189

Toxophilite Society 24

trampoline 172, 176, 185–86

Trentin, Pierre 123

triathlon 317–23
cycling 320, 321; drafting 320, 322; history 318–21; Olympic history 322–23; pacing 322; running 321; sighting 322; slipstreaming 320; swimming 320, 321; transitioning 320, 322

triple jump 52

Trois Sports, Les, Joinville-le-Pont, France 318

tug of war 378–79, 378

Tulu, Derartu 66

U

UEFA 163

Ueno, Masae 211

Ukraine
archery 22

uneven bars 176, 178

Unified Team 192

Union des Sociétés Françaises de Sports Athlétiques 38

Union Internationale de Pentathlon Moderne (UIPM) 222, 223, 226, 227, 228

United States
archery 29; athletics 31, 58–59, 62; badminton 75; basketball 81, 87, 89, 90, 91, 91, 92; boxing 106, 107; declines to defer to royalty 16–17; diving 138; rowing 236–37, 237; softball 382; swimming 260, 270, 272; tennis 315; volleyball 326; women's football 163, 170

Uranus 147

Uruguay
football 168, 384

US Overseas Expeditionary Force 326

US Triathlon Series 320

USSR
athletics 64; basketball 90–91; boxing 106; diving 138; football 169; gymnastics 187; water polo 334, 330–41; see also Russia

V

Valerie the Female Gladiator 346

van den Hoek, Aad 128

Van Dyken, Amy 274

van Innis, Hubert 28

Van Koeverden, Adam 109

Vandeville, Charles de 269

vault, the 176, 177

Vezzali, Valentina 149, 158

Vicru, Nicolae 180

Viren, Lasse 64

Vitray, Tamás 273

volleyball 324–33
beach volleyball 325, 326–27, 327, 329, 331, 333; etiquette 333; history 325–27; indoor volleyball 325, 327–29; dig, set, spike! 328; points, set, match 329; serving up 328–29; the special one 329; substitutions 329; Olympic history 331–33

Vöros, Zsuzsanna 228

W

Wade, Dwyane 92

Waikiki Swim Club 319

Waldner, Jan-Ove 297, 387
Walker, Keith 108
Walker, Melanie 49
walking 56
Wang, Kenan 135
Wang Liquin 291
Wangenheim, Lieutenant
   Konrad, Freiherr von 147
Wangila, Robert 108
Wanjiru, Samuel 47
Washington Canoe Club 118
Water Ballet Club, University
   of Chicago 278
water polo 334–42
   history 335–37; Hungary
   vs USSR 334, 340–41,
   341, 385; Olympic history
   340–42; the pool 337–38;
   rules 338
Waterford Crystal 148, *148*
Webb, Captain 262
weightlifting 343–54
   disc loading system of
   weights 346; doping record
   350–51; dumbbells *344*, 346,
   352; equipment 349; format
   347; history 344–47; long,
   springy bar 346; Olympic
   history 351–52; rules
   347–48; shot-loaded globe
   barbell 346; Suleymanoglu
   352–54, *353*; technique
   348–49; women's competitions 347
Weissmuller, Johnny 270, 271,
   271, 278
West Germany
   cycling 128; fencing 159; *see
   also* GDR; Germany
Westerhof, Lisa 239
Westminster, Constance
   Edwina Cornwallis West,
   Duchess of 248

Whitfield, Simon 318, 322,
   323
Wilde, Oscar 310
Wilkinson, Elizabeth 98
Williams, Esther 278–79, *279*
Williams sisters 311
Wilson, William 335
Wimbledon 308, 309
windsurfing 249
Wing, John Ian 374
Wingfield, Major Walter
   309–10
Winklevoss, Cameron 236–37,
   237
Winklevoss, Tyler 236–37, *237*
Winters, Frederick *344*
Wonder, Stevie 376
World Amateur Boxing
   Championships 98
World Badminton Federation
   79–80
World Basketball Champion-
   ships (2010) 81
World Cup 161, 165, 168,
   169, 200
World Fair (Paris, 1900) 16
World Taekwondo Federation
   (WTF) 301, 302
World University Games
   (1983) 132
wrestling 355–66
   Aleksandr Karelin 366,
   366; catch-as-catch-can
   348; Cumberland wrestling
   357; dress code 359; flat
   hand (French classical) 358;
   freestyle 357, 358, 360–61,
   363, 364, 365; glima 357;
   Greco-Roman wrestling
   357, 358, 360, 362–65;
   history 356–58; how a bout
   is won 360–61; how points
   are scored 361–62; kalo

pale (ground wrestling) 357;
   the mat 359; the officials
   359–60; Olympic history
   364–65; orthia pale (upright
   wrestling) 357; structure
   of the tournament 360;
   women's competition 365

X

Xiao Qin 183
Xu Yiming 138

Y

Yale University 237
Yamashita, Yasuhiro 219
Yin Jiàn 249
YMCA 82, 83, 89, 325–26
Young, John Paul 377
Young, Kevin 49
Yugoslavia
   badminton 91

Z

Zador, Ervin 341, *341*
Zagunis, Mariel 149
Zátopek, Emil 63, 69–70,
   69, 385
Zenovka, Eduard 227
Zhou Enlai 290, *290*
Zhuang Zedong 290
Ziegler, Dr John 350, 351
Zubiera, Constantin
   Henriquez de 379
Zuckerberg, Mark 236